Advances in Psychology and Law

Volume 3

Series editors
Brian H. Bornstein, University of Nebraska-Lincoln, Lincoln, USA
Monica K. Miller, University of Nevada, Reno, USA

More information about this series at http://www.springer.com/series/11918

Monica K. Miller • Brian H. Bornstein
Editors

Advances in Psychology and Law

Volume 3

Springer

Editors
Monica K. Miller
Department of Criminal Justice
Interdisciplinary Social Psychology PhD Program
University of Nevada
Reno, NV, USA

Brian H. Bornstein
Department of Psychology
University of Nebraska-Lincoln
Lincoln, NE, USA

ISSN 2366-6099 ISSN 2366-6102 (electronic)
Advances in Psychology and Law
ISBN 978-3-030-09343-3 ISBN 978-3-319-75859-6 (eBook)
https://doi.org/10.1007/978-3-319-75859-6

Printed on acid-free paper

This Springer imprint is published by the registered company Springer International Publishing AG part of Springer Nature.
The registered company address is: Gewerbestrasse 11, 6330 Cham, Switzerland

To Matt, for enriching my life every day.
—MM

To Christie, for embarking with me on new adventures.
—BB

Preface

With much excitement, we offer the third volume in the *Advances in Psychology and Law* book series. The initial vision for the series was to contribute to the legal psychology field by providing a book series that publishes thorough reviews of existing research with legal and policy implications. The two previous volumes have done just that—and the current volume continues this theme by providing nine chapters on some of the most current legal issues. We would like to thank Springer, and especially Sharon Panulla and Sylvana Ruggirello, for helping make this book series a reality.

This volume contains nine chapters, each focusing on a different topic within psychology and law. Each chapter provides a thorough but focused review of the legal issue, including a discussion of relevant laws, case law, and legal procedures. Then, the chapters provide a synthesized review of the psychology research and apply it to the relevant legal issues, leading to suggested reforms to the legal system. Authors for each chapter conclude by identifying gaps in the literature that are ripe for further investigation.

This volume's first two chapters address topics related to juries. Ruva reviews the research on the effects of pretrial publicity (PTP), with a focus on how the media landscape has changed due to social media and the Internet. Based on a review of the mechanisms that underlie the PTP effects, Ruva offers some remedies that could prevent PTP from improperly influencing jurors' verdicts.

Myers, Johnson, and Nuñez review the three U.S. Supreme Court decisions concerning the permissibility of victim impact statements, which are testimony that jurors hear regarding the effects the crime has had on the victim and family. They then discuss the legal and psychological controversies: (1) whether impact statements are relevant to the defendant's blameworthiness and capacity, (2) whether they distract jurors from their principal role as decision makers, and (3) whether their inflammatory nature promotes arbitrariness in jurors' decisions.

The next four chapters address issues related to justice for defendants, suspects, and trial litigants. Kelly and colleagues review the law and psychology surrounding *Miranda* warnings. The tension between suspects' rights (e.g., to remain silent and request a lawyer) and the mission of law enforcement (e.g., to obtain a confession or evidence to help solve crime) has created a body of law fraught with inconsistencies and requirements that are difficult to translate into psychological terms and principles. The body of work reviewed here highlights the implications of these court rulings for suspects.

In the fourth chapter, Brank and Groscup provide an overview of the law and the psychology related to the U.S. Constitution's Fourth Amendment protection from unlawful "search and seizure." The case law in this area makes psychological assumptions about behavior that are not always supported by research. Current issues in this area include the use of canines to search a person and his possessions and the validity of a suspect's consent to be searched.

The next chapter investigates the possibility that litigants (including defendants, but civil litigants as well) might be disadvantaged by biased mental health assessments. Neal and colleagues challenge the assumption that mental health experts who testify in court are "objective" and untainted by bias. They review relevant research from cognitive neuroscience, cognitive psychology, and social psychology to support their contention that forensic experts are likely affected by a variety of cognitive biases that affect their judgments.

The final chapter in this grouping discusses the increasing use of restorative justice principles in legal systems worldwide. Saulnier and Sivasubramaniam provide an overview of the academic literature associated with restorative justice, with a focus on the discrepancy between legal and lay notions of justice and how this discrepancy can hinder the advancement of restorative justice procedures.

The next two chapters address issues related to juveniles who are involved in the legal system. In chapter "Examining the Presenting Characteristics, Short-Term Effects, and Long-Term Outcomes Associated with System-Involved Youths," Taylor and colleagues discuss the variety of ways in which the juvenile justice system can be detrimental to juveniles' short-term and long-term life outcomes. Short-term outcomes include mental health issues, substance abuse, and suicidal tendencies. Long-term outcomes include persistent offending, challenges in obtaining employment, and difficulties establishing relationships.

Pfeifer and colleagues next provide an overview of the research and programs related to Indigenous youth crime across four jurisdictions that have substantial Indigenous populations (Australia, Canada, New Zealand, and the United States). Authors provide a conceptual framework that identifies the various factors that contribute to youth crime and categorizes these factors as systemic or individual. The analysis highlights the role of culture in providing for the needs of youth in each country.

Finally, Reed and colleagues provide a thorough assessment of publication patterns in legal psychology-themed scholarly journals. Their analysis identifies the substantive topics and types of articles published, as well as author characteristics. This analysis helps readers, as well as researchers working in the area, gauge the current state of the law-psychology field.

As this preview of the chapters included in Volume 3 illustrates, the field of psychology and law encompasses a wide variety of diverse topics, which involve the actions of suspects, offenders, witnesses, litigants, factfinders (e.g., juries and judges), and others. These topics invoke a number of different psychological theories and processes and legal issues. It is our hope that this series will continue to be useful to academics, students, and those in legal occupations.

As with the others in the series, this third volume of *Advances in Psychology and Law* will interest researchers in legal psychology and related disciplines (e.g., criminal justice) as well as practicing attorneys, trial consultants, and clinical psychologists

Reno, NV, USA
Lincoln, NE, USA

Monica K. Miller
Brian H. Bornstein

Contents

Contributors

Cyndi Banks Capilano University, North Vancouver, BC, Canada

Brian H. Bornstein Department of Psychology, University of Nebraska-Lincoln, Lincoln, NE, USA

Eve M. Brank Department of Psychology, University of Nebraska-Lincoln, Lincoln, NE, USA

Leah Brogan Violence Prevention Initiative Center for Injury Research and Prevention, Children's Hospital of Philadelphia, Wynnewood, PA, USA

Kimberly S. Dellapaolera University of Nebraska-Lincoln, Lincoln, NE, USA

Naomi E. S. Goldstein Department of Psychology, JD/PhD Program in Law and Psychology, Juvenile Justice Research & Reform Lab, Drexel University, Philadelphia, PA, USA

Jennifer L. Groscup Department of Psychology, Scripps College, Claremont, CA, USA

Cassandra Hamza School of Social and Behavioral Sciences, New College of Interdisciplinary Arts & Sciences, Arizona State University, Glendale, AZ, USA

Morgan Hight School of Social and Behavioral Sciences, New College of Interdisciplinary Arts & Sciences, Arizona State University, Glendale, AZ, USA

Brian C. Howatt School of Social and Behavioral Sciences, New College of Interdisciplinary Arts & Sciences, Arizona State University, Glendale, AZ, USA

Fiona Hutton Institute of Criminology, Victoria University, Victoria University Institute of Criminology, School of Social and Cultural Studies, Wellington, New Zealand

Sarah Johnson Department of Psychology, University of North Carolina Wilmington, Wilmington, NC, USA

Sharon Kelley Institute of Law, Psychiatry, and Public Policy, UVa School of Medicine, University of Virginia Health Systems, Charlottesville, VA, USA

Sarah Monod de Froideville Institute of Criminology, Victoria University, Victoria University Institute of Criminology, School of Social and Cultural Studies, Wellington, New Zealand

Philip Mulvey Department of Criminal Justice Sciences, Illinois State University, Normal, IL, USA

Bryan Myers Department of Psychology, University of North Carolina Wilmington, Wilmington, NC, USA

Tess M. S. Neal School of Social and Behavioral Sciences, New College of Interdisciplinary Arts & Sciences, Arizona State University, Glendale, AZ, USA

Narina Nuñez Department of Psychology, University of Wyoming, Laramie, WY, USA

Jeffrey E. Pfeifer Department of Psychological Sciences, Centre for Forensic Behavioural Science, Swinburne University of Technology, Melbourne, VIC, Australia

Krystia Reed Cornell University, Ithaca, NY, USA

Kristan Russell Interdisciplinary Social Psychology PhD Program, University of Nevada, Reno, Reno, NV, USA

Christine L. Ruva Department of Psychology, University of South Florida Sarasota-Manatee, Sarasota, FL, USA

Alana Saulnier Department of Interdisciplinary Studies, Lakehead University, Orillia, ON, Canada

Diane Sivasubramaniam Faculty of Health, Arts and Design, Department of Psychological Sciences, Swinburne University of Technology, Hawthorn, VIC, Australia

Melanie Taylor Department of Criminal Justice, University of Nevada, Reno, Reno, NV, USA

Brice Terpstra Department of Criminal Justice Sciences, Illinois State University, Normal, IL, USA

Sarah Thimsen South Dakota State University, University Center-Sioux Falls, Sioux Falls, SD, USA

Justin S. Trounson Department of Psychological Sciences, Centre for Forensic Behavioural Science, Swinburne University of Technology, Melbourne, VIC, Australia

John Winterdyk Department of Economics, Justice, and Policy Studies, Mount Royal University, Calgary, AB, Canada

Heather Zelle Department of Public Health Sciences, Institute of Law, Psychiatry, and Public Policy, UVa School of Medicine, University of Virginia Health Systems, Charlottesville, VA, USA

From the Headlines to the Jury Room: An Examination of the Impact of Pretrial Publicity on Jurors and Juries

Christine L. Ruva

Pretrial publicity (PTP) encompasses all media coverage of a case occurring prior to trial (Greene & Wade, 1988; Studebaker & Penrod, 1997). There is great variance in the amount and type of pretrial coverage that cases receive (Bruschke & Loges, 1999). More serious crimes are likely to receive greater amounts of PTP, and this PTP is likely to be anti-defendant (Lieberman & Sales, 2007; Simon & Eimermann, 1971) and contain information that the American Bar Association (ABA, 2016; see ABA Standards, Rule 3.6) regards as potentially prejudicial (Imrich, Mullin, & Linz, 1995; Tankard, Middleton, & Rimmer, 1978). Importantly, substantial PTP that is prejudicial and anti-defendant in nature can bias jurors' opinions of the defendant's character and increase the likelihood of a guilty verdict (see Steblay, Besirevic, Fulero, & Jimenez-Lorente, 1999 for review).

Over the past decade there have been dramatic changes in how the media covers, and the public follows, criminal and civil cases. Coverage of cases by nontraditional media sources (e.g., blogs, Facebook, Twitter, Netflix, YouTube, and Internet news sources) has increased the public's access to case information and removed geographical boundaries. The public's interest in, and the media coverage of, some high-profile cases have resulted in these cases being treated similar to popular TV dramas—with both traditional and social media following them from time of arrest, through the trial process, and beyond (e.g., *Arizona v. Arias*, 2013; *Florida v. Anthony*, 2011; *Florida v. Zimmerman*, 2013; and *Wisconsin v. Avery*, 2007). In such high-profile cases, the clash between citizens' First Amendment right of freedom of speech/press and a defendant's constitutional Sixth Amendment right to a fair trial is highlighted. All of these factors present new challenges for the courts that might not be resolved by traditional court remedies (Brickman, Blackman, Futterman, & Dinnerstein, 2008; Mastromauro, 2010).

C. L. Ruva (✉)
Department of Psychology, University of South Florida Sarasota-Manatee, Sarasota, FL, USA
e-mail: ruva@usf.edu

M. K. Miller, B. H. Bornstein (eds.), *Advances in Psychology and Law*,
Advances in Psychology and Law 3,
https://doi.org/10.1007/978-3-319-75859-6_1

In consideration of the above, this chapter begins by providing a summary of important court decisions involving PTP, as well as the American Bar Association's ethical rules for the dissemination of pretrial information by litigating attorneys (see ABA Standards, Rule 3.6). The second section of this chapter explores the amount and type/slant of PTP (negative-defendant, positive-defendant, and negative-victim) found in various media sources. This section also covers the changing media landscape resulting from the birth of Internet and social media coverage of cases.

The chapter then turns to reviewing the social science research. The third section of the chapter examines methods used by social scientists to explore PTP's effects on juror and jury decisions, summarizing their benefits, limitations, and general findings. The chapter's fourth section explores mechanisms through which PTP influences jurors' decisions, given that in order to make educated decisions regarding how to address PTP bias, researchers must understand the mechanisms that underlie it. In the fifth section of the chapter, the current remedies available to address PTP bias are examined. These remedies are examined in regard to the following: past research, mechanisms responsible for PTP's biasing effects on juror/jury decisions, and the increasing accessibility of pretrial information. Finally, the chapter concludes with future directions for PTP research and policy implications.

The Courts and Pretrial Publicity

This section of the chapter begins by reviewing important Supreme Court decisions involving PTP. It then examines the American Bar Association's ethical rules for the dissemination of pretrial information (see ABA Standards, Rule 3.6). The Supreme Court's decisions, and the ABA's ethical rules, focus on the prejudicial influence PTP can have on a defendant's right to a fair trial.

Important Court Decisions Involving Pretrial Publicity

In criminal cases, a defendant's right to a fair trial is guaranteed under the Sixth Amendment of the US Constitution, and the Fifth Amendment's Due Process Clause. The First Amendment of the US Constitution guarantees freedom of press/speech and the public's right to be informed of criminal proceedings. In high-profile trials containing large amounts of anti-defendant pretrial publicity (PTP), these constitutional amendments are likely to clash. The courts in such cases must decide how to balance these conflicting rights. These attempts to balance defendants' right to a fair trial with the public's right to free speech have, at times, made it to the Supreme Court, which during the 1960s and 1970s made several significant decisions regarding PTP. These decisions spoke to the problems arising from pervasive prejudicial PTP, guidelines for applying remedies for PTP bias, and who has the burden of demonstrating harm from pretrial information.

The first significant Supreme Court decision in the 1960s that dealt with PTP was *Irvin v. Dowd* (1961). The defendant, Leslie Irvin, was granted a change of venue, but then claimed that the widespread inflammatory PTP had also adversely impacted the jury pool in the new venue. The defense requested a second change of venue, which was denied. The Court in *Irvin v. Dowd* (1961) ruled that if a defendant's right to a fair trial would be threatened as a result of adverse effects of PTP, then a defendant's motion for a change of venue should be granted. In addition, the Court ruled that a trial by jury is not fair unless the jury members are impartial. The Court voided the conviction of Leslie Irvin and remanded the case back to District Court for further proceedings. The second major Court ruling in the 1960s was in *Rideau v. Louisiana* (1963), which concluded that when highly prejudicial PTP, as determined by its content and pervasiveness, creates a prejudicial environment, then a change of venue is required to protect a defendant's due process rights.

Following the *Rideau v. Louisiana* (1963) ruling, the Court reversed two lower court convictions due to substantial, pervasive, and prejudicial publicity surrounding the trials. In the first of these cases, *Estes v. Texas* (1965), the Court reversed the swindling conviction of Billy Sol Estes, stating that Mr. Estes' right to a fair trial was violated—mostly due to the large amount of publicity surrounding a televised two-day pretrial hearing. In this decision the Court expressed that "[T]he freedom granted to the press under the First Amendment must be subject to the maintenance of absolute fairness in the judicial process, and, in the present state of television techniques such freedom does not confer the right to use equipment in the courtroom which might jeopardize a fair trial, the atmosphere for which must be preserved at all costs" (U.S. 539-540, p. 381). Then, in *Shepard v. Maxwell* (1966), the Court reversed the murder conviction of Dr. Samuel Shepard, stating that it was impossible for Dr. Shepard to receive a fair trial given the pervasive and massive amount of prejudicial publicity surrounding his trial.

In *Murphey v. Florida* (1975) the court found that defendants could challenge a court's denial of change of venue, but to be successful this challenge must pass the "totality of the circumstances" test. Specifically, the defense has the obligation at voir dire of proving that potential jurors hold "actual" or "inherent prejudice" that makes the granting of a fair trial impossible.

Since the 1970s, there has been only one significant Supreme Court decision in reference to prejudicial PTP, and it was in *Mu'Min v. Virginia* (1991). Mu'Min had been convicted of murder and sentenced to death for killing a woman while out of prison on work detail. Extensive pretrial publicity surrounded the case, and eight of the 12 jurors on his jury admitted, during voir dire, to having seen or heard something about the case. Mu'Min asserted that his right to a fair trial had been violated because the trial judge refused to question prospective jurors as to the specific pretrial information they had been exposed to. The Supreme Court held that the Fourteenth Amendment's due process clause does not mandate that prospective jurors be queried about specific case information they have seen or heard. Further, the Sixth Amendment's impartial jury requirement is satisfied when prospective jurors refrain from stating that they have been prejudiced by pretrial publicity. This ruling clarified the extent to which the voir dire need delve into specific PTP information and juror bias.

American Bar Association and Pretrial Information

Along with the Supreme Court's decisions in regard to PTP's potential to impede a defendant's right to a fair trial, the American Bar Association has formulated ethical rules for the dissemination of pretrial information by litigating attorneys (ABA, 2016; see ABA Standards, Rule 3.6). These ethical rules indicate categories of information considered prejudicial, and that should therefore not be disseminated to the press (Rule 3.6—Comment). These categories include: (1) character, credibility, reputation, or criminal record of the accused; (2) possibility of guilty pleas, existence of a confession, admission, or statement or refusal to make statement; (3) performance/results on or refusal of any tests (e.g., DNA, polygraph); (4) opinions of guilt or innocence of defendant; (5) information that is likely inadmissible as evidence in courts; and (6) statement that the defendant is accused of crime, unless accompanied by statements that this is merely an accusation and defendant is innocent until proven guilty. Under Rule 3.8 (ABA, 2016), prosecutors have the additional obligation to refrain from making statements that are likely to increase condemnation of the defendant.

The ABA Standards (2016) also include a "Right to Reply" (Rule 3.6)—a lawyer may "make a statement that a reasonable lawyer would believe is required to protect a client from the substantial undue prejudicial effect of recent publicity not initiated by the lawyer or the lawyer's client." This right of reply, however, is limited only to "such information as is necessary to mitigate the recent adverse publicity." This right has come into question in recent high-profile cases (e.g., see Mosteller, 2007 for a review of the 2006 Duke Lacrosse Case; *FL v. Zimmerman*, 2013), and will be discussed further below.

Amount and Types of Pretrial Publicity in High-profile Cases

Cases making their way towards trial vary widely in the amount and type of pretrial media coverage they receive (Bruschke & Loges, 1999). This section of the chapter explores how the amount and type/slant of PTP (negative-defendant, positive-defendant, and negative-victim) affects juror bias. It also examines how the changing media landscape is influencing the amount and type of pretrial information disseminated to the public (Mastromauro, 2010).

Although the Supreme Court and the ABA have provided strong statements as to the threats that prejudicial publicity imposes on a defendant's right to a fair trial, there are ample examples of recent cases in which the pervasiveness of highly prejudicial PTP call into question the violation of this fundamental right (e.g., Scott

Peterson's 2004 first-degree murder conviction and subsequent death sentence, Phil Spector's 2009 conviction for second-degree murder at his second trial, Rod Blagojevich's 2011 convictions on 17 corruption charges, and Jodi Arias' 2013 first-degree murder conviction and subsequent life sentence without possibility of parole). Also of concern, content analyses of media sources have found that more serious crimes are likely to receive greater media coverage than less serious crimes, and news stories about crime are likely to contain information that the ABA (2016) has indicated impedes a defendant's right to a fair trial (i.e., negative statements about the defendant's character, reference to the defendant's guilt, reports of confessions, and prior criminal record of the accused; Imrich et al., 1995; Simon & Eimermann, 1971; Tankard, Middleton, & Rimmer 1978).

How the Amount of Publicity Affects Juror Bias

Shaffer (1986) suggests there might be a cumulative effect of PTP on jurors' attitudes and decisions, which is supported by the small amount of research exploring the influence of PTP quantity on juror bias. For example, DeLuca (1979) found that mock-jurors exposed to three pieces of anti-defendant information were more likely to render guilty verdicts than jurors exposed to only one or two pieces of this information. In a more recent study, Daftary-Kapur, Penrod, O'Connor, and Wallace (2014) exposed jurors to either five (low amount condition) or ten (high amount condition) pretrial news stories that were either anti-defendant, pro-defendant, or unrelated to the case. They found that, for jurors exposed to anti-defendant articles, those receiving high amounts of PTP were more likely to vote guilty than those receiving low amounts of PTP. For the pro-defendant PTP, jurors exposed to high amounts were less likely to vote guilty than those exposed to low amounts of PTP.

Surveys of potential jurors also indicate that as the amount of PTP exposure increases, so does potential juror bias. For example, surveys of jury eligible adults conducted by Costantini and King (1980/1981; three murder cases) and Moran and Cutler (1991; two drug cases) found that, as potential jurors' reported knowledge of a case increased, so did bias against the defendant. Importantly, Moran and Cutler found that potential jurors' knowledge about a case was not related to their self-reported ability to be impartial. Finally, Shaffer (1986) found that, for the five murder cases explored, the number of PTP articles appearing in a newspaper, as well as respondents' estimates of their amount of PTP exposure, were predictors of attributions of guilt.

The research above suggests that, as the quantity of PTP increases, so does its biasing effect on jurors' decisions, supporting both the Supreme Court's decisions and the ABA's ethical rules regarding the biasing influence of pervasive anti-defendant PTP. Importantly, the pervasiveness of PTP in high-profile cases is likely to increase in the future. This is due to changes in how high-profile cases are covered, especially the implementation of both Internet and social media, which the chapter now turns.

The Changing Media Landscape

The Supreme Court's decisions regarding PTP, in the 1960s and 1970s, came at a time of dramatic change in the manner in which trials were covered by the press. The emergence of broadcast journalism—radio in the 1930s followed by television in the 1950s and 1960s (New York Film Academy, 2015)—not only allowed journalists to reach a much larger audience but also allowed for the broadcasting of pretrial hearings and entire trials. In recent history, the media landscape has once again dramatically changed—mostly resulting from the birth of the Internet and social media—allowing for new forms of communication and ways of broadcasting information surrounding trials (e.g., Facebook, Twitter, personal websites and blogs, YouTube, iTunes podcasts, and Netflix).

These new forms of pretrial coverage have increased the reach of prejudicial pretrial information, and in recent years have outpaced traditional news sources (Mastromauro, 2010). The Pew Research Center for Internet, Science, and Technology (2017a) found that today nearly 70% of Americans use some type of social media "to connect with one another, engage with news content, share information and entertain themselves," which is up from just 5% in 2005 when they began tracking social media use (see also, Greenwood, Perrin, & Duggan, 2016). Americans' Internet use has also increased dramatically over the past 16 years, from approximately 50% of all American adults being online in 2000 to 90% in 2016 (Pew Research Center, 2017b).

Not only do these nontraditional news sources have the potential of reaching greater numbers of people, experiencing no geographical bounds, but they also allow for the dissemination of pretrial information that is more prejudicial, gruesome, erroneous, and that makes direct accusations of the defendant (Mastromauro, 2010). Nontraditional Internet news sources do not have the same standards as traditional media sites and are often unchecked or uncensored (Mastromauro, 2010). In addition, online media sources often contain comment sections, which encourage viewers/readers to provide their opinions of the case and defendant. Therefore, these online sources contain opinions and information not found in traditional media sources (Ward, 2008). High-profile trials also provide the perfect fodder for bloggers, who can work for newspapers, be ordinary citizens, or legal professionals/attorneys (Duncan, 2009). The *American Bar Journal* coined the term "blawggers" to refer to law bloggers (McDonough, 2015) and has published articles informing attorneys on how to develop and promote legal blogging (Lear, 2015). The end result of these commentary pages and blogs is that ordinary citizens (potential jurors) and attorneys are not only consumers of the news but also reporters of it and commenters on it (Rainie, 2005; Ward, 2008).

Finally, neither traditional nor nontraditional media websites are confined to a specific moment in time. Instead, the Internet allows access to pretrial information days, weeks, or even years after the original posting, and allows for an individual to access the material over and over again. This makes it more complicated for the courts, in high-profile cases, to seat a jury that has not been exposed to prejudicial media coverage.

In some high-profile cases, the social media coverage began in force prior to arrest, and might have played a role in securing an arrest. For example, on March 8th of 2012, the parents of 17-year-old Trayvon Martin, who was shot and killed in Sanford, Florida on February 26th 2012, created a petition on Change.org. This petition called for a full investigation of their son's death and the arrest of George Zimmerman, who was the acknowledged shooter. On March 17th 2012, after the release of the 911 call, the Zimmerman case became the first story of the year to have more traditional media coverage (19% of available newspaper and broadcast space) than the presidential race (14% of available newspaper and broadcast space; Pew Research Center, 2012). Also during this time, 21% of Twitter conversation expressed outrage at Zimmerman/calls for justice (Pew Research Center, 2012). By March 22, 2012 the Change.org petition had more than 2.2 million signatures that were presented to the Sanford City Commission by civil rights leader Jesse Jackson. Subsequently, a special prosecutor appointed by Florida Governor Rick Scott charged George Zimmerman with murder. Hence, this pre-arrest/pre-indictment publicity might have been influential in securing a murder charge in this case.

The anti-defendant media coverage of George Zimmerman followed the defendant throughout his trial and beyond. To counter the "avalanche of misinformation," George Zimmerman's attorney, Mark O'Mara, used the Internet and social media, setting up a Legal Defense website (http://gzlegalcase.com/), Twitter page, and Facebook account (Brook, 2012; Weis, 2012). The judge in the Zimmerman case refused the prosecution's request for a gag order that would prevent Mr. O'Mara from blogging. As mentioned above, the ABA Standards do provide litigating attorneys with the "Right to Reply" (Rule 3.6) to substantial prejudicial PTP in order to mitigate adverse effects caused by such PTP.

As the Zimmerman case demonstrates, the increasing use of the Internet and social media by the public and attorneys is likely to result in significant changes in the amount and types of pretrial information surrounding cases. How these new forms of pretrial coverage will affect juror bias, and the courts' ability to successfully protect defendants' right to a fair trial, are questions that the chapter will delve into below.

Types of Slants of PTP

The prosecution typically has the advantage regarding media coverage in high-profile cases (Dexter, Cutler, & Moran, 1992), with most PTP being pro-prosecution or anti-defendant (Imrich et al., 1995; Lieberman & Sales, 2007). As the media coverage surrounding *FL v. Zimmerman* (2013) demonstrates, some media savvy defense attorneys and defendants are taking the initiative to counter the anti-defendant coverage, getting their version of the story out. For example, some defendants and/or defense attorneys have set up websites, used Facebook, Twitter, blogs,

YouTube or radio, and TV interviews (e.g., George Zimmerman, Casey Anthony, and Steven Avery) in an attempt to present themselves in a positive light, or portray the victim in a negative one. In their article on PTP's influence on the courtroom, Lofink and Mullaney (2013) suggest that defense attorneys deal with PTP by "framing the media narrative early in the process" through the use of blogs, social media, and the Internet. They also suggest that defense attorneys "challenge the prosecution's narrative and the public's presumption about facts" by using these forms of media, and in essence pushing the limits of the ABA's guidelines for contact with the media and right to reply. Therefore, these new forms of media, and attorneys' increasing knowledge and use of them, has resulted in multiple types or slants of prejudicial PTP (e.g., anti-defendant, anti-victim, or pro-defendant) in some high-profile cases. The chapter now examines the research exploring how these various types or slants of PTP can influence jurors' decisions and impressions.

Negativity Bias

Research on the negativity bias has found that negative information has a greater effect than positive or neutral information on people's perceptions of others and impression formation (Kisley, Wood, & Burrows, 2007; Rozin & Royzman, 2001; Vaish, Grossmann, & Woodward, 2008). Ruva and McEvoy (2008) found some evidence for negativity bias, with negative-defendant PTP having a larger effect on guilt measures than positive-defendant PTP. In contrast, Daftary-Kapur et al. (2014) found that pro-defense PTP had a greater impact on guilt decisions than anti-defendant PTP. Also of interest, Bornstein, Whisenhunt, Nemeth, and Dunaway (2002) examined whether PTP could bias jurors against defendants or plaintiffs in a civil trial. They found that anti-defendant PTP had a stronger effect on liability judgments and perceptions of plaintiff sympathy, as compared to anti-plaintiff PTP. Therefore, the relative influence of different PTP slants might be case- or defendant-specific. Some defendants might benefit greatly from positive-defendant PTP or anti-plaintiff PTP, while others will not. The research discussed below suggests that all types or slants of PTP can significantly influence jurors' impressions of defendants and guilt decisions.

Negative-defendant PTP: Given that negative-defendant PTP is most prevalent and can threaten a defendant's right to a fair trial, especially in high-profile cases, it is not surprising that PTP researchers have focused most of their attention on negative-defendant PTP. Extensive research supports the contention that negative-defendant PTP can bias juror decision making by rendering a juror incapable of determining a verdict based solely on trial evidence (see Steblay et al., 1999 for review). Specifically, research has found that jurors who are exposed to negative-defendant PTP are more likely to find the defendant guilty and view the defendant as less credible than jurors who are not exposed to PTP (Kerr, Niedermeier, & Kaplan, 1999; Kramer, Kerr, & Carroll, 1990; Otto, Penrod, & Dexter, 1994; Ruva, McEvoy, & Bryant, 2007). Negative-defendant PTP also influences jurors' interpretation of trial evidence (Hope, Memon, & McGeorge, 2004; Otto et al., 1994; Ruva, Guenther, & Yarbrough, 2011; Ruva, Mayes, Dickman, & McEvoy, 2012) and the way jurors discuss ambiguous trial evidence during jury deliberations (Ruva & Guenther, 2015; Ruva & LeVasseur, 2012), pushing both toward an anti-defendant slant. In addition, negative-defendant PTP elicits negative emotional responses in jurors (Kramer et al., 1990; Ruva et al., 2011). Finally, exposure to negative-defendant PTP can influence jurors' memory for trial evidence by making it difficult for jurors to distinguish information obtained prior to trial (PTP) from information obtained during trial (source memory errors; Ruva & Guenther, 2015; Ruva & McEvoy, 2008; Ruva et al., 2007).

Positive-defendant PTP: As compared to negative-defendant PTP, far less research has focused on the biasing effects of positive-defendant or pro-defendant PTP. Positive-defendant PTP paints the defendant in a positive light, and is most likely to exist in trials involving rape or murder, as well as those in which the defendant is a celebrity or police officer (Daftary-Kapur et al., 2014). Some of the research examining how positive-defendant PTP influences jurors' decisions and impressions has used general PTP (not case-specific; Greene & Wade, 1988; Kovera, 2002; Woody & Viney, 2007). Research using case-specific positive-defendant PTP has found that it too influences jurors' decisions, impressions, interpretation of trial evidence, and memories. Specifically, jurors exposed to pro-defendant PTP are more likely to vote *not* guilty and perceive the defendant as *more* credible when compared with no-PTP controls, thus resulting in a pro-defense bias (Daftary-Kapur et al., 2014; Ruva, Dickman, & Mayes, 2014; Ruva et al., 2011; Ruva & McEvoy, 2008). In addition, jurors exposed to pro-defendant PTP are more likely, compared to jurors exposed to negative-defendant PTP or no-PTP controls, to misattribute the source of this PTP information to the trial (Ruva & McEvoy, 2008) and interpret trial evidence in favor of the defendant (Ruva et al., 2011; Ruva et al., 2012).

Negative-victim PTP: Negative-victim PTP involves using negative language to describe victims and/or portraying their actions as contributing to their victimization. While it is common for the media to focus on the accused, in certain cases the media has focused on blaming the victim by portraying the victim, at some level, to be at fault for the alleged crime (Taylor, 2009). Negative-victim PTP is prevalent for certain types of crime (e.g., rape, sexual assault, and domestic violence), and has been found to have an effect on jurors' decisions (Franiuk, Seefelt, Cepress, & Vandello, 2008; Taylor, 2009). For example, Franiuk et al. (2008) found that when mock-jurors were presented with anti-victim stories, as opposed to pro-victim stories, they were more likely to believe that the defendant was *not* guilty and that the victim was lying. In addition, Daftary-Kapur et al. (2014) found that jurors in the pro-defense PTP condition (consisting of a mixture of pro-defendant and anti-victim PTP) were less likely to find the defendant guilty than the no-PTP controls. Similarly, Ruva and Guenther (2017) found that jurors exposed to anti-victim PTP were more likely to find the defendant *not* guilty, rate the defendant as more credible, and the trial evidence as being more supportive of the defendant than jurors not exposed to PTP. They also found that the effect of PTP on guilt ratings was mediated by jurors' ratings of trial evidence and defendant credibility. Specifically, PTP imparted its biasing effects on jurors' guilt ratings by pushing their ratings of defendant credibility and trial evidence in the direction of the PTP bias (toward favoring the defendant if jurors were exposed to anti-victim PTP). Caution should be taken in interpreting the effect of negative-victim PTP on juror bias, given the small amount of research examining its influence on jurors' decisions.

Mixed PTP exposure: In their review of naturally occurring PTP, Daftary-Kapur et al. (2014) and Franiuk et al. (2008) discovered that, for some high-profile cases, multiple types of PTP (e.g., anti-defendant and anti-victim) are present. The prevalence of multiple types of PTP in high-profile case is only likely to increase as the accessibility to, and use of, nontraditional media outlets increases (e.g., Facebook, Twitter, and YouTube), as well as their implementation into the litigation process. Therefore, along with understanding how each type of PTP independently influences jurors' decisions and impressions, it is also important to understand how exposure to multiple PTP slants influences them.

Only two studies (Ruva et al., 2012, 2014) have explored how PTP effects on guilt decisions differ for jurors exposed to pure-PTP (e.g., exposure to only negative-defendant PTP) as opposed to jurors exposed to mixed-PTP (e.g., exposure to both negative-defendant and positive-defendant PTP). Ruva et al. (2012, 2014) exposed participants to either pure PTP or a mixture of pro-defendant and anti-defendant PTP over a period of 10–12 days. The mixed PTP exposure occurred either in an *alternating* (exposure episodes alternated between pro-defendant and anti-defendant) or *blocked* (jurors were exposed to all of the PTP articles of one slant before being exposed to the articles of the other slant) fashion. Both studies found that pure negative-defendant PTP jurors were more likely to vote guilty than pure positive-defendant PTP jurors. These studies also found that mixed PTP exposure presented in an alternating fashion resulted in a reduction of PTP bias (resembling no-PTP controls). However, Ruva et al. (2012) found that mock jurors who received a blocked mixture of negative-defendant PTP followed by positive-defendant PTP showed a primacy effect (i.e., negative-defendant PTP had the greatest impact), and their verdicts did not differ from pure negative-defendant PTP jurors. Interestingly, jurors in the blocked condition who received pro-defendant PTP first were most similar to jurors in the no-PTP control, suggesting a leveling of PTP bias. Ruva et al.'s (2014) findings differ from Ruva et al.'s (2012) in that the former found a reduction of PTP bias on verdicts for both the blocked and alternating groups. However, Ruva et al.'s (2014) guilt rating analyses (combination of guilt and confidence) suggested a recency effect, with those receiving negative-defendant PTP last closely resembling those in the pure negative-defendant PTP condition.

Although the results of these mixed PTP studies suggest that juror exposure to certain combinations of differing PTP slants might result in a reduction of bias, it should be noted that it is unlikely that equal amounts of negative-defendant and positive-defendant PTP would surround an actual case. Even more unlikely would be for traditional or social media to present these two types of PTP in an alternating fashion, and then for jurors to be exposed to this information in an alternating fashion. Therefore, much more research is needed before conclusions can be made on how various slants of PTP work in combination to bias jurors' decisions.

The research above suggests that all types or slants of PTP can influence jurors' guilt decisions, with negative-defendant PTP being especially problematic given its ability to bias the jury pool against the defendant–hence denying the defendant his/her right to a fair trial by an impartial jury. That being said, both positive-defendant and negative-victim PTP challenge the associated burden of proving guilt, which is placed on the prosecution. Therefore, understanding the influence of all PTP types/slants on juror bias is important. Social scientists have various methods they can employ to study these influences, with each having its benefits and limitations. These methods are the focus of the next section of this chapter.

Research Methodologies Used to Explore Pretrial Publicity's Biasing Effects

The effect of PTP on juror bias has been examined using three main methods: (1) surveys of actual or potential jurors, (2) jury simulation research/experiments, and (3) meta-analysis. Given that most of the research using these various methods is presented elsewhere in this chapter, only a brief discussion of the methodology will be presented here.

Survey Research

Survey studies exploring PTP's effects on prospective juror bias can be conducted solely for research purposes, but many have been conducted to assess the level of anti-defendant bias held by potential jurors in actual criminal cases (Studebaker & Penrod, 1997). Several of these survey studies have shown a strong relationship between the amounts of case information prospective jurors can report and their perceptions of defendant guilt (Costantini & King, 1980/1981; Moran & Cutler, 1991; Nietzel & Dillehay, 1983). For example, Moran and Cutler (1991) conducted surveys of prospective jurors in two high-profile cases and found a significant correlation between knowledge of case specifics and perceived culpability of the suspects. However, knowledge of case specifics was not correlated with prospective jurors' self-reported ability to be impartial. The authors concluded that negative-defendant PTP could prejudice potential jurors against a defendant and that self-reports of impartiality should not be taken at face value.

Surveys of prospective jurors benefit from high verisimilitude or realism, in that they query actual potential jurors about case relevant information. Realism is important given that judges might highly value it and some have dismissed scientific research due to a lack of it (e.g., *Ballew v. Georgia*, 1978; *Lockhart v. McCree*, 1986). Survey research also has several limitations. First, survey research does not clearly link exposure to PTP with biased jury decision making. The impact of PTP could be attenuated by the presentation of evidence at trial and jury deliberations. Therefore, the relationship between exposure to negative-defendant PTP and jury decision making might not be as strong as would be expected from survey research (Otto et al., 1994). Second, survey research does not allow for exact measurement of types and amounts of PTP that prospective jurors are exposed to. Instead, survey research relies on self-reports or indirect measures (e.g., memory reports) of PTP exposure. Finally, surveys suffer from a lack of control over extraneous variables, and without this control, researchers cannot make causal inferences (e.g., that exposure to PTP causes bias). Properly conducted jury simulation research does not suffer from these limitations, and has consistently shown that trial evidence presentation alone cannot eliminate the biasing effects of PTP (see Steblay et al., 1999 for review). That being said, no research method is perfect and below we review both the benefits and limitations of jury simulations.

Jury Simulation Research

Much of the research cited in this chapter consists of jury simulations or controlled experiments, which involve manipulations of variables under controlled conditions, resulting in increased internal validity over survey research. This control allows researchers to determine causal relationships between exposure to PTP and juror bias. One major advantage of jury simulations is that they allow researchers to systematically vary the amount and type of pretrial publicity that participants are exposed to, obviously something that is not possible with actual jurors. This systematic manipulation of amount and type of pretrial publicity makes it possible to determine their effects on juror decisions and impressions.

Another major advantage of jury simulation research is that it allows for the examination of the processes that influence jurors' and juries' decisions. As Bornstein et al. (2017) point out, it is important to explore not only the types of decisions jurors and juries make but also how they arrive at these decisions. At the juror-level these processes include, but are not limited to, how individual jurors' impressions, attitudes, memories, perceptions, and emotions influence their decisions. At the jury level the focus is on the deliberation process and how both individual and group-level mechanisms (e.g., group polarization, leniency shift, collaborative memory, and social decision schemes) influence jury decisions. As the review of mechanisms responsible for PTP's influence on guilt decisions will reveal, much has been learned about these processes through jury simulation research.

Experimental simulations do come with some costs. First, the systematic control over variables, which is the hallmark of experiments, results in lowered ecological validity and realism than field research (e.g., research on actual juries in a courtroom setting). That being said, most jury simulations attempt to create a realistic trial experience in a controlled experimental setting. These jury simulations differ widely in the degree of ecological validity or realism. It is a balancing act in which researchers need to maintain control over variables studied (internal validity), in order to infer causation, while at the same time attempting to make their stimuli and procedures as close to the real world as possible (ecological validity). PTP researchers can increase the ecological validity of their jury simulations by using actual news stories surrounding an actual trial. Additionally, they can have jurors deliberate to attempt to come to a unanimous verdict. The ecological validity of the trial stimuli can vary from trial transcripts (e.g., Daftary-Kapur et al. 2014; Hope et al., 2004) to videotape footage of actual trials (e.g., Otto et al., 1994; Ruva et al., 2007) to simulated reenactments with the roles of judges and attorneys being played by actual judges and attorneys (e.g., Kramer et al., 1990). The modality of PTP presentations can also vary from several written news articles (e.g., Daftary-Kapur et al., 2014; Ruva & McEvoy, 2008) to audiotaped presentations (e.g., Kramer et al., 1990) to videotaped television broadcasts (e.g., Ogloff & Vidmar, 1994; Wilson & Bornstein, 1998).

A second limitation of simulation research is that much of it uses college students as mock-jurors, which brings up questions regarding the representativeness of these samples, and hence their generalizability to the population of interest (i.e., actual jurors). In a recent meta-analysis of 53 jury simulation studies (40 criminal and 13 civil: $N = 17{,}716$), Bornstein et al. (2017) examined whether type of sample (student vs. nonstudent) had an effect on various outcome measures for criminal (i.e., guilty verdicts, continuous guilt/culpability, and sentencing) and civil (i.e., liability verdicts, continuous liability, and damages) cases. Bornstein and colleagues found no significant differences between samples for guilty verdicts, culpability ratings, and damage awards. That is, students were not more likely to find the defendant guilty, rate the defendant as more culpable, or award more in damages than nonstudents. The only statistically significant differences found between sample types were for liability judgments (both dichotomous and continuous measures), which had contradictory effects and therefore make the results difficult to interpret. Specifically, when compared to nonstudents, students were more likely to find defendants liable (liability verdict $d = 0.19$), but rated defendants lower in liability ($d = -0.11$). As for moderator effects, the authors note that "with the exception of trial presentation medium, moderator effects were small and inconsistent" (Bornstein et al., 2017, p. 13). Trial presentation medium (written summaries vs. others) moderated the effect of sample type on both guilty verdicts and culpability ratings. Specifically, student samples were more likely to render guilty verdicts and rate the defendant as more culpable when written summaries were used; however, no differences between sample types were found when other types of trial stimuli were used. This finding suggests that trial stimuli having greater ecological validity (e.g., videotaped trials or live trial simulations) might eliminate sample differences in regard to verdicts and culpability ratings. Bornstein et al. suggest that their findings could help to lessen the concern associated with the use of student samples in jury simulation research.

Meta-Analysis

Meta-analysis is a statistical procedure for combining the results from multiple studies in order to determine the overall effect of a variable (PTP) on a number of outcome variables (verdicts and impressions). To date, only one published meta-analysis on PTP effects has been conducted (Steblay et al., 1999). This meta-analysis included both jury simulation and survey research from 23 studies. These studies consisted of 44 empirical tests representing 5755 participants. Consistent with the research reviewed above, Steblay et al. found that mock-jurors exposed to negative-defendant PTP were significantly more likely to find that defendant guilty than those not exposed to PTP. Additionally, Steblay et al. found larger PTP effects in studies that included the following: nonstudents as opposed to students, actual PTP, multiple PTP components (e.g., crime details, arrest information, confession, prior record, and incriminating evidence), exposure to PTP at multiple points in time, a more serious charge (e.g., murder or sexual abuse), a greater delay between PTP exposure and decision, and surveys as opposed to jury simulations. They also observed that while PTP's effect was greatest prior to trial presentation, it persisted throughout pre- and post-deliberation verdict decisions.

In summary, all of the methods discussed above converge on a single conclusion—exposure to negative-defendant PTP biases jurors against the defendant. The chapter will now explore the important question of how PTP influences jurors' decision.

Mechanisms Responsible for PTP's Influence on Jurors' Decisions

It has been well established that PTP can have powerful effects on jurors' decisions regarding a defendant's guilt. To inform the courts on the types of remedies that will be most effective in reducing PTP bias, social scientists must understand the mechanisms that are responsible for this bias. Research has found that PTP imparts its biasing effects on jurors' decisions by influencing jurors': interpretation of trial evidence (Carlson & Russo, 2001; Hope et al., 2004; Ruva et al., 2011), impressions of defendants and attorneys (Kramer et al., 1990, Otto et al., 1994; Ruva & Guenther, 2015), emotional responses (Kramer et al., 1990; Ruva et al., 2011), and ability to discriminate the source of case information (PTP vs. trial; Ruva et al., 2007; Ruva & McEvoy, 2008). Therefore, research suggests that multiple mechanisms are responsible for PTP's biasing effects. Each of these mechanisms is reviewed in the subsections below.

Evidence Interpretation

It is a common assumption that people can be unbiased if they set their mind to it. Unfortunately, there is a wealth of social science research and theory that suggests otherwise (Kramer et al., 1990; Nisbett and Wilson 1977). Exposure to PTP biases jurors' processing of subsequent case information. Specifically, exposure to PTP influences what trial evidence jurors pay attention to, how much weight they give to this evidence, and whether they interpret this evidence as supporting the defense's or prosecution's case.

Primacy effects: Primacy effects have been found in a variety of situations and simply refer to early information being better remembered, or having greater influence on decisions and impressions, than later information (see Hurlstone, Hitch, & Baddeley, 2014 for review). Recency effects refer to situations in which information presented last has a greater influence on decisions and impressions than information presented earlier (Hurlstone et al., 2014 for review). Importantly for the discussion of PTP bias, research suggests that recency effects disappear with the institution of a delay, but primacy effects remain (Craik, 1970; Greene, 1986; Luchins & Luchins, 1970; Mayo & Crockett, 1964; Tan & Ward, 2000). The attention decrement hypothesis has been employed to explain how primacy effects occur. Specifically, when only a single judgment is required at the end of information presentation (e.g., verdict), primacy effects result from the reduced attention to information presented later, after an impression or decision is formed (Anderson, 1971). These primacy effects have also been explained via belief perseverance. Once an idea/belief is formed, it is resistant to change even after the basis for the belief has been refuted (Anderson, Lepper, & Ross, 1980; Anderson & Lindsay, 1998; Ross, Lepper, & Hubbard, 1975). All of this suggests that case information presented first (PTP) will have a greater influence on jurors' impressions and decisions than case information presented later at trial.

There is evidence of early case information having an influence on jurors' evaluation of later case information. For example, Schum (1993) found that 48% of his participants either ignored testimony that conflicted with prior evidence or interpreted it as agreeing with the earlier testimony. Schum attributed these findings to a type of primacy effect in which early information biases the interpretation and weight given to subsequent information. PTP is not trial evidence and therefore its effect on the jurors' interpretation of later case evidence might operate differently. That being said, Davis, Spitzer, Nagao, and Stassen (1978) found that jurors' pretrial biases (pro-prosecution or pro-defense) influenced the evaluation and weight given to the trial evidence. The results from both of these studies are consistent with Anderson's (1971) discounting explanation discussed above. Also consistent with the discounting explanation, Devine and Ostrom (1985) found that mock-jurors discounted inconsistent testimony in order to create a story that explained the trial events. This desire of jurors to create a coherent and complete trial story is explained by the story model, which the chapter now discusses.

The story model: The story model provides an explanation of how PTP influences jurors' decisions (Pennington & Hastie, 1986, 1993), which incorporates processes related to primacy effects discussed above. The story model posits that jurors use both information presented at trial and information that they come to trial with (e.g., PTP and knowledge about crime categories) to create cognitive frameworks through which all subsequent trial information is filtered and interpreted. Jurors have a desire to create a complete and coherent trial story. If jurors can create a complete story from early PTP information, later PTP or trial information that does not fit this story might be ignored or devalued, resulting in a primacy effect in which early information (PTP) has a greater effect on jurors' judgments than later information (Trial). Predecisional distortion theory also posits that early case information can bias jurors' interpretation of later case information.

Predecisional distortion theory: Predecisional distortion theory (Carlson & Russo, 2001) proposes that rather than weighing trial evidence according to its actual probative value, jurors will distort evidence to support their favored side (prosecution or defense). Research has shown that this distortion increases throughout the trial, as jurors' confidence that the favored side will win increases, and ultimately influences verdicts (Carlson & Russo, 2001; Russo, Meloy, & Medvec, 1998; Russo, Meloy, & Wilks, 2000). Jurors who are exposed to PTP are likely to come to trial with a favored side (e.g., negative-defendant PTP = prosecution favored), and might begin distorting trial evidence to support their favored side early during trial evidence presentation.

In order to examine whether PTP does result in predecisional distortion in the direction of the PTP bias, Hope et al. (2004) and Ruva et al. (2011) exposed mock-jurors to either negative-defendant PTP or unrelated news stories. Results from both studies found significantly higher levels of predecisional distortion (biased toward the prosecution) for jurors exposed to negative-defendant PTP, as well as an increase in the percentage of guilty verdicts. Both researchers suggested that primacy effects played a role. Specifically, when jurors are exposed to negative-defendant PTP and then early at trial favor the prosecution's case, it will be very difficult for mitigating evidence to be accurately weighed due to predecisional distortion. Additionally, Ruva et al. (2011) found that jurors exposed to positive-defendant PTP had significantly lower predecisional distortion scores (biased toward the defense), and were less likely to vote guilty than jurors in the no-PTP and negative-defendant PTP conditions. Importantly, both sets of researchers found that predecisional distortion of trial evidence mediated the effect of PTP on juror decisions. Therefore, exposure to PTP resulted in jurors interpreting trial evidence to favor the side that was favored in the PTP (prosecution or defense), and these biased interpretations influenced their guilt decisions. It should be noted that Ruva et al.'s findings suggest that both negative-defendant and positive-defendant PTP influence jurors' decisions through predecisional distortion.

The research above focuses on juror-level decisions, but there is also jury-level research that suggests predecisional distortion (or similar primacy effects) can affect how jurors discuss trial evidence during deliberations. As part of their analyses for two large jury studies, Ruva and associates (Ruva & Guenther, 2015; Ruva &

LeVasseur, 2012) content analyzed the videotaped deliberations of 60 mock-juries (30 per study). Half of these juries consisted of mock-jurors who had been exposed to negative-defendant PTP and the other half were exposed to unrelated news stories. They found that during deliberations, jurors who were exposed to negative-defendant PTP were significantly more likely, compared to no-PTP controls, to discuss ambiguous trial evidence (which did not support either side or was neutral) as if it supported the prosecution. Additionally, Ruva and Guenther (2015) found that discussion of ambiguous trial information in a pro-prosecution manner significantly mediated the effect of PTP on juries' guilt decisions. Therefore, jurors exposed to negative-defendant PTP were more likely to discuss ambiguous evidence in a pro-prosecution manner, and this biased discussion of evidence influenced juries' guilt decisions.

The research and theory above suggests that, in cases having a lot of PTP, it is likely that trial information will be distorted in a way that favors this PTP, regardless of its true probative value. As the discussion below will reveal, predecisional distortion, belief perseverance, and similar primacy effects are some, but not all, of the hurdles that the defense would have to overcome when pervasive negative-defendant PTP exists.

Impression Formation

The primacy effects described above are also important to this discussion of impression formation. Jurors who are exposed to PTP are likely to come to trial having already formed an impression of the defendant. Most of the research focusing on PTP's effects on jurors' perceptions of a defendant's credibility has focused on negative-defendant PTP. This research has found that jurors exposed to negative-defendant PTP rate the defendant as less credible, or have more negative impressions of the defendant, than jurors not exposed to PTP (Dexter et al., 1992; Kramer et al., 1990, Otto et al., 1994; Ruva et al., 2007). That being said, the small amount of research exploring the effect of positive-defendant PTP on jurors' impressions has found that exposure to pro-defendant PTP results in jurors rating the defendant as more credible than no-PTP controls (Ruva et al., 2011; Ruva & Hudak, 2013; Ruva & McEvoy, 2008). Importantly, these defendant credibility ratings have been found to mediate PTP's effect on jurors' guilt decisions (Ruva et al., 2011; Ruva & McEvoy, 2008). Thus, PTP influences jurors' impressions of the defendant and these impressions then influence jurors' guilt decisions.

In addition to influencing jurors' impressions of defendants, exposure to PTP influences jurors' impressions of litigating attorneys. Ruva and McEvoy (2008) found that jurors exposed to negative-defendant PTP rated the prosecuting attorney more favorably (higher in likability and ability), and the defense attorney less favorably (lower in likability and ability), than jurors exposed to positive-defendant PTP or no PTP. They also found that jurors exposed to positive-defendant PTP provided less favorable ratings of the prosecuting attorney than no-PTP controls. Similarly, Ruva and Guenther

(2015) found that jurors exposed to negative-defendant rated the prosecuting attorney as more favorable, and the defense attorney as less favorable, than the no-PTP controls. In both of these studies, jurors' ratings of the prosecuting attorney mediated the effect of PTP on guilt decisions. As with the defendant credibility ratings, exposure to PTP influenced jurors' impressions of key trial players (prosecuting attorney), and these biased impressions influenced their guilt decisions.

Ruva and associates suggest that Pennington and Hastie's (1988, 1993) story model can explain how jurors' impressions of defendants and attorney can mediate PTP's influence on jurors' decisions. Jurors exposed to PTP used this information as a framework for analyzing subsequent case information (i.e., trial evidence) in order to create a coherent story. Those jurors exposed to negative-defendant PTP come to court with a story that the defendant is not credible and is likely guilty. This results in subsequent trial evidence being encoded in a manner that agrees with this anti-defendant original story.

Emotional Responses

Recently, researchers have begun to explore the influence of emotions on jurors' decisions and impressions (see Nunez, Estrada-Reynolds, Schweitzer, & Myers, 2016 for review). According to Feigenson and Park (2006), emotions can affect jurors' decisions by biasing information processing in the direction of the emotion and providing informational cues. Therefore, PTP could influence verdict outcomes by eliciting negative emotional responses (e.g., anger, hostility, disgust, and anxiety) that then influence jurors' processing of trial information and ultimately their verdicts (Salerno & Bottoms, 2009). Obviously, emotional responses elicited by PTP are extralegal in nature, and become problematic when they bias jurors' decisions.

Negative-defendant PTP elicits negative emotional responses in jurors and influences both juror (Kramer & Kerr, 1989) and jury (Kramer et al., 1990) decisions. Much of this research suggests that emotional PTP has a more damaging effect on jurors' decisions than factual PTP. For example, Kramer et al. (1990) found that during voir dire mock-jurors exposed to negative-defendant PTP reported more negative emotions and held a stronger bias against the defendant than jurors exposed to factual PTP. They also found that a time delay between exposure to PTP and voir dire was only able to reduce the effects of factual PTP, whereas the effects of emotional PTP did not diminish over time.

Honess, Charman, and Levi (2003) examined jurors who were naturally exposed to PTP by having them recall the PTP they were exposed to. They then evaluated the content of these recalls as either factual or affective/evaluative. Jurors were then exposed to a briefing by the trial judge, along with prosecution and defense opening statements. Jurors who recalled affective/evaluative PTP showed more bias against the defendant in their reasoning, evaluations of the defense's arguments, and confidence in the defendant's guilt. Contrary to these findings, Wilson and Bornstein (1998) found that, when controlling for the information's diagnosticity, both factual and emotional PTP biased jurors' decisions, with no significant difference between them in regard to jurors' verdicts.

According to the Appraisal-Tendency Framework (Lerner & Keltner, 2000, 2001), not all negative emotions (e.g., anger, disgust, anxiety, and sadness) are equally influential on judgments and decisions (see Feigenson & Park, 2006, for review). Anger influences perceptions, beliefs, reasoning, choices, and punitiveness (Bodenhausen, Sheppard, & Kramer, 1994; Lerner, Goldberg, & Tetlock, 1998; Lerner & Tiedens, 2006). Importantly, anger can carry over to judgments and decisions regardless of whether the emotional state is related to the final decision (Loewenstein & Lerner, 2003; Zillmann, 1983).

Unfortunately, the research discussed above exploring the effects of emotional PTP on juror bias did not employ measures that could distinguish among different types of emotions. It only addressed whether the response was affective/emotional, and in some cases its valence (negative, neutral, or positive). Therefore, the specific emotions elicited by PTP in each study are unknown, and it is possible that the emotions elicited across the studies differed, resulting in conflicting findings. To rectify this, and explore whether anger acts as a unique emotional mechanism, Ruva et al. (2011) used two different emotional measures: (1) Spielberger's State-Trait Personality Inventory (STPI; Spielberger, 1983; Spielberger & Reheiser, 2003) and (2) a PTP recall and emotional response task. The STPI measures both the state and trait forms of anger, anxiety, depression, and curiosity, with Ruva and colleagues focusing on the state or transitory form (Spielberger & Reheiser, 2009). The emotion measure associated with the PTP recall task required participants to select emotion words, from an emotion word list (each word was part of a specific emotion category), that described their emotional responses to the PTP information they recalled. The jurors in Ruva et al.'s (2011) study were exposed to either negative-defendant PTP, positive-defendant PTP, or no PTP. Jurors exposed to negative-defendant PTP were angrier after viewing the trial than those in the positive-defendant or no PTP conditions. This anger acted as an emotional mechanism through which PTP influenced jurors' decision—with those exposed to negative-defendant PTP being angrier, which resulted in a greater propensity to vote guilty. In addition, jurors exposed to positive-defendant PTP were significantly more likely than jurors in the negative-defendant and no PTP conditions to use positive emotion words to describe their PTP recalls. The proportion of positive emotion words used to describe PTP recalls mediated guilt decisions. Positive emotional responses to PTP also acted as an emotional mechanism through which PTP influenced jurors' decision—with those exposed to positive-defendant PTP indicating more positive emotional responses, which resulted in a greater propensity to vote not guilty.

Dumas, Lepastourel, and Testé (2014) also explored whether anger mediated PTP's effect on jurors' decisions. They found that jurors were more likely to find the defendant guilty after reading negative-defendant PTP containing both incriminating (includes implicating evidence against the accused, such as results of a search warrant or admissions of guilt) and crime story information (details of the crime committed). They also found that the amount of anger jurors expressed increased as the number of crime story elements increased, while the amount of incriminating evidence did not influence the level of anger. Mediation analyses showed that incriminating evidence had a direct effect on verdicts; crime story information indirectly affected verdicts by eliciting negative emotional responses. Therefore, consistent with Ruva et al. (2011), this study suggests negative-defendant PTP influences jurors' verdicts by increasing juror anger, which then increases the likelihood of voting guilty.

Why does anger result in such biased decisions? People who are made to feel angry are less cautious in their decision making than those who feel other forms of negative affect, such as sadness (Bodenhausen et al., 1994; Tiedens, 2001). When deciding guilt, angry people are more influenced by stereotypes than people who express neutral emotions or sadness (Bodenhausen, et al., 1994; Tiedens & Linton, 2001). Therefore, anger can lead to automatic, superficial, and heuristic processing which could result in jurors' feeling increased confidence in their preconceived judgments and less likely to consider further information (Feigenson & Park, 2006; Lerner & Keltner, 2001; Lerner & Tiedens, 2006).

Source Memory

Memory might also be an important means by which PTP imparts its biasing effects on jurors' guilt decision. How information is encoded (brought into the memory system) has a significant effect on how strong and durable memory will be. In addition to the strength of the memory trace, the accuracy of people's source attributions (Johnson, Hashtroudi, & Lindsay, 1993) regarding where they learned particular facts about the case has important implications in regard to PTP's influence on juror bias, as well as jurors' ability to correct for this bias. Finally, as already discussed, cognitive biases such as predecisional distortion and belief perseverance can bias how jurors encode trial information. This section focuses on source memory, given that it is a mechanism through which PTP imparts its bias on jurors' decisions.

Otto et al. (1994, p. 457) discuss two methods by which PTP can bias jury decision making:

> Pretrial publicity may operate … by leading potential jurors to spontaneously form an impression of the defendant, which may then influence their judgments. … Jurors may not use the information received from the pretrial publicity in forming an impression, but might instead simply encode this information into long-term memory. Jurors would then be making memory-based judgments … in which they would have both the information gained from the pretrial publicity and the evidence actually presented in the trial to draw upon in making their judgments.

If in fact jurors do encode PTP and later retrieve it when making decisions about guilt, are they *aware* of the source of this information? This question pertains to the area of *source monitoring,* which "refers to a set of processes involved in making attributions about the origins of memories, knowledge, and beliefs" (Johnson et al.,

1993, p. 3). Memories are not tagged or labeled with specific sources, but instead contain informational clues that allow us to distinguish their source (Lindsay, 1994). At times, people consciously struggle to identify a source, but more often they are not conscious of this process (Lindsay, 1994). Source misattributions can arise because recollecting information about an event and the source of that information are believed to be two separate cognitive acts (Johnson et al., 1993), and memory performance for event information (e.g., PTP information) is generally better than memory for source information (Kelly, Carroll, & Mazzoni, 2002).

Ruva and associates have examined source monitoring in jurors exposed to PTP by using the *reverse suggestibility paradigm*. Research has demonstrated that people's memory for an event can be significantly influenced by *information presented before* (PTP) the to-be-remembered event (Trial), which is labeled the reverse suggestibility effect (Rantzen & Markham, 1992; Ruva et al., 2007). Ruva and associates have explored whether jurors exposed to PTP are more likely to misattribute information provided only in the PTP to trial, and refer to these errors as critical source memory errors. They have found that mock-jurors exposed to PTP are more likely than no-PTP controls to believe with a high level of confidence that information presented only in the PTP was presented at trial (Ruva & Guenther, 2015; Ruva & McEvoy, 2008; Ruva et al., 2007). In addition, jurors who deliberated made as many of these errors as the no-deliberation controls (Ruva & Guenther, 2015; Ruva et al., 2007). Also of interest, these source misinformation effects were found regardless of the slant/type of PTP exposure (i.e., negative-defendant or positive-defendant; Ruva & McEvoy, 2008). Importantly, these source misattributions were found to be a mechanism through which PTP biases juror decisions. That is, research suggests that mock-jurors do misattribute information presented in the PTP to the trial and these source misattributions influence guilt decisions.

Ruva and associates warn that source memory tasks of actual jurors, as compared to mock-jurors, are likely more difficult due to the increased delay between PTP exposure and trial testimony, as well as the increased delay between evidence presented early in trial and jury deliberations. A longer time delay between encoding and retrieval of information increases source misattributions (Frost, Ingraham, & Wilson, 2002; Hekkanen & McEvoy, 2005). To explore this using a mock-juror paradigm, Ruva and McEvoy (2008) manipulated the delay (no delay vs. 2 days) between trial exposure and completion of the source memory test. They found that jurors who experienced a delay made three times as many critical source-memory errors as those who did not experience a delay.

Also of interest, the jurors in Ruva and Guenther's (2015) study all experienced a 2-day delay between viewing the trial and jury deliberations, after which they completed the source memory test. Such a delay had not been instituted in prior jury deliberation studies exploring the effect of PTP on source-memory errors. Ruva and Guenther (2015) found that the PTP-exposed jurors made nearly three times the critical source-memory errors as jurors in previous research without a similar delay. In addition, the level of critical source memory errors was similar to those found in Ruva and McEvoy's (2008) delay condition. These findings are also interesting given that Steblay et al.'s (1999) meta-analysis found PTP effects increased as the delay between PTP exposure and verdict decision increased. Thus, the increased effects of PTP with increased delays could be at least partially due to increases in source memory errors.

In summary, there are multiple mechanisms responsible for PTP's biasing effects on juror and jury guilt decisions. These mechanisms are likely to be outside of jurors' awareness and therefore outside of their control (Feigenson & Park, 2006; Johnson et al., 1993; Wilson & Brekke, 1994; Wilson, Centerbar, & Brekke, 2002). In order to effectively remedy the effects of PTP on juror and jury decisions, it is important for the courts to be aware of the mechanisms responsible for theses biasing effects. It is also important for the courts to realize that jurors are unlikely to be able to self-correct for the effects of PTP, and are likely unaware of how this bias will influence their impressions of the defendant and their interpretation and memory for trial evidence.

Effectiveness of Court Remedies in Reducing or Ameliorating PTP Bias

Trial motions related to the effects of prejudicial PTP on defendants' right to a fair trial are prevalent and have increased over time (Minnow & Cate, 1991; Spano, Groscup, & Penrod, 2011). The courts have several remedies that can be used to combat the biasing effects of prejudicial PTP (e.g., continuance, voir dire, jury deliberations, judicial instruction, change of venue, and bench trial as opposed to jury trial). Many of these remedies are addressed, or alluded to in the significant decisions handed down by the Supreme Court. PTP researchers have examined the effectiveness of continuance, voir dire, deliberations, and judicial instruction. This section of the chapter focuses on this research and related theory. It also covers how the increasing Internet and social media coverage of cases making their way towards trial could impact the effectiveness of these remedies.

Continuance

Common sense might suggest that the influence of PTP should diminish over time. That is, a delay or continuance of a trial might be enough to significantly reduce or eliminate the bias associated with PTP. This is the stance that some courts have taken by refusing to accept the notion that the biasing effects of PTP can persist over a long period of time (*Irvin v. Dowd*, 1961). Therefore, in some cases a continuance or delay has been instituted to remedy the effects of prejudicial PTP (*United States v. Dioguardi*, 1956). Although *Rideau v. Louisiana* (1963) does not directly speak to continuance, it does refer to the effect of a delay on PTP bias. It suggests that a delay should be expected to alleviate PTP bias, "[U]nless the adverse publicity is shown by the record to have fatally infected the trial." This remedy of a delay is also thought to be effective, given that the majority of PTP surrounding a case occurs at the time of incident and arrest (*Sheppard v. Maxwell*, 1966).

Contrary to the courts' beliefs that a delay will diminish or eliminate the biasing effects of pervasive and prejudicial PTP, social science research suggests it is unlikely to be an effective remedy. In cases having large amounts of PTP, in which the exposure to the PTP is repeated over a long period of time, memory traces can be so strong that such memories could last over several years, if not a lifetime. The reasons for this are many. First, as already discussed above, emotional PTP is resistant to delay (Kramer et al., 1990). Second, research going back over a century has found that when learning episodes are spaced across time, rather than presented only once or over a short period of time, memory is enhanced, resulting in increased retention over longer periods of time (see Cepeda, Pashler, Vul, Wixted, & Rohrer, 2006 for review). The size of this distributed or spaced learning effect is often large (see Donovan & Radosevich, 1999 and Janiszewski, Noel, & Sawyer, 2003 for reviews), making these memory traces strong enough to withstand significant delays. Third, one problem with a continuance as a remedy for PTP bias is that, in the real world, the media typically reinstates the PTP at the time of pretrial hearings and just prior to trial (Dexter et al., 1992; Moran & Cutler, 1991).

Finally, given that the majority of American adults are now online (90%), and that the average Internet user accesses news through online media sources, blogs, and social media (Mastromauro, 2010; Pew Research Center, 2017b), the effectiveness of a continuance is questionable. This is because people can readily access stories and videos (e.g., YouTube, Netflix, iTunes podcasts) about a case from the distant past, and hence the influence of PTP might not fade with time due to continued exposure. Therefore, even if in the past the courts could count on the majority of PTP occurring at the time of the incident and arrest, nontraditional media sources could easily keep the PTP going throughout the delay or continuance.

Voir Dire

In cases having pervasive prejudicial PTP, the voir dire is used to assess potential jurors' knowledge of the PTP surrounding the case and potential bias against the defendant. In high-profile cases it might be difficult, if not impossible, to find jurors who have not seen or heard anything about the case. In such cases, the courts may allow more extensive questioning of potential jurors and additional peremptory challenges (see *United States v. Meredith*, 1987). Such focused questioning is thought by the courts to be an effective remedy for PTP bias (Kramer et al., 1990). The use of voir dire to remedy PTP bias assumes that attorneys and judges are able to determine whether potential jurors can be impartial, and that potential jurors can assess their own bias and honestly report on it (Shahani, 2005). The latter is of great importance, given that a juror is often defined by the courts as being free from prejudice if he/she reports the ability to set aside opinion and render a verdict based solely on the evidence presented at trial.

The social science research exploring the effectiveness of voir dire as a remedy for PTP bias suggests that it is unlikely that potential jurors can adequately assess their own bias. For example, Sue, Smith, and Pedroza (1975) found that jurors who were exposed to PTP and answered "yes" to the question, "Can you, in view of the publicity you have seen, judge the defendant in a fair and unbiased manner," were more likely to find the defendant guilty than jurors not exposed to PTP. Thus, despite the belief that they could put aside bias associated with exposure to PTP, these jurors could not and this was reflected in their verdicts. It should also be noted that jurors who answered "no" to this question, and hence believed that PTP had biased them, also were more likely to find the defendant guilty than the no-PTP controls.

Similarly, Kerr, Kramer, Carroll, and Alfini (1991), during voir dire, asked jurors exposed to PTP, "[C]an you put out of your mind any information you might have received from the newspapers or television and decide this case solely upon the evidence to be presented in court?" They found no relationship between jurors' responses to this question and their verdicts. That is, jurors who believed they could set aside bias associated with PTP exposure convicted the defendant at similar rates to those who doubted their ability to set aside PTP bias. It is not clear from this study, or Sue et al. (1975) above, whether jurors were unaware that PTP had influenced them, erroneously believed that they could correct for PTP bias, or were dishonest in their reporting of PTP's influence on them. Thus, jurors' assertions of being unbiased are clearly not enough.

Can attorneys and judges accurately assess potential juror bias associated with PTP exposure? Kramer et al. (1990) explored this question by having a sample of experienced defense attorneys, prosecutors, and judges evaluate videotapes of mock-jurors responding to questions during voir dire. These judges and attorneys also had access to background questionnaires and PTP summaries. They were to use all of this information to make decisions regarding which of the potential jurors they would excuse in their role as judge or attorney. Kramer and associates found that neither judges nor attorneys' exclusion decisions were related to juror verdicts. That is, jurors excused by judges and attorneys were no more likely to render guilty verdicts than those accepted, with jurors exposed to PTP being more likely to convict than no-PTP controls.

The effectiveness of voir dire as a remedy for PTP bias rests on a number of assumptions related to jurors' ability to identify and correct cognitive biases, many of which are also required for remedies of judicial instruction and deliberation. First, it presumes that potential jurors are aware that such bias exists. Second, potential jurors must understand how this bias can influence their decisions (size and direction of bias). Third, prospective jurors must be willing to report any bias they are aware of. Fourth, it presumes that once exposed to PTP, jurors are capable of disregarding it, and then encode trial information as if never exposed to PTP (see discussion on primacy effects, predecisional distortion theory, and story model above). Fifth, after being exposed to PTP and trial evidence, jurors would have to accurately identify the source of these two types of information (see discussion on source memory above). The research presented in previous sections of this chapter suggests that jurors exposed to PTP will find it difficult, if not impossible, to meet any, let alone all of these assumptions (see also Wilson & Brekke, 1994; Wilson et al., 2002), suggesting that traditional voir dire is likely ineffective at alleviating PTP bias.

The question now turns to whether more elaborate probing of juror bias and/or attempts to educate jurors about potential bias are effective remedies. Dexter et al. (1992) examined the effectiveness of an extended voir dire as a remedy for jury bias caused by negative-defendant PTP. In the extended voir dire the defense attorney sought to educate prospective jurors about their potential biases rather than to eliminate those biases. The attorney warned jurors that it would take "conscious effort to monitor one's thinking and to censor oneself" (p. 824). In the minimal voir dire, superficial questions were asked of the mock juries and there was no attempt to educate jurors. Despite the juror education, the extended voir dire did not reduce the effect of negative-defendant PTP on verdict decisions, which again is expected given the cognitive biases discussed above.

Qualls (2015) suggests that the courts should use more "'well-developed' 'and' 'widely accepted'" assessment instruments to determine whether prospective jurors hold bias against the defendant, as well as the amount of juror bias. Qualls suggests that such survey instruments should use Likert-type scales or semantic differentials to assess prospective jurors' attitudes toward the defendant, case, and crime, which would be a dramatic improvement over questions requiring only a "'yes' 'or' 'no'" response. Whether this type of questioning would be better able to ferret out juror bias in cases involving pervasive and prejudicial PTP has not been thoroughly tested.

Others have suggested that Internet and social media research could help identify juror bias during voir dire. In addition to the Internet and social media being a source for pretrial information, both have been extensively employed to conduct research on prospective jurors (Browning, 2016). Although it cannot correct for cognitive biases that jurors are unaware of, some have called for the use of the Internet ("voir Google") and social media ("Facebooking the jury") to investigate juror dishonesty during voir dire (see Browning, 2016 for review). The courts have a variety of opinions in regard to litigating attorneys conducting online or social media research on prospective jurors. Some judges have banned online research during voir dire, fearing that it could have a "chilling effect on jury service," resulting in citizens being unwilling to participate for fear that their privacy would be violated (Browning, 2016). A survey of federal judges conducted in 2014 found that 26% of respondents indicated that they banned social media use by attorneys during voir dire (Dunn, 2014). The main reasons provided for these social media bans were protecting jurors' privacy, fear that its use would be distracting and prolong the voir dire process, and the belief that traditional voir dire would be sufficient to uncover juror bias.

Although 26% of judges ban Internet and social media research, the courts are increasingly recognizing the right of attorneys to use them when conducting juror research (Dunn, 2014), and in some jurisdictions (e.g., New Jersey, Missouri, and

Florida) have suggested an imposition of their use (Browning, 2016). For example, in *Carino v. Muenzen* (2011; medical malpractice case) the New Jersey appellate court indicated that the lower court acted unreasonably by prohibiting the use of the Internet by the plaintiff's counsel during voir dire. In *Johnson v. McCullough* (2010; medical malpractice case), the Missouri Supreme Court indicated that competent representation in the digital age implied a duty to conduct online juror research during voir dire. Specifically, the court stated that "a party *must* use reasonable efforts to examine the litigation history on Case.net of those jurors selected but not empaneled and present to the trial court any relevant information prior to trial" (p. 559).

In addition to legal decisions regarding the use of online research during voir dire (see Browning, 2016 for review), the ABA has provided guidance in Formal Opinion 14-466, "Lawyer Reviewing Jurors' Internet Presence" (ABA, 2014). The ABA opined that it is not unethical for litigating attorneys to conduct a review of prospective jurors, so long as they do not have direct or indirect contact with them, and the law or court order does not prohibit it. The ABA also noted that there is a strong public interest in identifying biased or tainted jurors.

Clearly, the use of the Internet and social media to conduct juror research is still in its infancy, and it is likely to see dramatic changes over the next several years. Given that much of the bias associated with PTP exposure is a result of cognitive mechanisms outside of conscious control, it is unlikely that such research will ferret out all, or even most, of the PTP bias in prospective jurors. That being said, it could provide insight into how much pretrial information jurors have been exposed to and whether they have posted biased comments about the case online or on social media. The question now turns to whether, given voir dire's likely ineffectiveness at eliminating PTP bias, PTP bias can be corrected by court remedies occurring after voir dire; specifically, jury deliberation and judicial instructions.

Jury Deliberations

It is commonly assumed that jury deliberation enables jurors to correct errors, reject irrelevant information, and control biases. However, research suggests that this assumption is idealistic in that deliberation intensifies PTP bias (Kramer et al., 1990; Otto et al., 1994; Ruva et al., 2007; Studebaker & Penrod, 1997). This results in the responses of groups being more extreme than those of individuals, an effect which has been labeled group polarization (Moscovici & Zavalloni, 1969). Consistent with group polarization effects, Kerr et al. (1999) found that jurors exposed to PTP were more likely to vote guilty after deliberation than prior to it. In a similar study, Kramer et al. (1990) found that PTP's biasing effect was stronger in juries than jurors.

Other research has found that deliberation does not increase or reduce the PTP's biasing influence on verdicts. Across two large jury studies, Ruva and associates (Ruva & Guenther, 2015; Ruva et al., 2007) found that jurors who were exposed to PTP and then deliberated did not significantly differ in guilty verdicts from jurors exposed to PTP who did not deliberate (nominal jurors). Similarly, Otto et al. (1994) found that deliberation did not significantly reduce PTP-induced biases. Although deliberation did not increase the number of guilty verdicts, Ruva et al. (2007) found that it did increase PTP bias, in that jurors who deliberated rated the defendant more negatively than those who did not deliberate.

Also of interest, Ruva and Guenther (2015) found that jurors who were not exposed to PTP were less likely to vote guilty after deliberation than prior to it, which has been referred to as a leniency shift (Kerr, 1993). This leniency shift was not found for jurors exposed to negative-defendant PTP. Instead, these PTP-exposed jurors were just as likely to vote guilty after deliberations as they were prior to them. One explanation for the leniency shift is that, during jury deliberations, the defendant protection norm and reasonable doubt standard are highlighted (Kerr, 1993; Waters & Hans, 2009). The defendant protection norm is the preference of erroring on the side of acquitting a guilty defendant, as opposed to convicting an innocent one (Davis, Stasser, Spitzer, & Holt, 1976). This norm is thought responsible for the finding that initial majorities favoring not guilty verdicts prevail more often than those favoring guilty verdicts (see MacCoun & Kerr, 1988 for review). Interestingly, Ruva and Guenther (2015) found that juries exposed to PTP spent significantly less time, compared to juries not exposed to PTP, discussing jury instructions and the fact that there was a lack of evidence to convict. This could explain why deliberation had no effect on PTP-exposed jurors' verdicts, but did affect the verdicts of jurors not exposed to PTP. These results, along with those mentioned above, suggest that the corrective effect of juries on their individual members might not occur when jurors had been exposed to PTP.

Why are deliberations ineffective at reducing PTP bias? First, as noted above, the bias associated with PTP influences how trial evidence is encoded. By the time jurors begin deliberations, they have formulated a trial story and have encoded trial evidence in a manner consistent with this story. Then, according to persuasive argument theory, during deliberations jurors will spend more time discussing, and making better arguments for, the side they prefer (e.g., prosecution; Vinokur & Burnstein, 1974), which could result in polarization effects. Such biased interpretation and discussion of trial evidence was supported by Ruva and associates' finding that, when compared to no-PTP controls, juries whose members were exposed to negative-defendant PTP were more likely to discuss ambiguous trial evidence as if it supported the prosecution and were less likely to discuss it as supporting the defense (Ruva & Guenther 2015; Ruva & LeVasseur, 2012).

Additionally, PTP's influence on jurors' decisions can persist after deliberations due to jurors mistaking PTP for trial information (source memory error), and then discussing PTP during deliberations as if it came from the trial. Ruva and associates (Ruva & Guenther, 2015; Ruva & LeVasseur, 2012) found that jurors do discuss PTP during deliberations, and often fail to identify it as PTP and thus treat it as trial evidence. Such discussion can also result in jurors who were not originally exposed to PTP being exposed to it during deliberations, or it could act as a memory cue for jurors who might have forgotten some of the PTP they were exposed to. A recent study by Ruva and Guenther (2017) demonstrated that, during deliberations, PTP bias can be spread from PTP exposed jurors to those not previously exposed to PTP. Specifically, no-PTP jurors who deliberated with jurors exposed to negative-defendant PTP were more likely to vote guilty after deliberations, as compared to no-PTP jurors who deliberated on juries made up only of no-PTP jurors. Thus, instead of reducing PTP bias, deliberations can result in a spread of PTP bias. The discussion of PTP during deliberations and the spread of bias are further explored in the section on judicial instructions that follow.

Judicial Instructions

The remedy of judicial instructions assumes that jurors are aware of any potential bias from PTP and are able and willing to correct for it. The discussion above has already provided evidence that this is unlikely due to a number of cognitive biases and errors. Research examining the effectiveness of judicial instructions to disregard PTP provides further evidence that such judicial admonishments are ineffective at combating PTP bias (see Lieberman & Arndt, 2000 and Steblay, Hosch, Culhane, & McWethy, 2006 for reviews). In fact, research has found that jurors are likely to discuss PTP during jury deliberations even when admonished not to (Kline & Jess, 1966; Kramer et al., 1990; Ruva & Guenther, 2015; Ruva & LeVasseur, 2012). Ruva and LeVasseur (2012) and Ruva and Guenther (2015) videotaped and content analyzed 60 mock-jury deliberations. Prior to deliberations, these juries were admonished not to discuss PTP or use it to make verdict decisions. Ruva and LeVasseur (2012) found that all 14 of their PTP-exposed juries discussed PTP during deliberations, and spent, on average, 6.53% of their total deliberation time discussing PTP. These PTP-exposed juries rarely corrected their members who discussed PTP (only 10% of the time). Instead of correction, a common reaction to the mention of PTP was for jury members to acknowledge that the information being discussed was PTP, and then continue to discuss it anyway (occurred 44% of the time). Similarly, Ruva and Guenther (2015) found that all 15 of their PTP-exposed juries discussed PTP during deliberations, spending, on average, 8% of their total deliberation time discussing PTP. These jurors offered some form of correction only 28% of the time, with this correction working (jurors stopped discussing the PTP) only 19% of the time. Thus, contrary to the courts' assumption that judicial instruction is an effective remedy, the majority of the time that PTP was discussed no correction was made.

Why would jurors discuss PTP during deliberations after being admonished not to? Jurors might unknowingly discuss PTP during deliberations due to source confusions. That is, they unknowingly discuss information they have been instructed not to use. Kramer et al. (1990), Ruva and LeVasseur (2012), and Ruva and Guenther (2015) all suggest that some instances of PTP discussion during mock-jury deliberations, as well as failure to correct discussion of PTP, might have been due to source errors (i.e., confusing PTP with trial evidence).

Jurors might knowingly discuss PTP because it corresponds with their initial assumption about the defendant's culpability (Story Model; Pennington & Hastie, 1988, 1993). In addition, jurors might knowingly discuss PTP and not correct fellow jurors because they consider PTP information to be vital to the trial and their decision-making process (Devine, Clayton, Dunford, Seying, & Pryce, 2001). For example, Sommers and Kassin (2001) found that mock-jurors are likely to selectively comply with judicial instructions to disregard inadmissible evidence due to their motivation to arrive at a "just" verdict. According to Sommers and Kassin (2001) a "just" verdict indicates accuracy regarding whether the defendant committed the crime and is deserving of punishment. They found that jurors were likely to disregard judicial instructions regarding inadmissible evidence they deemed reliable, but would adhere to instructions when this same evidence was considered unreliable. This same selective compliance might be used for PTP, with jurors using what they consider reliable PTP information during jury deliberations, even when admonished not to.

Interestingly, both Davis (1986) and Ruva and Guenther (2015) found that jurors exposed to negative-defendant PTP discussed judicial instructions at a significantly lower rate than jurors exposed to unrelated or neutral PTP. That is, discussion of judicial instructions varied as a function of PTP exposure. It is not clear why jurors exposed to PTP discussed judicial instructions less frequently than juries not exposed to PTP. Perhaps, the negative-defendant PTP exposed juries avoided discussion of judicial instructions because these juries believed the defendant to be guilty, and therefore wanted to avoid discussion of information that would favor a not guilty verdict (e.g., reasonable doubt) or prohibited the discussion of case information pointing toward guilt (PTP).

Change of Venue

Although *Irvin v. Dowd* (1961), *Rideau v. Louisiana* (1963), *Murphy v. Florida* (1975), and *Sheppard v. Maxwell* (1966) all speak to change of venue in cases involving pervasive PTP, historically changes of venue are infrequently granted (Moran & Cutler, 1991). This could be partially due to the courts' use of the "totality of circumstances" test established by *Murphy v. Florida* (1975). This test places on the defense the burden of demonstrating that PTP resulted in juror bias that would make a fair trial impossible.

The effectiveness of change of venue has not been experimentally explored by social scientists. That being said, social scientists have explored, through field research involving actual trials, prospective juror bias as a function of whether these people resided inside or outside the trial venue. For example, Nietzel and Dillehay (1983) conducted venue survey studies for five murder trials. They found that respondents residing within the trial venues reported reading or hearing more about the case than those residing in other counties. Those residing within the venue counties also knew more case details (both admissible and inadmissible), and were more likely to believe the defendant was guilty than those residing outside of the trial venues.

The small amount of research on change of venue, as well as research showing that, as PTP exposure increases so does bias against the defendant, suggests that change of venue might currently be the most promising remedy for reducing PTP bias. That being said, caution should be taken in regard to the general acceptance of any remedy's effectiveness. It is also important to consider the significant costs of a change of venue, relative to any potential benefit. Advances in technology have affected how civil and criminal cases are covered by both traditional and nontraditional media. These relatively new media outlets suggest that changes might be needed in how the courts protect a defendant's Sixth Amendment right to a fair trial in cases having substantial amounts of prejudicial PTP. As mentioned above, Internet and social media coverage of cases have removed geographical boundaries, and for those cases that capture the nation's attention, finding a venue where a defendant can receive a fair trial might prove extremely challenging.

Conclusions and Future Directions

Given the present media culture, the threats of prejudicial PTP on defendants' right to a fair trial are only likely to increase. No longer are citizens passive participants of the news—through social media, media websites, and blogging they are now active agents in the news—they share, comment on, and in some cases report on cases making their way to trial. How might this more interactive form of news transmission affect the jury pool and jurors' ability to decide a verdict based solely on the evidence presented at trial? What can the courts practically do to remedy or reduce bias associated with PTP? Traditional and nontraditional media coverage are not going away—instead they are likely to increase and become more accessible. Therefore, the courts need to find a way to reduce, if not eliminate, PTP's influence on juror/jury decisions. All of this opens up new areas to be explored by PTP researchers, with questions unique to the changing media landscape surrounding how people are exposed to news, and the almost inescapable nature of PTP in high-profile cases.

For example, although social media coverage of both criminal and civil cases has increased over the past decade, PTP researchers have yet to explore whether exposure to PTP via social media has similar effects as exposure via traditional news outlets. Also of importance is whether PTP exposure via social media outlets affects jurors' decisions through the same mechanisms as traditional PTP exposure? In addition, content analyses of PTP surrounding actual trials, which include both traditional media and social media, are needed. The content analyses of media sources discussed in this chapter were conducted over 20 years ago (Imrich et al., 1995; Simon & Eimermann, 1971; Tankard et al., 1978), long before jurors could follow and comment on cases via social media. Along with a comparative analysis of the content of these different media sources, research should examine the relative amount of PTP exposure jurors receive through the various media sources and the perceived influence of them on decisions and impressions. Finally, the multiple sources from which prospective jurors can receive pretrial information could result in juries being composed of jurors who are exposed to different types of PTP (e.g., negative defendant, negative victim, or pro-defendant). Ruva and Guenther (2017) explored differences between heterogeneous and homogeneous PTP exposure at the jury level and found evidence of both bias transfer and reduction. More research on heterogeneous PTP exposure at the jury level is needed. This research should explore outcomes and biases using different trials, in juries having different majority or minority biases (e.g., majority negative defendant vs. negative victim), and should then content analyze these jury deliberations to explore how bias is transferred or reduced.

Also of interest, is how the effect of PTP coverage outside of the courtroom differs from coverage inside the courtroom. For high-profile cases having several pretrial hearings, or multiple defendants whose trials are severed, prospective jurors have the opportunity to observe the defendant in a courtroom setting prior to trial. This could be especially problematic when the defendant acts out (verbally or physically), demonstrates low emotional involvement or is shown in restraints (Antonio, 2006; Pryor and Buchanan 1984) or a prison (jail) orange jumpsuit. How does exposure to pretrial hearings influence prospective jurors? Does the effect of these hearings vary as a function of whether cameras are inside or outside of the courtroom? How does exposure to a trial of a co-defendant affect juror bias? In addition to biasing impressions of defendants, these pretrial hearings (or coverage of co-defendant trials) could impact prospective jurors' memory for trial. Source memory research finds that the more similar two sources of information are, the more difficult it is for people to discriminate between these sources (Johnson et al., 1993). Therefore, any pretrial footage of court proceedings could be especially problematic for jurors discriminating between pretrial and trial information.

On a positive note, over the past decade a lot has been learned about the mechanisms responsible for PTP bias. Therefore, PTP researchers and the courts are armed with valuable information regarding how PTP influences the decisions of jurors and juries. Understanding these mechanisms is just the first step in combatting PTP bias. Researchers must now explore whether it is possible to reduce PTP bias in the tainted juror. This will be extremely challenging, given that multiple mechanisms are responsible for PTP's biasing effects on jurors, many of which are out of the conscious control of jurors.

In summary, in cases that attract a lot of publicity and public interest, the courts have their work cut out for them in regard to protecting defendants' Sixth Amendment right to a fair trial. The methods for informing the public of both criminal and civil cases have dramatically changed over the past decade and are likely to continue to evolve in the future. Therefore, both the courts and social scientists have much work ahead of them if they are to ensure that defendants are provided the fair trial they are guaranteed by the Constitution.

References

American Bar Association. (2016). *Model rules of professional conduct.* Retrieved from http://www.americanbar.org/groups/professional_responsibility/publications/model_rules_of_professional_conduct/model_rules_of_professional_conduct_table_of_contents.html

American Bar Association. (2014). Formal opinion 466: Lawyer reviewing jurors' Internet presence. Retrieved from http://www.americanbar.org/content/dam/aba/administrative/professional_responsibility/formal_opinion_466_final_04_23_14.authcheckdam.pdf

Anderson, N. H. (1971). Integration theory and attitude change. *Psychological Review, 7*, 172–206. https://doi.org/10.1037/h0030834

Anderson, C. A., Lepper, M. R., & Ross, L. (1980). The perseverance of social theories: The role of explanation in the persistence of discredited information. *Journal of Personality and Social Psychology, 39*, 1037–1049. https://doi.org/10.1037/h0077720

Anderson, C. A., & Lindsay, J. J. (1998). The development, perseverance, and change of naive theories. *Social Cognition, 16*, 8–30. https://doi.org/10.1521/soco.1998.16.1.8

Antonio, M. E. (2006). Arbitrariness and the death penalty: How the defendant's appearance during trial influences capital jurors' punishment decisions. *Behavioral Sciences and the Law, 24*, 216–234. https://doi.org/10.1002/bsl.673

Ballew v. Georgia, 435 U.S. 223 (1978).

Bodenhausen, G. V., Sheppard, L. A., & Kramer, G. P. (1994). Negative affect and social judgment: The differential impact of anger and sadness. *European Journal of Social Psychology, 24*, 45–62. https://doi.org/10.1002/ejsp.2420240104

Bornstein, B. H., Golding, J. M., Neuschatz, J., Kimbrough, C., Reed, K., Magyaries, C., & Luecht, K. (2017). Mock juror sampling issues in jury simulation research: A meta-analysis. *Law and Human Behavior, 41*, 13–28. https://doi.org/10.1037/lhb0000223

Bornstein, B. H., Whisenhunt, B. L., Nemeth, R. J., & Dunaway, D. L. (2002). Pretrial publicity and civil cases: A two-way street? *Law and Human Behavior, 26*, 3–17. https://doi.org/10.1023/A:1013825124011

Brickman, E., Blackman, J., Futterman, R., & Dinnerstein, J. (2008). How juror Internet use has changed the American jury trial. *Journal of Court Innovation, 1*, 287–302. Retrieved from http://www.courtinnovation.org/sites/default/files/Brickman.pdf

Brook, J. (2012). Social media adds a new twist to pretrial publicity ethical issues. *Continuing education of the bar blog*. California: California University. Retrieved from https://blog.ceb.com/2012/05/02/social-media-adds-a-new-twist-to-pretrial-publicity-ethical-issues/

Browning, G. (2016). Voir dire becomes voir google: Ethical concerns of 21st century jury selection. *The Brief: Tort Trial & Insurance Practice Section, 45*(2). Retrieved from http://www.americanbar.org/publications/the_brief/2016_17/winter/voir_dire_becomes_voir_google_ethical_concerns_of_21st_century_jury_selection.html

Bruschke, J., & Loges, W. E. (1999). Relationship between pretrial publicity and trial outcomes. *Journal of Communication, 49*, 104–120. https://doi.org/10.1111/j.1460-2466.1999.tb02819.x

Carino v. Muenzen, 13 A.3d 363 (N.J. 2011).

Carlson, K. A., & Russo, J. E. (2001). Biased interpretation of evidence by mock jurors. *Journal of Experimental Psychology: Applied, 7*, 91–103. https://doi.org/10.1037//1076-898X.7.2.91

Cepeda, N. J., Pashler, H., Vul, E., Wixted, J. T., & Rohrer, D. (2006). Distributed practice in verbal recall tasks: A review and quantitative synthesis. *Psychological Bulletin, 132*, 354–380. https://doi.org/10.1037/0033-2909.132.3.354

Costantini, E., & King, J. (1980/1981). The partial juror: Correlates and causes of prejudgment. *Law and Society Review, 15*, 9–40. https://doi.org/10.2307/3053221

Craik, F. I. M. (1970). The fate of primary memory items in free recall. *Journal of Verbal Learning and Verbal Behavior, 9*, 143–148. https://doi.org/10.1016/S0022-5371(70)80042-1

Daftary-Kapur, T., Penrod, S. D., O'Connor, M., & Wallace, B. (2014). Examining pretrial publicity in a shadow jury paradigm: Issues of slant, quantity, persistence and generalizability. *Law and Human Behavior, 38*, 462–477. https://doi.org/10.1037/lhb0000081

Davis, J. H., Spitzer, C. E., Nagao, D. H., & Stassen, G. (1978). Bias in social decisions by individuals and groups: An example from mock juries. In H. Brandstatter, J. H. Davis, & H. Schuler (Eds.), *Dynamics of group decisions* (pp. 33–52). Beverly Hills, CA: Sage.
Davis, J. H., Stasser, G., Spitzer, C. E., & Holt, R. W. (1976). Changes in group members' decision preferences during discussion: An illustration with mock juries. *Journal of Personality and Social Psychology, 34*, 1177–1187. https://doi.org/10.1037/0022-3514.34.6.1177
Davis, R. W. (1986). Pretrial publicity, the timing of the trial, and mock jurors' decision processes. *Journal of Applied Social Psychology, 16*, 590–607. https://doi.org/10.1111/j.1559-1816.1986.tb01161.x
DeLuca, A. (1979). *Tipping the scales of justice: The effects of pretrial publicity*. (Unpublished master's thesis). Iowa State University, Ames.
Devine, D. J., Clayton, L. D., Dunford, B. B., Seying, R., & Pryce, J. (2001). Jury decision making: 45 years of empirical research on deliberating groups. *Psychology, Public Policy, & Law, 7*, 622–727. https://doi.org/10.1037//1076-8971.7.3.622
Devine, P. G., & Ostrom, T. M. (1985). Cognitive mediation of inconsistency discounting. *Journal of Personality and Social Psychology, 49*, 5–21. https://doi.org/10.1037/0022-3514.49.1.5
Dexter, H. R., Cutler, B. L., & Moran, G. (1992). A test of voir dire as a remedy for the prejudicial effects of pretrial publicity. *Journal of Applied Social Psychology, 22*, 819–832. https://doi.org/10.1111/j.1559-1816.1992.tb00926.x
Donovan, J. J., & Radosevich, D. J. (1999). A meta-analytic review of the distribution of practice effect: Now you see it, now you don't. *Journal of Applied Psychology, 84*, 795–805. https://doi.org/10.1037/0021-9010.84.5.795
Dumas, R., Lepastourel, N., & Testé, B. (2014). Press articles and influence processes: The different effects of incriminating information and crime story information on judgments of guilt. *Psychology, Crime & Law, 20*, 659–672. https://doi.org/10.1080/1068316X.2013.854790
Duncan, S. H. (2009). Pretrial publicity in high-profile trials: An integrated approach to protecting the right to a fair trial and right to privacy. *University of Louisville Law: Legal Studies Research Paper Series, 34*, 754–795. Retrieved from http://ssrn.com/abstract=1117864
Dunn, M. (2014). Jurors' and attorneys' use of social media during voir dire, trials, and deliberations: A report to the judicial conference committee on court administration and case management. *Federal Judicial Center, 13*, 1–52. Retrieved from https://www.nacdl.org/WorkArea/DownloadAsset.aspx?id=38031&libID=38001
Estes v. Texas, 382 U.S. 875 (1965).
Feigenson, N., & Park, J. (2006). Emotions and attributions of legal responsibility and blame: A research review. *Law and Human Behavior, 30*, 143–161. https://doi.org/10.1007/s10979-006-9026-z
Florida v. Anthony, 08-CF-15606-AO (FL. 2011).
Florida v. Zimmerman, 592012CF001083A (FL. 2013).
Franiuk, R., Seefelt, J. L., Cepress, S. L., & Vandello, J. A. (2008). Prevalence and effects of rape myths in print journalism: the Kobe Bryant case. *Violence Against Women, 14*, 287–309. https://doi.org/10.1177/1077801207313971
Frost, P., Ingraham, M., & Wilson, B. (2002). Why misinformation is more likely to be recognised over time: A source monitoring account. *Memory, 10*, 179–185. https://doi.org/10.1080/09658210143000317
Greene, R. L. (1986). A common basis for recency effects in immediate and delayed recall. *Journal of Experimental Psychology: Learning, Memory, and Cognition, 12*, 413–418. https://doi.org/10.1037/0278-7393.12.3.413
Greene, E., & Wade, R. (1988). Of private talk and public print: General pretrial publicity and juror decision-making. *Applied Cognitive Psychology, 2*, 123–135. https://doi.org/10.1002/acp.2350020204
Greenwood, S., Perrin, A., & Duggan, M. (2016). Social media update 2016: Facebook usage and engagement is on the rise, while adoption of other platforms holds steady (Research Report No. 202.419.4372). Retrieved from Pew Research Center for Internet, Science & Technology website.: http://www.pewinternet.org/2016/11/11/social-media-update-2016/

Hekkanen, S. T., & McEvoy, C. (2005). Source monitoring in eyewitness memory: Implicit associations, suggestions, and episodic traces. *Memory and Cognition, 33*, 759–769. https://doi.org/10.3758/BF03193072
Honess, T. M., Charman, E. A., & Levi, M. (2003). Factual and affective/evaluative recall of pretrial publicity: Their relative influence on juror reasoning and verdict in a simulated fraud trial. *Journal of Applied Social Psychology, 33*, 1404–1416. https://doi.org/10.1111/j.1559-1816.2003.tb01955.x
Hope, L., Memon, A., & McGeorge, P. (2004). Understanding pretrial publicity: Predecisional distortion of evidence by mock jurors. *Journal of Experimental Psychology: Applied, 10*, 111–119. https://doi.org/10.1037/1076-898X.10.2.111
Hurlstone, M. J., Hitch, G. J., & Baddeley, A. D. (2014). Memory for serial order across domains: An overview of the literature and directions for future research. *Psychological Bulletin, 140*, 339–373. https://doi.org/10.1037/a0034221
Imrich, D. J., Mullin, C., & Linz, D. (1995). Measuring the extent of prejudicial pretrial publicity in major American newspapers: A content analysis. *Journal of Communication, 45*(3), 94–117. https://doi.org/10.1111/j.1460-2466.1995.tb00745.x
Irvin v. Dowd, 366 U.S. 717, 81 (1961).
Janiszewski, C., Noel, H., & Sawyer, A. G. (2003). A meta-analysis of the spacing effect in verbal learning: Implications for research on advertising repetition and consumer memory. *Journal of Consumer Research, 30*, 138–149. https://doi.org/10.1086/374692
Johnson, M. K., Hashtroudi, S., & Lindsay, D. S. (1993). Source monitoring. *Psychological Bulletin, 114*, 3–28. https://doi.org/10.1037/0033-2909.114.1.3
Johnson v. McCullough. 306 S. W. 3d 551 (Mo. 2010).
Kelly, A., Carroll, M., & Mazzoni, G. (2002). Metamemory and reality monitoring. *Applied Cognitive Psychology, 16*, 407–428. https://doi.org/10.1002/acp.803
Kerr, N. L. (1993). Stochastic models of juror decision making. In R. Hastie (Ed.), *Inside the juror: The psychology of jury decision making* (pp. 116–135). New York, NY: Cambridge University Press.
Kerr, N. L., Kramer, G. P., Carroll, J. S., & Alfini, J. J. (1991). On the effectiveness of voir dire in criminal cases with prejudicial pretrial publicity: An empirical study. *American University Law Review, 40*, 665–701. Retrieved from https://www.wcl.american.edu/journal/lawrev/40/kerr.pdf
Kerr, N. L., Niedermeier, K. E., & Kaplan, M. F. (1999). Bias in jurors vs. bias in juries: New evidence from the SDS perspective. *Organizational Behavior and Human Decision Processes, 80*, 70–86. https://doi.org/10.1006/obhd.1999.2855
Kisley, M. A., Wood, S., & Burrows, C. L. (2007). Looking at the sunny side of life: Age-related change in an event-related potential measure of the negativity bias. *Psychological Science, 18*, 838–843. https://doi.org/10.1111/j.1467_9280.2007.01988.x
Kline, F. G., & Jess, P. H. (1966). Prejudicial publicity: Its effect on law school mock juries. *Journalism Quarterly, 43*, 113–116. https://doi.org/10.1177/107769906604300115
Kovera, M. B. (2002). The effects of general pretrial publicity on juror decisions: An examination of moderators and mediating mechanisms. *Law and Human Behavior, 26*, 43–72. https://doi.org/10.1023/A:1013829224920
Kramer, G. P., & Kerr, N. L. (1989). Laboratory simulation and bias in the study of juror behavior: A methodological note. *Law and Human Behavior, 13*, 89–99. https://doi.org/10.1007/bf01056165
Kramer, G. P., Kerr, N. L., & Carroll, J. S. (1990). Pretrial publicity, judicial remedies, and jury bias. *Law and Human Behavior, 14*, 409–438. https://doi.org/10.1007/BF01044220
Lear, D. (2015). So you want to write a law blog. *American Bar Association Journal, 4*(8). Retrieved fromhttp://www.americanbar.org/publications/gpsolo_ereport/2015/march_2015/so_you_want_to_write_a_law_blog.html.
Lerner, J. S., Goldberg, J. H., & Tetlock, P. E. (1998). Sober second thought: The effects of accountability, anger and authoritarianism on attributions of responsibility. *Personality and Social Psychology Bulletin, 24*, 563–574. https://doi.org/10.1177/0146167298246001

Lerner, J. S., & Keltner, D. (2000). Beyond valence: Toward a model of emotion-specific influences on judgement and choice. *Cognition and Emotion, 14*, 473–493. https://doi.org/10.1080/026999300402763

Lerner, J. S., & Keltner, D. (2001). Fear, anger, and risk. *Journal of Personality and Social Psychology, 81*, 146–159. https://doi.org/10.1037//0022-3514.81.1.146

Lerner, J. S., & Tiedens, L. Z. (2006). Portrait of the angry decision maker: How appraisal tendencies shape anger's influence on cognition. *Journal of Behavioral Decision Making, 19*, 115–137. https://doi.org/10.1002/bdm.515

Lieberman, J. D., & Arndt, J. (2000). Understanding the limits of limiting instructions: Social psychological explanations for the failures of instructions to disregard pretrial publicity and other inadmissible evidence. *Psychology, Public Policy, and Law, 6*, 677–711. https://doi.org/10.1037//1076-8971.6.3.677

Lieberman, J. D., & Sales, B. D. (2007). *Scientific jury selection*. Washington, DC: American Psychological Association.

Lindsay, D. S. (1994). Memory, source monitoring, and eyewitness testimony. In D. F. Ross, D. J. Read, & M. P. Toglia (Eds.), *Adult eyewitness testimony: Current trends and developments* (pp. 27–55). New York: Cambridge University Press.

Lockhart v. McCree 476 U.S. 162, 106 S. Ct. 1758, 90 L. Ed. 2d 137 (1986).

Loewenstein, G., & Lerner, J. (2003). The role of affect in decision making. In R. Davidson, K. Scherer, & H. Goldsmith (Eds.), *Handbook of affective sciences* (pp. 619–642). Oxford: Oxford University Press.

Lofink, C. R., & Mullaney, M. (2013). Pretrial publicity and the courtroom umami. *The Jury Expert: The Art of Science & Litigation, 25*(3), 1–7. Retrieved from http://www.thejuryexpert.com/wp-content/uploads//1305/JuryExpert_1305_Umami.pdf

Luchins, A. S., & Luchins, E. H. (1970). The effects of order presentation of information and explanatory models. *Journal of Social Psychology, 80*, 63–70. https://doi.org/10.1080/00224545.1970.9712520

MacCoun, R. J., & Kerr, N. L. (1988). Asymmetric influence in mock jury deliberation: Jurors' bias for leniency. *Journal of Personality and Social Psychology, 54*, 21–33. https://doi.org/10.1037/0022-3514.54.1.21

Mastromauro, M. (2010). Pre-trial prejudice 2.0: How YouTube generated news coverage is set to complicate the concepts of pre-trial prejudice doctrine and endanger Sixth Amendment Fair Trial Rights. *Journal of High Technology Law, 10*, 289–356. Retrieved from http://www.suffolk.es/documents/jhtl_publications/mastromauro.pdf

Mayo, C. W., & Crockett, W. H. (1964). Cognitive complexity and primacy-recency effects in impression formation. *Journal of Abnormal and Social Psychology, 68*, 335–338. https://doi.org/10.1037/h0041716

McDonough, M. (2015). What is the state of the legal blogosphere? *American Bar Association Journal, 4*(12) Retrieved from http://www.abajournal.com/magazine/article/the_state_of_the_legal_blogosphere.

Minnow, N. N., & Cate, F. H. (1991). Who is an impartial juror in an age of mass media? *The American University Law Review, 40*, 631–648. Retrieved from http://www.repository.law.indiana.edu/facpub/749

Moran, G., & Cutler, B. L. (1991). The prejudicial impact of pretrial publicity. *Journal of Applied Social Psychology, 21*, 345–367. https://doi.org/10.1111/j.1559-1816.1991.tb00524.x

Moscovici, S., & Zavalloni, M. (1969). The group as a polarizer of attitudes. *Journal of Personality and Social Psychology, 12*, 125–135. https://doi.org/10.1037/h0027568

Mosteller, R. P. (2007). The Duke Lacrosse case, innocence, and false identifications: A fundamental failure to do justice. *Fordham Law Review, 76*, 1337–1412. Retrieved from http://scholarship.law.duke.edu/faculty_scholarship/1668

Mu'Min v. Virginia, 500 U.S. 415 (1991).

Murphy v. Florida, 421 U.S. 794 (1975).

New York Film Academy. (2015). A brief look at the history of broadcast journalism. Retrieved from New York Film Academy website: https://www.nyfa.edu/student-resources/history-of-broadcast-journalism/

Nietzel, M. T., & Dillehay, R. C. (1983). Psychologists as consultants for changes of venue: The use of public opinion surveys. *Law and Human Behavior, 7*, 309–335. https://doi.org/10.1007/BF01044735

Nisbett, R. E., & Wilson, T. D. (1977). Telling more than we can know: Verbal reports on mental processes. *Psychological Review, 84*, 231–259. https://doi.org/10.1037/0033-295X.84.3.231

Nunez, N., Estrada-Reynolds, V., Schweitzer, K., & Myers, B. (2016). The impact of emotions on juror judgments and decision making. In B. H. Bornstein & M. K. Miller (Eds.), *Advances in psychology and law* (Vol. 2, pp. 55–92). Cham, Switzerland: Springer.

Ogloff, J. R. P., & Vidmar, N. (1994). The impact of pretrial publicity on jurors: A study to compare the relative effects of television and print media in a child sex abuse case. *Law and Human Behavior, 18*, 507–525. https://doi.org/10.1007/BF01499171

Otto, A. L., Penrod, S. D., & Dexter, H. R. (1994). The biasing impact of pretrial publicity on juror judgments. *Law and Human Behavior, 18*, 453–469. https://doi.org/10.1007/BF01499050

Pennington, N., & Hastie, R. (1986). Evidence evaluation in complex decision making. *Journal of Personality and Social Psychology, 51*(2), 242–258. https://doi.org/10.1037/0022-3514.51.2.242

Pennington, N., & Hastie, R. (1988). Explanation-based decision making: Effects of memory structure on judgment. *Journal of Experimental Psychology: Learning, Memory, and Cognition, 14*, 521–533. https://doi.org/10.1037/0278-7393.14.3.521

Pennington, N., & Hastie, R. (1993). The story model for juror decision making. In R. Hastie (Ed.), *Inside the juror: The psychology of juror decision-making* (pp. 192–221). New York: Cambridge University Press.

Pew Research Center: Journalism & Media. (2012). *How blogs, Twitter and mainstream media have handled the Trayvon Martin case*. Retrieved from http://www.journalism.org/2012/03/30/special-report-how-blogs-twitter-and-mainstream-media-have-handled-trayvon-m/

Pew Research Center for Internet, Science & Technology. (2017a). *Social media fact sheet*. Retrieved from http://www.pewinternet.org/fact-sheet/social-media/

Pew Research Center for Internet, Science & Technology. (2017b). *Internet/broadband fact sheet*. Retrieved from http://www.pewinternet.org/fact-sheet/internet-broadband/

Pryor, B., & Buchanan, R. W. (1984). The effects of defendant's demeanor on juror perceptions of credibility and guilt. *Journal of Communication, 34*, 92–99. https://doi.org/10.1111/j.1460-2466.1984.tb02176.x

Qualls, K. F. (2015). The answer to trial publicity is a better question. *Journal of Criminal Justice and Legal Issues, 3*, 1–15. Retrieved from http://www.aabri.com/manuscripts/152308.pdf

Rainie, L. (2005). *The State of Blogging* (Research Report No. 202-419-4500). Retrieved from the Pew Internet & American Life Project website: http://www.pewinternet.org/files/old-media/Files/Reports/2005/PIP_blogging_data.pdf.pdf

Rantzen, A., & Markham, R. (1992). The reversed eyewitness testimony design: More evidence for source monitoring. *The Journal of General Psychology, 119*, 37–43. https://doi.org/10.1080/00221309.1992.9921156

Rideau v. Louisiana, 373 U.S. 723 (1963).

Ross, L., Lepper, M. R., & Hubbard, M. (1975). Perseverance in self-perception and social perception: Biased attributional processes in the debriefing paradigm. *Journal of Personality and Social Psychology, 32*, 880–892.

Rozin, P., & Royzman, E. B. (2001). Negativity bias, negativity dominance, and contagion. *Personality and Social Psychology Review, 5*, 296–320. https://doi.org/10.1207/S15327957PSPR0504_2

Russo, J. E., Meloy, M. G., & Medvec, V. H. (1998). Predecisional distortion of product information. *Journal of Marketing Research, 35*, 438–452.

Russo, J. E., Meloy, M. G., & Wilks, T. J. (2000). Predecisional distortion of information by auditors and salesperson. *Management Science, 46*, 13–27. https://doi.org/10.1287/mnsc.46.1.13.15127

Ruva, C. L., & Hudak, E. (2013). Pretrial publicity and juror age affect juror decision making. *Psychology, Crime, & Law, 19*, 179–202. https://doi.org/10.1080/1068316X.2011.616509
Ruva, C. L., Dickman, M. C., & Mayes, J. L. (2014). Exposure to both positive and negative pretrial publicity reduces or eliminates mock-juror bias. *International Journal of Psychology and Behavioral Sciences, 4*, 30–40. https://doi.org/10.5923/j.ijpbs.20140401.05
Ruva, C. L., & Guenther, C. C. (2015). From the shadows into the light: How pretrial publicity and deliberation affect mock jurors' decisions, impressions, and memory. *Law and Human Behavior, 39*, 294–310. https://doi.org/10.1037/lhb0000117
Ruva, C. L., & Guenther, C. C. (2017). Keep your bias to yourself: How deliberating with differently biased others affects mock-jurors' guilt decisions, perceptions of the defendant, memories, and evidence interpretation. *Law and Human Behavior, 41*, 478–493. https://doi.org/10.1037/lhb0000256
Ruva, C. L., Guenther, C. C., & Yarbrough, A. (2011). Positive and negative pretrial publicity: The roles of impression formation, emotion, and predecisional distortion. *Criminal Justice and Behavior, 38*, 511–534. https://doi.org/10.1177/0093854811400823
Ruva, C., & LeVasseur, M. (2012). Behind closed doors: The effect of pretrial publicity on jury deliberations. *Psychology, Crime and Law., 18*, 1–22. https://doi.org/10.1080/1068316X.2010.502120
Ruva, C. L., Mayes, J. L., Dickman, M. C., & McEvoy, C. (2012). Timing and type of pretrial publicity affect mock-jurors' decisions and predecisional distortion. *International Journal of Psychology and Behavioral Sciences, 2*, 108–119. https://doi.org/10.5923/j.ijpbs.20120204.06
Ruva, C. L., & McEvoy, C. (2008). Negative and positive pretrial publicity affect juror memory and decision making. *Journal of Experimental Psychology: Applied, 14*, 226–235. https://doi.org/10.1037/1076-898X.14.3.226
Ruva, C., McEvoy, C., & Bryant, J. D. (2007). Effects of pre-trial publicity and jury deliberation on juror bias and source memory errors. *Applied Cognitive Psychology, 21*, 45–67. https://doi.org/10.1002/acp.1254
Salerno, J. M., & Bottoms, B. L. (2009). Emotional evidence and jurors' judgments: The promise of neuroscience for informing psychology and law. *Behavioral Sciences and the Law, 27*, 273–296. https://doi.org/10.1002/bsl.861
Schum, D. A. (1993). Argument structuring and evidence evaluation. In R. Hastie (Ed.), *Inside the juror: The psychology of juror decision making* (pp. 175–191). New York, NY: Cambridge University Press.
Shaffer, R. A. (1986). Pretrial publicity: Media coverage and guilt attribution. *Communication Quarterly, 34*, 154–169. https://doi.org/10.1080/01463378609369630
Shahani, V. R. (2005). Change the motion, not the venue: A critical look at the change of venue motion. *American Criminal Law Review, 42*, 93–120.
Sheppard v. Maxwell, 384 U.S. 333 (1966).
Simon, R. J., & Eimermann, T. (1971). The jury finds not guilty: Another look at media influence on the jury. *Journalism Quarterly, 48*, 343–344. Retrieved from http://journals.sagepub.com.ezproxy.lib.usf.edu/doi/pdf/10.1177/107769907104800219
Sommers, S. R., & Kassin, S. M. (2001). On the many impacts of inadmissible testimony: Selective compliance, need for cognition, and the overcorrection bias. *Personality and Social Psychology Bulletin, 27*, 1368–1377. https://doi.org/10.1177/01461672012710012
Spano, L. M., Groscup, J. L., & Penrod, S. D. (2011). Pretrial publicity and the jury: Research and methods. In R. L. Wiener & B. H. Bornstein (Eds.), *Handbook of trial consulting* (pp. 217–244). New York: Springer.
Spielberger, C. D. (1983). *Manual for the State-Trait Anxiety Inventory (Form Y)*. Palo Alto, CA: Consulting Psychologists Press.
Spielberger, C. D., & Reheiser, E. C. (2003). Measuring anxiety, anger, depression, and curiosity as emotional states and personality traits with the STAI, STAXI, and STPI. In M. J. Hilsenroth, D. L. Segal, & M. Hersen (Eds.), *Comprehensive handbook of psychological assessment* (Vol. 2.: *Personality assessment*, pp. 70–86). Hoboken, NJ: John Wiley.

Spielberger, C. D., & Reheiser, E. C. (2009). Assessment of emotions: Anxiety, anger, depression, and curiosity. *Applied Psychology: Health and Well-Being, 1*, 271–302. https://doi.org/10.1111/j.1758-0854.2009.01017.x
Steblay, N. M., Besirevic, J., Fulero, S. M., & Jimenez-Lorente, B. (1999). The effects of pretrial publicity on juror verdicts: A meta-analytic review. *Law and Human Behavior, 23*, 219–235. https://doi.org/10.1023/A:1022325019080
Steblay, N. M., Hosch, H. M., Culhane, S. E., & McWethy, A. (2006). The impact on juror verdicts of judicial instruction to disregard inadmissible evidence: A meta-analysis. *Law and Human Behavior, 30*, 469–492. https://doi.org/10.1007/s10979-006-9039-7
Studebaker, C. A., & Penrod, S. D. (1997). Pretrial publicity: The media, the law, and common sense. *Psychology, Public Policy, and Law, 3*, 428–460. https://doi.org/10.1037/1076-8971.3.2-3.428
Sue, S., Smith, R. E., & Pedroza, G. (1975). Authoritarianism, pretrial publicity, and awareness of bias in simulated jurors. *Psychological Reports, 37*, 1299–1302. https://doi.org/10.2466/pr0.1975.37.3f.1299
Tan, L., & Ward, G. (2000). A recency-based account of the primacy effect in free recall. *Journal of Experimental Psychology: Learning, Memory, and Cognition, 26*(6), 1589–1625. https://doi.org/10.1037/0278-7393.26.6.1589
Tankard, J. W., Jr., Middleton, K., & Rimmer, T. (1978). Compliance with American bar association fair trial-free press guidelines. *Journalism Quarterly, 56*, 464–468. https://doi.org/10.1177/107769907905600302
Taylor, R. (2009). Slain and slandered: A content analysis of the portrayal of femicide in crime news. *Homicide Studies: An Interdisciplinary & International Journal, 13*, 21–49. https://doi.org/10.1177/1088767908326679
Tiedens, L. Z. (2001). The effect of anger on the hostile inferences of aggressive and nonaggressive people: Specific emotions, cognitive processing, and chronic accessibility. *Motivation and Emotion, 25*, 233–251. https://doi.org/10.1023/A:1012224507488
Tiedens, L. Z., & Linton, S. (2001). Judgment under emotional certainty and uncertainty: The effects of specific emotions on information processing. *Journal of Personality & Social Psychology, 81*, 973–988. https://doi.org/10.1037//0022-3514.81.6.973
United States v. Dioguardi 147 F. Supp. 421 (S. D. N. Y. 1956).
United States v. Meredith, 824 F.2d 1418, 1423 (4th Cir. 1987).
Vaish, A., Grossmann, T., & Woodward, A. (2008). Not all emotions are created equal: The negativity bias in social-emotional development. *Psychological Bulletin, 134*, 383–403. https://doi.org/10.1037/0033-2909.134.3.383
Vinokur, A., & Burnstein, E. (1974). Effects of partially shared persuasive arguments on group-induced shifts: A group-problem-solving approach. *Journal of Personality and Social Psychology, 29*, 305–315. https://doi.org/10.1037/h0036010
Ward, S. F. (2008). Full court coverage what happens when defense counsel and ordinary citizens blog about high-profile trials? *American Bar Association Journal, 94*, 34–39. Retrieved from http://www.jstor.org/stable/pdf/27846654.pdf
Waters, N. L., & Hans, V. P. (2009). A jury of one: Opinion formation, conformity, and dissent on juries. *Journal of Empirical Legal Studies, 6*, 513–540. https://doi.org/10.1111/j.1740-1461.2009.01152.x
Weis, D. C. (2012). Judge in Trayvon Martin case refuses to ban defense lawyer's blog and comments. Retrieved from the American Bar Association Journal website: http://www.abajournal.com/news/article/judge_in_trayvon_martin_case_refuses_to_ban_defense_lawyers_blog_and_commen
Wilson, J. R., & Bornstein, B. H. (1998). Methodological considerations in pretrial publicity research: Is the medium the message? *Law and Human Behavior, 22*, 585–597. https://doi.org/10.1023/A:1025743614951
Wilson, T., & Brekke, N. (1994). Mental contamination and mental correction: Unwanted influences on judgments and evaluations. *Psychological Bulletin, 116*, 117–142. https://doi.org/10.1037/0033-2909.116.1.117

Wilson, T., Centerbar, D., & Brekke, N. (2002). Mental contamination and the debiasing problem. In T. Gilovich, D. Griffin, & D. Kahneman (Eds.), *Heuristics and biases: The psychology of intuitive judgment* (pp. 185–200). Cambridge: Cambridge University Press.
Wisconsin v. Avery, 2005CF381 (WI. 2007).
Woody, W. D., & Viney, W. (2007). General pretrial publicity in sexual assault trials. *Psychological Reports, 101*, 527–530. https://doi.org/10.2466/pr0.101.2.527-530
Zillmann, D. (1983). Transfer of excitation in emotional behavior. In J. Cacioppo & R. Petty (Eds.), *Social psychophysiology* (pp. 215–240). New York: Guilford.

Victim Impact Statements in Capital Sentencing: 25 Years Post-*Payne*

Bryan Myers, Sarah Johnson, and Narina Nuñez

In the penalty phase of the trial *State v. Fain*, the mother of the murder victim had the following exchange with the prosecutor: "Q: Could you tell the Court, Mrs. Johnson, how the loss of Daralyn Johnson has affected you personally? A: I would say probably devastation is the best description. I think someone could probably have cut off my right arm, and I would not have missed it as much as my daughter" (cited in Joh, 2000, p. 17).

The above quote exemplifies Victim Impact Statements (VIS) introduced in capital trials. They are personal and often emotionally compelling accounts of the suffering experienced by relatives or close friends or associates of the victim (i.e., victim survivors). Since *Payne v. Tennessee* (1991) was decided more than 25 years ago, VIS have elicited substantial controversy, with both legal scholars and psycholegal researchers devoting considerable attention to the merits of that decision. These statements are controversial because their relevance to the sentencing decision jurors must make is unclear, and because both justices and scholars contend their emotional appeal invites irrationality and capriciousness into the sentencing process (e.g., *Booth v. Maryland*, 1987, Austin, 2010; Logan, 1999; Shanker, 1999). We begin with a description of VIS and trace their development in capital sentencing proceedings. We then proceed to address the issues of controversy surrounding VIS, focusing specifically on the three U.S. Supreme Court decisions regarding their constitutionality: *Booth v Maryland*, *South Carolina v. Gathers*, and *Payne v. Tennessee*. Next, we consider the empirical research that has addressed the impact of VIS on jurors; much of this research consists of juror simulation studies. We end

B. Myers (✉) · S. Johnson
Department of Psychology, University of North Carolina Wilmington, Wilmington, NC, USA
e-mail: myersb@uncw.edu; sjohn192@vols.utk.edu

N. Nuñez
Department of Psychology, University of Wyoming, Laramie, WY, USA
e-mail: narina@uwyo.edu

M. K. Miller, B. H. Bornstein (eds.), *Advances in Psychology and Law*,
Advances in Psychology and Law 3,
https://doi.org/10.1007/978-3-319-75859-6_2

with a discussion of how the research on VIS can inform the debate surrounding admissibility, and we identify areas that warrant important future research directions.

Victim Impact Statements: Definition and Admissibility

VIS refers to statements given in court that detail the impact of crimes on victims or, in the case of capital crimes, victim survivors. Typically, they indicate economic and psychological hardships experienced as a consequence of the crime (e.g., see *Booth v. Maryland*, 1987; Myers & Greene, 2004; Schroeder, 2010). VIS may come in the form of written statements read either by witnesses or court officials, or they may come in the form of witness allocution testimony arising from direct examination by prosecutors.

Victims were not always granted such a prominent place in capital trial proceedings. The role victims have in the sentencing process has evolved and continues to evolve as both state and federal courts grapple with the competing goals of allowing both the families of victims and the community an opportunity to express their loss, while simultaneously protecting the rights of the accused (Logan, 2006). Prior to the 1970s, there was little opportunity for victims to be involved in the criminal justice process. While minimal attention was paid to victims of crimes in the form of "victim compensation" in the 1960s, it was not until the mid-1970s that victims began to play an active role in the outcome of criminal trials (Henderson, 1985). The 2004 Crime Victims' Rights Act guarantees crime victims the right to participate in virtually all public criminal proceedings in federal courts (Kyle, Twist, & Higgins, 2005). As of 2009, all 50 states provide expansive participatory and protective rights for victims and many have extended these rights for inclusion in their state constitutions (Roberts, 2009). Currently, 29 of the 31 states that enforce the death penalty allow for VIS during the penalty phase of the trial (Death Penalty Information Center, 2017).

In rare cases, state legislators have imposed restrictions on the content or manner in which VIS are introduced into the trial (Logan, 2005). One restriction that has been imposed infrequently is that VIS may not refer to defendants, and witnesses may not present their opinion regarding appropriate punishment.[1] While other restrictions exist in some jurisdictions, for the most part, witnesses are given wide latitude in a VIS (see Logan, 1999, 2005; Sanderford, 2012).

[1] It is typical for most states that allow VIS to limit content to include the characteristics of the victim and the effects of the crime (e.g., N.C. Gen Stat. § 15A-833(a)). In some instances, courts limit threats directed at or characterizations of the defendant, including recommendations for punishing the defendant (Robert Montgomery, Senior Deputy Attorney General, North Carolina Criminal Division, personal communication, November 7, 2016).

Debate Surrounding VIS and Capital Sentencing

Victim impact statements are controversial—particularly so for capital trial proceedings. Much of the controversy surrounding VIS and capital sentencing has been raised by the U.S. Supreme Court in the three instances in which they decided on the constitutionality of VIS, and legal commentators have, for the most part, echoed these sentiments. Central to the debate surrounding VIS in capital sentencing is whether information concerning the victim is relevant to the jury's task of determining the blameworthiness of the defendant (Myers & Greene 2004). On the side of those advocating for the inclusion of these statements, issues of balance and fairness pervade much of the discussion (Deise & Paternoster 2013). Supporters have contended that allowing testimony of this nature balances the scales of justice as there are precious few limits on testimony concerning the defendant during this phase of the trial (see fuller discussions surrounding this point in Logan, 2006; Sullivan, 1998). In comparison to unfettered access to information concerning the defendant, allowing testimony concerning the victim is important because it "keeps the balance true" (*Payne v. Tennessee*, 1991, p. 827), portrays the victim as more than a "faceless stranger" (p. 825), and provides jurors with more than a "quick glimpse of the life" (p. 822) of the victim. Others have taken the imbalance in attention a step further and have suggested that greater attention to the victim could improve the quality of sentencing decisions. This view suggests that providing the jury with information concerning the harm experienced by victims or even victim survivors is necessary to determine blameworthiness and thereby achieve fairer sentencing decisions (Cassell, 2009; Kilpatrick & Otto, 1987; Mulholland, 1995; Shanker, 1999) and that decisions will be more in line with the principle of proportionality (Erez, 1999).

Ultimately, for some (e.g., Cassell, 2009), VIS in capital sentencing are viewed as just a small element in a greater movement toward expanding the role of victims in the criminal justice system. The Victims' Rights Movement can be traced to the 1970s as crime victims became increasingly frustrated with their role in the criminal justice process (Hall, 1991; Henderson, 1985; Hillenbrand & Smith, 1989; President's Task Force on Victims of Crime, 1982). The growing support for greater participation by crime victims in the criminal justice process culminated in the Crime Victims' Rights Act (2004) which allows victims "to be reasonably heard" at any public legal proceeding. In this vein, advocates have argued that VIS affirm the dignity of the victims by allowing them some role in the process (Mulholland, 1995), or aiding victim catharsis by allowing closure (Mosteller, 2003). For some, the introduction of a VIS into the sentencing process is beneficial because it educates the defendant about the consequences of his acts (Cassell, 2009). For others, the introduction of VIS is justified and necessary because of the benefits it provides to victims and their relatives, and not merely because it assists the jury in recommending an appropriate sentence (Roberts, 2009).

However, the benefits of VIS on victim survivors have not been clearly established (Bandes, 2009). Although allowing a witness to make a VIS has been suggested to provide such benefits as improved emotional recovery (Lens, Pemberton, & Bogaerts, 2013), victim closure and related cathartic effects (Mosteller, 2003), support for these benefits has been questioned (Bandes, 1999, 2009; Davis & Smith, 1994). More critically, some have contended that prosecutors have used victims as a tool to achieve their own crime control goals (Henderson, 1985). They argue that prosecutors have their own agenda which may override the wishes of the victim survivors (Bandes, 2009). Some fear that many prosecutors employ VIS for the sole purpose of securing a death penalty verdict (Flamm, 1999), and regard the use of victim survivors in this role as "exploitive" (Burr, 2003). This perspective suggests that prosecutors would be far less interested in victims were their opinions less effective in promoting harsh sanctions.

Chief among the criticisms surrounding the introduction of VIS into capital sentencing is the belief that this information is irrelevant (see Blumenthal, 2001). According to this perspective, VIS are irrelevant because the suffering and harm experienced by the victim survivors was unknown to the defendant at the time of his act, and so this information arises from fortuitous circumstances and is unrelated to the defendant's decision to kill (Hills & Thomson, 1999). Further, by focusing on characteristics of the victim, a VIS serves as a distraction from the characteristics of the defendant, which should be the chief focus during sentencing. VIS distract jurors because they change the focus to the victim, and therefore allow sentencing decisions to be arbitrarily made according to qualities of the victim, rather than according to the qualities of the defendant (Greene, 1999). Moreover, victim character information is relatively unimpeachable evidence and nearly impossible for the defense to rebut (Blume, 2003; Curry, 2011; Logan, 1999). Attempting to challenge this testimony would only lead to a "mini-trial" that would distract the jury from their critical role in considering the defendant's character and crime circumstances (Frankel, 2008, p. 95). By directing attention to the victim, VIS signal an abrupt turn away from the offender's characteristics and toward the pain of the victim. This normally prompts a need for vengeance that naturally accompanies this focus (Joh, 2000). By introducing the story of the victim, jurors may be inclined to identify with the victim's perspective, and are therefore less willing to consider the perspective of the defendant (Minot, 2012). VIS are, according to this view, not only a possible distraction, but they also bias jurors toward the perspective of the victim and leave jurors comparatively deaf to the perspective of the defendant. This shift in focus toward the plight of the victim is seen by some as part of a larger progression toward greater punitiveness toward offenders (Haney, 1997); a so-called ever-expanding "empathic divide" that is already prominent in capital sentencing procedures (e.g., see Lynch & Haney, 2012).

While relevance figured prominently in the three U.S. Supreme Court decisions regarding the constitutionality of VIS in capital sentencing proceedings, a second matter of debate concerned the potential for the emotionality accompanying these statements to prejudice jurors and lead to arbitrary and capricious decisions. These decisions will be reviewed with a focus on the matters that have framed much of the empirical research conducted on VIS that follow in later sections of this chapter.

The Constitutionality of Victim Impact Statements: *Booth*, *Gathers*, and *Payne*

Three critical U.S. Supreme Court decisions have addressed the constitutionality of VIS in capital sentencing proceedings. Rarely does the U.S. Supreme Court return to the same issue three times in a four-year span, and as in this case, overturn earlier opinions. Thus, this triad of decisions in this brief span reflects the degree to which the Court struggled with the constitutionality of VIS. The first of these decisions was *Booth v. Maryland* (1987), in which the U.S. Supreme Court reviewed the Maryland Court of Appeals' decision to uphold a lower court's refusal to bar the VIS from the sentencing phase of the trial. In the original trial, the jury found the defendant, John Booth, guilty of two counts of murder. Booth had robbed and killed two of his elderly neighbors, Irvin and Rose Bronstein. Although his initial goal was robbing the elderly couple, Booth ultimately decided to stab the couple to death after having first bound and gagged them. As required by law, a pre-sentence report which included a VIS was introduced into the penalty phase of the trial. The VIS was based principally on interviews conducted with four members of the Bronsteins' family. The statement that arose from these interviews contained information surrounding the degree to which the couple would be missed, how family members experienced psychological harm such as depression, constant fear and anxiety, and how a family member's wedding was ruined because the bride canceled the honeymoon in order to attend the Bronsteins' funeral. In hearing the VIS, the jury learned the opinions of the victims' relatives about such matters as the crime itself and the defendant's deserved punishment. For example, it was noted that the defendant "butchered them like animals" and that the defendant "could never be rehabilitated" (p. 500). The official who conducted the interviews and prepared the statement ended by adding that, to the Bronstein family, the murder of this couple "permeated every aspect of their daily lives" and that they would be "haunted by the memory" of the attack (*Booth v. Maryland,* 1987, p. 500). The jury sentenced Booth to death, and the Maryland Court of Appeals upheld the conviction.

In a 5-4 vote, the U.S. Supreme Court in *Booth v. Maryland* (1987) reversed the decision of the Maryland Court of Appeals and ruled that "the Eighth Amendment prohibits a capital sentencing jury from considering victim impact evidence" (p. 502). Justice Powell wrote the majority opinion and outlined the Court's rationale for prohibiting VIS in capital sentencing proceedings. The information contained in the VIS prompted two areas of concern. The first area of concern was information that described the victim and focused on the victim's individual characteristics and on the emotional damage experienced by the surviving family. The second area concerned the family's opinions about the defendant and his crimes. However, the Court failed to specifically identify which of the two types of information they were referring to when they ultimately concluded that "this information is irrelevant to a capital sentencing decision, and its admission creates a constitutionally unacceptable risk that the jury may impose the death penalty in an arbitrary and capricious manner" (p. 503).

The *Booth* Court argued that VIS are unconstitutional because they promote arbitrariness in sentencing. Arbitrariness in sentencing is a violation of the cruel and unusual punishment clause of the 8th Amendment, as articulated years earlier in *Furman v. Georgia* (1972). In the *Furman* decision, the Court overturned Furman's death sentence based on the grounds that capital sentencing decisions had become "wantonly and freakishly imposed" (*Furman v. Georgia*, 1972, p. 238). At this time, capital sentencing lacked explicit guidance from the court, leading to selective and irregular use of the death penalty (Costanzo & Costanzo, 1994). With the decision in *Furman,* death sentences imposed without statutory guidelines were invalidated (Dorland & Krauss, 2005). In *Gregg* v. *Georgia* (1976) the U.S. Supreme Court established directions for proper considerations during sentencing proceedings (e.g., weighing aggravating and mitigating factors; Shaked-Schroer, Costanzo, & Marcus-Newhall, 2008) with the goal of reducing the substantial variability and apparent arbitrariness with which death sentences were imposed. The *Booth* Court contended that ruling VIS as inadmissible in sentencing proceedings because they are unrelated to defendant blameworthiness would ultimately reduce arbitrariness in sentencing.

In *South Carolina v. Gathers* (1989), the U.S. Supreme Court again visited the constitutionality of VIS in capital sentencing, and in so doing, reaffirmed the ruling in *Booth* that VIS be barred from the capital sentencing penalty phase. Demetrius Gathers had attacked a homeless man in the park and brutally beaten him until he died. The issue that drew the Court's attention was not a particular statement by a witness, but rather, information provided by the prosecutor. The prosecutor, in addressing the jury during the penalty phase of the trial, insisted that while the victim was a homeless man of little means, he nevertheless was a citizen of this country and deserved the right to enjoy the public parks without fear. He then read extensively some literature found in the victim's possession that was designed to convey the victim's personal philosophy and his values. In their 5-4 decision, the Court noted that the prosecutor's statement bore little relevance to the sentencing task, and they added that it mattered little whether this information came in the form of a statement by the prosecutor or from testimony by a witness. The *Gathers* decision mirrored the earlier position the Court took in *Booth* by emphasizing that VIS share little relevance to sentencing and their inflammatory nature posed a threat that their capacity to invite prejudice might outweigh any probative value (see Myers & Greene, 2004).

In *Payne v. Tennessee* (1991) the U.S. Supreme Court again addressed the constitutionality of VIS in capital sentencing. In this case, the defendant, Pervis Payne, had entered the apartment of a neighbor and single mother, Charisse Christopher, whom he attacked after she refused his sexual advances. In his attack, he repeatedly stabbed her, inflicting 84 separate wounds which lead to her death. Payne also brutally attacked Christopher's two-year-old daughter, Lacie, who also died as a result of stab wounds to multiple areas on her body, including her head. Only 4-year-old Nicholas Christopher managed to survive, despite enduring multiple stab wounds that led to massive and critical blood loss. During the victim impact statement, the mother of Charisse Christopher, Mary Zvolanek, spoke of raising a grandson who was forced to live with the loss of a mother and a baby sister. "He cries for his mom. He doesn't seem to understand why she doesn't come home. And he cries for his sister Lacie. He comes to me many times during the week and asks me, Gandmama, do you miss my Lacie. And I tell him yes. He says, I'm worried about my Lacie." (p. 814).

In question was whether information that the small boy still missed and asked about his mother and his sister was relevant to the sentencing decision. Once again, the Court also questioned the inflammatory potential of the victim impact statement. However, in this instance, their 6-3 decision overruled *Booth* and *Gathers*, and in doing so argued that VIS is "simply another form or method of informing the sentencing authority about the specific harm caused by the crime in question, evidence of a general type long considered by sentencing authorities" (*Payne v. Tennessee*, 1991, p. 825) . Chief Justice Rehnquist, in delivering the opinion of the Court, challenged the contention in *Booth* and *Gathers* that the information contained in a VIS is irrelevant because it is unrelated to the defendant's blameworthiness. He noted that "wherever judges in recent years have had discretion to impose sentence, the consideration of the harm caused by the crime has been an important factor in the exercise of that discretion" (*Payne v. Tennessee*, 1991, p. 820). He further argued that VIS represent just another method of informing the factfinder about the consequences of the defendant's actions. "Two equally blameworthy criminal defendants may be guilty of different offenses solely because their acts cause differing amounts of harm" (p. 819). Consequently, the Court reasoned that barring VIS is overly restrictive and prevents the jury from hearing relevant information. In quoting *Gregg v. Georgia* (1976), Rehnquist reiterated the long tradition of avoiding unnecessary restrictions on information that will aid the factfinder: "We think it desirable for the jury to have as much information before it as possible when it makes the sentencing decision" (p. 821), and that a VIS "is designed to show instead each victim's 'uniqueness as an individual human being'" (p. 823). The Court's apparent abrupt pivot in *Payne v. Tennessee* (1991) surprised many and was regarded as an endorsement of VIS in capital sentencing, but in reality it only supported the introduction of VIS so long as this testimony did not invite prejudice (Levy, 1993). The *Payne* Court therefore ruled that there may be instances in which the VIS serves no purpose other than to inflame the passions of the jury, but there is no constitutional basis for restricting *all* VIS, and consequently VIS are not per se inadmissible in capital sentencing proceedings.

Empirical Research on Victim Impact Statements and Juror Judgments

The extensive debate surrounding VIS therefore largely centered around whether the introduction of VIS promotes arbitrariness and capriciousness in capital sentencing. These possibilities emerge when evidence is introduced that is irrelevant and distracts jurors from their principal role of assessing the blameworthiness of the defendant, or when the evidence promotes a mindset in jurors which impedes their capacity to remain impartial and reasoned in their decision making. These are concerns that lend themselves to empirical examination, and a number of studies by psycholegal researchers have shed important light on these questions.

Whereas much of the empirical research on VIS relies on jury simulation methodology (for reviews, see Myers & Greene, 2004; Nuñez, Estrada-Reynolds, Schweitzer, & Myers, 2016), some studies have investigated the effects of VIS using information obtained from actual capital sentencing decisions or post-trial interviews with capital jurors. For example, Eisenberg, Garvey, and Wells (2003) examined capital sentencing cases from South Carolina in the period between 1985 and 2001. The analysis consisted of post-trial interviews with jurors and analysis of jury verdicts. They found that the introduction of VIS correlated with jurors' self-reported ratings of the degree to which the victim was admired, which in turn was related to the perceived seriousness of the offense. However, neither perceptions of the victim nor the presence or absence of VIS was directly related to sentencing judgments. In a more recent analysis of VIS in capital trials, Aguirre, Davin, Baker, and Lee (2010) examined 154 capital cases in California comprising the years just prior to *Payne* and the years immediately following the *Payne* decision. They noted that prosecutors in California were reluctant to introduce VIS prior to *Payne*, and so when looking only at post-*Payne* cases ($n = 75$), juries were nearly 1.5 times more likely to vote for death when a VIS was present than when it was not; this difference was statistically significant. Specifically, 70.5% of juries who were presented with a VIS voted for death, whereas 48.4% of juries voted for death when a VIS was not presented.

Emotions and VIS: Are VIS Inflammatory?

A mother of a 14-month-old daughter who died in the explosion of the Oklahoma City Federal Building in 1995 delivered this message in her VIS during the Timothy McVeigh trial: "And I think in the end, by the time they finally told us that they found her body, it had been seven days, and I was just so incredibly thankful that they found her at all; and I felt lucky that I got to hold her wrapped in a beautiful receiving blanket made by my friend, Joyce. And that's the last thing I held" (cited in Burr, 2003, p. 524).

Evidence of this sort carries the potential to move jurors emotionally. The U.S. Supreme Court certainly recognized this potential. Citing *Gardner v. Florida* (1977), the Court in *Booth* noted that capital sentencing decisions must "be, and appear to be, based on reason rather than caprice or emotion" (*Booth v. Maryland*, 1987, p. 508). In the *Payne* decision, despite ruling that VIS are not per se inadmissible, the Court still warned of the dangers that the emotionality of VIS might overwhelm jurors. Justice O'Connor, in referencing the VIS in the *Payne* case, conceded: "I have no doubt that the jurors were moved by this testimony—who would not have been?" (p. 832). But, while recognizing the emotional appeal of VIS, the majority in *Payne* did not see anything in the Eighth Amendment that justified an outright bar of VIS from all capital sentencing penalty phases. Instead, the Court argued that should VIS be "so unduly prejudicial that it renders the trial fundamentally unfair, the Due Process Clause of the Fourteenth Amendment provides a mechanism for relief" (p. 825).

Much of the legal commentary critical of VIS has addressed the emotional appeal of this testimony (Deise & Paternoster, 2013; Myers & Greene, 2004). According to Blumenthal (2001), those who fear VIS believe that the jury "could be so inflamed by emotion that it does not make its decisions rationally" (p. 77). This is a common assumption: within the legal community, an emotional juror is typically seen as an irrational juror (Feigenson, 2000; Shaunessy, 1992). Little question exists that VIS can be moving, and prosecutors encourage this (Bandes, 2009; Burr, 2003). A field study of 125 transcripts containing VIS was conducted where the researchers analyzed both emotional content using the Linguistic Inquiry and Word Count program (LIWC; Pennebaker, Francis, & Booth, 2001) along with subjective ratings of participants who read the transcripts. The findings revealed that: (1) linguistically, emotional language pervades most VIS, and (2) a high proportion of participants who read these transcripts reported experiencing sadness (Nuñez, Egan-Wright, Kehn, & Myers, 2011).

Regardless of the widespread belief that VIS promote irrationality in jurors, there is a need to examine the issue empirically. The questions surrounding the inflammatory appeal of VIS can be evaluated and informed both by basic science research on emotions and judgment and with more applied research on juror decision making. This research indicates that, while VIS might elicit emotional responses in jurors, all emotions do not necessarily interfere with rational decision making, and there is a need to understand the complex effects of different emotions and how they might impact judgments. As Bandes and Blumenthal (2012) aptly put it: "the folk concept of emotions as unknowable and untamable is incorrect" (p. 171). Instead, in certain contexts, some emotions can detract from jurors' ability to reason and fully process information in their decision either as a result of reduced cognitive processing, more rapid judgments, or a biased search for information in making their judgments (see Feigenson & Park, 2006, for a review). However, in other instances, emotions can actually enhance information processing and jurors' capacity to reason (Bandes & Blumenthal, 2012; Myers, Weidemann, & Pearce, 2006; Wiener, Bornstein, & Voss, 2006). Some of the basic social-cognitive theories on emotions and judgment will be explored prior to examining the research in the jury decision-making literature.

Social Cognition Research on Emotions and Decisions

How emotions affect juror judgments regarding punishment and sentencing is an issue worthy of empirical analysis, and we will only briefly examine this issue as this topic has been addressed in much greater detail elsewhere (e.g., see Feigenson

& Park, 2006; Nuñez et al., 2016). A variety of social-cognitive theories explain the manner and degree to which distinct emotions (as well as moods and affect in general) influence judgments. For example, the Affect Infusion Model (AIM; Forgas, 1995) suggests that emotions are most likely to influence decision making when the decisional task is either substantive (e.g., a complex decisional task in which accuracy is required) or heuristic (e.g., a task in which quick judgments are required or motivation to process information is low). Both conditions can arise in a trial context. Multiple theories of emotion and judgment suggest that the emotional valence and the decision are consonant, either because the decision maker uses the emotion to inform the judgment (e.g., affect-as-information; Schwarz & Clore, 1983) or because the emotions activate thoughts consistent with that emotion (e.g., affective priming; Bower, 1981).

Research on emotions and judgment also indicates that specific emotions could have unique effects on decisions (Keltner, Ellsworth, & Edwards, 1993). According to the Appraisal Theory by Tiedens and Linton (2001), emotions such as anger prime feelings of certainty, whereas sadness evokes feelings of uncertainty. Feelings of certainty promote a heuristic processing style in which individuals have little motivation to carefully process information but are instead motivated to act (Feigenson & Park, 2006). By contrast, sadness and corresponding feelings of uncertainty promote careful and extensive information processing as individuals seek to gather information, presumably to restore a greater sense of certainty. Indeed, research has shown that angered individuals rely more on expertise or stereotypes and less on the strength of argument when making judgments—a finding that supports the theory that anger promotes heuristic processing (Tiedens & Linton 2001). Supporting evidence also comes from research indicating that information processing is less systematic when the individual is experiencing anger (Bodenhausen, Sheppard, & Kramer, 1994). According to this perspective, jurors might be expected to be less rational in their judgments (if we equate extensive information processing as more rational) when VIS promote angry responses than when VIS promote sad responses.

Other models suggest that emotions can guide the search for information and suggest how that information is weighed in judgments. Feigenson and Park (2006) characterize these models as *affective valence* models whereby emotions promote judgments consistent with the valence of that emotion (e.g., good or bad) and do so relatively automatically. According to this view, any rational information processing that arises serves only to justify the decision post-hoc rather than to inform the decision. Haidt's (2001) Moral Intuitionist Model and Alicke's (2000) Culpable Control Model are two examples of affective valence models.

Other related models suggest that the specific emotion motivates individuals to find information that might support their need to act on emotions (e.g., punish when angered). For example, the Intuitive Prosecutor Model (Tetlock, 2002) suggests that when angered, individuals shift into "intuitive prosecutor" mode, whereby events that specifically evoke anger lead individuals to judge a perpetrator's acts as more responsible for the harm and warranting harsher punishment (Goldberg, Lerner, & Tetlock, 1999). Haidt's, Alicke's and Tetlock's models share the view that *specific* emotions (rather than emotion in general) will influence what information is sought and attended to, and consequently influence judgments. The appraisal model proposed by Tiedens and Linton suggests that *specific* emotions (such as anger) promote less rational judgments because individuals are directed to make quicker judgments based on less information processing. None of these theories indicate that *all* emotions are antithetical to reasoned and impartial decisions.

Consequently, it is clear from the research on emotions and judgments that it would be inappropriate to paint emotions with a broad brush in the way justices and legal scholars have done thus far. Not all emotions are equally detrimental to the decision-making process of jurors, and so the effects of emotions on how information is processed and integrated into sentencing judgments is not uniform across emotions. Moreover, in the few studies conducted on emotions and judgments in the context of VIS and sentencing, a pattern of findings has emerged recently that mirror the findings in the social cognition literature.

VIS, Emotions, and Juror Judgments

A number of studies have focused specifically on the emotional appeal of VIS and the potential to influence juror sentencing judgments (e.g., Myers, Lynn, & Arbuthnot, 2002; Nuñez, Myers, Wilkowski, & Schweitzer, 2017; Nuñez, Schweitzer, Chai, & Myers, 2015; Paternoster & Deise, 2011; Platania & Berman, 2006; Tsoudis & Smith-Lovin, 1998; Wevodau, Cramer, Kehn, & Clark, 2014). Evidence for the prejudicial effects of VIS would more appropriately come from demonstrating that VIS elicit emotional responses in jurors, and these emotions can be directly linked to their sentencing decisions. A handful of studies on VIS have measured how jurors' emotions varied in response to VIS, but many of these studies have failed to differentiate among the different emotions and instead showed only that jurors' affective states predicted sentencing. A more recent pattern of findings suggest that when discrete emotional states are assessed, jurors who experience anger show a greater tendency to punish the defendant whereas sad jurors do not appear to be more punitive.

One of the first studies to examine emotionality associated with VIS was conducted by Tsoudis and Smith-Lovin (1998). In this investigation, college students read vignettes that included VIS that varied according to the emotional demeanor of the victim. They manipulated witness emotionality by embedding nonverbal expression cues into the transcript (e.g., "lifts head, eyes tearing"). Participants were told these descriptions were included to help them better visualize what took place during the testimony. Although the emotion displayed by the witness appeared to be sadness, the researchers did not assess emotional responses to the testimony. Jurors rated their perceptions of the victim's emotion, and their beliefs about the victim's identity (e.g., good—bad), beliefs about the criminal act (e.g., how serious), and recommended a sentence for the defendant. They found that the emotional display by the victim led to differences in how positively they perceived the victim's identity to be, which in turn was related to sentencing judgments. However, contrary to predictions, victims who displayed greater sadness were not judged to have experienced a more severe crime. Because the findings indicate that emotions displayed by the witness were related to sentencing, but not to beliefs about the criminal act, they support the contention that the emotionality of VIS might promote decisions based on factors that are irrelevant to the blameworthiness of the defendant. However, it is unclear whether jurors themselves became emotional, and thus it is difficult to trace the sentencing decision back to the emotionality of the jurors.

An early study that examined the emotional responses of jurors as a result of VIS comes from Myers et al. (2002). In this study, they randomly assigned participants to one of four trials containing a victim impact statement that crossed harm information (mild/severe) with the demeanor of the witness (stoic/emotional) and measured punishment ratings along with negative affect as measured by the PANAS (Watson, Clark, & Tellegen, 1988). Harm information, not emotional demeanor, significantly affected sentencing judgments. Although harm information also significantly affected negative affectivity, emotion ratings failed to mediate the relationship between harm and sentencing judgments. Instead, harm had a direct effect on sentencing (rather than because it led to strong emotions). Moreover, although the demeanor of the witness influenced jurors' emotions, it failed to influence their sentencing judgments. Importantly, the researchers failed to measure the discrete emotional responses in participants, so it is difficult to determine whether the emotion evoked in jurors was one of sadness or anger. But, post-hoc evaluation of the content of the statement and witness demeanor suggests that the jurors likely experienced sadness as a result of the VIS.

Two additional studies that have examined emotions and VIS have failed to find convincing evidence that VIS might be inflammatory. For example, Platania and Berman (2006) randomly assigned participants to watch a videotaped VIS which varied the emotional demeanor of the witness. The two emotional demeanor groups failed to differ significantly from one another on sentencing. Moreover, an instruction to use caution when considering the VIS negated any sentencing differences that emerged between a VIS and a No-VIS control. More recently, Wevodau et al. (2014) investigated the effects of VIS and measured overall negative affectivity along with sentencing. Although VIS produced significant changes in negative affect, these emotional responses did not significantly predict sentencing judgments. Consequently, studies have consistently shown that VIS can elicit emotional reactions in jurors. However, these same studies have not measured discrete emotional responses to victim impact testimony, nor have they demonstrated that general emotional reactions in jurors are directly related to the sentencing judgments they recommend.

Affective valence models of emotion and judgment argue that the effects of emotion on judgment depend on the particular emotion elicited. Accordingly, sadness has little effect on sentencing, but anger might promote harsher sentencing judgments. The studies reviewed thus far have failed to identify the particular emotion jurors experienced as a result of the VIS. In those that have assessed emotions but have found the emotions unrelated to sentencing (e.g., Myers et al., 2002; Wevodau et al., 2014), there is reason to contend that the impact testimony mainly evoked feelings of sadness in participants. In the studies reviewed next, there emerges a pattern of findings indicating that anger (but not sadness) influences sentencing judgments.

For example, Paternoster and Deise (2011) exposed mock jurors to a videotaped penalty phase that varied the presence of VIS. They found that, when jurors watched the trial containing this testimony, they were four times more likely to vote for death (62.5%) than were participants in the control condition (17.5%). In this study, neither harm nor the emotional aspect of the VIS was varied. However, the emotional responses of the death-qualified jury eligible participants were measured. The researchers found that when a VIS was present, there were greater reported feelings of anger and vengefulness on the part of jurors, and those emotions partially mediated the relationship between the VIS and sentencing judgments.

Further support for the effects of anger on sentencing comes from Georges, Wiener, and Keller (2013), who asked jurors to read a transcript of a capital case. Researchers measured their emotional responses (e.g., anger and sadness) at various points throughout the trial. Although this study examined capital trial sentencing but did not involve VIS, the authors nevertheless found that increased anger was associated with a greater likelihood of rendering death penalty decisions, whereas increased sadness was not related to sentencing. Similarly, Nuñez et al. (2015) presented jurors a penalty phase of a trial that included a VIS. The researchers held the content of the VIS constant and measured the specific emotions that mock jurors reported feeling during the trial (as measured by the PANAS-X pre- and post-trial). They found that participants who reported increases in anger during the trial were more likely to sentence the defendant to death, whereas increases in sadness had no effect on sentencing decisions.

In each of these instances in which anger led to more punitive sentencing, VIS was not manipulated in order to elicit a discrete emotional response. However, most recently, Nuñez et al. (2017) randomly assigned death-qualified mock jurors to watch one of six videotaped trials that crossed three levels of victim impact statement (No-VIS, Sad-VIS, Angry-VIS) with two levels of mitigating factors (weak vs. strong). The researchers pilot tested more than a hundred actual VIS from capital cases, and identified those testimonies that exhibited high emotional content using linguistic software that measures the emotional content in language (i.e., LIWC; Pennebaker et al., 2001). These same statements were given to jury eligible adults who rated their level of anger and sadness after reading each statement. Finally, a script containing a VIS was produced that contained numerous quotes from various VIS that were identified (based on both linguistic scoring and subjective ratings) as highly emotional. A videotaped penalty phase for a capital trial was produced in which the victim impact testimonies (control, sad, angry) varied. The distinct emotion of sadness versus anger was manipulated by altering the demeanor of the witness who played the mother of the deceased victim. The researchers found that participants who saw the angry witness were significantly more likely to sentence the defendant to death than participants who saw no victim impact witness or a witness who was sad. Participants rated their level of anger and sadness using the

PANAS-X (Watson & Clark, 1994), and individuals who became more angry after witnessing the VIS were more likely to sentence the defendant to death compared to those who became more sad after the VIS. Moreover, those who became angry after witnessing the statement rated the mitigating evidence as less important to their decision.

Therefore, while the U.S. Supreme Court in *Booth* and later in *Payne* highlighted the potential inflammatory effects of VIS, only a small number of the published empirical studies on VIS and sentencing have focused on the emotionality surrounding VIS, and only a few of these have assessed the specific emotions participants experienced after they were exposed to victim impact evidence. Content analysis of transcripts containing VIS reveals that these testimonies are often rich in emotion-laden language and evoke emotional responses from participants who read these statements, but that the most typical emotion experienced is sadness (Nuñez et al., 2011). There is mounting evidence to suggest that statements that elicit anger in jurors are more likely to result in death penalty judgments than statements that either fail to evoke an emotional response, or statements that elicit sadness (Nuñez et al., 2017; Paternoster & Deise, 2011).

Relevance of VIS to Blameworthiness: Victim and Defendant Characteristics

As previously noted, the second major issue of contention in U.S. Supreme Court cases concerning VIS and capital sentencing was whether information about the victim is relevant to judgments of defendant blameworthiness. Information concerning the characteristics of the victim and the loss suffered by the family holds little relevance to sentencing because the defendant typically has no knowledge of the victim's family or their characteristics when engaging in the criminal conduct. As a consequence, VIS might invite the jury to base their decision on information that arises fortuitously but is nevertheless unrelated to the defendant's culpability. Justice Powell, in delivering the majority opinion in *Booth*, noted that during sentencing, the focus must remain on the defendant and his acts, whereby the jury assesses whether the death penalty is warranted "based on the character of the individual and the circumstances of the crime" (p. 502, in citing *Zant v. Stevens*, 1983). Consistency in sentencing can be further eroded by the degree to which some victim survivors can articulate their suffering and loss. The personal and idiosyncratic nature of the statement might introduce arbitrariness in sentencing decisions, as the Justices noted in *Booth*: "We are troubled with the implication that defendants whose victims are assets to their community are more deserving of punishment than those whose victims are perceived to be less worthy. Of course, our system of justice does not tolerate such distinctions" (*Booth v. Maryland,* 1987, p. 506 in citing *Furman v. Georgia*, 1972, p. 242).

In writing the majority opinion in *Payne*, Justice Rehnquist clarified his position that victim character information should not lead to perceptions of worth when he argued: "as a general matter, victim impact evidence is not offered to encourage comparative judgments of this kind—for instance, that the killer of a hardworking devoted parent deserves the death penalty, but the murderer of a reprobate does not" (*Payne v. Tennessee*, p. 823). Still, the *Payne* Court reasoned that information concerning the loss of the victim should not be distinguished from other information in the trial that conveys the harm produced by the defendant's actions. Here it was noted that a VIS "is simply another form or method of informing the sentencing authority about the specific harm caused by the crime in question" (*Payne v. Tennessee*, 1991, p. 825). In other words, VIS are relevant if they convey the harm produced by the defendant's act.

If information fails to convey harm but instead alters perceptions of the value of the decedent (i.e., social value; see Myers & Greene, 2004), decisions could turn on factors that are irrelevant. Blame attributions have long been related to the characteristics of both those who cause harm and those who experience harm. Defendant personal characteristics have consistently been found to influence both punishment and guilt ratings (e.g., Kaplan & Kemmerick, 1974; Nadler & McDonnell, 2012; Nemeth & Sosis, 1973). Comparatively less research has addressed victims, but it nevertheless suggests that individuals are less opposed to punishing perpetrators who harm more likeable victims than less likeable victims (e.g., Deitz, Littman, & Bentley, 1984; Jones & Aronson, 1973). Supportive evidence for this finding comes from an examination of court records, which reveals that killing disreputable victims tends to be treated more leniently than when the victims are more reputable (Baumer, Messner, & Felson, 2000).

In the VIS literature, the identity and character of the victim can influence critical judgments. For example, gender of the victim might be important in juror sentencing judgments generally (Curry, Lee, & Rodriguez, 2004). Forsterlee, Fox, Forsterlee, and Ho (2004) examined the gender of the victim and sentencing judgments in the context of VIS. The researchers manipulated the presence or absence of a VIS along with the gender of the defendant and the gender of the victim. A defendant gender by VIS interaction emerged so that while participants punished the male defendant more severely, the disparity in punishment between the genders was significantly smaller when a VIS was present. The authors reported no significant main effects or interactions concerning the gender of the victim. Importantly, other than varying the gender of the victim, no other characteristics of the victim were varied in this study.

In two early studies on VIS (Greene, 1999; Greene, Koehring, & Quiat, 1998), researchers manipulated various personal qualities of the victim, and measured mock jurors' beliefs about the severity of the crime, their level of compassion for the victim's surviving family, as well as their opinion of the defendant. Greene et al. (1998) discovered that when victims were described as high in respectability (married and never previously divorced, prominent members of the community), participants rated the crime as more severe and expressed greater sympathy for the victim survivors than when the victim was described as less respectable (divorced and remarried, unemployed with little financial means, and minimal communication with family). Later, Greene (1999) confirmed this pattern, finding again that characteristics of the victim influenced a number of beliefs that could ultimately impact sentencing decisions. Specifically, when the victim was characterized as a loyal friend and devoted father, victim likeability, compassion for the surviving family, and perceptions of harm were all significantly higher than when the victim was characterized as a convicted felon who had minimal contact with family. Therefore, variations in victim respectability--information that is unrelated to the blameworthiness of the defendant--nevertheless influenced judgments that could directly affect sentencing.

These studies by Greene and her colleagues point to the dangers of VIS communicating aspects of "victim worth" that could ultimately influence sentencing judgments. One of the advantages of jury simulation research is that it reveals decisions based on factors of which jurors might be unaware. When Sundby (2003) conducted a large post-trial survey of jurors on the factors that influenced their sentencing judgments, respondents indicated that most victim characteristics were unlikely to influence their decisions. While this may cause one to doubt the effects of victim characteristics on sentencing, it is important to note that responses on post-trial surveys, while useful, might also be plagued by impression management (e.g., social desirability) goals which might mask respondents' true opinions.

A recent study by Mitchell, Myers, and Broszkiewicz (2016) affirm the findings by Greene (1999) and Greene et al. (1998), while narrowing the type of victim characteristics that have the greatest impact on sentencing judgments. Mitchell et al. (2016) examined how information about the victim provided in VIS was directly related to sentencing decisions, and how perceived harm mediated this relationship. The researchers distinguished between information which reveals the character of the victim (i.e., good/bad) and victim information which relays their significance to the surviving family. Information about the personal qualities of the victim is considered to be irrelevant to sentencing, unless it conveys the degree of harm the family experienced. Mitchell et al. (2016) crossed information about the personal character of the victim with information concerning the victim's significance to the surviving family (e.g., degree of presence in their lives and extent to which they were dependent on him) in trial summaries presented to mock jurors in the form of a VIS. They discovered that when victims were described as highly significant or essential to the overall well-being of the surviving family, participants rated the murder as more harmful to the family, and they were significantly more likely to sentence the defendant to death than when they read about a victim with low family significance. By contrast, whether the victim had good character (e.g., admirable doctor and philanthropist) or bad character (e.g., corrupt doctor accused of fraud) had no significant effect on mock jurors' perceptions of harm, nor on their sentencing decisions. In other words, victim information that communicates the level of harm the surviving relatives will experience due to the loss of the victim is most likely to affect sentencing decisions.

Testimony that identifies unique personal characteristics of the victim might allow the jury to see the victim as more than a "faceless stranger" (see *Payne v.*

Tennessee, 1991, p. 825), but it also opens up the possibility that jurors might reach conclusions about the social worth of the victim. For example, a recent study by Schweitzer and Nuñez (2017) examined how VIS might convey irrelevant information about the victim's social class, and whether information of this sort might influence sentencing decisions. They varied the VIS presented by the victim's daughter, which conveyed information regarding the victim's social class (either middle or working class). The testimony was delivered by a theater major who presented the testimony in either a working class or middle class speech style. Details about the deceased victim were altered by changing her occupation (salesperson or manager at a furniture store), housing (trailer or house), and a recent vacation she had taken (camping trip or cruise). The education level and occupation of the victim's daughter were also varied. The researchers found that mock jurors were significantly more likely to give the death penalty to the defendant who killed the middle class rather than the working class victim. Thus, it appears that differences in the social class of the victim, which was gleaned from the VIS (and reflected in juror's estimates of the victim's SES), ultimately affected sentencing decisions. The findings by Schweitzer and Nuñez (2017) provide an interesting empirical counterpoint to Chief Rehnquist's remarks in *Payne* that VIS are "not offered to encourage comparative judgments of the kind—for instance, that the killer of a hardworking, devoted parent deserves the death penalty, but the murderer of a reprobate does not" (*Payne v. Tennessee*, 1991, p. 823). Indeed, when considered in light of the earlier studies described in this section, these findings support the argument that VIS which communicate information about the characteristics of the victim might promote sentencing decisions that arise in an arbitrary manner.

In some cases, VIS can offer the witness an opportunity to characterize the defendant, and not just the victim. Some scholars have noted the concern that the capital sentencing process is already structured in a way that eases our natural reluctance to kill others (Haney 1997, 2005; Haney, Weill, & Lynch, 2015; Osofsky, Bandura, & Zimbardo, 2005). The introduction of an angry witness who delivers a VIS in a fashion that dehumanizes the defendant has the potential to exacerbate jurors' already developing reluctance to regard the defendant as human and worthy of compassion. Dehumanizing a punishment target prompts a degree of moral disengagement which counters our efforts not to harm others (Bandura, Barbaranelli, Caprara, & Pastorelli, 1996; Bandura, Underwood, & Fromson, 1975; Kelman, 1973). Examples of dehumanizing language applied to defendants include terms such as "parasite" (*Williham v. State*, 1997) and "piece of trash" (*Conover v. State*, 1997). Indeed, Duncan (1994) notes that metaphors for filth and slime are routinely directed at defendants during the course of the trial.

In one of the few studies to examine VIS and the effects of dehumanizing language on punishment, Myers, Godwin, Latter, and Winstanley (2004) randomly assigned mock jurors to read one of four brief summaries of a VIS that crossed defendant dehumanization (present/absent) and victim humanization (present/absent) along with a fifth condition in which participants did not read a VIS. Dehumanizing language included wording that portrayed the defendant in less-than-human terms (e.g., "a monster," a "piece of filth"), whereas humanizing language portrayed positive human qualities about the victim (e.g., "warm" and "caring"). Humanizing language directed toward the victim had no significant effect on sentencing judgments. However, the researchers found a significant effect of dehumanizing language on sentencing, as there was a significantly greater proportion of death penalty judgments selected when the defendant was dehumanized than when he was not.

Overall, it appears that jurors may be willing to consider factors unrelated to the defendant when judging the appropriate punishment. Studies that have varied characteristics of the victim have demonstrated significant effects on measures such as victim sympathy and perceived harm (e.g., Greene, 1999; Greene et al., 1998). Moreover, when participants learn that the victim has played a significant role in the lives of the surviving relatives, they judge the harm produced by the crime as significantly greater and are more willing to sentence the defendant to death (Mitchell et al., 2016). Indeed, even information about the qualities of the victim survivors (e.g., SES)—information that surely fails to establish relevance to sentencing judgments--nevertheless impacts the severity of the penalty imposed (Schweitzer & Nuñez, 2017). While this greater scrutiny toward the victim might be designed to balance the virtually unrestricted information that can be offered on behalf of the defendant, the greater focus on the victim could come at a cost to the fairness by which life and death decisions are made.

Victim Impact Statements and Jurors: How Trial and Juror Characteristics Moderate Effects

A number of studies have been conducted on VIS and juror judgments that have focused on aspects of the trial in which a VIS is introduced, or individual characteristics of the jurors that may play a role in how a VIS is perceived and processed (e.g., Boppre & Miller, 2014; Luginbuhl & Burkhead, 1995; Myers, Roop, Kalnen, & Kehn, 2013). In some cases, these studies have tended to focus on specific elements within the trial that accompany VIS and potentially enhance or attenuate the effects on sentencing. In other instances, researchers have focused on specific judgments jurors must make during the course of the trial, and how VIS might influence those judgments (e.g., how mitigating factors are weighed). In addition, procedural variations in how a VIS is introduced (e.g., who may present a VIS, the inclusion of limiting instructions, etc.) could affect juror sentencing judgments. Other studies concerning VIS have focused on individual difference measures and how these juror characteristics may interact with VIS on sentencing. These areas all merit careful scrutiny in order to understand the effects of VIS in capital sentencing cases.

Trial Characteristics

VIS have the potential to inform jurors about the extent of suffering experienced by the victim's family. In some jurisdictions, witnesses are afforded the opportunity to describe aspects of the crime they found upsetting, and this could include aspects about the brutality of the event. Researchers have considered how the effects of VIS could interact with the brutality of the crime. For example, in the earliest published study on VIS and juror judgments, Luginbuhl and Burkhead (1995) asked 100 participants to read brief vignettes about either a murder case that was moderately aggravated (an innocent bystander was killed during the robbery of a fast-food store), or a case that was severely aggravated (an elderly victim was stabbed repeatedly while tied to a chair). The vignette also manipulated the presence or absence of a VIS. The statement was based on the *Booth* case, and contained extensive information about the characteristics of the victim along with the grown children's reactions to their parent's death. The researchers found that participants presented with a VIS were significantly more likely to vote for death (51%) than were those in the control group (20%). Importantly, the presence of a VIS interacted with the crime such that the relationship between the VIS and death penalty judgments was substantially higher in the severely aggravated condition (29% chose death when a VIS was absent and 74% chose death when it was present) than was the relationship in the moderately aggravated condition (24% chose death when a VIS was absent versus 55% when it was present).

In the *Payne* decision, Justice O'Connor addressed the belief that the impact of VIS may vary to some extent according to the characteristics of the crime. Here, she noted: "I do not doubt that the jurors were moved by this testimony—who would not have been? But surely this brief statement did not inflame their passions more than did the facts of the crime" (*Payne v. Tennessee*, 1991, p. 832). This argument implied that any effects of VIS on sentencing are likely to be overwhelmed by the brutality of the crime itself, suggesting that VIS are likely to have the greatest effects on jurors when the crime is not particularly heinous. Myers et al. (2013) tested this hypothesized interaction by varying the heinousness of the crime along with the presence or absence of a VIS. The statement was provided by the victim's spouse who detailed the experience of finding her husband's dead body, her emotional devastation since his murder, and the financial strain she experienced as a result of his death. In the less heinous condition, the victim died of a single gunshot to the heart, whereas in the more heinous condition, the victim was pistol whipped and then shot 14 times in various parts of the body and then sodomized with an umbrella in a manner similar to the case in *South Carolina v. Gathers* (1989). They found that heinousness significantly predicted death penalty sentencing, and the effect of the VIS was only marginally significant. Further, the VIS failed to interact with crime heinousness on sentencing judgments. Jurors were not significantly more likely to choose a death sentence when a VIS came in the context of a less heinous crime than when it came in the context of a more heinous crime.

Elements present in a capital trial other than the brutality of the crime might ultimately enhance or detract from the influence of VIS on juror judgments. One example is testimony that might provide a counterbalance to the effects of VIS. Execution Impact Evidence (EIE) refers to statements presented during the penalty phase of a capital trial in which relatives of the defendant describe how they would likely be affected by the execution of the defendant, as well as their opinions regarding why the defendant deserves to live. These statements have frequently arisen in capital sentencing proceedings since the mid-1990s (Wolff & Miller, 2009). Not surprisingly, EIE is controversial and, as Logan (1999) has argued, it might allow for some balance against the effects of VIS. Boppre and Miller (2014) tested the possibility that EIE might promote positive views of the defendant and crossed EIE testimony with a VIS on a sample of death-qualified participants who read a trial scenario and, depending on condition, read a 200-word VIS and/or a 300-word EIE statement. While no main effects emerged for sentencing for either EIE or the VIS, those who read the EIE statement judged the defendant to be more remorseful than those not exposed to the EIE. Moreover, while the VIS led to more positive impressions of the victim, this effect did not emerge for participants who had also read the EIE statement.

In some instances, researchers have focused on critical decisions jurors must make during the penalty phase of the trial in addition to sentencing. One measure of critical importance is the degree to which jurors are willing to consider mitigating factors (i.e., reasons why the death penalty should not be imposed). *Lockett v. Ohio* (1978) addressed the importance of jurors properly considering mitigating evidence when sentencing the defendant in capital cases. In this decision, the U.S. Supreme Court ruled that jurors *must* consider "any aspect of a defendant's character or record and any of the circumstances of the offense that the defendant proffers as a basis for a sentence less than death" (p. 604). Indeed, one of the concerns regarding VIS is that by focusing on characteristics of the victim, the jury's attention is diverted from their intended role of considering the more relevant aspects of the defendant (Bandes, 1996; Phillips, 1998). Mitigating factors represent one of the more critical factors jurors must consider during the penalty phase of the trial. Focusing on the victim may detract from a juror's capacity to focus on the defendant and properly evaluate the mitigating evidence. One fear, according to Arrigo and Williams (2003), is that as jurors begin to feel closer to the victim as a consequence of hearing the VIS, their capacity to empathize with the defendant may ultimately be reduced. Indeed, in his dissent in *Payne*, Justice Marshall noted that VIS could have "an inherent capacity to draw the jury's attention away from the character of the defendant and the circumstances of the crime" (*Payne v. Tennessee*, 1991; p. 846).

The degree to which jurors are willing to use mitigating evidence in forming their decisions about whether a defendant should receive the death penalty has been examined by researchers in a number of instances. For example, Brewer (2004) analyzed sentencing judgments for 865 respondents as part of a large grant-funded study on sentencing called the Capital Juror Project. Brewer reported that, as receptivity to mitigation increased a single unit, the odds that the defendant would not get the death penalty increased more than 100%.

In some instances, researchers have employed jury simulation approaches to examine the degree to which jurors are receptive to mitigating factors and how VIS influence acceptance of mitigators. For example, Gordon and Brodsky (2007) varied the presence or absence of a VIS and found that they had no effect on participants' ratings of mitigating factors. In the previously reported study by Nuñez et al. (2017), the researchers crossed a VIS (no-VIS/VIS-Sad/VIS-Angry) with the strength of mitigating evidence (Weak/Strong) and found that when a VIS elicited anger (but not sadness), mock jurors rated the mitigating evidence as less important to their decision. Although more research in this important area is clearly needed, this most recent finding by Nuñez et al. (2017) suggests that when VIS provoke anger responses, receptivity to mitigation evidence will be negatively affected.

Procedural Factors

There are a number of procedural factors that could either amplify or reduce the effects of VIS on sentencing decisions, and only a small proportion of these issues have been given empirical scrutiny. For example, many states grant wide latitude regarding who and how many witnesses may testify to present victim impact evidence (Logan, 2005). McGowan and Myers (2004) held the content of the VIS constant, but varied the identity of the witness who delivered it (no-VIS control, spouse, coworker, first-responder). Although the testimony by the spouse led to the highest ratings of harm the defendant inflicted, sentencing judgments for this group failed to differ significantly from the no-VIS control group. Unexpectedly, they instead found that only testimony by the coworker led to significantly more death penalty judgments. The researchers argued that perhaps some of the influence of VIS on sentencing might be related to the degree to which harm and suffering information is unexpected. As Weidemann (2008) later theorized, jurors likely assume the spouse of the victim would experience extensive harm as a result of the crime, but that coworkers and friends might experience considerable loss is less expected and, for that reason, more influential. However, this remains conjecture, and so the explanation for the findings in McGowan and Myers (2004) remain unclear and warrant follow-up investigation.

Jurors frequently have difficulty understanding their responsibilities in capital cases (Eisenberg & Wells, 1993; Garvey, Johnson, & Marcus, 2000; Wiener, Pritchard, & Weston, 1995), particularly surrounding their use of aggravating and mitigating factors (Garvey, 1998). The capital trial process might be uniquely complicated due to the bifurcated process and the fact that some of the procedures in the penalty phase differ from the guilt phase of the trial. Consequently, how to integrate VIS into their sentencing decisions represents a considerable challenge for jurors. VIS are not aggravating factors, but they are likely to be misjudged as such. For a number of reasons, jurors might benefit considerably from greater instruction regarding how to use VIS in their decision making.

Platania and Berman (2006) investigated the effects of specific judicial instructions concerning VIS on mock juror sentencing judgments. Specifically, they randomly assigned death-qualified college participants to watch a videotaped trial in one of six conditions crossing a VIS that varied in emotional content (VIS-high emotion/VIS-low emotion/no-VIS) with type of instructions (standard/specific). In the high emotion condition, jurors witnessed the decedent's mother sobbing while testifying, whereas the same testimony was given in a stoic manner in the low emotion condition. In the specific instructions, jurors were informed they were free to assign the VIS whatever weight in their decision that they felt appropriate, but that the VIS could not substitute for state-enacted aggravating factors. The researchers found that the VIS did not affect sentencing judgments. However, instructions were significantly related to sentencing, as 60% of participants who heard general instructions voted for death, whereas only 40% did so when specific instructions were used. Moreover, specific instructions lowered the importance jurors assigned the VIS to their sentencing judgments.

Blumenthal (2009) examined how expert testimony might serve to attenuate the impact of VIS on sentencing. Specifically, he noted that the research findings on affective forecasting (see Wilson & Gilbert, 2003) indicate that judging future emotional impact for events is frequently overestimated. He hypothesized that expert testimony informing participants about the research on affective forecasting would reduce the effects of VIS. To test this, a sample of death-qualified college students were asked to read a modified summary of the facts used previously in Butler and Moran (2002) and were randomly assigned to one of three conditions that varied VIS along with expert testimony about affective forecasting (i.e., no-VIS/VIS/VIS + expert). Although the introduction of expert testimony about affective forecasting negated the effects of the VIS, he was unable to replicate these findings in a second study in which expert testimony increased death penalty judgments relative to those who heard a VIS without expert testimony. Although the findings do not present conclusive evidence that expert testimony might attenuate the effects of VIS, by focusing on misconceptions individuals have about future emotional suffering, Blumenthal (2009) addressed an important gap in the literature surrounding VIS: namely, that more research should be directed toward understanding what aspects of VIS jurors find influential in their sentencing judgments.

An additional procedural factor that might moderate the influence of VIS is the deliberation process. Deliberation could influence juror judgments for a number of reasons. For example, post-deliberation juries are more apt to follow the judge's instructions (Kerwin & Schaffer, 1994; London & Nightingale, 1996), and they are more likely to remember the evidence (Ellsworth, 1989) than are individual jurors. Biased attitudes jurors hold could be less likely to affect final judgments after a period of group deliberation (Kaplan & Miller, 1978), and juries show improved reasoning following deliberation (McCoy, Nuñez, & Dammeyer, 1999), in addition to showing a reduced likelihood of relying on inadmissible evidence (London & Nuñez, 2000). Nevertheless, researchers have generally failed to examine the role group deliberation might play on VIS and sentencing. One exception is a study by Myers and Arbuthnot (1999), who performed a rather crude analysis that showed that post-deliberation death sentences were significantly more likely when a VIS was present (compared to when it was not), while this effect failed to emerge for pre-deliberation sentencing judgments. However, systematic analysis of the content of the deliberations was not provided, and so little is known about what jurors discussed during deliberations.

Juror Characteristics

Any analysis of juror decision making would be incomplete without examining individual difference characteristics and how those characteristics can shape interpretation of evidence and decision making. One of the more critical individual difference characteristics in capital sentencing judgments is attitudes toward the death penalty. For capital trials, the voir dire includes the death qualification process whereby individuals are removed from serving if their attitudes "impair" their ability to carry out their duties (*Wainwright v. Witt*, 1985). Yet, despite this initial screening process, substantial variation in attitudes toward the death penalty remain even in death-qualified juries (Unnever, Cullen, & Roberts, 2005).

Death penalty attitudes have been shown to be a robust predictor of sentencing in capital cases (Haney, Hurtado, & Vega, 1994). The degree to which death penalty attitudes influence perceptions of VIS was first explored by Luginbuhl and Burkhead (1995) in a study that was described previously in this chapter. Participants who rated themselves as neutral or moderately supportive of the death penalty were most likely to show the effects of VIS on their sentencing judgments. Only this subgroup of participants was significantly more likely to vote for death in the presence of a VIS (than when a statement was absent). By contrast, when attitudes toward the death penalty were strong, no differences in sentencing emerged between participants in the VIS and the no-VIS groups.

Butler (2008) examined the relation between death qualification status, VIS, and sentencing. A sample of 200 jury eligible community members read a summary of a murder case that either did, or did not, contain a VIS. The statement included testimony by multiple witnesses who all described the emotional devastation they experienced as a result of the crime. While the victim impact evidence did not directly predict sentencing judgments, VIS interacted with death qualification status such that death-qualified participants were more likely to sentence the defendant to death when a VIS was present than when it was not, but these differences did not emerge for the nonqualified participants. Similarly, Myers et al. (2004) also found that VIS predicted sentencing, but only for those who were death-qualified. With the exception of the study by Weidemann (2008), who was unable to find that VIS interacted with death penalty attitudes, the findings in this area generally show that VIS might require a narrow window of moderate support for the death penalty in order for VIS to produce significant effects on sentencing.

Because VIS are typically delivered in an emotional fashion, the degree to which individuals are receptive to emotional appeals could be important in understanding the effects of VIS (Nadler & Rose, 2003). Need for Affect (NFA: Maio & Esses, 2001) reflects the degree to which individuals seek emotional experiences, process emotional information, and are affected by emotions in their judgment processes. Wevodau et al. (2014) investigated whether the effects of VIS on sentencing judgments might be moderated by individual differences in NFA. They found that jurors high in NFA made lengthier sentencing recommendations than those low on the scale, but these individual differences failed to interact with the presence or absence of VIS.

Individuals better able to empathize with victims might also be more impacted by VIS. Butler (2008) found the presence of a VIS led participants to experience greater empathy for the victim's survivors and to rate the survivors as significantly more likable. One question which emerges is whether the presentation of a VIS directs individuals to empathize with the victim to the defendant's detriment. As Arrigo and Williams (2003) have argued, empathy may be a zero-sum game in which increased empathy for the victim comes at the expense of the defendant. Support for this notion comes from Paternoster and Deise (2011), who found that, in the presence of a VIS, participants reported significantly greater empathy and sympathy for the victim, and viewed the victim's family more positively, but they regarded the defendant less positively. Similarly, Henry et al. (2014) found that individual differences in Empathic Concern (EC), as measured with the Interpersonal Reactivity Index (IRI: Davis, 1983), significantly and negatively correlated with death penalty judgments. Moreover, individuals exposed to a VIS reported a significantly greater discrepancy between their rated empathy for the victim and their empathy for the defendant. However, individual differences in EC failed to significantly moderate the relationship between VIS and sentencing.

To summarize, a number of researchers have explored the role of individual difference variables that tap a general willingness to attend to or experience emotional information or the emotions of others (e.g., Need for Affect, Empathy, Empathic Concern). While these studies have generally found that these measures tended to predict how either the defendant or the victim was judged, and in some instances have predicted the final sentencing judgment, there has been little evidence to date that these measures have interacted with VIS on sentencing. By contrast, measures of death penalty attitudes have both directly predicted sentencing judgments, and also interacted with VIS, such that VIS have the greatest impact on sentencing when jurors hold moderate attitudes toward the death penalty.

VIS and Capital Sentencing: Implications and Future Directions

As Myers and Greene (2004) noted earlier, while the *Payne* decision ruled that VIS is not per se prejudicial, the Court nevertheless provided little guidance on how VIS might be administered in capital trials in a way that would reduce the likelihood of prejudice. Consequently, individual states have varied considerably in how VIS have been implemented. The variability in how VIS are administered only adds to the concern that those who receive the death penalty and those who do not might vary according to arbitrary factors. Moving forward, in order for researchers to better account for the effects of VIS on juror decision making, greater focus on these various procedural factors (e.g., who may testify, how many, and any restrictions placed on testimony) is warranted. Moreover, establishing a clear model of how VIS influence capital sentencing decisions remains an unfulfilled goal. A number of possible models exist that could account for the effects of VIS on sentencing (e.g., an affect model, a harm model). As we note in the next section, clarifying and refining these models represents a critical next step in understanding VIS and juror judgments.

Diversity in Methods and Models

The literature on VIS, to date, suffers from a lack of diversity in approaches as it has primarily relied on jury simulation research. Limitations with this approach have been articulated elsewhere (e.g., Diamond, 1997), including the research specifically devoted to examining VIS (e.g., Myers et al., 2006), and will not be detailed here. Consequently, there is a need for other approaches that could provide support for the findings obtained through simulation methodology. This could rely on data from court transcripts, or on examination of actual jury decisions and post-trial interviews with jurors (e.g., see Eisenberg et al., 2003 for an excellent example). While the alternative approaches we mention here suffer from their own limitations, some degree of convergence in findings between trial simulations and these alternative approaches would enhance our understanding of VIS and the potential effect on capital sentencing decisions.

Some diversity in the proposed models by which VIS render their effects on jurors have been observed. For example, some studies have suggested that VIS affect sentencing by eliciting emotions such as anger which promotes a prosecutorial mindset (e.g., Nuñez et al., 2017). Indeed, this model has been supported by a number of studies (e.g., Nuñez et al., 2015; Paternoster & Deise, 2011). But other models exist that could explain the effects of VIS on sentencing that do not rely on emotion. As we noted, some studies have suggested that VIS influence sentencing judgments because they effectively communicate harm information, and perceived harm is related to sentencing (e.g., Mitchell et al., 2016). Moreover, VIS which violate our initial expectations about experienced harm are likely most impactful (McGowan & Myers, 2004). Although this proposition needs further testing (see Weidemann, 2008), researchers have noted the importance of expectancy violations in juror judgments (Ask & Landstrom, 2010; Hackett, Day, & Mohr, 2008; Lens, van Doorn, Lahlah, Pemberton, & Bogaerts, 2016; Rose, Nadler, & Clark, 2006). Other models suggest that researchers consider the characteristics of who was harmed in understanding how jurors form blame assessments. In line with social psychological research on blame attributions, it may be that jurors seek to punish defendants who have harmed victims who are liked more than they are willing to punish defendants who harm victims who are less liked. Empirical findings on actual jury decisions (Baumer et al., 2000), as well as jury simulation research suggesting that status of the victim matters (e.g., Greene et al., 1998; Schweitzer & Nuñez, 2017), would indicate that perceptions of the qualities of the victim do guide judgments about the case.

Moving forward, there is a need to begin to test the limits of these models. As this chapter suggests, the effects of VIS on sentencing are not robust, and this illustrates the need to move toward a better understanding of why jurors might be influenced by this testimony. What is the information contained in a VIS that jurors regard as relevant to their sentencing? A recent study by Johnson et al. (2016) suggests that when participants were asked if they felt it was important to hear a victim's mother testify prior to rendering a sentencing judgment, 30% indicated they would prefer *not* to hear a VIS. Interestingly, their reported reasons for not wanting to hear a statement mirrored the arguments that the courts have expressed when arguing against the admissibility of VIS testimony (e.g., irrelevant to decision, emotions could bias judgments).

Procedural Discrepancies Regarding VIS

What the research on VIS and juror judgments has thus far failed to adequately mine is the potentially rich source of data surrounding the variability by which VIS are implemented procedurally. Because there is a concern that VIS might invite arbitrariness in sentencing (see *Booth v. Maryland*, 1987), the effects of the numerous variations in how VIS are implemented merit investigation. For example, to our knowledge, no studies have investigated how the number of statements could impact sentencing. Yet, as Logan (2005) has noted, courts generally place few restrictions on how many can testify. In cases of crimes that lead to multiple victims such as the bombing of the Federal Building in Oklahoma City in 1995 (see Logan, 2000), or the bombing during the Boston Marathon in 2013 (Seelye, 2015), a large number of witnesses provided lengthy and gripping accounts of the grief and suffering experienced by numerous relatives, friends, and even emergency first responders. In their field study which examined more than a hundred VIS taken from capital trials, Nuñez et al. (2011) found that there were many instances of multiple witnesses presenting VIS for a single victim. Ogul (2000) has suggested that as more witnesses testify, the odds that a given witness will provide testimony that invites prejudice also increase. This specific concern was raised in *New Jersey v. Muhummad* (1996), in which the court expressly limited the number of witnesses who may testify. Multiple victim impact witnesses might have greater impact on sentencing than a single witness for a number of reasons (e.g., greater perceptions of harm, enhanced credibility of testimony). Moreover, the likelihood that a particular witness's story will resonate with a juror increases as the number of individuals testifying increases. Alternatively, jurors might reach an early saturation point with respect to victim survivor suffering, and added testimony by victim survivors could do little to change their initial beliefs about the case. Indeed, multiple witnesses might desensitize jurors to the suffering or, even worse, produce a level of cynicism in jurors as they begin to feel manipulated by these emotional appeals. Consequently, empirical evidence is needed to assess the potential for the numerous possible outcomes associated with statements from multiple victim survivors.

Another procedural variation on the administration of VIS which has generated controversy is the introduction of videos, pictures, and music to accompany a VIS. Currently, courts have not dealt with this issue uniformly (Kennedy, 2008; Schroeder, 2010). For example, Schroeder (2010) notes that in *People v. Kelly* (2007), the court permitted a VIS that involved a 20-minute display of photos covering the life of the victim accompanied by music by Enya. But, by contrast, in *United States v. Sampson* (2004) and in *Salazar v. State* (2002), similar videos and picture montages set to music were deemed to be unduly prejudicial. Harden (2010) agrees that these video montages are "unduly prejudicial" and should be disallowed under Federal Rule of Evidence 403. One court disallowed pictures of the victim because they failed to depict the victim as he was at the time of the murder. Here, the court reasoned that the excessive childhood photos were apt to send the message that the defendant "killed this laughing, light-hearted child" (*Salazar v. State*, 2002, p. 330). Despite substantial discrepancies in the restrictions placed on photos, videos, and music to accompany VIS, little empirical research has explored this issue.

Emotionality and VIS

The concern that VIS may be inflammatory and influence capital sentencing judgments because jurors might fail to decide in an impartial and rational fashion due to strong emotions is frequently addressed by legal commentators. Most recently, a pattern of results indicates that anger is the specific emotion associated with harsher sentencing. Sadness, by contrast, appears to have little impact on sentencing judgments. Research on VIS and emotions has overlooked other emotions and how they might influence judgments. Fear appears to be a worthy candidate for investigation. The research on mortality salience and Terror Management Theory (TMT) suggests that a capital sentencing task might be particularly likely to encourage individuals to aggress against others to maintain their worldview (e.g., see Judges, 1999; Kirchmeier, 2008). Moreover, as Jones and Weiner (2011) note, the effects of TMT are most pronounced when the jurors consider their own death rather than that of the victim or the defendant. The degree to which jurors identify with the victim, a process Arrigo and Williams (2003) argue is aided by VIS, could promote a focus on one's own mortality and a corresponding tendency to use aggression in response to these feelings.

The fact that researchers have restricted their focus to anger and sadness is partly justified as anger and sadness appear to be the dominant emotions jurors experience (e.g., see Nuñez et al., 2011). A critical next step would be to apply closer scrutiny to the content of VIS, and identify the types of information most frequently associated with angry reactions. Only a few studies thus far have addressed the content of VIS and how it relates to emotions. Some recent data by Myers, Nuñez, Mitchell, Kehn, and Wilkowski (2017) indicate that VIS typically describe surviving relatives' emotional suffering and financial harm, and they frequently relate to the jury the positive aspects of the victim's character. Englebrecht and Chavez (2014) found other commonalities such as the experience of grief and how the witness has mourned the loss of a loved one. These findings are perhaps not surprising, and similar results have been observed by Younglove, Nelligan, and Reisner (2009). But some unexpected themes have emerged when examining victim impact statement content. One example was the tendency for witnesses to share their experience of first learning of the fate of the deceased (Myers et al., 2017). It may be that witnesses (and prosecutors) recognize this experience as a fear that individuals universally contemplate, and so this narrative consistently finds itself in victim survivors' testimony. Identifying specific content that triggers problematic emotional states in jurors may be the critical next step if research is to influence policy regarding VIS.

Concluding Remarks

Victim impact statements remain highly controversial in capital sentencing and continue to generate lengthy debate among legal scholars regarding their admissibility. Furthermore, because VIS often concern issues that are highly emotional, the topic itself represents an area that has long been considered ripe for investigation and empirical analysis by psychologists (e.g., Myers & Greene, 2004). Some important developments in this area have emerged, particularly with regard to our understanding of how specific emotions such as anger may promote a greater tendency to endorse the death penalty. However, other findings of critical importance to this debate have emerged as well, such as the tendency for victim character information to influence sentencing decisions, particularly when the information informs jurors about the level of harm the victim survivors have experienced. Other areas of importance to the debate about VIS and capital sentencing have garnered much less study and warrant greater focus. These include procedural matters such as restrictions on who, how many, and the manner in which testimony is introduced (e.g., with accompanying photo montages). These issues, along with a greater need to investigate VIS utilizing research methods other than jury simulations, represent new directions that could generate important findings in years to come.

References

Aguirre, A., Davin, R. P., Baker, D. V., & Lee, K. (2010). Sentencing outcomes, race, and victim impact evidence in California: A pre- and post-Payne comparison. *The Justice Professional: A Critical Journal of Crime, Law and Society, 11*, 297–310. https://doi.org/10.1080/1478601X.1999.9959510

Alicke, M. D. (2000). Culpable control and the psychology of blame. *Psychological Bulletin, 126*, 556–574. https://doi.org/10.1037//0033-2909.126.4.556

Arrigo, B. A., & Williams, C. R. (2003). Victim vices, victim voices, and impact statements: On the place of emotion and the role of restorative justice in capital sentencing. *Crime & Delinquency, 49*(4), 603–626. https://doi.org/10.1177/0011128703252408

Ask, K., & Landstrom, S. (2010). Why emotions matter: Expectancy violation and affective response mediate the emotional victim effect. *Law Human Behavior, 34*, 392–401. https://doi.org/10.1007/s10979-009-9208-6

Austin, R. (2010). Documentation, documentary, and the law: What should be made of victim impact videos? *Cardozo Law Review, 31*, 979–1017.

Bandes, S. A. (1996). Empathy, narrative, and victim impact statements. *The University of Chicago Law Review, 63*(2), 361–412.

Bandes, S. A. (1999). Reply to Paul Cassell: What we know about victim impact statements. *Utah Law Review, 2*, 545–552.

Bandes, S. A. (2009). Victims, "closure," and the sociology of emotion. *Law and Contemporary Problems, 72*, 1–29.

Bandes, S. A., & Blumenthal, J. A. (2012). Emotion and the law. *Annual Review of Law and Social Science, 8*, 161–181. https://doi.org/10.1146/anurev-lawosci-102811-173825

Bandura, A., Barbaranelli, C., Caprara, G. V., & Pastorelli, C. (1996). Mechanisms of moral disengagement in the exercise of moral agency. *Journal of Personality and Social Psychology, 71*, 364–374. https://doi.org/10.1037/0022-3514.71.2.364

Bandura, A., Underwood, B., & Fromson, M. E. (1975). Disinhibition of aggression through diffusion of responsibility and dehumanization of victims. *Journal of Research in Personality, 9*, 253–269. https://doi.org/10.1080/0305724022014322

Baumer, E. P., Messner, S. F., & Felson, R. B. (2000). The role of victim characteristics in the disposition of murder cases. *Justice Quarterly, 17*(2), 281–307. https://doi.org/10.1080/07418820000096331

Blume, J. H. (2003). Ten years of *Payne*: Victim impact evidence in capital cases. *Cornell Law Review, 88*, 257–281.

Blumenthal, J. A. (2001). The admissibility of victim impact statements at capital sentencing: Traditional and nontraditional perspectives. *Drake Law Review, 50*, 67–91.

Blumenthal, J. A. (2009). Affective forecasting and capital sentencing: Reducing the effect of victim impact statements. *American Criminal Law Review, 46*, 107–125.

Bodenhausen, G. V., Sheppard, L. A., & Kramer, G. P. (1994). Negative affect and social judgment: The differential impact of anger and sadness. *European Journal of Social Psychology, 24*, 45–62. https://doi.org/10.1002/ejsp.2420240104

Booth v Maryland. 482 U.S. 496. 1987.

Boppre, B., & Miller, M. K. (2014). How victim and execution impact statements affect jurors' perceptions, emotions, and verdicts. *Victims and Offenders: An International Journal of Evidence-based Research, Policy, and Practice, 9*, 413–435. https://doi.org/10.1080/15564886.2013.845124

Bower, G. H. (1981). Mood and memory. *American Psychologist, 36*(2), 129–148. https://doi.org/10.1037/0003-066X.36.2.129

Brewer, T. W. (2004). Race and jurors' receptivity to mitigation in capital cases: The effect of jurors', defendants', and victims' race in combination. *Law and Human Behavior, 28*, 529–545. https://doi.org/10.1023/B:LAHU.0000046432.41928.2b

Burr, R. (2003). Litigating with victim impact testimony: The serendipity that has come from *Payne v. Tennessee*. *Cornell Law Review, 88*, 517–529.

Butler, B. (2008). The role of death qualification in venirepersons' susceptibility to victim impact statements. *Psychology, Crime & Law, 1492*, 133–141. https://doi.org/10.1080/10683160701483534

Butler, B. M., & Moran, G. (2002). The role of death qualification in venirepersons' evaluations of aggravating and mitigating circumstances in capital trials. *Law and Human Behavior, 26*(2), 175–184. https://doi.org/10.1023/A:1014640025871

Cassell, P. G. (2009). In defense of victim impact statements. *Ohio State Journal of Criminal Law, 6*, 611–648.

Conover v. State 933 P. 2d. 1074, 1085–1086 (Okla Crim. App. 1997).

Costanzo, S., & Costanzo, M. (1994). Life or death decisions: An analysis of capital jury decision-making under the special issues framework. *Law and Human Behavior, 18*, 151–170. https://doi.org/10.1007/BF01499013

Crime Victim's Rights Act. 18 U.S.C. § 3771. 2004.

Curry, T. R., Lee, G., & Rodriguez, S. F. (2004). Does victim gender increase sentence severity? Further explorations of gender dynamics and sentencing outcomes. *Crime & Delinquency, 50*(3), 319–343. https://doi.org/10.1177/0011128703256265

Curry, L. (2011). The elusive right to cross-examine individuals presenting victim impact statements in Arizona capital sentencing proceedings. *Arizona State Law Journal, 43*, 563–589.

Davis, M. (1983). Measuring individual differences in empathy: Evidence for a multidimensional approach. *Journal of Personality and Social Psychology, 44*(1), 113–126. https://doi.org/10.1037/0022-3514.44.1.113

Davis, R. C., & Smith, B. E. (1994). Victim impact statements and victim satisfaction: An unfulfilled promise? *Journal of Criminal Justice, 22*, 1. https://doi.org/10.1016/0047-2352(94)90044-2

Death Penalty Information Center (2017). .Legal issues: States that allow victim impact statements. Retrieved from www.deathpenalty.org/legalissues.

Deise, J., & Paternoster, R. (2013). More than a "quick glimpse of the life": The relationship between victim impact evidence and death sentencing. *Hastings Constitutional Law Quarterly, 40*(3), 611–652.

Deitz, S. R., Littman, M., & Bentley, B. J. (1984). Attribution of responsibility for rape: The influence of observer empathy, victim resistance, and victim attractiveness. *Sex Roles, 10*(3/4), 261–280. https://doi.org/10.1007/BF00287780

Diamond, S. (1997). Illuminations and shadows from jury simulations. *Law and Human Behavior, 21*(5), 561–571. https://doi.org/10.1023/A:1024831908377

Dorland, M., & Krauss, D. (2005). The danger of dangerousness in capital sentencing: Exacerbating the problem of arbitrary and capricious decision-making. *Law & Psychology Review, 29*, 63–105.

Duncan, M. G. (1994). In slime and darkness: The metaphor of filth in criminal justice. *Tulane Law Review, 68*, 725–801.

Eisenberg, T., Garvey, S. P., & Wells, M. T. (2003). Symposium: Victims and the death penalty: Inside and outside the courtroom: Victim characteristics and victim impact evidence in South Carolina capital cases. *Cornell Law Review, 88*, 306–342.

Eisenberg, T., & Wells, M. T. (1993). Deadly confusion: Juror instructions in capital cases. *Cornell Law Review, 79*(1), 1–17.

Ellsworth, P. (1989). Are twelve heads better than one? *Law and Contemporary Problems, 52*, 205–224. https://doi.org/10.2307/1191911

Englebrecht, C. M., & Chavez, J. M. (2014). Whose statement is it? An examination of victim impact statements delivered in court. *Victims & Offenders, 9*(4), 386–412. https://doi.org/10.1080/15564886.2013.838615

Erez, E. (1999). Who's afraid of the big bad victim? Victim impact statements as victim empowerment and enhancement of justice. *Criminal Law Review, 1*, 345–356.

Feigenson, N. (2000). *Legal blame: How jurors think and talk about accidents*. Washington D.C.: American Psychological Association.

Feigenson, N., & Park, J. (2006). Emotions and attributions of legal responsibility and blame: A research review. *Law and Human Behavior, 30*, 143–161. https://doi.org/10.1007/s10979-006-9026-z

Flamm, J. D. (1999). Due process on the "unchartered seas of irrelevance": Limiting the presence of victim impact evidence in capital sentencing after Payne v. Tennessee. *Washington & Lee Law Review, 56*, 295–342.

Forgas, J. P. (1995). Mood and judgment: The affect infusion model (AIM). *Psychological Bulletin, 117*(1), 39–66. https://doi.org/10.1037/0033-2909.117.1.39

Forsterlee, L., Fox, G. B., Forsterlee, R., & Ho, R. (2004). The effects of a victim impact statement and gender on juror information processing in a criminal trial: Does the punishment fit the crime? *Australian Psychologist, 39*(1), 57–67. https://doi.org/10.1080/00050060410001660335

Frankel, J. (2008). Payne, victim impact statements, and nearly two decades of devolving standards of decency. *New York City Law Review, 12*, 87–128.

Furman v. Georgia, 408 U.S. 238 (1972).

Gardner v. Florida, 430 U.S., 349 (1977).

Garvey, S. P. (1998). Aggravation and mitigation in capital cases: What do jurors think? *Columbia Law Review, 98*, 1538–1576. https://doi.org/10.2307/1123305

Garvey, S. P., Johnson, S., & Marcus, P. (2000). Correcting deadly confusion: Responding to jury inquiries in capital cases. *Cornell Law Review, 85*, 627–655.

Georges, L. C., Wiener, R. L., & Keller, S. R. (2013). The angry juror: Sentencing decisions in 1st degree murder. *Applied Cognitive Psychology, 27*, 156–166. https://doi.org/10.1002/acp.2880

Goldberg, J. H., Lerner, J. S., & Tetlock, P. E. (1999). Rage and reason: The psychology of the intuitive prosecutor. *European Journal of Social Psychology, 29*, 781–795. https://doi.org/10.1002/(SICI)1099-0992(199908/09)29:5/6<781::AID-EJSP960>3.0.CO;2-3

Gordon, T. M., & Brodsky, S. L. (2007). The influence of victim impact statements on sentencing in capital cases. *Journal of Forensic Psychology Practice, 7*(2), 45–52. https://doi.org/10.1300/J158v07n02_03

Greene, E. (1999). The many guises of victim impact evidence and effects on jurors' judgments. *Psychology, Crime & Law, 5*, 331–348. https://doi.org/10.1080/10683169908401776

Greene, E., Koehring, H., & Quiat, M. (1998). Victim impact evidence in capital cases: Does the victim's character matter? *Journal of Applied Social Psychology, 28*(2), 145–156. https://doi.org/10.1111/j.1559-1816.1998.tb01697

Gregg v. Georgia, 428 U.S. 153 (1976).

Hackett, L., Day, A., & Mohr, P. (2008). Expectancy violation and perceptions of rape victim credibility. *Legal and Criminological Psychology, 13*, 323–334. https://doi.org/10.1348/135532507X228458

Haidt, J. (2001). The emotional dog and its rational tail: A social intuitionist approach to moral judgment. *Psychological Review, 108*(4), 814–834. https://doi.org/10.1037/0033-295X.108.4.814

Hall, D. J. (1991). Victims' voices in criminal court: The need for restraint. *American Criminal Law Review, 38*, 233–266.

Haney, C. (1997). Violence and the capital jury: Mechanisms of moral disengagement and the impulse to condemn to death. *Stanford Law Review, 49*, 1447–1486. https://doi.org/10.2307/1229350

Haney, C. (2005). *Death by design: Capital punishment as a social psychological system*. New York, NY: Oxford University Press.

Haney, C., Hurtado, A., & Vega, L. (1994). "Modern" death qualification. *Law and Human Behavior, 18*, 619–633. https://doi.org/10.1007/BF01499328

Haney, C., Weill, J., & Lynch, M. (2015). The death penalty. In B. L. Cutler & P. Zapf (Eds.), *APA handbook of forensic psychology, Criminal investigation, adjudication, and sentencing outcomes* (Vol. 2, pp. 451–510). Washington, DC: American Psychological Association.

Harden, A. N. (2010). Drawing the line at pushing "play": Barring video montages as victim impact evidence at capital sentencing trials. *Kentucky Law Journal, 99*, 845–879.

Henderson, L. N. (1985). The wrongs of victim's rights. *Stanford Law Review, 37*, 937–985. https://doi.org/10.2307/1228587

Henry, S., Barlow, M., Mitchell, K., Broszkiewicz, N., & Myers, B., et al. *Eliciting empathy in capital jurors: The effect of victim impact statements*. Poster presented at the annual conference of the American Psychology-Law Society (Div 41), New Orleans, LA, March 2014.

Hillenbrand, S. W., & Smith, B. E. (1989). *Victims rights legislation: An assessment of its impact on criminal justice practitioners and victims*. Washington, D.C.: American Bar Association, Criminal Justice Section, Victim Witness Project.

Hills, A. M., & Thomson, D. M. (1999). Should victim impact influence sentence? Understanding the community's justice reasoning. *Behavioral Sciences and the Law, 17*, 661–671. https://doi.org/10.1002/(SICI)1099-0798(199923)17:5<661::AID-BSL369>3.0.CO;2-N

Joh, E. E. (2000). Narrating the pain: The problem with victim impact statements. *Southern California Interdisciplinary Law Journal, 10*, 17–37.

Johnson, S., Thorpe, K., Prichard, K., Phillips, D., Moore, A., et al. (2016). *Public attitudes toward victim impact statements in capital cases: Individual differences and the willingness to hear the victim's perspective*. Atlanta, GA, March: Poster presented at the annual conference of the American Psychology-Law Society.

Jones, C., & Aronson, E. (1973). Attribution of fault to a rape victim as a function of respectability of the victim. *Journal of Personality and Social Psychology, 26*(3), 415–419. https://doi.org/10.1037/h0034463

Jones, M. B., & Weiner, R. L. (2011). Effects of mortality salience in capital punishment sentencing decisions. *Basic and Applied Social Psychology, 33*(2), 167–181. https://doi.org/10.1080/01973533.2011.568852

Judges, D. P. P. (1999). Scared to death: Capital punishment as authoritarian terror management. *University of California Davis Law Review, 33*, 155–249.

Kaplan, M. F., & Kemmerick, G. D. (1974). Juror judgment as information integration: Combining evidential and non-evidential information. *Journal of Personality and Social Psychology, 30*, 493–499. https://doi.org/10.1037/h0037034

Kaplan, M. F., & Miller, L. E. (1978). Reducing the effects of juror bias. *Journal of Personality and Social Psychology, 36*, 1443–1455. https://doi.org/10.1037/0022-3514.36.12.1443

Kelman, H. C. (1973). Violence without moral restraint: Reflections on the dehumanization of victims and victimizers. *Journal of Social Issues, 29*, 25–61. https://doi.org/10.1111/j.1540-4560.1973.tb00102

Keltner, D., Ellsworth, P. C., & Edwards, K. (1993). Beyond simple pessimism: Effects of sadness and anger on social perception. *Journal of Personality and Social Psychology, 64*(5), 740–752. https://doi.org/10.1037/0022-3514.64.5.740

Kennedy, C. M. (2008). Victim impact videos: The new wave of evidence in capital sentencing hearings. *Quinnipiac Law Review, 26*, 1069–1105.

Kerwin, J., & Schaffer, D. R. (1994). Mock jurors versus juries: The role of deliberations in reactions to inadmissible testimony. *Personality and Social Psychology Bulletin, 20*, 153–162. https://doi.org/10.1177/0146167294202002

Kilpatrick, D. G., & Otto, R. K. (1987). Constitutionally guaranteed participation in criminal justice proceedings for victims: Potential effects of psychological functioning. *Wayne State Law Review, 34*, 7–28. Retrieved from http://heinonline.org/HOL/Page?handle=hein.journals/waynlr34&id=17

Kirchmeier, J. L. (2008). Our existential death penalty: Judges, jurors, and terror management. *Law and Psychology Review, 32*, 55–107.

Kyle, J., Twist, S. J., & Higgins, S. (2005). On the wings of their angels: The Scott Campbell, Stephanie Roper, Wendy Preston, Louarna Gillis, Nila Lyn Crime Victims' Rights Act. *Lewis & Clark Law Review, 9*, 581–611. Retrieved from http://heinonline.org/HOL/Page?handle=hein.journals/lewclr9&g_sent=1&id=601

Lens, K. M. E., Pemberton, A., & Bogaerts, S. (2013) Heterogeneity in victim participation: A new perspective on delivering a Victim Impact Statement. *European Journal of Criminology 10* (4), 479–495

Lens, K. M. E., van Doorn, J., Lahlah, E., Pemberton, A., & Bogaerts, S. (2016). Observer's reactions to victim impact statements: A preliminary study into the affective and cognitive responses. *International Review of Victimology, 22*(1), 45–53. https://doi.org/10.1177/0269758015610851

Levy, J. H. (1993). Limiting victim impact evidence and argument after *Payne v. Tennessee*. *Stanford Law Review, 45*, 1027–1060. https://doi.org/10.2307/1229203

Lockett v. Ohio, 438 U.S., 586 (1978).

Logan, W. A. (1999). Through the past darkly: A survey of the uses and abuses of victim impact evidence in capital trials. *Arizona Law Review, 41*, 143–192.

Logan, W. A. (2000). Opining on death: Witness sentence recommendations in capital trials. *Boston College Law Review, 41*, 517–547.

Logan, W. A. (2005). Victims, survivors and the decisions to seek and impose death. *William Mitchell Legal Studies Research Paper No. 12*; *FSU College of Law, Public Law Research Paper No. 235*. Retrieved from SSRN: https://ssrn.com/abstract=715021.

Logan, W. A. (2006). Victim impact evidence in federal capital trials. *Federal Sentencing Reporter, 19*(5), 05. https://doi.org/10.1525/fsr.2006.19.1.05

London, K., & Nightingale, N. N. *The impact of inadmissible evidence on jury deliberations*. Poster presented at the biennial meeting of the American Psychology-Law Society, Hilton Head, S.C, March 1996.

London, K., & Nuñez, N. (2000). The effect of jury deliberations on jurors' propensity to disregard inadmissible evidence. *Journal of Applied Psychology, 85*, 932–939. https://doi.org/10.1037/0021-9010.85.6.932

Luginbuhl, J., & Burkhead, M. (1995). Victim impact evidence in a capital trial: Encouraging votes for death. *American Journal of Criminal Justice, 20*(1), 1–17. https://doi.org/10.1007/BF02886115

Lynch, M., & Haney, C. (2012). Looking across the empathic divide: Radicalized decision making on the capital jury. *Michigan State Law Review, 2011*, 573–607.

Maio, G. R., & Esses, V. M. (2001). The need for affect: Individual differences in the motivation to approach or avoid emotions. *Journal of Personality, 69*, 583–615. https://doi.org/10.1111/1467-6494.694156

McCoy, M. L., Nuñez, N., & Dammeyer, M. M. (1999). The effect of jury deliberations on jurors' reasoning skills. *Law and Human Behavior, 23*(5), 557–575. https://doi.org/10.1023/A:1022348229558

McGowan, M. G., & Myers, B. (2004). Who is the victim anyway? The effects of bystander victim impact statements on mock juror sentencing decisions. *Violence and Victims, 19*(3), 357–374. https://doi.org/10.1891/vivi.19.3.357.65763

Minot, D. (2012). Silenced stories: How victim impact evidence in capital trials prevents the jury from hearing the constitutionally required story of the defendant. *The Journal of Criminal Law and Criminology, 102*(1), 227–251.

Mitchell, K., Myers, B., & Broszkiewicz, N. (2016). Good or essential? The effects of victim characteristics and family significance on sentencing judgments and perceptions of harm. *Psychiatry, Psychology, and Law, 23*, 651. https://doi.org/10.1080/13218719.2015.1084662

Mosteller, R. P. (2003). Symposium: Victims and the death penalty: Inside and outside the courtroom: Victim impact evidence: Hard to find the real rules. *Cornell Law Review, 88*, 543–554.

Mulholland, C. L. (1995). Sentencing criminals. *Missouri Law Review, 60*, 731–748.

Myers, B., & Arbuthnot, J. (1999). The effects of victim impact evidence on the verdicts and sentencing judgments of mock jurors. *Journal of Offender Rehabilitation, 29*(3/4), 95–112. https://doi.org/10.1300/J076v29n03_05

Myers, B., Godwin, D., Latter, R., & Winstanley, S. (2004). Victim impact statements and mock juror sentencing: The impact of dehumanizing language on a death qualified sample. *American Journal of Forensic Psychology, 22*(2), 39–55.

Myers, B., & Greene, E. (2004). The prejudicial nature of victim impact statements: Implications for capital sentencing policy. *Psychology, Public Policy, and Law, 10*(4), 492–515. https://doi.org/10.1037/1076-8971.10.4.492

Myers, B., Lynn, S. J., & Arbuthnot, J. (2002). Victim impact testimony and juror judgments: The effects of harm information and witness demeanor. *Journal of Applied Social Psychology, 32*(11), 2393–2412. https://doi.org/10.1111/j.1559-1816.2002.tb01869

Myers, B., Nuñez, N., Mitchell, K., Kehn, A., & Wilkowski, B. M. (2017). *The heterogeneity of victim impact statements: A content analysis of capital trial penalty transcripts*. Unpublished manuscript.

Myers, B., Roop, A., Kalnen, D., & Kehn, A. (2013). Victim impact statements and crime heinousness: a test of the saturation hypothesis. *Psychology, Crime & Law, 19*(2), 129–143. https://doi.org/10.1080/1068316X.2011.614244

Myers, B., Weidemann, E., & Pearce, G. (2006). Psychology weighs in on the debate surrounding victim impact statements and capital sentencing: Are emotional jurors really irrational? *Federal Sentencing Reporter, 19*, 13–20. https://doi.org/10.1525/fsr.2006.19.1.13

Nadler, J., & Rose, M. R. (2003). Victim impact testimony and the psychology of punishment. *Cornell Law Review, 88*, 419–456. https://doi.org/10.2139/ssrn.377521.

Nadler, J., & McDonnell, M. (2012). Moral character, motive, and the psychology of blame. *Cornell Law Review, 97*(2), 1–44.

Nemeth, C., & Sosis, R. (1973). A simulated jury study: Characteristics of the defendant and the jurors. *Journal of Social Psychology, 90*(2), 221–229. https://doi.org/10.1080/00224545.1973.9712562

*New Jersey v. Muhummad.*145 N.J. 23, 54 [678 A. 2d 164, 180] (N.J. 1996).

Nuñez, N, Egan-Wright, D., Kehn, A., & Myers, B. *Impact of different methods of victims impact statement delivery at capital trials: Emotionality of statements and its impact on sentencing decisions.* Talk presented at the 4th International Congress of Psychology and Law, Miami, FL, March 2011.

Nuñez, N., Estrada-Reynolds, V., Schweitzer, K., & Myers, B. (2016). The impact of emotions on juror judgments and decision-making. In B. H. Bornstein & M. Miller (Eds.), *Advances in Psychology and Law* (Vol. 2, pp. 346–385).

Nuñez, N., Myers, B., Wilkowski, B. M., & Schweitzer, K. (2017). The impact of angry versus sad victim impact statements on mock jurors' sentencing decisions in a capital trial. *Criminal Justice and Behavior, 44*(6), 862–886. https://doi.org/10.1177/0093854816689809

Nuñez, N., Schweitzer, K., Chai, C. A., & Myers, B. (2015). Negative emotions felt during trial: The effect of fear, anger, and sadness on juror decisions. *Applied Cognitive Psychology, 29*, 200–209. https://doi.org/10.1002/acp.3094

Ogul, M. (2000). Capital cases: Dealing with victim impact evidence (part 1). *Champions, 24*, 43–47.

Osofsky, M. J., Bandura, A., & Zimbardo, P. (2005). The role of moral disengagement in the execution process. *Law and Human Behavior, 29*, 371–393. https://doi.org/10.1007/s10979-005-4930-1

Paternoster, R., & Deise, J. (2011). A heavy thumb on the scale: The effect of victim impact statements on capital decision making. *Criminology, 49*(1), 129–161. https://doi.org/10.1111/j.1745-9125.2010.00220

Payne v. Tennessee. 501 U.S. 808. 1991.

Pennebaker, J. W., Francis, M. E., & Booth, R. J. (2001). *Linguistic Inquiry and Word Count: LIWC 2001*. Mahwah, NJ: Lawrence Erlbaum.

People v. Kelly, 171 P.3d 548, (Cal. 2007).

Phillips, A. K. (1998). Thou shalt not kill any nice people: The problem of victim impact statements in capital sentencing. *American Criminal Law Review, 35*, 93–118.

Platania, J., & Berman, G. (2006). The moderating effect of judge's instructions on victim impact testimony in capital cases. *Applied Psychology in Criminal Justice, 2*(2), 84–101.

President's Task Force on Victims of Crime. (1982). *Final report*. Washington, DC: U.S. Government Printing Office.

Roberts, J. V. (2009). Listening to the crime victim: Evaluating victim input at sentencing and parole. *Crime and Justice, 38*, 347–403. https://doi.org/10.1086/599203

Rose, M. R., Nadler, J., & Clark, J. (2006). Appropriately upset? Emotion norms and perceptions of crime victims. *Law Human Behavior, 30*, 203–219. https://doi.org/10.1007/s10979-006-9030-3

Salazar v. State, 90 S.W.3d 330, 337 (Tex. Crim. App. 2002).

Sanderford, D. (2012). Victim impact evidence, state by state. Retrieved from http://www.deathpenaltyinfo.org/legal-issues-states-allow-victim-impact-statements.

Shaked-Schroer, N., Costanzo, M., & Marcus-Newhall, A. (2008). Reducing racial bias in the penalty phase of capital trials. *Behavioral Sciences & the Law, 26*(5), 603–617. https://doi.org/10.1002/bsl.829

Schroeder, E. A. (2010). Comment: Sounds of prejudice: Background music during victim impact statements. *Kansas Law Review, 58*, 473–505.

Schwarz, N., & Clore, G. L. (1983). Mood, misattribution, and judgments of well-being: Informative and directive functions of affective states. *Journal of Personality and Social Psychology, 45*(3), 513–523. https://doi.org/10.1037/0022-3514.45.3.513

Schweitzer, K., & Nuñez, N. (2017). Victim impact statements: How victim social class affects juror decision-making. *Violence and Victims, Online First., 32*, 521. https://doi.org/10.1891/0886-670

Seelye, K. Q. (2015, March 30). Prosecution in Boston Marathon trial closes with raw details of killings. *The New York Times, A-16*.

Shanker, N. (1999). Getting a grip on *Payne* and restricting the influence of victim impact statements in capital sentencing: The Timothy McVeigh Case and various state approaches compared. *Hastings Constitutional Law Quarterly, 26*, 711–740.

Shaunessy, J. M. (1992). Booth v. Maryland, insights into the contemporary challenges to judging. *Washington & Lee Law Review, 49*, 249–291.

South Carolina v. Gathers. 490 U.S. 805. 1989.

Sullivan, B. E. (1998). Harnessing *Payne*: Controlling the admission of victim impact statements to safeguard capital sentencing hearings from passion and prejudice. *Fordham Urban Law Journal, 25*, 601–639.

Sundby, S. E. (2003). Inside and outside the courtroom: The capital jury and empathy: The problem of worthy and unworthy victims. *Cornell Law Review, 88*, 343–381. https://doi.org/10.2139/ssrn.358521.

Tetlock, P. E. (2002). Social functionalist frameworks for judgment and choice: Intuitive politicians, theologians, and prosecutors. *Psychological Review, 109*, 451–471. https://doi.org/10.1037/0033-295X.109.3.451

Tiedens, L. Z., & Linton, S. (2001). Judgment under emotional certainty and uncertainty: The effects of specific emotions on information processing. *Journal of Personality and Social Psychology, 81*, 973–988. https://doi.org/10.1037/0022-3514.81.6.973

Tsoudis, O., & Smith-Lovin, L. (1998). How bad was it? The effects of victim and perpetrator emotion on responses to criminal court vignettes. *Social Forces, 77*(2), 695–722. https://doi.org/10.2307/3005544

Unnever, J. D., Cullen, F. T., & Roberts, J. V. (2005). Not everyone strongly supports the death penalty: Assessing weakly-held attitudes toward capital punishment. *American Journal of Criminal Justice, 20*, 187–216. https://doi.org/10.1007/BF02885735

United States v. Sampson, 335 F. Supp. 2d 166, 192-93 (D. Mass. 2004).

Wainwright v. Witt, 469 U.S. 412 (1985).

Watson, D., & Clark, L. A. (1994). *The PANAS-X: Manual for the positive and negative affect schedule-expanded form*. Iowa City: University of Iowa. https://doi.org/10.13072/midss.438

Watson, D., Clark, L. A., & Tellegen, A. (1988). Development and validation of brief measures of positive and negative affect: The PANAS scales. *Journal of Personality and Social Psychology, 54(6)*, 1063–1070. https://doi.org/10.1037/0022-3514.54.6.1063

Weidemann, E. J. (2008). *Victim impact statements: The role of expectations in juror judgments*. Wilmington, NC: Unpublished Master's Thesis.

Wevodau, A. L., Cramer, R. J., Kehn, A., & Clark, J. W. (2014). Why the impact? Negative affective change as a mediator of the effects of victim impact statements. *Journal of Interpersonal Violence, 29*, 1–20. https://doi.org/10.1177/0886260514527170

Wiener, R. L., Bornstein, B. H., & Voss, A. (2006). Emotion and the law: A framework for inquiry. *Law and Human Behavior, 30*, 231–248. https://doi.org/10.1007/s10979-006-9025-0

Wiener, R. L., Pritchard, C. C., & Weston, M. (1995). Comprehensibility of approved jury instructions in capital murder cases. *Journal of Applied Psychology, 80*(4), 455–467. https://doi.org/10.1037/0021-9010.80.4.455

Williham v. State, 947 P.2d 1074, 1085-1086 (Okla Crim. App. 1997).

Wilson, T. D., & Gilbert, D. T. (2003). Affective forecasting. In M. P. Zanna (Ed.), *Advances in experimental social psychology* (Vol. 35, pp. 345–411). San Diego, CA: Academic Press. https://doi.org/10.1111/j.0963-7214.2005.00355

Wolff, K. T., & Miller, M. K. (2009). Victim and execution impact statements: What judges know about case and psychological research. *Judicature, 92*, 148–157.

Younglove, J. A., Nelligan, P. J., & Reisner, R. L. (2009). Victim character evidence in death penalty cases: How many songs is too many? *Criminal Justice Review, 34*, 536–552. https://doi.org/10.1177/0734016809338559

Zant v. Stevens. (1983). 462 U.S. In *862*.

Review of Research and Recent Case Law on Understanding and Appreciation of *Miranda* Warnings

Sharon Kelley, Heather Zelle, Leah Brogan, and Naomi E. S. Goldstein

"You have the right to remain silent." So begins nearly every version of the *Miranda* warnings—the set of advisements given to people who are being interrogated by police. In doing so, the warnings intend to convey the cornerstone of the right against self-incrimination: Suspects in criminal investigations do not have to speak to the police. The statement, "You have the right to remain silent," and the ones that follow (in one variation or another) might seem easy to understand—you do not have to speak with the police; if you do speak with the police the statements you make can be used as evidence against you; you have the right to an attorney; if you cannot afford one, an attorney will be appointed to represent you; and you can exercise these rights at any point during the interrogation. However, these statements—and the Constitutional rights they convey—are deceptively complex. That complexity, and its effect on the suspects who hear or read the *Miranda* warnings, is the focus of this chapter.

S. Kelley (✉)
Institute of Law, Psychiatry, and Public Policy, UVa School of Medicine, University of Virginia Health Systems, Charlottesville, VA, USA
e-mail: Smk8n@virginia.edu

H. Zelle
Department of Public Health Sciences, Institute of Law, Psychiatry, and Public Policy, UVa School of Medicine, University of Virginia Health Systems, Charlottesville, VA, USA
e-mail: Zelle@virginia.edu

L. Brogan
Violence Prevention Initiative Center for Injury Research and Prevention, Children's Hospital of Philadelphia, Wynnewood, PA, USA
e-mail: BROGANL1@email.chop.edu

N. E. S. Goldstein
Department of Psychology, JD/PhD Program in Law and Psychology, Juvenile Justice Research & Reform Lab, Drexel University, Philadelphia, PA, USA
e-mail: Neg23@drexel.edu

M. K. Miller, B. H. Bornstein (eds.), *Advances in Psychology and Law*,
Advances in Psychology and Law 3,
https://doi.org/10.1007/978-3-319-75859-6_3

This chapter provides an overview of the legal and psychological landscape of the *Miranda* warnings. It begins with *Miranda*'s inception in 1966 and the cases that shaped the warnings over the following decades. Then, it covers the translation of *Miranda*'s legal requirements into psychological criteria suitable for evaluation by forensic mental health professionals. Based on this foundation, it covers recent advances in the *Miranda* warnings, both in terms of the contributions of researchers in measuring and identifying fundamental problems in understanding and appreciating the warnings and the judiciary's treatment of the *Miranda* decision over the past decade. Finally, the chapter concludes with recommendations for future research and policy work.

The Law Surrounding *Miranda* Warnings and Waivers.

In *Miranda v. Arizona* (1966), the Supreme Court of the United States issued a decision about when suspects' confessions could be used as evidence against them at trial. The following sections discuss the *Miranda* decision, place this landmark case in the broader context of confession and criminal procedure law in the twentieth century, and describe how the *Miranda* holding was refined and applied in subsequent decades.

Miranda v. Arizona

Miranda v. Arizona (1966) represents the Supreme Court's decision in four separate cases that were consolidated because they all presented the same fundamental question: Are statements made by suspects during police interrogation admissible as evidence if the suspects were not informed of their rights to silence and counsel? In each of these four cases, the defendants (Ernesto Miranda, Michael Vignera, Carl Calvin Westover, and Roy Allen Stewart) had been interrogated by police without being informed of their rights. And, in each case, the defendants ultimately made incriminating statements that were used against them at trial.

The central question in *Miranda v. Arizona* (1966), and the focus of this chapter, concerns a balancing act. On one side of the scale are the rights of individuals when they are questioned by police about a crime, and on the other side are the authority and rights of the state (i.e., police, prosecutors, and the public) when investigating and prosecuting criminal offenses. As one might imagine, a confession—a statement in which a suspect admits that he or she committed a crime—and other incriminating statements are extremely powerful evidence and potentially the *most important* form of evidence (e.g., Kassin & Neumann, 1997). Thus, police seek confessions, often zealously, and in ways that have the potential to jeopardize individuals' rights. As a result, in the *Miranda* decision, the Supreme Court of the

United States recognized an imbalance in the scale that favored the state and attempted to correct it with a set of warnings.

Like the *Miranda* warnings, the *Miranda* decision is more complex than many people appreciate. A simple summary of *Miranda v. Arizona*'s holding is: To secure the admissibility of a suspect's statements at trial, (1) police must inform the suspect of his rights, specifically the right to remain silent, intent to use a suspect's statements as evidence against him, the right to counsel—even if he is indigent—and the ability to assert rights at any time; and (2) if the suspect waives (i.e., gives up) the rights, that waiver must be provided knowingly, intelligently, and voluntarily to be considered valid. The set of rights about which suspects have to be informed, now known as the *Miranda* warnings, and the waiver requirements form the basis of forensic mental health evaluations of *Miranda* waivers (i.e., did the suspect have the capacity to execute a knowing, intelligent, and voluntary waiver?).

Miranda is better understood with some context and nuance. The law on the admissibility of confessions had been developing for 30 years prior to *Miranda*, beginning with a 1936 case in which the Court held that the state's use of confessions that had been extracted through physical torture violated the Fourteenth Amendment's Due Process clause ("[N]or shall any State deprive any person of life, liberty, or property, without due process of law"; *Brown v. Mississippi*, 1936). Thereafter, courts would look to the *totality of the circumstances*—all of the factors surrounding the interrogation and confession—to determine whether a confession was voluntary, that is, whether the defendant's "will was overborne" by law enforcement (*Haynes v. Washington*, 1963, p. 513). The *totality of the circumstances* analysis is, by definition, case specific and done *after* the interrogation—which made it nearly impossible for police or prosecutors to predict which statements would be admissible in court.

The *Miranda* decision was issued by the Supreme Court in 1966, the height of the Warren Court's criminal procedure revolution, and authored by Chief Justice Earl Warren himself. The decision followed a line of cases that gradually expanded rights for suspects and defendants, such as: expanding the definition of involuntary confessions (e.g., *Haynes v. Washington*, 1963; *Spano v. New York*, 1959), establishing that evidence from illegal searches and seizures would be excluded from trial (*Mapp v. Ohio*, 1961), recognizing the right to counsel for indigent suspects (*Gideon v. Wainwright*, 1963), and determining that suspects have the right to counsel during interrogations (*Escobedo v. Illinois*, 1964). Chief Justice Warren came to the bench with 22 years of law enforcement experience (18 as a district attorney and 4 as state attorney general), giving him a "keen awareness of the opportunities for coercion and exploitation of confusion in the custodial interrogation setting" (Kamisar, 2005, p. 11). Thus, he was cognizant of actual police interrogation tactics: the third-degree (i.e., infliction of physical pain) practices of the 1930s, and the more subtle—yet still intimidating—psychological strategies that had risen to prominence by the 1960s. As explained by popular interrogation manuals of the time (e.g., Inbau & Reid, 1962), the crux of this latter set of strategies involved isolation of the suspect augmented by persistent, often lengthy questioning, hostility, and deception.

Against this backdrop, the *Miranda* court articulated the primary holding of the case—not the *Miranda* warnings—but the fact that the Fifth Amendment's prohibition of compulsory self-incrimination ("Nor shall any person … be compelled in any criminal case to be a witness against himself") applies to informal pressure to speak during a custodial interrogation. Put another way, the inherently coercive environment of a custodial interrogation is equivalent to being compelled to testify against oneself. The Court stated,

> It is obvious that [the] interrogation environment is created for no purpose other than to subjugate the individual to the will of his examiner. The atmosphere carries its own badge of intimidation. To be sure, this is not physical intimidation, but it is equally destructive of human dignity. The current practice of incommunicado interrogation is at odds with one of our Nation's most cherished principles—that the individual may not be compelled to incriminate himself (pp. 457–458).

The Court could have stopped there, holding that the privilege against self-incrimination applies to custodial interrogations. This would have left it up to Congress, the states, or individual police departments to craft appropriate safeguards. However, in the wake of the *totality of the circumstances* framework and the *Escobedo v. Illinois* (1964) holding that only vaguely described the new scope of a defendant's right to counsel—both of which left police, prosecutors, and judges with substantial uncertainty and discretion—the Court elected to describe a safeguard that would sufficiently dispel the coercion of police interrogation: a set of advisements of suspects' rights, since coined "the *Miranda* warnings."

Thus, the *Miranda* warnings were offered as a practical solution so that police, prosecutors, and judges could easily distinguish statements that were admissible from those that were not. This point brings into focus two other, related aspects of the *Miranda* decision. First, it articulates a rule of admissibility, *not* a rule of police conduct. Police are not required to read suspects the *Miranda* warnings as a general rule; they only have to do so to preserve a prosecutor's ability to admit the suspect's statements into evidence at trial. Although this framework generally incentivizes officers to read suspects their rights (but see Clymer, 2002), it is quite different from requiring it as a matter of course. Second, as referenced above, it reflects the Court's attempt to balance suspects' rights with the needs of law enforcement—not an attempt to tip the scales in favor of suspects. Thus, in many ways, the decision was designed to allow interrogations to proceed, but with better-informed suspects and better-prepared police officers.

Of course, interrogations were only supposed to proceed once the suspect waived the *Miranda* rights. Like other waivers of constitutional rights, a waiver of the *Miranda* rights must be knowing, intelligent, and voluntary in order to be considered valid. Generally, knowing and intelligent refer to the suspect's comprehension of the warnings, and voluntary refers to the absence of coercion in waiving the rights. Subsequent cases elaborated on the meaning of these waiver components, and some jurisdictional differences emerged with respect to the knowing and intelligent requirements. While some states require only a basic understanding of the warnings (e.g., *Illinois v. Bernasco*, 1990; *Michigan v. Daoud*, 2000), others also require evidence that the suspect appreciated the personal significance of the rights and the consequences of waiving them (*Arkansas v. Bell*, 1997; *Pennsylvania v. DeJesus*, 2001). The Supreme Court issued a definitive opinion on the voluntariness requirement in 1986, holding that a statement is only involuntary if it is the product of governmental coercion (*Colorado v. Connelly*). Thus, the Court effectively foreclosed broader inquiries into the suspect's free will.

One year after the *Miranda* decision, the Supreme Court addressed the rights of juvenile suspects (*In re Gault*, 1967). *Gault* extended several due process protections (e.g., right to counsel, right to confront witnesses) to juveniles, including, by implication, the *Miranda* warnings and waiver requirements. The following decade, the Court also held that juvenile waivers would be evaluated using the *totality of the circumstances* approach used for adult waivers (*Fare v. Michael C.*, 1979).

The Aftermath of Miranda

Despite *Miranda*'s potential to dramatically change the landscape of interrogations and courts' admissibility analyses, in many ways it did not (Leo, 2001). Prior to the decision, many law enforcement agencies, including the Federal Bureau of Investigation, were already in the habit of administering a set of warnings prior to interrogation (Kamisar, 2005). After the decision (and a relatively brief adjustment period) other police departments followed suit. Nevertheless, many suspects waived their rights, meaning that any challenge to the validity of their waivers or admissibility of their statements was analyzed using the familiar *totality of the circumstances* framework (i.e., the same framework used prior to *Miranda*).

Under this flexible framework, no specific factors are required to be considered, and no one factor is dispositive across all cases. When courts evaluate the *totality of the circumstances* of a *Miranda* waiver, they generally focus their inquiry on two broad categories: characteristics of the suspect and situational conditions of the interrogation. Cases using this approach have referenced suspect-specific factors such as age, intelligence, apparent comprehension of rights, prior experience with police, and interrogation-specific factors such as length of questioning, promises of leniency, or denial of basic needs (e.g., food, drink, sleep; *Coyote v. United States*, 1967; *West v. United States*, 1968). The relationship between these factors and *Miranda* comprehension are discussed further in the following sections.

From the outset, *Miranda*'s scope was limited to suspects subjected to *custodial interrogation*, and the Court elaborated on these terms in subsequent cases. Specifically, custody was subsequently defined as whether a reasonable person would have felt he or she was at liberty to terminate the interrogation and leave given the circumstances surrounding the interrogation (*Thompson v. Keohane*, 1995). The Court defined interrogation as "any words or actions on the part of the police ... that the police should know are reasonably likely to elicit an incriminating response from the suspect" (*Rhode Island v. Innis*, 1980, pp. 301–302). Thus, certain situations, including traffic stops (*Berkemer v. McCarty*, 1984) and even interviews at the police station in which the suspect is technically free to leave (*Oregon v. Mathiason*, 1977), are outside of *Miranda*'s scope. Additionally, through a series of cases, the Court also clarified that there were uses for un-*Mirandized* statements. For instance, when police elicit un-*Mirandized* statements from a suspect under the auspices of public safety, those statements can be introduced as part of the prosecution's case-in-chief (*New York v. Quarles*, 1984), meaning the portion of the trial in which the prosecution presents evidence in an effort to satisfy its burden of proof (i.e., beyond a reasonable doubt). Further, un-*Mirandized* statements can be used to impeach (i.e., undermine the credibility and reliability of) a defendant's testimony at trial (*Harris v. New York*, 1971). In all of these cases (i.e., cases in which *Miranda* does not apply and cases in which un-*Mirandized* statements are used), the only requirement is that the suspect's statement must have been voluntary.

Although the impact of *Miranda* was less significant than anticipated (see Leo, 2001), Congress passed a federal statute shortly after the decision that made the admissibility of suspects' statements turn on voluntariness only (18U.S.C. § 3501). However, the statute was not used to challenge *Miranda* until over three decades later. Given the substantial narrowing and carving-out of *Miranda*, described above, there was some speculation that the *Miranda* decision might be overturned. However, the Supreme Court rejected the attempt to legislatively "overrule" *Miranda*, holding that 18U.S.C. § 3501 was unconstitutional and reaffirming the constitutionality of the 1966 decision in *Dickerson v. United States* (2000).

Translating Legal Requirements into Psychological Constructs

Psychological testing and evaluation can help inform a court's *totality of circumstances* analysis of whether a suspect's waiver of rights was valid. Forensic evaluators typically assess the "cognitive" requirements: whether a waiver was knowing and intelligent (Goldstein & Goldstein, 2010; Oberlander & Goldstein, 2001; Oberlander, Goldstein, & Goldstein, 2003). Voluntariness may also be assessed by forensic evaluators; however, because of the primary focus of voluntariness on situational aspects rather than suspect features (*Colorado v. Connelly*, 1986), voluntariness challenges cannot contain cognitive questions (Grisso, 1998). This section, therefore, focuses on translation of the knowing and intelligent requirements.

The knowing, intelligent, and voluntary waiver standard, like many other concepts in criminal law, developed out of case law and analysis of legal principles, not out of empirical investigation of police interrogations. It is the nature of the law as an idiographic field to develop constructs in this manner, just as it is the nature of psychology as a nomothetic field to develop constructs empirically. This difference between the fields is not a problem, per se, but it does lead to the need for translation of terms and concepts. Legally meaningful terms like "insanity" have no direct equivalent in psychology; rather, legal concepts must be understood at the operational level and then linked to relevant concepts in psychology.

As with other questions of defendant abilities to take part in the criminal justice system (e.g., competence to stand trial), the knowing and intelligent requirements indicate the need for a person to be able to *function* in a certain legal *context*. Grisso (2003) clearly describes the functional and contextual nature of legal competencies:

> Legal competence constructs focus on person-context interactions. A legal competence question does not merely ask the degree of functional ability or deficit that a person manifests. It asks further, "Does this person's level of ability meet the demands of the specific situation with which the person will be … faced?" Defined more formally, a decision about legal competence is in part a statement about the *congruency or incongruency between (a) the extent of a person's functional ability and (b) the degree of performance demand that is made by the specific instance of the context in that case*. Thus an interaction between individual ability and situational demand, not an absolute level of ability, is of special significance for legal competence decisions … The individual's level of ability will be important to consider, yet the fact finder can assess its significance only when it is weighed against the demands of the individual's specific situation (pp. 32–33, emphasis in the original).

With this general framework in mind, scholars have looked to case law to discern the functional abilities in which courts seem interested for each legal context and identified several broad abilities that are particularly relevant to most legal competencies. Appelbaum and Grisso (1988) identified four abilities that appeared to be of interest to the courts in cases in which the ability to make medical treatment decisions was at issue. The four "tiers" of ability are sufficiently general, however, that they have proven to be a sound basis for many other legal competencies. Depending on the context, a competence standard might require just one of the abilities, some of the abilities, or all four abilities. The following are the four competence-related abilities:

- *Communicating choices* refers to the basic ability to convey a choice consistently as evidence of decision-making ability.
- *Understanding relevant information* is the ability to comprehend information relevant to decision making.
- *Appreciating the situation and its consequences* is a concept that encapsulates the need for a person to grasp what information means *in his or her own case*.
- *Manipulating information rationally* is the ability to use logical thinking (reasoning) to weigh risks and benefits of options.

For *Miranda* waiver analyses, the knowing and intelligent components of the legal standard have been equated by scholars to the understanding and appreciation components in the Appelbaum and Grisso (1988) model of necessary abilities for legal decision making (Goldstein & Goldstein, 2010; Grisso, 1981). In the context of *Miranda* waivers, understanding denotes an individual's ability to understand the basic meaning of the warnings, and appreciation refers to an individual's ability to grasp the importance of the warnings in the legal context and to recognize the consequences of waiving the rights (Grisso, 1981, 2003). Drawing a distinction between knowing and intelligent is important from a theoretical standpoint, as it creates a need for distinguishing and operationally defining two constructs. It is significant in practice also because it establishes a context in which a suspect can meet one requirement but fail another (e.g., a suspect may understand that she has a right to have an attorney present before and during questioning, but fail to appreciate the consequences of waiving that right; Frumkin & Garcia, 2003; Grisso, 1998). What is more, distinguishing between knowing and intelligent establishes a hierarchy of comprehension in which understanding basic details is necessary before someone can appreciate the significance of the rights and rights waivers.

The theoretical work just described is sound, yet it is important to recognize that it is based upon a general model of legal decision-making ability and that *Miranda* case law, unfortunately, does not provide a detailed or consistent operationalization of knowing and intelligent. As noted in the prior section of this chapter, lower courts have varied in their descriptions of knowing and intelligent, and the United States Supreme Court has not provided detailed guidance. Appellate decisions in many states appear to require two distinct abilities (e.g., *Arkansas v. Bell*, 1997; *Clay v. Arkansas*, 1994; *Pennsylvania v. DeJesus*, 2001; *In re Patrick W.*, 1978; *Tennessee v. Stephenson*, 1994). Additionally, a distinction between the knowing and intelligent requirements appears in United States Supreme Court opinions, as well—perhaps most notably in *Moran v. Burbine* (1986) where the Court indicated that an individual must be aware of both the nature and consequences of a *Miranda* waiver (see also *Brady v. United States*, 1970; *Escobedo v. Illinois*, 1964; *Fare v. Michael C.*, 1979).

Although an operational legal definition of knowing and intelligent remains elusive, some state courts require only a basic understanding of the *Miranda* rights in order to find a waiver valid (e.g., *Michigan v. Daoud*, 2000; *Michigan v. Cheatham*, 1996; *Illinois v. Bernasco*, 1990). Some of those courts, though, demonstrate ambivalence across opinions. In *Illinois v. Young* (2006), the Appellate Court of Illinois held that a waiver would be valid if the suspect had an awareness of the basic parts of the warning (i.e., that he could remain silent, he could request a lawyer, that his statements could be used against him). Yet, two years later, the same court seemed to describe a somewhat higher level of required comprehension in which a suspect had "a full awareness of both the nature of the right being abandoned and the consequences of the decision to abandon it" (*In re Dante W.*, 2008, p. 1044).

In between these poles, several courts have outlined intermediate approaches to *Miranda* waiver requirements—for example, holding that a suspect should have some understanding of waiver consequences but stating that a suspect does not need to be aware of every potential consequence (e.g., *Colorado v. Al Yousif*, 2002; *New Hampshire v. Bushey*, 1982). The Supreme Court also offered what seems to be an intermediate definition. The year after *Moran v. Burbine*, the Court noted that a suspect does not need to "know and understand every possible consequence of waiver of the Fifth Amendment privilege;" rather, recognition of at least some consequences of revocation of rights would suffice (*Colorado v. Spring*, 1987, p. 574). The Court also seemed to suggest that recitation of the *Miranda* warnings was sufficient to protect the Fifth Amendment privilege, however, even though the warnings do little to explain the consequences of a waiver. So, it seems that the Court requires appreciation of consequences, but namely just the consequence of having a suspect's statements used against him, as that was the only consequence described in the warnings used in that case (*Colorado v. Spring*, 1987; King, 2006).

To date, it appears that the Court does not consider the terms knowing and intelligent to be synonymous, but it has done little to establish operational definitions that distinguish them clearly (Grisso, 2003). A survey of state court judges, however, did find that the large majority of judges (1) reported that their state required both knowing and intelligent as two different types of comprehension and (2) that knowing and intelligent, as distinct types of comprehension, should be required to find a waiver valid (Zelle, 2012). In addition, the judges' responses to case scenarios with varied levels of comprehension indicated that they found a waiver in which the suspect had good understanding and good appreciation to be significantly more valid than a waiver in which the suspect had good understanding but poor appreciation, which further suggests that judges look for both understanding and appreciation when considering waiver validity.

Given the general, if at times vague, direction of the courts and the soundness of the theoretically based translation of knowing and intelligent to understanding and appreciation, it remains good practice for the psychological assessment of waiver capacity (whether for legal cases or for research) to address both understanding and appreciation. Grisso (1998) developed the Instruments for Assessing Understanding and Appreciation of Miranda Rights in order to assess both constructs. Based upon the theoretical distinction between understanding and appreciation, he created four individual tools that target the two constructs separately (Grisso, 1998; the instruments were recently updated and maintain the four distinct instruments aimed at the two constructs, though they were renamed as the Miranda Rights Comprehension Instruments [MRCI], Goldstein, Zelle & Grisso, 2014). Each of the instruments is scored independently from the others, and normative data are available for each. The first instrument, the Comprehension of *Miranda* Rights (CMR), addresses understanding by asking evaluees to paraphrase each of the five warnings in their own words. Because paraphrasing the warnings requires evaluees to demonstrate understanding through verbal expressive abilities that might be beyond what some evaluees possess, the Comprehension of *Miranda* Rights—Recognition (CMR-R) instrument also assesses understanding but by a different method: evaluees are asked to recognize whether a variety of sentences mean the same thing or something different from the warnings. Assessing understanding via the two methods also helps identify errors that might not have been apparent on one of the instruments (e.g., an evaluee might not express confusion about the difference between an attorney and a social worker when paraphrasing the rights, but might demonstrate the error when presented with a sentence that equates appointment of a social worker with appointment of an attorney). The Comprehension of *Miranda* Vocabulary (CMV) instrument includes 16 words that often appear in warnings and, if misunderstood, could lead to misunderstanding of the rights. Although originally thought of as another measure of understanding, research suggests vocabulary comprehension is actually a prerequisite for understanding and appreciation (Zelle et al., 2008). Finally, the Function of Rights in Interrogation (FRI) instrument assesses appreciation by asking evaluees about how the rights apply to relevant legal contexts. Evaluees are presented with scenarios (e.g., a suspect being questioned by police, a suspect meeting with his attorney before interrogation) and asked what should happen if, for example, the vignette suspect tells police that he does not want to talk.

A second set of instruments is now also available, the Structured Assessment of *Miranda* Abilities (SAMA; Rogers, Sewell, Drogin, & Fiduccia, 2012). The SAMA includes measures of *Miranda* understanding (the Miranda Comprehension Template), misconceptions about *Miranda* rights (the Miranda Quiz), *Miranda* vocabulary (the Miranda Vocabulary Scale), and response style (the Miranda Acquiescence Questionnaire). Interestingly, the SAMA also includes an instrument aimed at assessment of "*Miranda* reasoning" (the Miranda Reasoning Measure), despite the courts' stated interest in, at most, only the appreciation of consequences of waiving the rights—not the ability to weigh risks and benefits when making a waiver decision. Assessment of and research concerning rational decision making in the context of *Miranda* may be important, however, for underscoring the shortcomings of the *Miranda* warnings as a prophylactic device. As the next two sections respectively discuss, there is far from universal comprehension of the *Miranda* warnings, undercutting their stated aim of balancing the scales between suspects and police, and recent case law has made the warnings more complicated to understand and to invoke. Evidence of people's misunderstandings and uninformed reasoning, therefore, might be quite relevant to future *Miranda* research and policy, if not evaluation practice.

Understanding and Appreciating *Miranda* Warnings: The State of the Science

The *Miranda* holding did not radically shift criminal investigations in the way that some might have anticipated, in large part because most people waive their *Miranda* rights. Based on observations of police interrogations and interviews with defendants, approximately 80% of adults and 90% of juveniles waive their rights and speak with police (Grisso & Pomicter, 1977; Leo, 1996; Viljoen, Klaver, & Roesch, 2005). The frequency of waivers raises questions about how they measure up against the knowing and intelligent standards. In this context, a review of the research on the factors associated with understanding and appreciation of the *Miranda* warnings is particularly important.

Beginning with Grisso's seminal work in the 1970s, decades of research have consistently shown that the *Miranda* warnings could be more difficult to comprehend than anyone might have predicted. As one might expect, certain individuals (e.g., juveniles, individuals with intellectual disabilities), as a group, have greater difficulties than others. In addition, other factors that might reasonably seem related to *Miranda* comprehension (e.g., prior legal experience, exposure to the warnings through television programs) have proven surprisingly unhelpful in predicting understanding or appreciation of legal rights. This section provides an overview of "the state of the science"—what nearly 40 years of research tells us about the factors that best predict *Miranda* comprehension, the parts of the warning that are most problematic, and how situational demands of police interrogation contribute to poor comprehension. The discussion is organized by common factors courts consider in a *totality of the circumstances* analysis and those identified by research as having some bearing on *Miranda* comprehension. These include suspect factors (e.g., age, prior legal experience) and situational factors (e.g., the language and delivery of the *Miranda* warnings).

Suspect Factors

Miranda comprehension is determined, in part, by characteristics of the individual hearing or reading the warnings. These individual characteristics, or *suspect factors*, can range from rather indelible qualities like intelligence to more dynamic factors such as symptoms of mental illness. The most salient suspect factors, as determined by research and court opinions, are reviewed below.

Intelligence: Across decades of research, intelligence has emerged as an important factor—and perhaps the *most* important factor—in *Miranda* comprehension. Among studies of justice-involved youth, for instance, IQ has consistently been associated with *Miranda* understanding and appreciation (e.g., Colwell et al., 2005; Goldstein et al., 2003; Grisso, 1981; Viljoen & Roesch, 2005). Though the full range of intellectual abilities (often reflected, operationally, as a Full Scale IQ score) has a strong relationship with *Miranda* comprehension, verbal intelligence has a particularly strong association with both understanding and appreciation (Colwell et al., 2005; Viljoen & Roesch, 2005).

Available research suggests that the importance of IQ in *Miranda* comprehension among youth may vary depending on age, though the specific nature of this interaction differs by study. Grisso's (1981) research indicated that IQ might be most influential for youth ages 14–16 because younger youth, as a class, were generally unable to demonstrate understanding or appreciation of rights and older youth, as a class, generally demonstrated understanding and appreciation comparable to adults. By contrast, Viljoen and Roesch (2005) found that intelligence was more important for younger than older youth.

Among adults, IQ has consistently been the most consistent predictor of *Miranda* comprehension. Unlike youth, for whom developmental status (for which age is often the best proxy) has the potential to strongly influence *Miranda* comprehension, adults' understanding and appreciation of legal rights seems to hinge more directly on intellect. For instance, Grisso (1981) found that IQ had the strongest relationship with *Miranda* understanding, even when controlling for age, gender, race, and socioeconomic status. Perhaps not surprisingly, adults with cognitive impairment show significant deficits in *Miranda* comprehension. In absolute terms, many individuals with intellectual disabilities demonstrate profound misunderstandings of the *Miranda* warnings as reflected in an inability to paraphrase the warnings or accurately categorize statements as conveying information that is either the same or different from one of the *Miranda* rights. For instance, in one study of *Miranda* comprehension among individuals with mild intellectual disability, 50% were unable to adequately paraphrase any component of the warnings, and only 2% scored significantly greater than chance when classifying statements as either meaning the same thing as or something different than a statement from the warnings (O'Connell, Garmoe, & Goldstein, 2005). In relative terms, individuals with intellectual disabilities often perform significantly worse on measures of *Miranda* comprehension than youth and the overwhelming majority of other adults (Fulero & Everington, 1995; O'Connell et al., 2005).

Age: Research has consistently revealed age as one of the most important factors in *Miranda* comprehension (e.g., Oberlander and Goldstein, 2001; Grisso, 1981; Colwell et al., 2005). Across the board, youth have more difficulty than adults with all elements of *Miranda* understanding and appreciation. Specifically, youth are less able to paraphrase or recognize the meaning of the rights, define vocabulary terms used in the *Miranda* warnings, or appreciate how the rights to silence and counsel function in practice (e.g., Grisso, 1981; Kelley, 2014). In addition to the distinction between youth and adults, there are important distinctions between younger and older youth. Across most studies that have explored the age-*Miranda* comprehension relationship, the greatest deficits are seen in youth under age 15, particularly in youth under age 13. By around age 15, most youth reach a plateau in their *Miranda* understanding, such that the ability to understand the basic meaning of one's legal rights does not seem to markedly improve past mid-adolescence (Abramovitch, Peterson-Badali, & Rohan, 1995; Goldstein, Condie, Kalbeitzer, Osman, & Geier, 2003; Grisso, 1981). In contrast, appreciation of the rights to silence and counsel and the ability to define critical *Miranda* vocabulary continue to improve throughout adolescence and into adulthood (Grisso, 1981; Kelley, 2014).

The types of errors youth tend to make often reflect fundamental misconceptions about the nature of rights. In the body of research on children's reasoning about rights, Melton (1980, 1983) described an age-related progression from egocentricity, perceiving rights in terms of what one can have or do (e.g., something allowed by an authority figure) to abstraction, considering rights based on morality and intangible principles (e.g., freedom of speech). Subsequent research has shown that this progression does not necessarily occur in a linear manner and certain developments may occur later than expected, depending on the context. Ruck et al. (1998) found that the majority of youth (ranging in age from 8 to 16) continued to define "right" as something one can or is allowed to do, not an entitlement. And, in contrast to some earlier findings, this research revealed that older children were *more* likely than younger children to believe that rights can be taken away. Additionally, whereas younger children most frequently contemplated that rights could be removed by parents, older children often conveyed that their rights could be revoked if they did something wrong (Ruck, Keating, Abramovitch, & Koegl, 1998).

Moving from the development of reasoning about rights generally to reasoning about *Miranda* rights specifically, the research reveals how these fundamental misconceptions can play out in a specific legal context. For instance, regarding the right to silence, Grisso (1981) found that the majority of youth did not recognize that police should stop questioning if a suspect refuses to talk. Multiple studies have also revealed errors in youths' appreciation of the right to counsel and the attorney-client relationship. For example, youth often mistakenly report that defense attorneys only protect innocent clients and that attorneys play a fact-finding role and reveal all client communications with the judge (Abramovitch, Peterson-Badali, & Rohan, 1995; Goldstein et al., 2003; Grisso, 1997). Finally, youth often struggle with certain *Miranda* vocabulary terms, an issue that is revisited below in the section on *Miranda* wording. In particular, youth have the most trouble defining the terms "consult," "interrogation," "entitled," and "right" (Grisso, 1981; Zelle, Riggs Romaine, & Goldstein, 2015).

Importantly, although adults' *Miranda* comprehension is generally strong in a relative sense (i.e., when compared to youths' *Miranda* comprehension), their understanding and appreciation of rights is often far from perfect (e.g., Grisso, 1981; Kelley, 2014; Rogers, Rogstad, et al. 2010b). Further, because many *Miranda* abilities plateau in mid-to-late adolescence or early adulthood, age is *not* a useful predictor of *Miranda* comprehension among adults. Finally, among youth and adults, individual differences abound—particularly when other factors, such as intelligence, are taken into account—emphasizing the importance of individualized evaluations of *Miranda* waivers.

Developmental factors: Given the robust relationship between age and *Miranda* comprehension, some research has explored different aspects of development—cognitive, psychosocial, and neurological—to better understand the factors that account for this association. Certainly, as a prerequisite to even a rudimentary understanding of the *Miranda* warnings, one must have developed basic cognitive abilities such as *verbal abilities* to comprehend the language used in the warnings, *attention* to focus on the warnings sufficiently enough to comprehend them, *memory* to recall the warnings after they have been administered, and *executive abilities* to reason about the warnings and make a decision about waiving or invoking them. Cognitive abilities develop throughout childhood and adolescence and partially explain the relationship between age and *Miranda* comprehension. Specifically, Viljoen and Roesch (2005) found that general intellectual abilities mediated the relationship between age and youths' abilities to paraphrase the *Miranda* warnings, recognize statements conveying the same content as the *Miranda* warnings, define *Miranda* vocabulary, and appreciate how the rights to silence and counsel function during interrogations and court proceedings. Research has also revealed that, of the array of cognitive abilities, *verbal abilities* have the strongest relationship with *Miranda* comprehension (Colwell et al., 2005; Viljoen & Roesch, 2005).

Mapping these results onto the age findings discussed in the section above, cognitive abilities are an important part of the age-*Miranda* comprehension picture. Remember that most youth reach a plateau in *Miranda* understanding around age 15 or 16 (Abramovitch et al., 1995; Goldstein et al., 2003; Grisso, 1981). This is roughly the age at which many basic cognitive abilities crystallize. For instance, research suggests that basic logical abilities are generally in place by age 16 (Cauffman & Steinberg, 2000), giving youth the capacity to use rational algorithms to make decisions just as adults do (Quadrel, Fischhoff, & Davis, 1993). Thus, the development of basic cognitive abilities seems to account for improvements in *Miranda* understanding over time. The continued development of *other Miranda* abilities, namely the ability to define key vocabulary and appreciate the function and significance of rights, must, then, involve additional capacities.

Another aspect of development is psychosocial maturity, or maturity of judgment, which refers to three broad categories of psychosocial factors that influence the process of decision making: responsibility, perspective, and temperance (Cauffman & Steinberg, 2000). Responsibility refers to autonomy, clarity of one's identity, and independence. Perspective refers to the ability to consider situations from multiple viewpoints and examine the short- and long-term consequences of decisions. Temperance refers to the ability to evaluate situations before acting and inhibit impulsive behavior. Early research in this area revealed that higher levels of psychosocial maturity were associated with more mature, socially responsible decision making (i.e., decision making that resulted in less antisocial or risky behavior; Cauffman & Steinberg, 2000). Research has also shown that younger adolescents are less likely to recognize the risks associated with legal decisions or recognize the long-term consequences of legal decisions (Grisso et al., 2003). Subsequent research on the relationship between psychosocial maturity and *Miranda* comprehension specifically indicated that responsibility significantly predicted youths' understanding and appreciation of the *Miranda* warnings (Colwell et al., 2005). Youth at lower levels of psychosocial maturity have also demonstrated significantly greater misconceptions about the *Miranda* rights and greater difficulty recalling the *Miranda* warnings than their more psychosocially mature peers (Rogers, Steadham, Fiduccia, Drogin, & Robinson, 2014).

Finally, the last couple of decades have seen remarkable advances in the understanding of neurological development, specifically age-related changes in both brain structures and connections. Much of this research has focused on the frontal lobes of the brain, the seat of executive functions such as decision making, regulating impulsivity, attention, planning, and problem solving (e.g., Gogtay et al., 2004; Steinberg, 2008). Imaging research has shown that these are the last part of the brain to reach maturity and that many important parts of frontal lobe development do not happen until the mid-twenties (e.g., Gogtay et al., 2004). At the same time, the limbic system, or socio-emotional center of the brain, is developed and highly active during adolescence (Kambam & Thompson, 2009). The activity of limbic system structures, such as the nucleus accumbens, seems to partially account for the increase in risky behavior seen in adolescence. The dopaminergic system—part of the brain's reward circuitry—is also remodeled during puberty, leading to a "rapid and dramatic increase in dopaminergic activity within the socioemotional system," followed by a decrease in activity and redistribution of dopamine receptors (Steinberg, 2008, p. 1764). This phenomenon has important implications for reward-seeking behavior in adolescence. The active, reward-sensitive limbic system combined with the immature frontal lobes—the structures that eventually control and regulate decision making—means that adolescents are more prone to risk-taking and reward-seeking behaviors than adults (Steinberg, 2008).

In the context of *Miranda* comprehension, these aspects of neurological development certainly have the potential to influence not only how youth understand and appreciate their rights, but also how youth make waiver decisions. For instance, under-developed frontal lobes can influence how youth appreciate the function of rights and the consequences of a waiver, both in terms of short-term outcomes (e.g., police questioning designed to elicit a confession) and long-term outcomes (e.g., incarceration). Additionally, police officers bring social (e.g., authority) and emotional (e.g., fear, stress) demands to an interrogation that are likely far more salient to youth than the purely logical calculus of reasoning about the meaning of the *Miranda* warnings and weighing the pros and cons of waiving rights.

Academic achievement: Academic skills, like intellectual abilities, can influence *Miranda* comprehension. In contrast to the larger body of literature on the relationship between age, IQ, and *Miranda* comprehension, the research on academic achievement is relatively sparse. Nonetheless, the studies that have investigated academic achievement found strong associations with *Miranda* understanding and appreciation (Kelley, 2014; Zelle, Riggs Romaine, & Goldstein, 2015). Indeed, it appears that skills specific to language comprehension—listening and reading comprehension—are the most important academic skills for *Miranda* comprehension, as might be expected. As further support of this premise, results from one study have shown that adults with a specific language impairment (i.e., SLI, language impairment in the absence of cognitive or neurological impairment) demonstrated significantly poorer understanding and appreciation of *Miranda* rights than peers without a SLI (Rost & McGregor, 2012).

Research on the relationship between placement in special education programming and *Miranda* comprehension has yielded conflicting results. One study found that youth with a history of special education demonstrated significantly lower comprehension than those without a special education history (Goldstein et al., 2003), but a larger study found that special education was not related to *Miranda* comprehension (Zelle et al., 2015). The authors of the second study noted that students can receive special education services for a wide variety of reasons, not all of which are related to learning disabilities (e.g., mental health issues, behavior problems). Therefore, academic skills relevant to *Miranda*, such as reading and listening comprehension, discussed above, are likely clearer indicators of comprehension (Goldstein & Goldstein, 2010).

Mental illness: Symptoms of mental illness can also influence *Miranda* comprehension, though research outcomes depend on the diagnosis and specific symptoms in question. Generally, available research suggests that symptoms of psychosis (e.g., hallucinations, delusions, disorganization) in psychiatric inpatients are related to *Miranda* understanding and appreciation, even after controlling for IQ (Cooper & Zapf, 2008; Viljoen, Roesch, & Zapf, 2002). In relative terms, Cooper and Zapf's (2008) study revealed that psychiatric inpatients generally performed worse than adults from Grisso's (1981) sample, either worse or comparable to Grisso's (1981) juveniles, and slightly better than offenders with intellectual disabilities from another study (Fulero & Everington, 1995). However, one study did *not* find an association between psychosis and *Miranda* comprehension, instead finding that cognitive and academic achievement variables were the most significant predictors of *Miranda* comprehension, even among an inpatient sample (Rogers, Harrison, Hazelwood, and Sewell, 2007a).

Beyond psychosis, other symptoms certainly have the potential to influence *Miranda* comprehension. For instance, the cognitive slowing, negative distortions about one's self and abilities, and hopelessness about the future associated with depression could negatively affect one's motivation to evaluate the rights or the consequences of waiving them (Goldstein & Goldstein, 2010). Similarly, individuals with clinical anxiety, which can lead to cognitive processing difficulties, might have difficulty evaluating the meaning of their rights, particularly during a stressful interrogation (Covington & Omelich, 1987). There is limited research on these symptoms, and the studies that have evaluated the relationship between depression or anxiety and *Miranda* comprehension have not found significant associations in juveniles (Olubadewo, 2009; Viljoen & Roesch, 2005). In fact, Viljoen and Roesch (2005) found that the only symptoms that were related to *Miranda* comprehension among youth were markers of psychomotor excitation associated with Attention-Deficit/Hyperactivity Disorder.

Finally, substance use also has a strong theoretical relationship with *Miranda* comprehension. Studies have demonstrated the impact of intoxication on executive functioning skills, such as decreased inhibition, attention, reasoning, and self-monitoring and increased impulsivity and risk-taking (e.g., Fromme, Katz, & D'Amico, 1997)—all of which have the potential to influence the cognitive and psychosocial abilities needed to understand and appreciate legal rights. This relationship is particularly important given evidence that a significant proportion of youth and adults are intoxicated while being questioned by police or used illicit drugs in the 24 hours prior (Ferguson & Douglas, 1970; Pearse, Gudjonsson, Clare, & Rutter, 1998; Viljoen, Klaver, & Roesch, 2005). However, as with research on other aspects of mental illness and *Miranda* comprehension, there is a dearth of work in this area. One study found that substance use problems were associated with significant deficits in *Miranda* comprehension among justice-involved youth (Olubadewo, 2009). However, with respect to relative performance, a study that examined comprehension of rights to silence and counsel among psychiatric inpatients found that adults with substance use disorders demonstrated significantly better understanding than adults with psychotic or affective disorders (Viljoen, Roesch, & Zapf, 2002).

Prior exposure to the Miranda warnings: There is, perhaps, no other factor for which commonsense notions differ so dramatically from results of research than prior experience with police. Often, courts assume that a history of arrests provides suspects with opportunities to learn their *Miranda* rights through repeated exposure to the warnings and, perhaps, the implications of waiving their rights (Grisso, 1981). Research, however, has consistently refuted the idea that history of arrests has a relationship with *Miranda* comprehension.

Researchers have investigated this relationship in a number of different ways. Conventionally, research participants are asked about their number of prior arrests (among other relevant demographic and personal history questions) and complete measures of *Miranda* understanding and appreciation. Statistical analyses then determine whether there is a significant relationship between the variables. Done this way, research has revealed that that understanding and appreciation of *Miranda* rights are unrelated to history of arrests for justice-involved youth (Grisso, 1981; Zelle et al., 2015), justice-involved adults (Grisso, 1981; Kelley, 2014; Rogers, Rogstad, Steadham, & Drogin, 2011), undergraduate students (Eastwood & Snook, 2010), and adults with mental illness (Cooper & Zapf, 2008; Rogers, Harrison, Hazelwood et al., 2007a; Viljoen & Roesch, 2005). In a more recent study, researchers administered five versions of the *Miranda* warnings in one sitting (interspersed with other tasks) and tested whether participants—pretrial detainees—demonstrated improved comprehension at the end of the session and again 2–4 weeks later (Rogers, Fiduccia, Robinson, Steadham, and Drogin, 2013b). Results revealed that, in general, improvements in comprehension were negligible at posttest (i.e., the end of the first session) or follow up (2–4 weeks later). Of low-performing participants—those who had most room to improve—less than one third (32%) improved with repeated administrations.

Finally, a small body of research recently investigated *Miranda* comprehension among the general population to address whether exposure to the rights—typically through popular media—has resulted in actual understanding of rights. As Zelle et al. (2015) summarized, "Despite the appeal of an osmotically based knowledge of rights, research suggests that exposure has not improved our *Miranda* comprehension" (p. 293). Results of other studies revealed that college students hold misconceptions about the *Miranda* warnings similar to those held by defendants, and jury-eligible adults similarly made significant errors both in terms of ability to recall the warnings and in their misconceptions (Rogers, Fiduccia, Drogin, et al., 2013a; Rogers, Rogstad, et al. Shuman, 2010b).

Although research does not support the notion of a relationship between prior arrests and global *Miranda* comprehension abilities, some studies have found a relationship between prior arrests and specific capacities. Among justice-involved youth, history of arrests has demonstrated a significant association with appreciation of the right to counsel (Grisso, 1981; Viljoen & Roesch, 2005). Among adults, number of prior felony arrests was significantly related to one aspect of *Miranda* understanding: ability to paraphrase rights, but unrelated to other aspects of understanding or any aspects of appreciation (Grisso, 1981). In sum, research suggests a few, narrowly carved relationships between arrests and certain aspects of *Miranda* comprehension, but generally refutes the notion that a history of arrests and police contact results in meaningful gains in understanding and appreciating legal rights.

Despite the general lack of association between arrest history and *Miranda* comprehension, research does suggest a positive relationship between *Miranda* comprehension and contact with attorneys. Viljoen and Roesch (2005) found that, among justice-involved youth, the number of hours spent with defense attorneys predicted multiple components of understanding and appreciation. Further, this contact was most important for youth with lower IQ scores. More recently, Zelle et al. (2015) observed a relationship between justice-involved youths' recollection of discussing *Miranda* rights with an attorney and recognition of the meaning of rights. Thus, while interactions with police do not appear to bolster *Miranda* comprehension, contact with attorneys might—perhaps because it allows for direct exposure to the meaning of rights, significance of waivers, and first-hand appreciation of how defense attorneys function (Goldstein & Goldstein, 2010).

Innocence and guilt: The final suspect factor we review is somewhat different than the others because it cannot be known with certainty (in contrast with age, for example) or otherwise assessed (in contrast with factors such as intelligence or academic achievement). Thus, this final factor also cannot be evaluated as part of a forensic mental health assessment of a defendant's *Miranda* waiver, nor can it be considered in a court's *totality of the circumstances* analysis. Nevertheless, research has shown that suspects' guilt or innocence is relevant to their interrogation experience.

The relationship between guilt/innocence and *Miranda* comprehension has not been a topic of direct inquiry. Indeed, one would not expect systematic differences in understanding of legal rights between guilty and innocent suspects. However, one's status as guilty or innocent *can* influence stress during interrogation, which, as described in the Situational Factors section below, can influence understanding and appreciation of *Miranda* rights. Research has shown that guilty "suspects" (i.e., participants in laboratory settings) experienced more stress than innocent suspects when confronted with an accusation of wrongdoing, potentially because innocent suspects believed that their innocence would be apparent, and therefore, they perceived less need to engage in self-protection (Guyll et al., 2013). Differences in physiologic stress levels, however, diminished over the course of interrogation. Further, among innocent suspects, the act of resisting confession over the course of interrogation led to elevated activation of the sympathetic nervous system, suggestive of cognitive resource depletion (Guyll et al., 2013). Generalizing these lab-based findings to actual interrogations, guilty and innocent suspects might be differentially affected depending on when *Miranda* rights are administered in the course of speaking with police.

Research has also revealed different rates of rights waivers among guilty and innocent suspects, with innocent suspects generally executing waivers at *much higher* rates. For instance, in a laboratory study in which participants were assigned to either guilty or innocent conditions, Kassin and Norwick (2004) found that, while only 36% of guilty suspects waived their rights, 81% of innocent suspects did so. And, although participants across both groups cited concerns about looking guilty if they did not waive their rights, nearly three-quarters (72%) of innocent suspects who waived their rights cited innocence as a factor in their waiver decisions. This result has been replicated in more recent research (Scherr & Franks, 2015). Findings such as these, paired with research on false confessions, has led to a body of work on the phenomenology of innocence, or the ways in which "innocence may put innocent people at risk" (Kassin, 2005, p. 215) of waiving their rights and ultimately offering a false confession. Interestingly, some of this research has shown that a suspect's guilt or innocence influences not only waiver rights, but how interrogations proceed after a *Miranda* waiver (for a review, see Kassin, 2005).

Although a detailed discussion of the relationship between innocence and false confessions is outside the scope of this chapter, recent research has attempted to "unpack" the phenomenology of innocence and its effect on *Miranda* waivers. Overall, this research has shown that strong *just world beliefs* (i.e., the belief that people's actions are generally met with appropriate consequences) are associated with increased rights waivers (Scherr & Franks, 2015) and that innocent suspects' willingness to waive their rights was positively associated with endorsement of just world beliefs (Scherr et al., 2016). Research that has explored the effect of just world beliefs *and* a particular interrogation strategy among guilty and innocent suspects revealed that the effect of the interrogation strategy depended not only on the suspect's guilt or innocence, but also on the strength of their just world beliefs (Scherr et al., 2016). The results of this research are reviewed in more detail in the Delivery of the Warning section, below.

Situational Factors

Miranda comprehension is not entirely determined by individual characteristics. The circumstances surrounding the interrogation and the *Miranda* warnings can influence how well suspects understand and appreciate their legal rights. These contextual influences, or *situational factors*, include how the warnings are worded and the stress associated with custodial interrogations. The most relevant situational factors, as determined by research and legal decisions, are reviewed below.

Miranda wording: The language used to convey the *Miranda* warnings varies across, and even within, jurisdictions. In fact, Rogers and colleagues (Rogers, Harrison, Shuman et al., 2007b; Rogers, Hazelwood, Sewell, Harrison, et al., 2008a; Rogers et al., 2012) collected 945 unique general *Miranda* warnings and 371 unique juvenile-specific *Miranda* warnings from 888 jurisdictions. Several important findings have come out of this line of research. First, the length and reading level of these different warnings vary dramatically, from 49 to 547 words, and from warnings that require a third grade reading level to warnings that require post-college education (i.e., an eighteenth grade reading level; Rogers, Hazelwood, Sewell, Harrison et al., 2008a). Additionally, *Miranda* warnings often include vocabulary words that require at least a tenth grade education such as "accord," "alleged," and "coerced" (Rogers, Hazelwood, Sewell, Harrison et al., 2008a). Second, these wording differences result in variability in the content of the warnings. For instance, some warnings only mention the rights, while others provide an explanation (e.g., You have the right to remain silent, that means you have no obligation to talk with police). Others specify, sometimes incorrectly, the timeframe in which the right to counsel and ability to reassert rights operate. For example, some suspects are told that attorneys are available only *during* questioning or that silence can only be asserted *until* an attorney is available (Rogers, Harrison, Shuman et al., 2007b). Third, juvenile *Miranda* warnings are typically longer and more difficult to read than their adult counterparts (Rogers, Hazelwood, Sewell, Shuman et al., 2008b; Rogers et al., 2012).

Far from being concerned with this variability, the Supreme Court has repeatedly held that it will not scrutinize the precise language used to convey the *Miranda* warnings. Instead, the Court only considers whether a particular set of warnings reasonably "conve[ys] [to a suspect] his rights as required by *Miranda*" (*California v. Prysock*, 1981, p. 361) or "touched all of the bases required by *Miranda*" (*Duckworth v. Eagan*, 1989, p. 203). In these and other decisions (e.g., *California v. Prysock*, 1981; *Duckworth v. Eagan*, 1989; *Florida v. Powell*, 2010), the Court reminded the parties that the warnings themselves are not constitutionally protected—the right against self-incrimination is—and, therefore, analysis of the language used to convey the warnings is somewhat relaxed.

Although variations in *Miranda* warnings do not always carry legal significance, researchers have investigated whether these variations might have practical significance. In other words, do changes in the wording of *Miranda* warnings influence comprehension? The research in this area is limited, but suggests that certain wording changes, for certain populations, have limited significance. Three studies have compared participants' *Miranda* comprehension after hearing two different versions of the warning. The first study (Ferguson & Douglas, 1970) compared adolescents' comprehension of the *Miranda* warnings used by the San Diego Police Department to a simplified version created by the authors. The other two studies compared comprehension of the *Miranda* warnings used in Grisso's (1998) original *Miranda* instruments to Goldstein and colleagues' (2012) version in the updated instruments that had a lower reading comprehension level among psychiatric inpatients (Cooper & Zapf, 2008) and detained youth (Messenheimer et al., 2009). In brief, all three studies found that simpler versions of the warning did *not* lead to improved comprehension.

In addition to addressing the relative complexity of entire *Miranda* warnings, research has also identified certain words and phrases that are most problematic. Rogers et al. (2011) identified the most challenging *Miranda* vocabulary as: "coercion/coerced," "demand," "proceedings," and "right"; depending on the word, from 56 to 86% of pretrial defendants in the study produced errors when defining these words. Some of the most problematic phrases were: (regarding the right to free legal services) "Have him present to advise you before we ask you any questions (86.1% made errors); (regarding the ability to reassert rights) "When you so desire, before or during the questioning" (73.9% made errors); and (regarding the right to silence) "This fact cannot be used against me" (60.4% made errors).

More recently, Gillard et al. (2014) explored the *Miranda* wording that framed the basis for the challenge in *Florida v. Powell* (2010) that conveyed, in relevant part, that suspects "have the right to talk to a lawyer *before* answering any [police] questions" (p. 1200, emphasis added). The defendant's contention, which was rejected by the Court, was that the law required police to inform him that he also had the right to an attorney *during* questioning. Gillard et al. (2014) found no differences in understanding between participants informed using the Powell language and those informed of the right to an attorney before and during questioning.

Delivery of the warning: Compared to research on other areas of *Miranda* comprehension, minimal research exists on how police actually administer or deliver the *Miranda* warnings. Based on review of numerous interrogation transcripts, Leo and White (1999) described three categories of delivery. In the first, officers deliver the *Miranda* warnings in a neutral manner, typically reading the warnings off of a pre-printed card, often before engaging in any conversation with the suspect. In this way, officers are simply "conveyors of legal information" (p. 433). In the second, officers de-emphasize the significance of the warnings. Leo and White (1999) observed that officers implemented this strategy in a multitude of ways, for example: (1) reading the warnings in a perfunctory tone; (2) rushing through the warnings without pausing or looking at the suspect; (3) explicitly calling to the suspect's attention the formality of the warnings, thereby conveying their unimportance; (4) referring to the warnings' dissemination in popular culture; (5) focusing the suspect's attention on the importance of sharing his side of the story and implying that the warnings are the sole impediment to him doing so; or (6) creating the appearance of a nonadversarial relationship in which the officer is there to help the suspect. Finally, in the third category, officers implicitly offer some benefit in exchange for the rights waiver. For example, similar to one of the de-emphasizing strategies, they might focus attention on the suspect being able to share his side of the story or provide a compelling justification for his actions. Skillful interrogators convey—without explicitly stating—that doing so may lead to reduced charges or a lighter sentence.

Delivery of the warnings certainly has the potential to influence both how suspects interpret the warning and how they make decisions about speaking with police. In fact, some legal scholars have argued that, despite the actual meaning of the *Miranda* rights—which serve as a warning or caution about speaking with police—delivery of *Miranda* can encourage suspects to cooperate, that is, to waive their rights:

> Skillfully presented, the *Miranda* warnings themselves sound chords of fairness and sympathy at the outset of the interrogation. The interrogator who advises, who cautions, who offers the suspect the gift of a free lawyer, becomes all the more persuasive by dint of his apparent candor and reasonableness (Malone, 1986, p. 371, cited in Leo, 2001).

Although researchers have not systematically investigated how each of these different delivery styles might influence suspects, recent studies have addressed two of these strategies using samples of "wrongly accused" (i.e., innocent) participants: trivializing the importance of a set of legal warnings and treating the opportunity to speak with the police (and provide one's own "side of the story") as a scarce, time-limited resource. With respect to trivializing, results indicated that participants who heard the rights and associated waiver form described in unimportant terms were more likely to execute a waiver and demonstrated worse comprehension of the rights than participants who heard the rights and waiver form described as significant (Scherr & Madon, 2013). In contrast, researchers found that the "scarcity" ploy did not influence whether participants waived or invoked their rights (Scherr, Alberts, Franks, & Hawkins, 2016).

Another set of studies investigated whether "social proof pressure," or influencing others to believe that certain behaviors (e.g., rights waivers) are normal, affected rights waivers of "guilty" and "innocent" participants. Results revealed that social proof pressure did influence rights waivers, but affected guilty and innocent participants differently based on their endorsement of just world beliefs. Social proof pressure led to increased waiver rates among guilty participants with *strong* just world beliefs and innocent participants with *weak* just world beliefs (Scherr & Franks, 2015). Interestingly, in a subsequent study, researchers initially employed social proof pressure among innocent participants, but then gave a subset of participants information *inconsistent* with that expectation (i.e., they were explicitly told they had a choice about whether to sign the rights waiver form). Results indicated that this disruption of participants' cognitive fluency—by explicitly informing them of their choice—led to *decreased* rights waivers (Scherr et al., 2016). In a similar experiment, participants who were specifically asked whether they wanted to waive their rights had lower rates of waivers (17%) than participants who were not (86%; for the latter set of participants, researchers read the *Miranda* warnings and immediately began questioning without asking for an explicit waiver decision; Gillard et al., 2014).

Other research in this area has explored basic questions about both delivery and the effect of delivery on comprehension. A large-scale survey of American and Canadian investigators found that 67% of officers informed suspects of the *Miranda* warnings orally and 29% did so in writing (Kassin et al., 2007). The studies that have evaluated how mode of delivery affected comprehension of rights found results at odds with officers' typical mode of delivery: participants' comprehension of rights improved (sometimes dramatically) when they were delivered in written, as opposed to oral, format (Eastwood & Snook, 2010; Rogers et al., 2011; Rogers, Fiduccia, Robinson et al., 2013b). A likely contributor to the difficulty with oral warnings is the rate at which law enforcement officers read them. Research suggests that rates of speech beyond 150–200 words per minute are problematic for understanding (e.g., Jester & Travers, 1966, cited in Snook et al., 2010). Problematically, Snook et al.'s (2010) study of administration of rights in Canada revealed that the average speed of delivery was 262.6 words per minute for the right to silence and 204.7 words per minute for the right to counsel. Such speedy delivery is likely to be particularly problematic for nonnative English speakers and individuals with low intelligence or little formal education.

What about suspects who are informed of their rights multiple times during the same interrogation? As referenced above in the "Prior Exposure to the *Miranda* Warnings" section, Rogers, Fiduccia, Robinson and colleagues (2013b) found that hearing multiple versions of the *Miranda* warning within one session did not result in any meaningful benefits, and actually produced short-term *detriments*. Specifically, after hearing multiple versions of the warnings, significantly more pretrial detainees inaccurately believed that statements could be retracted if law enforcement used deception and that police could not falsely inform a suspect about an eyewitness identification.

Stress: Police interrogations are stressful, often by design (Kassin et al., 2010). Most important in the context of *Miranda* comprehension, a body of literature supports the premise that stress can compromise cognitive functioning, particularly working memory (for a brief review, see Scherr & Madon, 2012). In short, stress consumes valuable cognitive resources that might otherwise be used for attending to, processing, and recalling novel information, leading individuals under stress to make more errors and rely more on cognitive shortcuts.

Research on *Miranda* comprehension specifically has found that stress (typically induced in experimental settings by an accusation of wrongdoing) undermines the ability to understand and appreciate legal rights (Rogers, Gillard, Wooley, & Fiduccia, 2010a; Scherr & Madon, 2012, 2013). When considered in the context of the linguistic and conceptual demands of the *Miranda* warnings, these findings are perhaps unsurprising. However, the magnitude of these results should also be considered. For instance, in one study, participants in the stressful condition demonstrated *Miranda* comprehension on par with juveniles and with adults with psychotic disorders (Scherr & Madon, 2012).

Presence of parents (for juvenile suspects): Requiring parents (or legal guardians) to be present for interrogations of their children has been a logical outgrowth of the documented problems with youths' poor comprehension of rights. Nevertheless, state laws vary tremendously regarding whether parents need to be notified of their child's interrogation or present during it, and they are often contingent on the youth's age (for a review see Cruise, Pitchal, & Weiss, 2008). Additionally, departments have their own local policies and practices—not codified as law—that influence whether parents might be present, though internal agreement about and implementation of these polices can vary (Meyer, Reppucci, & Owen, 2006). Parental presence laws and policies, as well as common calls to either implement or expand them (e.g., Huang, 2001), have posed interesting questions for researchers about whether parents will educate their children about important gaps in knowledge identified by research (i.e., the meaning of the rights and implications of waiving or invoking them).

Research on this topic suggests that parental presence is far from the panacea hoped for by advocates and theorized by scholars. Early research based on observations of interrogations of youths with their parents present found that most often (70% of the time) parents did not offer any advice about the youths' legal rights, a finding influenced by the fact that, about two-thirds of the time (66%), the parents and youth did not speak to one another at all (Grisso & Ring, 1979). Of the one-third of parents who did offer advice, 60% of them encouraged youth to waive their rights; only 16% of this group (4% of all parents) advised against waivers (Grisso & Ring, 1979). The results of a more recent study (Viljoen, Klaver, & Roesch, 2005) were similar when juvenile defendants were asked to report on their experiences during interrogation. Roughly one-quarter of defendants had one or both parents present during interrogation. Of this group, 40% reported that they did not know what their parent wanted them to do. Of the other 60% who indicated that they did know their parents' wishes, nearly 80% perceived that their parents wanted them to speak with the police (to confess [57%] or to "tell the truth" [11%]).

Though decades apart, these studies both found that, during their children's interrogations, parents often fail to embody the role of legal advocate. Some researchers have questioned the premise of these laws and policies—whether parents have the capacity to compensate for youths' interrogation-related deficits. Results of this research revealed that, although parents generally demonstrated better understanding of the *Miranda* rights than their children, both parents and children demonstrated significant misunderstandings about police practices (e.g., whether police are permitted to lie to suspects) (Woolard, Cleary, Harvell, & Chen, 2008). Thus, available evidence suggests that parents generally do not protect the legal rights of their children and that they have limited abilities to do so. Admittedly, legal advocacy is a role many parents have neither prepared nor asked for, and some parents may perceive their child's moral development (taking responsibility for a guilty act by confessing) as paramount to a legal defense. Therefore, other protections for youthful suspects must be explored.

Recent *Miranda* Jurisprudence and Implications for Research

Two years before the *Miranda* decision, the Warren Court expressed concern about a criminal justice system too dependent on confessions:

> We have learned the lesson of history, ancient and modern, that a system of criminal law enforcement which comes to depend on the 'confession' will, in the long run, be less reliable and more subject to abuses than a system which depends on extrinsic evidence independently secured through skillful investigation. … We have also learned the companion lesson of history that no system of criminal justice can, or should, survive if it comes to depend for its continued effectiveness on the citizens' abdication through unawareness of their constitutional rights. No system worth preserving should have to fear that if an accused is permitted to consult with a lawyer, he will become aware of, and exercise, these rights. If the exercise of constitutional rights will thwart the effectiveness of a system of law enforcement, then there is something very wrong with that system
>
> (*Escobedo v. Illinois*, 1964, pp. 488–490).

The quote above clearly conveys the Court's motivation to establish that constitutional protections apply not only to court settings but to interrogation settings as well. *Escobedo* was a Sixth Amendment (right to counsel) case, as opposed to the Fifth Amendment focus of *Miranda*, but the evocative language presages *Miranda* well as the Court grappled with how to establish a mechanism, standard, or rule that would provide protection beyond the basic voluntariness standard that applied—all too amorphously—to suspects' statements to police. *Escobedo* captures the spirit of *Miranda* well, therefore, through its direct expression of the need to avoid abuses not only in terms of physical force but also in terms of exploitation of citizens' unwitting interactions with government agents. The quote above puts into relief the most expansive sense of *Miranda*'s aim and provides a sharp contrast to how the case law has since evolved.

As Part I noted, cases subsequent to *Miranda* (only some of which are covered in this chapter) whittled away at the precedent, assuring a more modest impact. Part I ended with *Dickerson v. U.S.*, which seemed to cement *Miranda* as foundational and robust against further efforts to revert back to the voluntariness-only approach to suspect interactions with police. *Miranda* has been contracted further within the past decade, however, by several Supreme Court opinions, to the point that some scholars argue that case law has effectively returned to a voluntariness-only regime (e.g., Primus, 2015). Lower courts, including federal Circuit Courts, have struggled with, and in many cases abridged, *Miranda* in recent years. This section: (1) reviews recent Supreme Court cases, (2) reviews issues raised by exemplar lower court cases, and (3) highlights what these developments indicate for research.

Recent Supreme Court Case Law

Focusing on the past decade, the first Supreme Court case of interest is *Montejo v. Louisiana* (2009). This case concerned a change in the Court's perspective on whether the right to counsel should be presumed to be invoked during questioning if the defendant had exercised the right by obtaining counsel at a previous arraignment or similar proceeding. A prior opinion, *Michigan v. Jackson* (1986), had concluded that a waiver of the right to counsel after invocation at arraignment would be presumed invalid; however, in *Montejo*, the Court overruled *Jackson* and held that individuals would still be required to invoke their rights even if they had previously requested counsel at an arraignment. The decision is somewhat complex because it involves developments that cross over between Fifth Amendment rights during interrogation and Sixth Amendment rights during arraignment, with the Court ultimately determining that the protections already in place for the Fifth Amendment in the interrogation context were sufficient. For the purposes of this section, *Montejo* is noted because it was, perhaps, the first decision of the Roberts Court to suggest that the Court was headed toward reversing any outward expansion of *Miranda*. It also exemplifies how recent *Miranda*-related cases have created a labyrinth of narrow decisions that impact how suspects' rights may be exercised but that few people probably understand.

The following year, 2010, three Supreme Court opinions directly addressed the *Miranda* rights. One, *Florida v. Powell*, was relatively straightforward in that it reaffirmed the Court's standing position on the wording of the warnings: no particular form or wording is required—the warnings must merely "reasonably convey" the rights (p. 1201). The defendant in *Powell* argued that the warnings administered to him did not make it clear that he had a right to counsel *during* questioning because the warnings only mentioned a right to counsel *before* questioning.

A second 2010 case, *Maryland v. Shatzer*, set a sort of "expiration date" on *Miranda* rights invocations. The Court reasoned that the purpose of the warnings was to alleviate the inherent pressure that an interrogation context conveys and that such pressure dissipates after someone is released from police custody because the person is no longer in the interrogation context and, what is more, the person can seek advice from others. Thus, the Court reasoned, if a suspect invokes his rights during interrogation but is then released from custody, the rights invocation should be assumed to extend only for up to 14 days; after that time, if the person is again questioned by police, the person must re-invoke his rights if he wishes them to apply again.

The third and perhaps most impactful 2010 case was *Berghuis v. Thompkins*. In a previous case, *North Carolina v. Butler* (1979), the Court concluded that a rights waiver could be inferred based on a suspect's "course of conduct indicating waiver" (p. 373). In 1994, the Court held that an invocation of the right to *counsel* during interrogation must be explicitly made (*Davis v. United States*, 1994). This implicit waiver/explicit invocation paradigm was cemented in *Berghuis v. Thompkins*, which applied the same standard to the right to silence during interrogation. In other words, a suspect must now speak in order to remain silent, as remaining silent for nearly 3 hours (as the defendant in *Berghuis* did) is not sufficient to invoke the right to silence. And, as the Court's cases concerning invocation of the right to counsel have made clear, the Court expects that such explicit invocations be clear and unambiguous—suspects stating that they *think* they need a lawyer or otherwise seeming to question whether they do want to invoke either right will not be interpreted as invocations. The *Miranda* Court had envisioned a broader definition of invocation: "If, however, he indicates in any manner and at any stage of the process that he wishes to consult with an attorney before speaking, there can be no questioning. Likewise, if the individual is alone and indicates in any manner that he does not wish to be interrogated, the police may not question him" (pp. 444–45). *Berghuis*, however, has made clear that the modern Court is not interested in such a wide application of *Miranda* and the onus is on citizens to know the intricacies of how the rights, and waivers of those rights, actually work. What is more, citizens must be able to affirmatively, even forcefully, assert those rights in the face of the inherent coercion against which they want those rights to protect them.

Three years later, in *Salinas v. Texas* (2013), the Court again emphasized individuals' responsibility to invoke their rights during police interactions. The defendant in this case participated in a noncustodial interview—such that he was not informed of his *Miranda* rights—and when he remained silent but acted unusually in response to a question (he looked at the floor, shuffled his feet, bit his lip, clenched his hands, and "began to tighten up"), that silent reaction was later admissible in court as evidence of his guilt (p. 2178). Thus, the case underscored the limited application of *Miranda* as a protection for suspects (i.e., only suspects who are in custody are entitled to be informed of their rights to silence and counsel) and made clear that it is incumbent on citizens to invoke their right to silence.

Another recent Supreme Court case of interest, *J.D.B. v. North Carolina* (2011), concerned adolescents. The case was not directly about *Miranda waivers*; rather, it focused on whether an adolescent's age should be considered when applying the objective "reasonable person" standard to determine whether a suspect was in custody (and, thus, whether the *Miranda* warnings must be administered). Among the recent *Miranda*-related cases, *J.D.B.* is the one case that expands *Miranda*. The

Court held that adolescent age should be considered in the custodial determination based on the premise that youth are more likely than adults to believe they are in custody and unable to leave when faced with authority figures.

In contrast to the custody definition in *J.D.B.*, the Court in *Howes v. Fields* (2012) held that an adult prisoner who was removed from the general population and questioned about incidents unrelated to the charges for which he was sentenced was not in custody and, therefore, *Miranda* did not apply. The opinion is narrow in that it addressed whether inmates who are lawfully imprisoned upon conviction will be automatically considered "in custody" for purposes of *Miranda*. Nevertheless, the factual findings made by the Court demonstrate how narrowly the Court is restricting the application of *Miranda*. The prisoner, Fields, was taken from his cell by armed deputies during the night and taken to an interrogation room. Despite his requests to stop the interrogation, he was questioned for 5–7 hours. Nonetheless, the Court pointed to the fact that deputies told Fields he could ask to go back to his cell, the fact that he was not restrained or threatened, and the fact that the door was sometimes open as countering the idea that Fields was in custody. Moreover, the Court reasoned that prisoners are used to restrictions on their freedom, so questioning of the type that Fields experienced does not involve the inherent coercion about which *Miranda* precedent is concerned.

Although we will not review the cases in detail, it is worth noting that a parallel line of case law has developed concerning the use of un-Mirandized statements to impeach defendants when they choose to testify at their trials. As mentioned, the Supreme Court seemed to cement the constitutional status of *Miranda* in *Dickerson v. United States* (2000). However, the Court in that opinion was careful to describe *Miranda* as providing "constitutional guidance," and after that case, the Court quickly returned to emphasizing the *Miranda* warnings as a prophylactic measure, not a constitutional right. By characterizing the *Miranda* case law in this way, it allows the Court to hold that the use of un-Mirandized statements at trial is not a violation of the constitution; rather, it is simply a violation of a constitutionally related prophylactic rule. The distinction allows for a line of reasoning in which use of the statements for impeachment of a testifying defendant (i.e., to undermine the defendant's reliability as a witness), rather than for evidence of guilt, is permissible (see, e.g., *Kansas v. Ventris*, 2009; O'Neill, 2010; Todd, 2013). Although the difference between using evidence for impeachment rather than as evidence of guilt is an important *legal* distinction, in practice jurors have difficulty following the limiting instructions that direct them to make this distinction during deliberations (Tanford & Cox, 1988). In short, there is yet another angle of *Miranda* case law that circumscribes the protections—an angle about which few people are probably aware.

Collectively, these cases offer the following lessons. First, the Court requires suspects to be explicit with respect to invoking their rights: Witnesses not involved in custodial interrogations must assert the privilege against self-incrimination without first being informed of it (*Salinas v. Texas,* 2013), and suspects in custodial interrogations must unambiguously invoke their rights to silence and counsel (*Berghuis v. Thompkins,* 2010). Second, whereas invocations of rights must be explicit, waivers of *Miranda* rights may be implicit (*Berghuis v. Thompkins,* 2010).

Third, the Court will not scrutinize the language of *Miranda* warnings (*Florida v. Powell*, 2010). Fourth, the custody analysis remains highly contextual (e.g., being incarcerated, per se, does not amount to being "in custody;" childhood is a reasonable factor to be considered) (*Howes v. Fields*, 2011; *J.D.B v. North Carolina*, 2010). Finally, certain layers of prophylaxis around invocations of rights have been refined or removed, again placing a greater burden on suspects to assert their rights (*Montejo v. Lousiana*, 2009).

Lower Courts' Case Law

Review of a few lower court cases can help highlight how the Supreme Court's (lack of) precedent has led to (1) further narrowing of *Miranda* at the state court level, (2) differences between states in the application of *Miranda*, and (3) accidental and strategic administration variations by officers that undermine the purpose of the *Miranda* warnings.

The Supreme Court of the United States is not the only court to have hemmed in *Miranda* by focusing on the "underlying police-regulatory purpose" of the opinion (*Garner v. Mitchell*, 2009, p. 263). In *Garner v. Mitchell* (2009), the United States Court of Appeals for the Sixth Circuit considered appeals by the defendant, Garner, arguing that he did not validly waive his rights because his intellectual deficits led him to not understand the warnings. In short, the court found that Garner had knowingly and intelligently waived his *Miranda* rights based on his "conduct before and during the interrogation" and, more consequentially, established an "objective" police-perspective-based test for a suspect's misunderstanding of the warnings (p. 261). In determining that Garner's conduct was indicative of a knowing and intelligent waiver, the court noted a variety of externally-focused details, such as the fact that Garner "appeared 'perfectly normal' and 'very coherent,'" that the officers read the warnings at least twice, that Garner signed and dated a waiver form, that the officers asked after each warning if Garner understood the warning, and that Garner's statements about the crime indicated he knew of its wrongfulness (p. 272). The court also pointed to observations made by a psychologist in a competence to stand trial report, despite the focus of that report on a different topic (one for which it is common to educate an evaluee about the material) and different situational context of that evaluation. (As an aside, the case can also serve as an example of how some courts utilize apparent awareness of wrongfulness or attempts to lie to police as proxies for understanding constitutional rights, a nonempirical supposition that eases the way to finding a waiver valid.)

Ultimately, the court found that "even if Garner's mental capacity, background, age, and experience did somehow prevent him from actually understanding the *Miranda* warnings … the officers questioning Garner had no way to discern the misunderstanding in Garner's mind" (p. 262). The court supported its reasoning by focusing solely on the "police-regulatory" purpose of *Miranda*, wholly discounting the idea that police conduct was to be regulated by *meaningfully informing* citizen-suspects, arming them with knowledge that they could comprehend and utilize (p. 263). The Sixth Circuit concluded that waiver "circumstances be examined, in their totality, primarily from the perspective of the police" (p. 263). The holding seems contrary to the *Miranda v. Arizona* approach that was concerned with the suspect's perspective and also raises questions about when police would ever find reason to believe that a suspect misunderstood the warnings. Given the often rote and administratively toned delivery of the warnings, it may be only the rare case in which someone demonstrates misunderstanding so great that it cannot be overlooked. Or, as some cases mentioned below suggest, it seems that when suspects do ask questions, officers might respond with confusing responses and suspects might end up signing waivers in resignation. In sum, the *Garner* case is noted here because of the pains it goes to in order to restrain the application of *Miranda* and ultimately turn the prophylactic rule to serve interrogators rather than suspects. We encourage interested readers to review the case in full, including Judge Moore's thoughtful dissent.

The Garner case is not only illustrative of the ways that lower courts have narrowed *Miranda*; it also provides a foil for a conflicting line of case law in Illinois, demonstrating one instance of lower court conflict over the application of *Miranda*. Illinois cases have led to a policy under which *Miranda* waivers "can be invalid based solely on the subjective inability of a suspect to understand the warnings" (O'Neill, 2010, p. 429). Although the *Garner* majority cited an opinion by the circuit court that covers Illinois (the Seventh Circuit), it seems that their reliance on that circuit's precedent may have been misplaced (see Judge Cole's partial dissent), and it appears to be settled case law in Illinois that *Miranda* waivers can be found invalid based on the subjective comprehension of the suspect-defendant. We will forego in depth review of the Illinois case law for the sake of space (see O'Neill, 2010 for a review), but the conflict is worth identifying because it demonstrates how lower courts are grappling with differing interpretations and that not all courts have accepted the narrow "police-regulatory" purpose approach to *Miranda*.

The Supreme Court's firm refusal to provide detailed guidance or expectations about how the warnings must be phrased has led to some startling exchanges between suspects and officers. It also seems that many officers might be unclear on how the rights function, and even if they mean well, can end up misleading suspects who ask questions about the rights. For example, the defendant in *United States v. Gray* (2015) seemed to have been talked out of asserting his rights due to a confusing conversation that took place after the defendant said "I want a lawyer present." Instead of stopping the interview, the officers talked with him about how he would get a lawyer and told him that he would only get an attorney appointed if he was arrested, which was not going to happen that day. The court noted that the defendant "said in apparent resignation: '[s]o fuck it. Let me sign that [waiver] then, I guess.'" (p. 2). Ultimately, the court suppressed his statement in that case. The Ninth Circuit Court of Appeals addressed similar problems in several cases. In one case, *Doody v. Ryan* (2011), an adolescent was administered the *Miranda* warnings using a juvenile-specific form with relatively uncomplicated language, including explanatory parentheticals. Nevertheless, the transcript of the warnings administration was

12 pages long because "of the detective's continuous usage of qualifying language" (p. 991) and deviations from the language of the form that were misleading. The Circuit Court ultimately found Doody's waiver to be invalid in that case, as well. (For additional examples, see *Alvarez v. Gomez*, 1999; *Sessoms v. Grounds*, 2014; *State v. Mayer*, 2015).

Finally, as noted in the Translating Legal Requirements section, state courts appear to be split on how they interpret the knowing and intelligent standard—whether it requires one level of understanding or two distinct levels. More generally, it is worth underscoring just how low the bar seems to be set by many courts. As the Seventh Circuit has noted, "It is only when the evidence in the case shows that the defendant could not comprehend even the most basic concepts underlying the *Miranda* warnings that the courts have found an unintelligent waiver" (*Collins v. Gaetz*, 2010, p. 588). Recognizing this, many scholars have begun to view the trajectory of *Miranda* and related confession law as returning to a focus solely on voluntariness (e.g., Primus, 2015) or to point out that *Miranda v. Arizona* (1966) effectively just incentivized officers to Mirandize suspects because Mirandized statements are virtually always found to be voluntary and admissible (Todd, 2013). There is also the interesting development of the Ninth Circuit utilizing the voluntariness standard for confessions in a relatively proactive way to suppress statements made by a young man with intellectual disability who was questioned using legal but problematic strategies (*United States v. Preston*, 2015), which falls in line with the presaged return to a focus on confession voluntariness. Any or all of these developments/realizations have implications for research, which, to date, has largely focused on assessing the knowing and intelligent prongs of the waiver standard.

Implications for Current Research

Why review so much case law? We feel it is imperative for social science researchers to attend to developments in the law because they have important implications for research, particularly given the apparent momentum toward substantive changes in *Miranda* precedent that had seemed relatively settled for decades. The psycholegal constructs appear to be evolving, or at least becoming increasingly complex and multifaceted, and the points for investigation are multiplying. The final part of this chapter points up future directions more specifically, but as a close to this part, we offer a brief review of what seem to be the most salient research implications from the case law.

First, researchers, us included, should broaden their view beyond examining the knowing and intelligent prongs of the waiver standard as laid out in *Miranda v. Arizona*. The focus on knowing and intelligent has been the keystone of *Miranda* research, and rightfully so given the apparent match of those cognitively-focused prongs to psychological constructs and psychologists' ability to provide relevant assessment of cognitive functioning. The courts, however, do not set the bar for knowing and intelligent very high, continue to differ in how they define the terms, and seem to accept the fact of *Miranda* administration as sufficient to establish a "knowing, intelligent, and voluntary" waiver in a number of cases. There may still be a need to advance research on this facet if social scientists can figure out how to effectively impress upon the courts that the many people do not actually know their rights or how they function—but the assumption of widespread knowledge of the rights has proved to be incredibly intractable. One new point to the knowing and intelligent research comes from the recent cases that have complicated how the rights function; in addition to measuring how much (or little) people know about what the rights mean, there is a need to measure how much (or little) people know about how to invoke their rights. The shrinking scope of the knowing and intelligent prongs also suggests against trying to expend research energies on assessing peoples' reasoning behind decisions to waive because the courts seem to have made clear how little they are interested in examining the "subjective" experience and considering the actual suspect. If nothing else, researchers should consider how courts might apply the voluntariness standard (e.g., *United States v. Preston*, 2015; Primus, 2015) rather than continuing with the general assumption that voluntariness is about police conduct and therefore does not leave much for psychologists to assess.

Not all research has been so focused on the knowing and intelligent aspects of a valid waiver, of course. As the research section of this chapter highlighted, many researchers have contributed important, novel work that broadens the scope of *Miranda* research. As some of the case law makes clear, there is definite need for this work—for example, further examination of the actual mechanics and practices of *Miranda* administration is clearly needed. The variation in how the warnings are administered, both procedurally and substantively, has led to the warnings effectively being just one more tool in officers' armament of interrogation strategies rather than a meaningful equalizer and protection for suspects. Courts often treat the mere fact of *Miranda* administration by officers as a proxy for finding that suspects knowingly, intelligently, and voluntarily waive the rights. Thus, more research is needed on how officers administer the rights and the impact of those practices on understanding, as well as the human factors that are at play when a person is faced with an authority figure using multiple strategies to induce compliance. As Smalarz, Scherr, and Kassin (2016) insightfully noted, for example, research is needed to examine "whether the act of eliciting a waiver by signature implies a contractual and irrevocable forfeiture of rights" (p. 458).

Some final upshots concern context: the context of interrogations and the context of today's criminal justice system. As the case law review section, and particularly the Supreme Court case law review section, highlights, courts are keen to restrain the application of *Miranda* by strictly defining what "in custody" means. The Court defined, over 20 years ago, what it meant to be in custody by applying a "reasonable person" standard, yet there is virtually no research that examines when the average person, let alone someone from a more vulnerable population, might feel at liberty to terminate an interrogation and leave. The current state of case law and police interrogation strategies leaves plenty of room for the artful creation of "noncustodial" interviews because it is presumed that most people feel at liberty to stop police questioning and leave. An escalating set of requests from police can lead to someone agreeing to go to the police station, and officers can defuse suggestions of custody with a statement that the person is free to go or that the interrogation room door is unlocked. Yet we do not actually know how citizens perceive these or other interactions with officers. The second context-related implication concerns taking into account the differences between the criminal justice system of the 1960s and now; because it is broader and less tied to the case law reviewed here, we discuss it in the next section.

Future Directions

Despite changes in the landscape of *Miranda* since the Supreme Court's decision decades ago, there are still many issues ripe for empirical examination and policy work. Future work in this area is reviewed below, organized by three broad domains: suspects, law enforcement, and the legal system.

Suspects

Perhaps one of the most consistent and important findings from the knowing and intelligent line of research is the vulnerability of certain populations to offering *un*knowing and *un*intelligent *Miranda* waivers. Youths and individuals with intellectual disabilities, in particular, struggle to understand language used to convey the warnings as well as the conceptual principles at stake (e.g., Fulero & Everington, 1995; Goldstein et al., 2003; Grisso, 1981; O'Connell et al., 2005). Research (e.g., Cooper & Zapf, 2008; Viljoen et al., 2002) suggests that individuals with certain mental health symptoms have difficulty fully comprehending the *Miranda* rights as well, though more research is needed on how such symptoms influence understanding and appreciation of legal rights.

Extant research underscores the need for enhanced protections of vulnerable populations during the *Miranda* warning and waiver process. It also indicates that merely having a parent or guardian present for interrogations of juveniles is insufficient (Grisso & Ring, 1979; Viljoen et al., 2005). Thus, future research and policy work should explore other options. Because there are questions about the developmental capacities of youth to sufficiently grasp the concepts conveyed in the *Miranda* warnings, regardless of whether they are clearly conveyed, researchers and advocates might explore possibilities such as a nonwaivable right to attorney or requiring consultation with counsel before effectuating a waiver (particularly for children and younger adolescents). Additionally, research could potentially assist law enforcement in identifying suspects vulnerable to poor *Miranda* comprehension through the development of brief screening instruments (of course, determining what to do following a problematic score on such an instrument would require additional policy work and consensus-building between advocates and law enforcement).

Developments from recent case law also raise concerns about members of the general population that are not part of these vulnerable groups. As a broad point, it would be interesting to explore people's beliefs, more generally, about exercising constitutional rights in the face of government authority (for a review of people's beliefs in the context of Fourth Amendment searches, see the chapter by Brank and Groscup in this volume). And, as discussed above, a narrower line of inquiry more directly related to case law involves perspectives on custodial interrogation. Research could then inform how a "reasonable person" appraises his or her circumstances when being questioned by the police. Finally, moving forward, research should assess individuals' understanding of implicit waivers and explicit invocations as set forth in *Berghuis v. Thompkins* (2010).

Law Enforcement

The Supreme Court essentially delegated to local law enforcement the task of determining *when* and *how* to convey the *Miranda* rights to suspects. Although the Court prescribed "custody" as a threshold condition for the *Miranda* warnings and later provided a working definition of this term, in all practicality law enforcement officers are the ones to decide, in the moment, whether a suspect is in custody and, therefore, whether to administer the warnings. This has led to a practice of officers conducting "noncustodial" interviews (as in *J.D.B. v. North Carolina*, 2011) under conditions in which (arguably) a reasonable person would *not* feel at liberty to terminate the interrogation (Leo, 2001). This phenomenon speaks to a need for research on how police officers operationally define custody in the course of their work and the accuracy of their perceptions of relevant factors (e.g., a youth's age).

Regarding how *Miranda* rights are conveyed, the Court's laissez-faire attitude has produced considerable variability in terms of the language used and how the warnings are administered. Some research has explored how wording and delivery affect comprehension, but there are a number of avenues still worthy of exploration. Although previous studies revealed nonsignificant effects of *Miranda* wording on comprehension, much more research is needed. In particular, future research might explore how deliberate changes in wording—reflected in objective measures of readability *and* listenability—affect comprehension in different populations. Clinicians performing evaluations of *Miranda* waivers should also be attuned to meaningful discrepancies between the suspect's reading comprehension level and the reading level of the warnings he or she was administered. Other variations in mode of administration could be explored as well. For instance, researchers might investigate whether giving the suspect time to read the warnings to themselves, followed by oral administration, produces meaningful improvements in comprehension.

Research, like actual interrogations, should also extend beyond a fixed set of warnings administered by a law enforcement officer. Given the fact patterns in *United States v. Gray* (2015) and *Doody v. Ryan* (2011), discussed above, police may (inadvertently or not) mislead suspects about the meaning and function of their rights. These cases point to a need for both evaluation of how well law enforcement officers understand the *Miranda* rights, as well as training for officers so that they can answer suspects' questions accurately. Evaluating, more broadly, officers' perspectives of the *Miranda* warnings could also reveal biases about the rights of suspects in criminal cases that could potentially be rectified with training and mentorship. Finally, given the holding in *Garner v. Mitchell* (2009), researchers could evaluate the accuracy of officers' conclusions about suspects' *Miranda* comprehension against other metrics, such as existing *Miranda* assessment tools.

The Legal System

Finally, it is worth considering whether the vast difference between today's criminal justice system and the criminal justice system in place at the time of the *Miranda* opinion calls for a new facet of *Miranda* research. The justice system context at the time of the *Miranda* opinion was one defined by the Warren Court's expansion of constitutional rights for criminal defendants, but also was one in trials were more common than they are today (see, e.g., Galanter, 2004; Bureau of Justice Statistics, 2013). When a defendant goes to trial, there is the opportunity to challenge statements and, perhaps, have them suppressed on invalid *Miranda* waiver grounds during a pretrial hearing—or at least to challenge the reliability of the statements if they are determined admissible. With so many cases resolved through plea bargaining in the current context, there are new areas for research. Research on plea bargaining has expanded rapidly in recent years (e.g., Daftary-Kapur & Zottoli, 2014; Kutateladze, Andiloro, & Johnson, 2016; Redlich, Bushway, & Norris, 2016), and innocence work has demonstrated that both false confessions and plea bargaining have roles in some convictions that are later overturned. Without pretrial hearings or a trial, it is unclear how inculpatory statements, that might otherwise have been found inadmissible because of an invalid waiver, are used. Are inculpatory statements leveraged by prosecutors regardless of their likely admissibility? If so, how often? Are plea bargains pushed in some cases because of concerns that statements might not be admissible at trial but seem damning enough to use as leverage during plea bargaining? As with other questions about *Miranda* waivers and the plea bargaining process, these concerns and others remain in shadow but should be brought into the light through research.

Conclusions

The Supreme Court's decision in *Miranda v. Arizona* (1966) entitled suspects in custodial interrogation to be informed of their rights to silence and counsel, an eponymous notification now known as the *Miranda* warnings. In many ways, the decision reflected the Court's appreciation of the psychologically coercive nature of police interrogation, which it viewed as problematic enough to warrant an effort to level the playing field between suspects and law enforcement. Not long after *Miranda* was decided, the requirement that waivers of *Miranda* rights be executed in a knowing, intelligent, and voluntary manner served as a call for psychological research about how well individuals—particularly individuals from vulnerable populations—understand and appreciate their rights during police interrogations. Early research efforts paved the way for a rich body of literature on individual factors (e.g., intelligence, age) and situational factors (e.g., *Miranda* wording and delivery, stress) that influence *Miranda* comprehension.

Over time, the courts have interpreted the *Miranda* decision in an increasingly narrow manner and underscored the obligation that individuals have to unambiguously assert their rights during interactions with police. The shift in jurisprudence creates an obligation for researchers to adjust lines of inquiry accordingly. Just as courts have tended to assume widespread knowledge of the *Miranda* warnings due to the passage of time and their presence in popular culture, researchers have arguably become somewhat complacent in assuming that *Miranda* jurisprudence is settled. Recent federal and state case law demonstrates the dynamic nature of *Miranda*, however, and researchers and policymakers should recognize the opportunity and obligation to inform jurisprudence with relevant empirically based material. In certain respects, researchers have responded to this call by developing studies to specifically address recent Supreme Court holdings (e.g., Gillard et al., 2014). In other respects, there is much work left to be done, particularly with respect to law enforcement (e.g., comprehension and delivery of *Miranda* rights) and the criminal justice system (e.g., given the increase in plea bargaining since the *Miranda* decision).

The *Miranda* Court set out to address the psychological coercion evident in police interrogation practices, and in doing so clearly noted that the issue was not about favoring suspects but about striking a balance between individuals' Fifth Amendment rights and society's interests in identifying and prosecuting offenders. The *Miranda* Court's admonition that "the accused must be adequately and effectively apprised of his rights and the exercise of those rights must be fully honored" (p. 467) is a modestly phrased one, which has proved to have hidden depths when put into practice. Consequently, there is a continuing need to unpack that principle empirically as law enforcement practices and court jurisprudence develop.

References

Abramovitch, R., Peterson-Badali, M., & Rohan, M. (1995). Young people's understanding and assertion of their rights to silence and legal counsel. *Canadian Journal of Criminology, 37*, 1–18.
Alvarez v. Gomez, 185 F. 3d 995 (1999).
Appelbaum, P. S., & Grisso, T. (1988). Assessing patients' capacities to consent to treatment. *New England Journal of Medicine, 319*, 1635–1638. https://doi.org/10.1056/NEJM198812223192504
Arkansas v. Bell, 948 S.W.2d 557 (Ark. 1997).
Berghuis v. Thompkins, 560 U.S. 370 (2010).
Berkemer v. McCarty, 468 U.S. 420 (1984).
Brady v. United States, 397 U.S. 742 (1970).
Brown v. Mississippi, 297 U.S. 278 (1936).
Bureau of Justice Statistics. (2013). Felony defendants in large urban counties, 2009. Retrieved from http://www.bjs.gov/content/pub/pdf/fdluc09.pdf.
California v. Prysock, 453 U.S. 355 (1981).
Cauffman, E., & Steinberg, L. (2000). (Im)maturity of judgment in adolescence: Why adolescents may be less culpable than adults. *Behavioral Sciences and the Law, 18*, 741–760. https://doi.org/10.1002/bsl.416
Clay v. Arkansas, 883 S.W.2d 822 (Ark. 1994).
Clymer, S. D. (2002). Are police free to disregard *Miranda*? *Yale Law Journal, 112*, 449–552. https://doi.org/10.2307/1562248
Colorado v. Al Yousif, 49 P.3d 1165 (Colo. 2002).
Colorado v. Connelly, 479 U.S. 157 (1986).
Colorado v. Spring, 479 U.S. 564 (1987).
Collins v. Gaetz, 612 F.3d 574 (7th Cir. 2010).
Colwell, L. H., Cruise, K. R., Guy, L. S., McCoy, W. K., Fernandez, K., & Ross, H. H. (2005). The influence of psychosocial maturity on male juvenile offenders' comprehension and understanding of the *Miranda* warning. *Journal of the American Academy of Psychiatry and the Law, 33*, 444–454.
Cooper, V. G., & Zapf, P. A. (2008). Psychiatric patients' comprehension of *Miranda* rights. *Law and Human Behavior, 32*, 390–405. https://doi.org/10.1007/s10979-007-9099-3
Covington, M. V., & Omelich, C. L. (1987). "I knew it cold before the exam": A test of the anxiety-blockage hypothesis. *Journal of Educational Psychology, 79*, 393–400. https://doi.org/10.1037/0022-0663.79.4.393
Coyote v. United States, 380 F.2d 305 (10th Cir. 1967).
Cruise, K. R., Pitchal, E. S., & Weiss, R. (2008, March). Parental involvement in the interrogation of juveniles: A review of state statutes and implications for research and practice. Paper presented at the annual conference of the American Psychology-law Society, Jacksonville, FL.
Daftary-Kapur, T., & Zottoli, T. M. (2014). A first look at the plea deal experiences of juveniles in adult court. *International Journal of Forensic Mental Health, 13*, 323–336. https://doi.org/10.1080/14999013.2014.960983
Davis v. United States, 512 U.S. 452 (1994).
Dickerson v. United States, 530 U.S. 428 (2000).
Doody v. Ryan, 649 F.3d 986 (2011).
Duckworth v. Eagan, 492 U.S. 195 (1989).
Eastwood, J., & Snook, B. (2010). Comprehending Canadian police cautions: Are the rights to silence and legal counsel understandable? *Behavioral Sciences and the Law, 28*, 366–377. https://doi.org/10.1002/bsl.898
Escobedo v. Illinois, 378 U.S. 478 (1964).
Fare v. Michael C., 442 U.S. 707 (1979).

Ferguson, A. B., & Douglas, A. C. (1970). A study of juvenile waiver of rights. *Juvenile Court Judges Journal, 21*, 12–22.

Florida v. Powell, 599 U.S. 50 (2010).

Fulero, S. M., & Everington, C. (1995). Assessing competency to waive *Miranda* rights in defendants with mental retardation. *Law and Human Behavior, 19*, 533–543. https://doi.org/10.1007/BF01499342

Fromme, K., Katz, E., & D'Amico, E. (1997). Effects of alcohol intoxication on the perceived consequences of risk taking. *Experimental and Clinical Psychopharmacology, 5*, 14–23. https://doi.org/10.1037/1064-1297.5.1.14

Frumkin, I. B., & Garcia, A. (2003). Psychological evaluations and the competency to waive *Miranda* rights. *Champions, 9*, 12–23.

Galanter, M. (2004). The vanishing trial: An empirical examination of trials and related matters in federal and state courts. *Journal of Empirical Legal Studies, 1*, 459–570. https://doi.org/10.1111/j.1740-1461.2004.00014.x

Garner v. Mitchell, 557 F.3d 257 (6th Cir. 2009).

Gideon v. Wainwright, 372 U.S. 335 (1963).

Gillard, N. D., Rogers, R., Kelsy, K. R., & Robinson, E. V. (2014). An investigation of implied Miranda waivers and Powell wording in a mock-crime study. *Law and Human Behavior, 38*, 501–508. https://doi.org/10.1037/lhb0000093

Gogtay, N., Giedd, J. N., Lusk, L., Hayashi, K. M., Greenstein, D., Vaituzis, A. C., ... Thompson, P. M. (2004). Dynamic mapping of human cortical development during childhood through early adulthood. *Proceedings of the National Academy of Sciences of the United States of America, 101*, 8174-8179. https://doi.org/10.1073/pnas.0402680101

Goldstein, A. M., & Goldstein, N. E. S. (2010). *Evaluating capacity to waive Miranda rights*. New York: Oxford University Press.

Goldstein, N. E. S., Condie, L. O., Kalbeitzer, R., Osman, D., & Geier, J. L. (2003). Juvenile offenders' *Miranda* rights comprehension and self-reported likelihood of offering false confessions. *Assessment, 10*, 359–369. https://doi.org/10.1177/1073191103259535

Goldstein, N. E. S., Zelle, H., & Grisso, T. (2014). *The Miranda rights comprehension instruments manual*. Sarasota, FL: Professional Resources Press.

Grisso, T. (1981). *Juveniles' waiver of rights: Legal and psychological competence*. New York: Plenum Press. https://doi.org/10.1007/978-1-4684-3815-4

Grisso, T. (1997). The competence of adolescents as trial defendants. *Psychology, Public Policy, and Law, 3*, 3–32. https://doi.org/10.1037//1076-8971.3.1.3

Grisso, T. (1998). *Instruments for assessing understanding and appreciation of Miranda rights*. Sarasota, FL: Professional Resource Press.

Grisso, T. (2003). *Evaluating competencies: Forensic assessments and instruments* (2nd ed.). New York: Kluwer Academic/Plenum Publishers.

Grisso, T., & Pomicter, C. (1977). Interrogation of juveniles: An empirical study of procedures, safeguards, and rights waivers. *Law and Human Behavior, 1*, 321–342. https://doi.org/10.1007/BF01048593

Grisso, T., & Ring, M. (1979). Parents' attitudes toward juveniles' rights in interrogation. *Criminal Justice and Behavior, 6*, 211–223.

Grisso, T., Steinberg, L., Woolard, J., Cauffman, E., Scott, E., Graham, S., ... Schwartz, R. (2003). Juveniles' competence to stand trial: A comparison of adolescents' and adults' capacities as trial defendants. *Law and Human Behavior, 27*, 333–363. https://doi.org/10.1023/A:1024065015717

Guyll, M., Madon, S., Yang, Y., Lannin, D. G., Scherr, K., & Greathouse, S. (2013). Innocence and resisting confession during interrogation: Effects on physiologic activity. *Law and Human Behavior, 37*, 366–375. https://doi.org/10.1037/lhb0000044

Harris v. New York, 401 U.S. 222 (1971).

Haynes v. Washington, 373 U.S. 503 (1963).

Howes v. Fields, 132 S. Ct. 1181 (2012).

Huang, D. T. (2001). Less unequal footing: State courts' per se rules for juvenile waivers during interrogations and the case for their implementation. *Cornell Law Review, 86*, 437–482.
Illinois v. Bernasco, 562 N.E.2d 958 (Ill. 1990).
Illinois v. Young, 850 N.E.2d 284 (Ill.App. 1 Dist. 2006).
In re Dante W., 890 N.E.2d 1030 (Ill.App. 1 Dist. 2008).
In re Gault, 387 U.S. 1 (1967).
In re Patrick W., 84 Cal.App.3d 520 (Cal. App. 1978).
Inbau, F. E., & Reid, J. E. (1962). *Criminal interrogation and confession*. Baltimore, MD: Williams & Wilkins.
J.D.B. v. North Carolina, 131 S. Ct. 2394 (2011).
Kambam, P., & Thompson, C. (2009). The development of decision-making capacities in children and adolescents: Psychological and neurological perspectives and their implications for juvenile defendants. *Behavioral Sciences and the Law, 27*, 173–190. https://doi.org/10.1002/bsl.859
Kansas v. Ventris, 556 U.S. 586 (2009).
Kamisar, Y. (2005). How earl Warren's twenty-two years in law enforcement affected his work as chief justice. *Ohio State Journal of Criminal Law, 3*, 11–32.
Kassin, S. M. (2005). On the psychology of confessions: Does innocence put innocents at risk? *American Psychologist, 60*, 215–228. https://doi.org/10.1037/0003-066X.60.3.215
Kassin, S. M., Drizin, S. A., Grisso, T., Gudjonsson, G. H., Leo, R. A., & Redlich, A. D. (2010). Police-induced confessions: Risk factors and recommendations. *Law and Human Behavior, 34*, 3–38. https://doi.org/10.1007/S10979-009-9188
Kassin, S. M., Leo, R. A., Meissner, C. A., Richman, K. D., Colwell, L. H., Leach, A. M., & La Fon, D. (2007). Police interviewing and interrogation: A self-report survey of police practices and beliefs. *Law and Human Behavior, 31*, 381–400. https://doi.org/10.1007/s10979-006-9073-5
Kassin, S. M., & Neumann, K. (1997). On the power of confession evidence: An experimental test of the fundamental difference hypothesis. *Law and Human Behavior, 21*, 469–484. https://doi.org/10.1023/A:1024871622490
Kassin, S. M., & Norwick, R. J. (2004). Why people waive their *Miranda* rights: The power of innocence. *Law and Human Behavior, 28*, 211–221. https://doi.org/10.1023/B:LAHU.0000022323.74584.f5
Kelley, S. L. (2014). *Addressing relative criteria for Miranda waivers: A comparison of juvenile justice youths' and adult offenders' understanding and appreciation of the rights to silence and legal counsel during police interrogations* (Doctoral dissertation). Retrieved from https://idea.library.drexel.edu/
King, K. J. (2006). Waiving childhood goodbye: How juvenile courts fail to protect children from unknowing, unintelligent, and involuntary waivers of *Miranda* rights. *Wisconsin Law Review, 2006*, 431–477.
Kutateladze, B. L., Andiloro, N. R., & Johnson, B. D. (2016). Opening Pandora's box: How does defendant race influence plea bargaining? *Justice Quarterly, 33*, 398–426. https://doi.org/10.1080/07418825.2014.915340
Leo, R. A. (1996). Inside the interrogation room. *Journal of Criminal Law and Criminology, 86*, 266–276.
Leo, R. A. (2001). Questioning the relevance of *Miranda* in the twenty-first century. *Michigan Law Review, 99*, 1000–1029.
Leo, R. A., & White, W. S. (1999). Adapting to *Miranda*: Modern interrogators' strategies for dealing with the obstacles posed by *Miranda*. *Minnesota Law Review, 84*, 397–472.
Mapp v. Ohio, 367 U.S. 643 (1961).
Melton, G. B. (1980). Children's concepts of their rights. *Journal of Clinical Child Psychology, 9*, 186–190. https://doi.org/10.1080/15374418009532985
Melton, G. B. (1983). Toward personhood for adolescents- autonomy and privacy as values in public-policy. *American Psychologist, 38*, 99–103. https://doi.org/10.1037/0003-066X.38.1.99

Messenheimer, S., Riggs Romaine, C. L., Wolbransky, M., Zelle, H., Serico, J. M., Wrazien, L., & Goldstein, N. E. S. (2009). Readability and comprehension: A comparison of the two versions of the *Miranda* rights assessment instruments. Presented at the annual conference of the *American Psychology-Law Society*, San Antonio, TX.
Meyer, J., Reppucci, N. D., & Owen, J. (2006, March). Criminal interrogation with young suspects: perspectives and practices of law enforcement. In J.L. Woolard (chair), Police interrogation of juvenile suspects. Paper presented at the annual conference of the American Psychology-Law Society, St. Petersburg, Florida.
Michigan v. Cheatham, 551 N.W.2d 355 (Mich. 1996).
Michigan v. Daoud, 614 N.W.2d 152 (Mich. 2000).
Michigan v. Jackson, 475 U.S. 625 (1986).
Miranda v. Arizona, 384 U.S. 436 (1966).
Montejo v. Louisiana, 556 U.S. 778 (2009).
Moran v. Burbine, 465 U.S. 412 (1986).
New Hampshire v. Bushey, 453 A.2d 1265 (N.H. 1982).
New York v. Quarles, 467 U.S. 649 (1984).
North Carolina v. Butler, 441 U.S. 369 (1979).
Oberlander, L. B., & Goldstein, N. E. (2001). A review and update on the practice of evaluating *Miranda* comprehension. *Behavioral Sciences and the Law, 19*, 453–471. https://doi.org/10.1002/bsl.453
Oberlander, L. B., Goldstein, N. E., & Goldstein, A. M. (2003). Competence to confess. In I. B. Weiner, D. K. Freedheim, & A. M. Goldstein (Eds.), *Handbook of psychology: Forensic psychology* (pp. 335–357). Hoboken, NJ: John Wiley & Sons, Inc..
O'Connell, M. J., Garmoe, W., & Goldstein, N. E. (2005). *Miranda* comprehension in adults with mental retardation and the effects of feedback style on suggestibility. *Law and Human Behavior, 29*, 359–369. https://doi.org/10.1007/s10979-005-2965-y
Olubadewo, O. (2009). The relationship between mental health symptoms and comprehension of Miranda rights in male juvenile offenders. *Dissertation Abstracts International, 69*, 5788.
O'Neill, T. P. (2010). Illinois courts and the law of Miranda waivers: A policy worth preserving. *Northern Illinois University Law Review, 30*, 429–444.
Oregon v. Mathiason, 429 U.S. 492 (1977).
Pearse, J., Gudjonsson, G. H., Clare, I. C. H., & Rutter, S. (1998). Police interviewing and psychological vulnerabilities: Predicting the likelihood of a confession. *Journal of Community and Applied Social Psychology, 8*, 1–21. https://doi.org/10.1002/(SICI)1099-1298(199801/02)8:13.0.CO;2-D
Pennsylvania v. DeJesus, 787 A.2d 394 (Pa. 2001).
Primus, E. B. (2015). The future of confession law: Toward rules for the voluntariness test. *Michigan Law Review, 114*, 1–56.
Quadrel, M. J., Fischhoff, B., & Davis, W. (1993). Adolescent (in)vulnerability. *American Psychologist, 48*, 102–116. https://doi.org/10.1037/0003-066X.48.2.102
Redlich, A. D., Bushway, S. D., & Norris, R. J. (2016). Plea decision-making by attorneys and judges. *Journal of Experimental Criminology, 12*, 537–561. https://doi.org/10.1007/s11292-016-9264-0
Rhode Island v. Innis, 466 U.S. 291 (1980).
Rogers, R., Fiduccia, C. E., Drogin, E. Y., Steadham, J. A., Clark, J. W., & Cramer, R. J. (2013a). General knowledge and misknowledge of *Miranda* rights: Are effective *Miranda* advisements still necessary? (2013). *Psychology, Public Policy, and Law, 19*, 432–442. https://doi.org/10.1037/a0033964
Rogers, R., Fiduccia, C. E., Robinson, E. V., Steadham, J. A., & Drogin, E. Y. (2013b). Investigating the effects of repeated *Miranda* warnings: Do they perform a curative function on common Miranda misconceptions? *Behavioral Sciences and the Law, 31*, 397–410. https://doi.org/10.1002/bsl.2071

Rogers, R., Gillard, N. D., Wooley, C. N., & Fiduccia, C. E. (2010a). Decrements in Miranda abilities: An investigation of situational effects via a mock-crime paradigm. *Law and Human Behavior, 38*, 501–508. https://doi.org/10.1037/lhb0000093
Rogers, R., Harrison, K. S., Hazelwood, L. L., & Sewell, K. W. (2007a). Knowing and intelligent: A study of *Miranda* warnings in mentally disordered defendants. *Law and Human Behavior, 31*, 401–418. https://doi.org/10.1007/s10979-006-9070-8
Rogers, R., Harrison, K. S., Shuman, D. W., Sewell, K. W., & Hazelwood, L. L. (2007b). An analysis of Miranda warnings and waivers: Comprehension and coverage. *Law and Human Behavior, 31*, 177–192. https://doi.org/10.1007/s10979-006-9054-8
Rogers, R., Hazelwood, L. L., Sewell, K. W., Harrison, K. S., & Shuman, D. W. (2008a). The language of Miranda warnings in American jurisdictions: A replication and vocabulary analysis. *Law and Human Behavior, 32*, 124–136. https://doi.org/10.1007/s10979-007-9091-y
Rogers, R., Hazelwood, L. L., Sewell, K. W., Shuman, D. W., & Blackwood, H. L. (2008b). The comprehensibility and content of juvenile Miranda warnings. *Psychology, Public Policy, and Law, 14*(1), 63–87. https://doi.org/10.1037/a0013102
Rogers, R., Rogstad, J. E., Gillard, N. D., Drogin, E. Y., Blackwood, H. L., & Shuman, D. W. (2010b). "Everyone knows their Miranda rights": Implicit assumptions and countervailing evidence. *Psychology, Public Policy, and Law, 16*, 300–318. https://doi.org/10.1037/a0019316
Rogers, R., Rogstad, J. E., Steadham, J. A., & Drogin, E. Y. (2011). In plain English: Avoiding recognized problems with Miranda miscomprehension. *Psychology, Public Policy, and Law, 17*, 264–285. https://doi.org/10.1037/a0022508
Rogers, R., Sewell, K. W., Drogin, E. Y., & Fiduccia, C. E. (2012). *Standardized assessment of Miranda abilities*. Lutz, FL: Psychological Assessment Resources.
Rogers, R., Steadham, J. A., Fiduccia, C. E., Drogin, E. Y., & Robinson, E. V. (2014). Mired in *Miranda* misconceptions: A study of legally involved juveniles at different levels of psychosocial maturity. *Behavioral Sciences and the Law, 32*, 104–120. https://doi.org/10.1002/bsl.2099
Rost, G. C., & McGregor, K. K. (2012). *Miranda* rights comprehension in young adults with specific language impairment. *American Journal of Speech-Language Pathology, 21*, 101–108. https://doi.org/10.1044/1058-0360(2011/10-0094)
Ruck, M. D., Keating, D. P., Abramovitch, R., & Koegl, C. J. (1998). Adolescents' and childrens' knowledge about rights: Some evidence for how young people view rights in their own lives. *Journal of Adolescence, 21*, 275–289. https://doi.org/10.1006/jado.1998.0153
Salinas v. Texas, 133 S. Ct. 2174 (2013).
Scherr, K. C., Alberts, K. M., Franks, A. S., & Hawkins, I. (2016). Overcoming innocents' naivete: Pre-interrogation decision-making among innocent suspects. *Behavioral Sciences and the Law, 34*, 564–579. https://doi.org/10.1002/bsl.2247
Scherr, K. C., & Franks, A. S. (2015). The world is not fair: An examination of innocent and guilty suspect' waiver decisions. *Law and Human Behavior, 39*, 142–151. https://doi.org/10.1037/lhb0000121
Scherr, K. C., & Madon, S. (2012). You have the right to understand: The deleterious effect of stress on suspects' ability to comprehend "Miranda". *Law and Human Behavior, 36*, 275–282. https://doi.org/10.1037/h0093972
Scherr, K. C., & Madon, S. (2013). "Go ahead and sign": An experimental manipulation of Miranda waivers and comprehension. *Law and Human Behavior, 37*, 208–218. https://doi.org/10.1037/lhb0000026
Sessoms v. Grounds, 776 F. 3d 615 (2014).
Smalarz, L., Scherr, K. C., & Kassin, S. M. (2016). *Miranda* at 50: A psychological analysis. *Current Directions in Psychological Science, 25*, 455–460. https://doi.org/10.1177/0963721416665097
Snook, B., Eastwood, J., & MacDonald, S. (2010). A descriptive analysis of how Canadian police officers administer the right-to-silence and right-to-legal-counsel cautions. *Canadian Journal of Criminology and Criminal Justice, 52*, 545–560. https://doi.org/10.1353/ccj.2010.0006
Spano v. New York, 360 U.S. 315 (1959).
State v. Mayer, 362 P.3d 745 (Wash. 2015).

Steinberg, L. (2008). A social neuroscience perspective on adolescent risk-taking. *Developmental Review, 28*, 78–106. https://doi.org/10.1016/j.dr.2007.08.002

Tanford, S., & Cox, M. (1988). The effects of impeachment evidence and limiting instructions on individual and group decision-making. *Law and Human Behavior, 12*, 477–497. https://doi.org/10.1007/BF01044629

Tennessee v. Stephenson, 878 S.W.2d 530 (Tenn. 1994).

Thompson v. Keohane, 516 U.S. 99 (1995).

Todd, J. P. (2013). Have United States Supreme Court decisions curtailed the Miranda rule too much or is the balance just right? *Phoenix Law Review, 7*, 371–394.

United States v. Gray, 2015 WL 8479064 (D. Ariz. Dec. 10, 2015).

United States v. Preston, 751 F.3d 1008 (9th Cir. 2015).

Viljoen, J. L., Klaver, J., & Roesch, R. (2005). Legal decisions of preadolescent and adolescent defendants: Predictors of confessions, pleas, communication with attorneys, and appeals. *Law and Human Behavior, 29*, 253–277. doi: doi.org/10.1007/s10979-005-3613-2.

Viljoen, J. L., & Roesch, R. (2005). Competence to waive interrogation rights and adjudicative competence in adolescent defendants: Cognitive development, attorney contact, and psychological symptoms. *Law and Human Behavior, 29*, 723–742. https://doi.org/10.1007/s10979-005-7978-y

Viljoen, J. L., Roesch, R., & Zapf, P. A. (2002). An examination of the relationship between competency to stand trial, competency to waive interrogation rights, and psychopathology. *Law and Human Behavior, 26*, 481–506. https://doi.org/10.1023/A:1020299804821

West v. United States, 399 F.2d 467 (5th Cir. 1968).

Woolard, J. L., Cleary, H. M. D., Harvell, S. A. S., & Chen, R. (2008). Examining adolescents' and their parents' conceptual and practical knowledge of police interrogation: A family dyad approach. *Journal of Youth and Adolescence, 37*, 685–698. https://doi.org/10.1007/s10964-008-9288-5

Zelle, H. (2012). *Judges' treatment of the knowing and intelligent requirements for Miranda waivers* (Doctoral dissertation). Retrieved from https://idea.library.drexel.edu/

Zelle, H., Goldstein, N. E. S., Riggs Romaine, C. L., Serico, J. M., Kemp, K., & Taormina, S. (2008, March). *Factor structure of the Miranda rights comprehension instruments-II*. Part of a symposium: The *Miranda Rights Comprehension Instruments-II*. Presented at the annual conference of the *American Psychology-Law Society*, Jacksonville, FL.

Zelle, H., Riggs Romaine, C. L., & Goldstein, N. E. S. (2015). Juvenile's *Miranda* comprehension: Understanding, appreciation, and totality of circumstances factors. *Law and Human Behavior, 39*, 281–293. https://doi.org/10.1037/lhb0000116

Psychology and the Fourth Amendment

Eve M. Brank and Jennifer L. Groscup

Psychology and the Fourth Amendment

Although a great deal of law-psychology research and attention is focused on criminal law (Wylie, Hazen, Hoeter, Haby, & Brank, 2018), very little attention has focused on the Fourth Amendment to the U.S. Constitution. This neglect is surprising given the Amendment's colorful legal history, relevance to law enforcement, and clear behavioral implications. The Fourth Amendment to the U.S. Constitution provides that people are to be "secure in their persons, houses, papers, and effects, against unreasonable searches and seizures." It further requires that warrants to perform such searches and seizures are based on probable cause with specific descriptions of what will be searched or seized.

Whereas the rest of the Bill of Rights provides absolute language guaranteeing, *inter alia*, speedy trials, free speech, and the right to counsel, the Fourth Amendment distinctively includes the word "unreasonable," thereby indicating that some searches and seizures may be *reasonable* (Loewy, 1983). At its core, the Fourth Amendment is precisely what law-psychology is about—behavioral assumptions in the law and subjective determinations. Add to that the Supreme Court's attention to the Fourth Amendment, especially considering how many cases focus on psychological assumptions and do not have majority opinions (Blumenthal, Adya, & Mogle, 2009; Bradley, 1985), and the area seems begging for empirical attention from law-psychology scholars.

E. M. Brank (✉)
Department of Psychology, University of Nebraska-Lincoln, Lincoln, NE, USA
e-mail: ebrank2@unl.edu

J. L. Groscup
Department of Psychology, Scripps College, Claremont, CA, USA
e-mail: jgroscup@scrippscollege.edu

M. K. Miller, B. H. Bornstein (eds.), *Advances in Psychology and Law*,
Advances in Psychology and Law 3,
https://doi.org/10.1007/978-3-319-75859-6_4

In the current chapter, we provide both the legal and psychological history. We focus on the current status of the Fourth Amendment and the empirical research that has addressed Fourth Amendment issues. In doing so, we provide a foundation for future research in this area.

Fourth Amendment Background

Historically, the Fourth Amendment spoke to what was essential to the American Revolution. Indeed, many historians point to the colonists' protests against writs of assistance as the beginning of the revolutionary movement (Sklansky, 2000). Under English common law, any person who had a "reasonable suspicion" of another's felonious activity could arrest and take that person into custody even if doing so required breaking into the offender's home to retrieve him or her (Barrett, 1960). No such sweeping permission existed for searches. English common law staunchly protected property rights with only robbery victims permitted to apply for a warrant. That warrant then sanctioned a law officer to go with the victim and search for the stolen property (Barrett, 1960).

In the mid-1700s, the colonists were tightly controlled by the British crown yet these scrappy new-world dwellers were creative in their efforts to circumvent what many viewed as unreasonable taxation and restrictions on trade. Most of their creative efforts involved smuggling and therefore hiding contraband within their homes and businesses. Enter writs of assistance – a form of warrant that required no specific suspicion or declared location of the search. With these easily granted writs, British officials could search shops and homes with little-to-no legal hurdles. In 1761, James Otis legally challenged the writs of assistance and although he lost the legal battle, he drew more attention to and anger toward the injustice of such general warrants (Davies, 1999). In fact, by the mid-1770s as the fires of independence were fanning, few British officials were dauntless enough to use the writs of assistance (Taslitz, 2006).

Within the next few years, the U.S. was no longer subject to the British crown. Once U.S. independence was won and the Constitution in place, memories of those writs of assistance and other British injustices led to concerns about the Constitution's neglect of personal protections. Indeed, the fact that there was no protection against general warrants was one of the major apprehensions with the Constitution as written. James Madison, a member of the U.S. House of Representatives, drafted a list of amendments for the First Congress to approve and the states to ratify. A subset of ten of these original amendments is now what we refer to as the Bill of Rights with the Fourth Amendment addressing the colonists' fears of arbitrary searches.

During the next century, law enforcement violations of the Fourth Amendment, if addressed at all, were done by categorizing the violation as a false imprisonment or trespass rather than focusing on the Fourth Amendment directly (Barrett, 1960). That ended in the early 1900s with the Supreme Court in *Weeks v. United States* (1914) excluding evidence illegally obtained and thereby removing law enforcements' incentive to disregard the Fourth Amendment. The Exclusionary Rule, as it is now known, was born because police and other government officials entered Fremont Weeks' Kansas City home without a search warrant and took papers that implicated Weeks' mailing of lottery tickets – a federal offense. Weeks' attorney argued that the Fourth Amendment was only lip service and not true protection unless the Court excluded illegally obtained evidence. In a unanimous decision, the Court agreed and held that the illegally gained papers must be excluded as evidence. A few years later in *Silverthorne Lumber Co. v. United* States (1920) the Court extended the Exclusionary Rule to evidence that was obtained because of illegally acquired information, which was later referred to as "fruit of the poisonous tree" (*Nardone v. United States,* 1939, p. 341). The rule was further extended and applied not only to federal prosecutions but also to state courts by *Mapp v. Ohio* (1961).

The goal of the Exclusionary Rule is to disincentivize government officials from ignoring the law to search and seize evidence that they could not lawfully obtain. Although not based on empirical evidence or empirically tested, the rule is meant to "prevent, not to repair" (*Elkins v. United States,* 1960, p. 217). A modern era of Fourth Amendment jurisprudence began with *Weeks* in the early part of the twentieth century, which led scholars to question and strongly criticize the quality and consistency of decisions courts were making about Fourth Amendment issues. For example, Dworkin (1973) called Fourth Amendment cases "a mess!" (p. 329). A decade later, Bradley (1985) characterized it as a "sticky" area for the Supreme Court (p. 1468). Two decades later, Amar (1994) called Fourth Amendment jurisprudence "an embarrassment" (p. 757) and a "sinking ocean liner—rudderless and badly off course" (p. 759). These criticisms originated mostly because there was a lack of a clear guiding rule or theory on which courts were making Fourth Amendment decisions, and a lack of clarity about guiding rules makes it unclear how future cases will be decided.

Despite the criticisms, very little empirical research has examined Fourth Amendment issues. Instead, modern Fourth Amendment research has largely been theoretical in scope. We focus on a few key areas within Fourth Amendment jurisprudence that deserve more (or any) empirical attention. We start by examining when a search or seizure becomes a Fourth Amendment issue including reasonable versus unreasonable expectations of privacy and searching and seizing people instead of places. Next, we focus on the warrant requirement and some exceptions to that requirement. We turn then to the infusion of digital technology, which may be influencing privacy notions. Finally, we examine people's willingness to consent to search requests and whether even subtle situational effects may have an influence on someone's willingness to consent to a search. We will address each of these theoretical and jurisprudential issues in turn, including what psychological research there is on each. In most instances, there is no specific psychological research and we will use this platform as an opportunity to suggest possible avenues for new lines of work. Because the legal landscape in Fourth Amendment jurisprudence relies almost exclusively on what nine (actually, a mere majority of five) Supreme Court justices say, it is an area ripe for new approaches that can be informed by law-psychology research findings.

Search and Seizure for the Purposes of the Fourth Amendment

The Fourth Amendment applies to both searches and seizures; therefore, the first and seemingly most simple question is whether a Fourth Amendment-invoking search or seizure has transpired (Dworkin, 1973). For nearly 200 years, defining a search or seizure was fairly straightforward and relied on the common understanding of physical intrusions. In fact, as late as 1928, the Supreme Court was still relying on a concrete understanding of physical intrusion and privacy when it ruled in *Olmstead v. United States*. Based on evidence obtained from a warrantless telephone wiretap, Olmstead was convicted of bootlegging in violation of the National Prohibition Act. Olmstead argued, unsuccessfully, that the incriminating evidence should have been excluded at his trial because the police violated his Fourth (and Fifth) Amendment rights. A five-justice majority of the Supreme Court disagreed, saying the wiretap did not constitute a search and seizure under the meaning of the Fourth Amendment. This physical notion of trespass remained for about four decades.

A Test beyond Physical Trespass: Reasonable Expectations

Justice Brandeis provided a dissent in *Olmstead* (1928) that focused on more subtle and, arguably, psychological definitions of intrusion. In his dissent, Brandeis argued that there should be no legal difference between government agents reading a sealed letter and listening to a phone conversation. Instead of concrete and physical definitions, Brandeis focused on Americans' "right to be let alone" (p. 478). Going several steps further, he also noted that "every unjustifiable intrusion by the Government upon the privacy of the individual, whatever the means employed, must be deemed a violation of the Fourth Amendment" (p. 478).

In hindsight, the Brandeis dissent provides poignant foreshadowing to *Katz v. U.S.* (1967). The Supreme Court in *Katz* rejected the physical trespass requirement of the *Olmstead* majority decision. In so doing, the Court abandoned the antiquated *Olmstead* construal of the Fourth Amendment and steered the Court toward a new understanding of Fourth Amendment rights. Although the majority opinion has largely been ignored (Winn, 2009), Justice Harlan's concurring opinion outlined a two-prong test that became the basis for future legal precedent in determining if the Fourth Amendment protections were triggered. The first consideration was whether the individual claiming an expectation of privacy had an actual, subjective expectation that the searched area or item was private. The second consideration was whether that subjective expectation is one that society is willing to recognize as reasonable (p. 361). As Dworkin (1973) notes, a search under *Katz* was defined not by what the searcher does, but instead by the "justifiability of the expectations of the person subjected to the search" (p. 335). In other words, a search only occurred if the searchee expected privacy and such expectation was justifiable. Unfortunately, this is an extremely difficult judgment for a police officer to make in the field, and that difficulty is compounded because the Court did not provide a basis for determining what would be justifiable (Dworkin, 1973).

Many academics have criticized Harlan's standard as circuitous at best and based on judicial decision-making whimsy. In contrast, Winn (2009) argued that Harlan's concurrence was much deeper and more nuanced than most critics recognize. Indeed, Winn (2009) focused specifically on one part of Harlan's opinion where he wrote, "As the Court's opinion states, 'the Fourth Amendment protects people, not places.' The question, however, was what protection it affords to those people. Generally, as here, the answer to that question required reference to a 'place'" (p. 361). With that, Harlan indirectly invoked a core social psychological principle first introduced by Kurt Lewin (1943). That is, behavior is a function of the person and his or her environment. In other words, privacy is situation specific. Therefore, even though the new privacy test established in *Katz* focused on protecting people rather than places, the place and situation still played an integral role in invoking the Fourth Amendment. The Supreme Court has applied the *Katz* logic in a variety of places finding that the Fourth Amendment does not apply to searches involving the police digging through garbage at the curb (*California v. Greenwood,* 1988), wired police informants (*U.S. v. White*, 1971), bank-maintained account records (*U.S. v. Miller,* 1976), a pen register on a telephone that records the phone numbers called (*Smith v. Maryland*, 1979), or the area beyond the curtilage of a home (*Oliver v. U.S.,* 1984). We detail later whether the Court's assumptions in these cases match those of laypersons.

As it turns out, most scholars believe that the Supreme Court's "reasonable" test ends up being anything but one simple reasonable test (Kerr, 2007). Kerr (2007) explains that there are four distinct models for the reasonable expectation of privacy. Even though these models are different, the Supreme Court seems to mix and match from the four when determining whether a person has a constitutionally protected expectation of privacy. Those four models are: probabilistic, private facts, positive law, and policy. We will detail these below and, when relevant, describe the psychological implications for each of these models.

According to Kerr (2007) the probabilistic model relies on the chance that a person would believe he had privacy in that situation. This model gets us the quintessential public opinion poll view of the Fourth Amendment. That is, if we ask 100 people whether the item being searched is private, do most of them think it is? Psychological research is well-suited to help in this model because of the skilled ability to accurately measure social norms and expectations. Additionally, psychologists are well-versed on matters of statistical probabilities. One clear problem for this model is the possibility that enough government intrusions could lead to people not expecting privacy. For example, if it was known that the government was listening to phone calls, then it would not be reasonable to expect one's phone calls to be private. According to Kerr (2007) the Supreme Court only relies on this model occasionally and often rejects it.

Kerr's (2007) second model he calls the private facts model because when the Court uses this model, it bases the search determination on whether the information collected is private. As such, this model moves away from how the information was obtained and focuses on what was obtained. It focuses more on what the justices believe to be private. The public opinion poll will not answer this question. Instead, psychological research on third-person versus first-person perspectives could provide empirical rationales for the justices and demonstrate that the justices' conceptions of what is private are unlikely to be absolute.

Kerr's (2007) third model, the positive law model, simply asks whether the government had to break the law to get the information. Said another way, the government obtaining information that is available to the general public does not violate a reasonable expectation of privacy. Although this model does not have obvious psychological footings, it should be noted that the government may have greater capabilities to conduct these legal activities. For example, one of the cases Kerr explains is that of *Florida v. Riley* (1989) in which investigators observed a marijuana greenhouse while flying a helicopter over the defendant's property at 400 feet altitude. Although not illegal to fly a helicopter over Riley's house, the opportunity to do so rested on having a helicopter, which is not especially common outside law enforcement circles.

Lastly, Kerr's (2007) fourth model is the policy model that relies on a policy question of whether a particular practice should fall under the warrant requirement because of the legal and practical consequences if the practice did not fall under the warrant requirement. This model rests on balancing between civil liberties and unnecessarily restricting government investigations. For example, courts have balanced the amount of privacy violation resulting from the use of technology to obtain massive amounts of data about a suspect's activities with the effect of restricting the use of such technologies on the ability to investigate (see *Kyllo v. U.S.*, 2001). Kerr argues that there is no one size fits all model for Fourth Amendment jurisprudence and having these four different models is appropriate and provides the most sensible outcomes in each of the particular cases. For at least two of Kerr's models, the lay public's opinion on the issue should play a role in judicial decisions. Indeed, we detail next the empirical research that has addressed the lay public's perceptions.

Slobogin and Schumacher (1993) conducted empirical research to examine what "society is prepared to recognize as reasonable" (p. 731, citing Harlan's concurrence from *Katz*). More precisely, the researchers sought to examine people's expectations of privacy for specific searched areas and in what kind of situations people would feel restrained by police action. In so doing, the study asked participants to read 50 search scenarios similar to court cases varied as to first- versus third-person and a description of the specific evidence being sought versus no description. The descriptions varied from looking at foliage in a public park to a body cavity search. For a number of the scenarios, the research findings suggest a disconnect between the Supreme Court holdings and public opinion. The researchers suggest that the Supreme Court should use the research as an impetus for a new Fourth Amendment standard that rests on how the public views the intrusiveness of searches. In addition, the results demonstrate that when people assess the intrusiveness of a search, they will see a search of themselves as more intrusive than that of a third person. Of course, a judge will always be making third-person assessments. Further, searches were rated as more intrusive when the purpose of the search was not articulated (i.e., no description of specific evidence sought).

Blumenthal et al. (2009) expanded and replicated the work of Slobogin and Schumacher (1993) by utilizing multidimensional scaling and focusing on other dimensions of privacy beyond intrusiveness. Although their results were consistent with the results of Slobogin and Schumacher (1993) on intrusiveness ratings, Blumenthal and colleagues also demonstrated with their college-student participants that privacy perceptions have multiple dimensions in determinations of what is private and reasonable. In addition, the seriousness of the crime also mattered to the participants such that they viewed the searches as less intrusive when the criminal activity was more serious.

As noted above, the first step is determining if the search is one that falls within the Fourth Amendment's purview. Moving away from an actual physical trespass requirement, the Court moved into the muddier area of reasonable expectations of privacy in their Fourth Amendment jurisprudence. Although Kerr's (2007) four models described above help clarify the Court's reasoning, what little empirical research that has been done demonstrates a potential disconnect between the Supreme Court and lay people's perceptions and expectations of privacy. We turn next to focus on searching and seizing people rather than places.

Searching and Seizing People Not Places

In contrast to searches of papers and effects, many searches are of a suspect's body. With the Court in *Katz* (1967) noting that the Fourth Amendment protects people, not places, it would follow there would be a bubble of safety around a person's body protecting from searches. But, as is often the case with Fourth Amendment jurisprudence, the cases do not always follow intuitive logic. The Court has said that no Fourth Amendment relevant seizure occurs when a reasonable person would feel free to leave the interaction with the police (*Florida v. Bostick,* 1991). That is, not every police seizure of a person will be unreasonable. In *Bostick*, the defendant was riding on a bus from Miami to Atlanta. A short while into the trip, two police officers boarded the bus, asked Terrance Bostick for his ticket and identification, and then asked to search his luggage. The officers found cocaine in the searched luggage and proceeded to arrest Bostick.

At the Florida Supreme Court level, the court held that this type of police action was an impermissible seizure. The court highlighted the fact that the officers had no "articulable reason" for boarding the bus and questioning passengers (p. 431). The U.S. Supreme Court reversed, noting that the officers gave Bostick the option to refuse and the officers were not threatening (e.g., they did not remove their guns as a "gun-wielding inquisitor" p. 432), therefore there was no seizure. Justice O'Connor, writing for the majority, did not ignore the tight quarters of the bus, but said such cramped confines were only one factor to be considered in determining if a seizure occurred. The Court said that Bostick's feeling that he was not free to leave was simply because he was a passenger on the bus and not because of the police encounter.

The dissent in *Bostick* seemed to rely on their basic understanding of human nature by focusing on the intimidating nature of these bus sweeps. Specifically, the dissent noted that they "occur within cramped confines, with officers typically placing themselves in between the passenger … and the exit of the bus" (p. 442). The dissent also noted the authority reigned from the officers' clothing, the presence of a weapon, and the physical positioning of the officers on the bus. Both the majority and the dissent made behavioral assumptions about how free a person would feel to leave or to end the police encounter; in both instances, they focused on the behaviors of the law enforcement agents.

In addition, the Supreme Court has developed a particular set of standards for body searches starting with the case of an Ohio detective suspicious of three men in downtown Cleveland, Ohio (*Terry v. Ohio*, 1968). After watching John Terry and two others appear to "case" a store for a "stick-up," the officer approached the three men, patted down the outside of Terry's clothing, and felt a pistol on Terry. Terry was charged with carrying a concealed weapon. The Supreme Court held that there was no Fourth Amendment violation and the weapon need not be excluded from evidence. The Court articulated that the Fourth Amendment applied even when there is no formal arrest. The Fourth Amendment is triggered "whenever a police officer accosts an individual and restrains his freedom to walk away" (p. 16). Additionally, a patting down of the outside of a person's clothing is a search. The question then became whether this search and seizure violated the defendant's rights. As such, the Court highlighted that the police action was "swift … . on-the-spot" (p. 20) and therefore did not fall under the warrant requirement, but rather the determination was whether the police action was an unreasonable search and seizure. The Court balanced the government's interest in crime control and the officer's safety against the intrusion of a search. For the Court, the scale tipped toward protecting the officer such that police can conduct what is now called a "stop-and-frisk" or *Terry* stop when police have a reasonable suspicion of criminal activity; to do so the police need not have probable cause to arrest. The Court's analysis focused on the fact that the officer in the *Terry* case was not searching to gather evidence, which would have made it unreasonable, but rather, was searching for other purposes such as protecting the police officer's own safety.

Once again, the Court seems to rely on very specific case facts in their decision making while ignoring psychological factors and making behavioral assumptions that may not be accurate. For example, Carbado (2002) argues that the suspect's perspective and personal characteristics such as race are important factors excluded from the Court's analysis in *Bostick*. Indeed, Carbado explains that "racial vulnerability" (p. 977) leads to more police encounters for people who are Black and therefore they are likely to react differently to these encounters. Although the majority in *Bostick* did not note the race of either Bostick or the officers, Bostick was Black and the officers were White. O'Connor and the majority indicated that the officers' behavior was routine and not coercive, but Carbado argues that Bostick's race creates an underlying circumstance that fundamentally changes the interaction for him. Similarly, in *Immigration and Naturalization Service (INS) v. Delgado* (1984), where INS officers surveyed Latina/o workers at a garment factory, the Court held that a seizure did not take place. Again, according to Carbado, the Court did not consider how race would contribute to the experience and change the situation for those being questioned. Other legal scholars make similar arguments relying on the disproportionate number of traffic stops minorities endure compared to nonminorities (MacLin, 1998; Thompson, 1999).

Although we know of no empirical research that has yet examined the influence of race on defining whether a Fourth Amendment search or seizure has occurred, research in other areas would suggest that race of the suspect plays a role in whether someone felt free to leave and free to deny consent. For example, Najdowski (2011) examined the effect of stereotype threat in Black suspects falsely confessing. In short, the fear of confirming a negative stereotype about one's group can lead to an increase in stereotype-confirming behaviors. As Najdowski notes, stereotype threat increases anxiety, physical arousal, cognitive load, and self-regulatory efforts. Although Najdowski was comparing the similar effects of stereotype threat to that of deception, it is clear that the effects of stereotype threat can have a real impact on how suspects interpret a situation and understands whether they are free to leave.

For almost two centuries, a Fourth Amendment search or seizure was defined in concrete ways relying on the physical dimensions of police activity. Although the Court has drifted from that focus somewhat by broadening the definition of intrusion, the justices have not fully embraced in their analyses the more nuanced psychological effects. There are glimmers the Court may move in that direction in the future. For example, the *Bostick* dissent detailed above highlighted in their seizure determination the cramped physical surroundings and their potential effects on how the suspect would interpret the situation. These types of questions from the Court (even if only in the dissent at this point) provide a call for law-psychology research to determine more nuanced definitions of a search or seizure.

Warrant Requirement

The plain language of the Fourth Amendment provides a warrant requirement based on probable cause. Although there is an academic debate about whether "reasonableness" was meant to apply to the whole amendment or only the second clause (Amar, 1994), the Fourth Amendment is generally regarded as two separate clauses: the Warrant Clause and the Reasonableness Clause. Historically, the Supreme Court focused on the Warrant Clause as the main crux of the issue (Sundby, 1994). So it would seem that once we establish there is a Fourth Amendment invoking search or seizure then there must be a warrant. Simply put, it is impossible to achieve agreement about this requirement beyond accepting that some of the time there will be some sort of warrant requirement. The Supreme Court's attention to the warrant requirement is anything but clear. The Court examined the warrant requirement in a 1948 case that involved illegal distilling and a search following an arrest (*Trupiano v. U.S.*). Waving high the flag of a warrant requirement, the five-Justice majority held that the evidence seized had to be excluded because the officers had ample opportunity to obtain a search warrant but did not do so. In so deciding, the Court noted that the point of the Fourth Amendment was to ensure that "the right to search and seize should not be left to the mere discretion of the police, but should as a matter of principle be subjected to the requirement of previous judicial sanction wherever possible" (pp. 709–710). The requirement was said to be at the "very essence" of the Fourth Amendment (p. 710).

With such a strong declaration in *Trupiano* (1948), it would seem warrants must be widely and broadly required. Although that seems the likely outcome, a case 2 years later heard by a Court that included a couple of new Justices involved a man selling forged postage and overturned *Trupiano*. In *U.S. v. Rabinowitz* (1950) the Fourth Amendment warrant requirement got sidelined after the Court declared warrants unnecessary if a search is reasonable and conducted during a lawful arrest. What, then, does "reasonable" mean? The Court in *Rabinowitz* says that there is no "fixed formula" (p. 63) for determining reasonableness and that always requiring a warrant is not a good solution. Instead, the Court held the facts and circumstances of the particular case would determine reasonableness. In the case, Rabinowitz was arrested in his small office, and the office was searched when he was arrested. For *Rabinowitz*, the reasonableness of the office search rested on the fact that the arrest was valid, that the search occurred as part of the arrest, and that the area searched was public and small enough to be under the control of the defendant.

Many legal scholars have discussed the warrant requirement and reasonableness. Davies (2008) advocates that the Fourth Amendment Framers did not separate the warrant requirement from the reasonableness requirement. According to Davies, the Framers were most concerned with the general warrants that were commonly used by the British at the time and to them, any search or seizure made pursuant to a general warrant was unreasonable. As such, Davies argues that the Framers would have never considered that the reasonableness standard would be used to conduct warrantless searches and the Framers would not have been able to fathom a world where warrantless searches were so commonplace. In contrast, Stuntz (1991, 1995) argues that a warrant requirement is an aberration in our legal culture because prescreening of conduct is more costly than a review after the conduct has taken place. In other words, it is more cost effective and efficient to only review offending conduct rather than pre-screen for offending conduct. Further, Stuntz (1991) argues that a warrant is less fair because defendants have no representation during a warrant request, whereas they would during a suppression hearing.

In contrast to Stuntz (1991), Slobogin (1991) proposed a new system for Fourth Amendment jurisprudence that was intended to guide police in their decision making by requiring pre-authorization. Slobogin's basic premise is that the government agent would have to obtain third-party authorization prior to any nonemergency search or seizure. That third-party decision should then be guided by the proportionality principle such that the level of certainty to authorize a search should be relatively proportional to the intrusiveness of the search or seizure. One caveat to Slobogin's proposal is that it was based in a time before modern, instant communication. Slobogin notes his new system would work by having one police officer wait with the car while the other officer took the suspect to the station to obtain a warrant. Of course, today it would be possible to have more instant approval through electronic communication.

The two proposals set forth by Stuntz (1991) and Slobogin (1991) set up an interesting empirical comparison question. Which option would lead to fewer unreasonable intrusions on privacy – a more universal warrant requirement (Slobogin, 1991) or the threat of suppression hearings (Stuntz, 1991)? Empirically this could be examined predictively from both the first- and third-person perspective. Of course, one basic question is what the public believes is private. This question seems to be evolving rapidly with each new technological advancement.

Expectations of Privacy in the Digital Age

One particularly important and timely context for Fourth Amendment jurisprudence is that of online communication and data storage. Supreme Court justices from just a few decades ago could have never imagined the scope of communication and data available today. When balancing the government's intrusion against its interest in conducting the search, some distinctions arise between outside or inside spaces (e.g., out in the open versus inside a suspect's home) (Kerr, 2010, 2012). But, as a searched item becomes more technological and virtual, the outside versus inside distinction is increasingly blurred. Does a person have a reasonable expectation of privacy to a picture on their laptop in the same way they would if the picture was inside their home? For instance, is a laptop sitting open at a restaurant searchable because it is in "plain view"? What if an incriminating picture was a desktop image (Bector, 2009)? Do the laptop's privacy and password settings matter? Despite how individuals may answer, at least one court held that a suspect did not have a reasonable expectation of privacy when police officers were able to view passwords on a computer screen over the suspect's shoulder (*U.S. v. David*, 1991). Indeed, password protection on a device is not dispositive, but only one factor considered in determining reasonable expectations of privacy (*U.S. v. Barrows*, 2007). Clearly, the inside versus outside distinction provides very little guidance with technology and the area seems ripe for empirical contributions. In addition, it seems the Court is moving away from relying on reasonable expectations because of the fear of how much and how efficiently information can be obtained with the use of technology.

The Supreme Court seemed particularly concerned with the efficiency of data collection in *Kyllo v. U.S.* (2001) when they held that obtaining data from thermal imaging was a search for the purposes of the Fourth Amendment. Government officials used thermal imaging outside Danny Kyllo's home to measure the level of heat emitting from his home. He was suspected of growing marijuana, the growing of which emits a large amount of heat. The officials used the imaging device from a public vantage point and only measured heat levels—no pictures, conversations, or other human activities. Because the results showed a great deal of heat coming from Kyllo's house, the officers obtained a search warrant to search his home for marijuana growing, which they did find. Kyllo argued the thermal imaging was an unlawful search and the Supreme Court agreed, noting that the officials did not have a search warrant when they used the thermal imaging device. The Court also noted that the thermal imaging device is not something commonly available and that contributes to the unreasonableness of the search. Justice Scalia seemed particularly concerned with the future technology that could be even more invasive than the thermal imaging device used on Kyllo's house and that the Fourth Amendment is particularly protective of the inside of the home.

With *Kyllo* (2001) there is a clear fear for what technology could do and how much information could be gleaned easily from a person's home with such technology. It seemed to provide a circle of protection around the home and not anything else, but *United States v. Jones* (U.S. v. Jones, 2012) demonstrates that the concern in *Kyllo* may have been less about the home and more about the technology. In the course of investigating Antoine Jones for narcotics violations, the police placed a Global Positioning System (GPS) device on Jones's car. They did so without obtaining a warrant beforehand and monitored Jones's movements for 24 hours per day for 4 weeks. Eventually, Jones was arrested for his involvement with possessing and distributing cocaine. His case made its way to the Supreme Court to determine if installing and using a warrantless tracking device on a car violates the defendant's Fourth Amendment rights.

In a departure from their lack of protection of cars on public roads (*U.S. v. Knotts*, 1983), the Supreme Court majority held that installing the GPS tracker was a trespass and therefore a search. Although the majority opinion in *Jones* stayed on the high ground of trespass, Justice Alito's statements during oral arguments foreshadowed his concurring opinion. Similar to the fear present in *Kyllo,* Justice Alito stated, "You know, I don't know what society expects and I think it's changing. Technology is changing people's expectations of privacy. Suppose we look forward 10 years, and maybe 10 years from now 90% of the population will be using social networking sites and they will have on average 500 friends and they will have allowed their friends to monitor their location 24 hours a day, 365 days a year, through the use of their cell phones. Then—what would the expectation of privacy be then?" (p. 44). Following this line of reasoning, the concurring opinion written by Justice Alito focused on the duration of the surveillance and contrasted the short-term monitoring with the month-long monitoring that occurred in *Jones*, saying that, "short-term monitoring of a person's movements on public streets accords with expectations of privacy that our society has recognized as reasonable" (p. 934). He went on to write, "the use of longer term GPS monitoring in investigations of most offenses impinges on expectations of privacy. For such offenses, society's expectation has been that law enforcement agents and others would not … secretly monitor and catalogue every single movement of an individual's car for a very long period" (p. 934) Justice Sotomayor also wrote a separate concurrence and rather than focusing on how long the monitoring occurred, focused on the efficiency with which any government monitoring can "ascertain, more or less at will, their political and religious beliefs, sexual habits, and so on" (p. 925) of the people being monitored.

The concurring opinions in *Jones* hinted that the Court was moving toward adopting what Kerr (2012) has called the "Mosiac Theory" of privacy. In previous cases, courts had considered each action taken by the police as part of a search independently. In *Jones*, the concurring opinions introduced the idea that a series of police actions could be considered a search when considered together, even if each individual action would not rise to the level of a search. Such a "mosaic" of information creates a picture of the suspect's activity that each individual search would not provide independently. However, as Kerr (2012) notes, in the past the practice of bringing together many sources of nonsearch information was considered appropriate and "good police work" (p. 328). Additionally, it is unclear what level of aggregation will offend the Court's sensitivities. Justice Alito said that the Court "need not identify with precision the point at which the tracking of this vehicle became a search, for the line was surely crossed before the 4-week mark" (p. 13). He went on to concede that other cases may be more difficult to decide, but failed to explain where a line might be drawn. Additionally, the Court did not provide any information about what level of aggregation was needed to trigger the exclusionary rule. Of course, changing technologies will forever continue to complicate the Court's job as developing technologies quickly outpace our court system.

Once again, the Court seemingly departed from long-standing Fourth Amendment precedent in *Riley v. California* (2014) because the case involved technology. Since the 1969 case of *Chimel v. California,* police have been permitted to search without a warrant the body and area where the suspect may reach in order to protect material evidence or the officer's safety. This rule is generally referred to as the search incident to a lawful arrest, as discussed above as an exception to the warrant requirement. The *Riley* case was a consolidated case of two separate cases (*Riley v. California,* 2014*U.S. v. Wurie,* 2013) involving police searches of cell phones incident to a lawful arrest. In separate situations, Riley and Wurie were being arrested, and in both cases the contents of their cell phones were searched without a warrant as incident to the arrest. In *Riley*, The Supreme Court noted that once the cell phone was determined not to be a threat to the officer's safety there should be no further searching. The Court was further unsympathetic to police desires to preserve material evidence stored on a phone. Instead, the Court called modern cell phones the "privacies of life" (p. 2495). What seemed to create the most consternation for the Justices was the vast amount of information available on modern cell phones.

In a sense, the Supreme Court seems to be trying to protect citizens from themselves. As the quote from Alito above notes, people's expectations are changing and that could mean that they have very little expectation for privacy. For example, many people use their cell phones as a way to let their friends and others know where they are and what they are doing, thinking, and eating. The Supreme Court seems uncomfortable letting the changing tides dictate what should be considered private. This shift effectively takes the power of determining privacy away from the public and into the hands of nine or fewer justices. How are the police who engage in searches to know what behaviors are appropriate? In today's society, more than ever before, communication is much less about a specific place or even a specific person. No longer are we concerned with letters through the mail and phone calls in phone booths, but the "cloud" around us that contains millions and millions of highly private bits of data. Should all searches and seizures be subject to a warrant requirement?

Slobogin (2013) argues a statutory provision is key to addressing the mire of technology that will continually confound at a rate much more rapidly than Court decisions. His proposed statutory language starts by saying that a search is "an effort by government to find or discern evidence of unlawful conduct" (p. 17). He then distinguishes a targeted (i.e., focused on a specific person or place) versus a general (i.e., not about a specific target) search. In Slobogin's definition of a search he does not distinguish between searching with and without technological aid. He equates a search of a file drawer of papers as the same as a search of computer files. Although Slobogin details quite specifically the warrant and court order requirements for a search, he still provides a consent exception in his statutory language. We address at length below the issue of people consenting to searches, but it is important to note here that the vast majority of people consent to searches when asked. Should that be of concern as we consider the possibility of legislative language regarding searches? Should we be concerned that the over-sharing of life details through technology may even increase a person's willingness to consent? Slobogin does a thorough job codifying what the Court seemed to be limping toward and addressed the sticky nature of courts deciding privacy issues related to technology; however, the proposed statutory provision still provides a consent exception and as we will detail below, people's willingness to consent to search requests may be among the greatest threats to privacy rights.

Law Enforcement Dogs: A Special Type of Searching "Technology"

Law enforcement dogs are a key aspect to many criminal investigations. Dogs can be trained to detect and alert to the presence of many different items, including most commonly drugs, explosives, and cadavers. Bomb-sniffing dogs are often used in airports and large public events to protect the public's safety. Bomb- and drug-sniffing dogs also are often used to identify people engaged in illegal behavior. In the past, the Supreme Court has determined that dog sniffs in a variety of situations are not searches (*City of Indianapolis v. Edmond*, 2000; *Illinois v. Caballes*, 2005; *U.S. v. Place*, 1983), and therefore they do not require probable cause to conduct. In *Place*, the Court determined that a dog sniffing for drugs does not invade a legitimate privacy interest because a dog only detects illegal contraband that is hidden from view, and people do not have a legitimate privacy interest in illegal material. In *Edmond* and *Caballes*, the Court determined that a dog sniff is not a search and does not invade privacy when conducted during a traffic stop. However, a frequently used means of obtaining probable cause to search is a "sniff" for the presence of illegal materials by a law enforcement dog, and the sniff itself requires little justification. When a dog alerts to illegal substances, this alert can be used as probable cause to justify a search. Therefore, law enforcement dogs are an important tool for the police to identify otherwise invisible illegal behavior.

The Supreme Court has recently placed some limitations on the use of drug-sniffing dogs in cases that raise interesting psychological questions. In *Florida v. Jardines* (2013), the Court determined that a dog sniff conducted in the space around a house constituted a search requiring a warrant. In *Jardines*, the police had an officer walk up to the front door of a house for which they received an anonymous tip that the house was being used to grow marijuana. An anonymous tip is not sufficient information on its own to conduct a warrantless search (*Florida v. J.L.*, 2000) or obtain a search warrant (*Illinois v. Gates*, 1983). When the dog approached the front door, it alerted to the presence of marijuana, and the police used the evidence of the dog's alert to obtain a warrant to search the house. The Supreme Court was asked to consider whether a dog sniff in this circumstance was itself a search requiring a warrant. The Court ruled that this particular dog sniff was a search because it trespassed onto the property, or more specifically encroached on the "curtilage" around the house. However, the Court did not expand their ruling beyond the area immediately surrounding the house, and it did not address how issues that have been raised in past dog sniff cases might differ for a house sniff, such as privacy expectations, embarrassment, anonymity, government interest, and public safety.

In another recent case, the Court addressed the reliability of drug sniffing dogs (*Florida v. Harris*, 2013). In *Harris*, the Court considered whether the reliability of the dog could impact the validity of any subsequent searches based on the dog's alert. The Court considered the relative impact of training quality, testing accuracy, field accuracy, and certification on the validity of a dog's alert to illegal substances in the field. Rules regarding certification and training vary widely by jurisdiction. The Court determined that training quality and testing accuracy were the most important determinant of a dog's reliability, with certification and field accuracy being less important. This case raised questions about how perceptions of the accuracy of a law enforcement dog can potentially impact people's feelings of their privacy being invaded during a dog sniff.

The Supreme Court also has considered whether the circumstances under which a dog sniff occurs at a traffic stop make the sniff unreasonable. In the past, courts have ruled that asking a driver to exit the vehicle, asking "off-topic" questions, and conducting a dog sniff of the vehicle are not intrusive and do not require reasonable suspicion to conduct during a traffic stop. For example, the Court ruled that a dog sniff conducted during a traffic stop is not an unreasonable search or seizure in *Illinois v. Caballes* (2005). In *U.S. v. Rodriguez* (2014), the Court considered whether holding a person after the completion of a traffic stop to wait for a dog sniff is more than a *de minimis* intrusion requiring at least reasonable suspicion. Rodriguez was pulled over for a traffic violation by a K-9 unit, and a ticket was issued. The police officer asked if his dog could sniff the car, and Rodriguez said no. The officer detained Rodriguez for 7–8 minutes until another officer arrived, at which time the dog sniffed the car and alerted to the methamphetamine that was later found when the car was searched based on the alert. Rodriguez's detainment after the ticket was issued to perform the dog sniff was found to be acceptable by the trial court and by the lower appellate courts. The Supreme Court ruled that a traffic stop cannot be extended to conduct a dog sniff without reasonable suspicion. However, the Court did not determine whether reasonable suspicion was present in this case or provide any guidance on reasonable time limits for a dog sniff co-occurring with a traffic stop.

In sum, courts have determined that dog sniffs are not searches requiring probable cause to conduct, unless they are conducted within the curtilage of a home. However, there has been little empirical research examining what factors impact expectations of privacy for dog sniffs. Slobogin and Schumacher (1993; described above) included as one of their 50 court case scenarios that participants rated for intrusiveness, a case involving a dog sniffing a person's body for drugs. Although the Court has held that a dog sniff does not constitute a search, participants ranked the dog sniff scenario as equally intrusive to a "frisk," which the Court has ruled to be a search. Therefore, there appears to be some disagreement between people's expectations of privacy in a dog sniff situation and how the Court views privacy and dog sniffs.

Addressing the issues raised by the Supreme Court decisions in *Jardines* and *Harris*, some research has been conducted on the location of the search and the accuracy of the dog. Research on actual dog sniffs has demonstrated the problem with field accuracy addressed by the Court in *Harris*, finding that dogs are only around 50% accurate in the field (Hinkel & Mahr, 2011). Some research also has been conducted on how perceptions of dog sniffs can be influenced by the accuracy of the dog and the location of the sniff. Bambauer (2012) conducted a survey of law students about privacy expectations during dog sniffs and whether they thought a dog sniff was a search in various situations. Participants read scenarios in which the dogs were either drug-sniffing, bomb-sniffing, or cadaver-sniffing. Within the multiple scenarios presented to the participants, the accuracy of the dog (100, 99, or 90%) was varied, and the location of the sniff was varied (car or home). Drug-sniffing dogs were perceived as more invasive than bomb- or cadaver-sniffing dogs, and this perception of invasiveness increased as the accuracy of the dog decreased. Participants were more likely to think the dog sniff was a search when the sniff target was a house compared to a car (Bambauer, 2012).

Bambauer (2013) also surveyed laypersons about invasions of privacy by dog sniffs. Participants were presented with a dog sniff scenario in which the dog was either sniffing for drugs or cadavers. The dog's field accuracy also was varied (100% accurate, 99%, or 90%). Similar to the results from law students in Bambauer (2012) laypersons felt the drug-sniffing dogs were more invasive than the cadaver-sniffing dogs, and the invasiveness increased as the accuracy of the dog decreased. The less accurate the dog was, the more invasive the sniff was perceived to be (Bambauer, 2013). Overall, Bambauer's research indicates that the context of the search and the perceived or actual accuracy of the dog can affect perceptions of privacy and intrusiveness.

In our own research on perceptions of dog sniffs, we have found results similar to Bambauer on the effect of the location searched and accuracy of the dog on perceptions of intrusiveness. In one study, we presented participants with vignettes in which the location of the search was varied to be either a home, apartment, hotel room, office, car during a traffic stop, luggage at an airport, or compartment on a train. Similar to Bambauer and consistent with the Court's ruling in *Jardines*, we found that sniffs by drug dogs of a home were perceived as more intrusive and more likely to be a trespass than searches of all other locations (Groscup, Rivera, Hoetger, & Brank, 2014). However, we also found that people expect the same amount of privacy for their cars and their homes, which is contrary to the Court's reasoning that a dog sniff of a car during a traffic stop does not violate perceived privacy. In a second study, we presented participants with a vignette about a traffic stop similar to the *Harris* case facts in which we varied the training, certification, and accuracy during testing of a drug-sniffing dog (Rivera & Groscup, 2014). Contrary to Bambauer's results, none of those factors affected the perceived intrusiveness of the dog sniff. However, good training, up-to-date certification, and higher levels of accuracy did increase perceptions that the dog was reliable and that the dog's alert indicated the presence of drugs (Rivera & Groscup, 2014). Taken together, this small body of extant research indicates that the Court's reasoning about the intrusiveness of dog sniffs may differ from laypersons' perceptions.

Overall, the Supreme Court in addressing law enforcement dogs has focused on the potential limits on the use of dog sniffs without a warrant. Although some research investigating perceptions of dog sniffs has been conducted, there are many psychological implications of the various uses for law enforcement dogs that could be further researched. For example, we know little about how privacy is perceived in the wide variety of dog sniff situations. We also know little about what makes a dog sniff intrusive enough to be a search. Similarly, we do not know whether the presence of a dog will make people more likely to consent to a search request. Research on these topics could assist courts in assessing the intrusiveness of these techniques and the voluntariness of the consents.

Consent Searches

As already noted, a search must be reasonable and ordinarily must be accompanied by a warrant to be valid; however, a search will not violate the Fourth Amendment if the official obtained consent to search (*Schneckloth v. Bustamonte*, 1973). Police officers do not need probable cause nor do they need to meet any legal standard to request consent to search. They can ask to search anyone at any time. A consent search will be valid, so long as the consent was voluntarily given. Voluntariness is determined by examining all of the facts of the case – the "totality of the circumstances." That is, courts are to consider the situational and person variables that were present at the time of the consent to determine whether the consent was voluntary – not coerced "by explicit or implicit means, by implied threat or covert force" (*Schneckloth v. Bustamonte*, 1973, p. 228; *U.S. v. Drayton*, 2002).

In assessing the "totality of the circumstances," courts have focused on whether a reasonable person would understand that he or she had the right to refuse (*U.S. v. Drayton*, 2002) or that he or she had the freedom to deny consent and terminate the police encounter (*Florida v. Bostick*, 1991; see *Brendlin v. California*, 2007 for a similar standard for perceived freedom in the seizure context). Therefore, whether the defendant reasonably felt free to say "no" and knew refusing consent was an option are among the many important factors in determining voluntariness (*Schneckloth v. Bustamonte*, 1973; *U.S. v. Drayton*, 2002; see Nadler, 2002; Tiersma & Solan, 2004; Kessler, 2009 on the related issue of seizures). Whether a person is in custody, the number of police officers present, and the emotional state of the suspect are all factors the courts have considered as part of the totality of circumstances (LaFave, Israel, King, & Kerr, 2009), but courts have not determined that any situational or personal factor makes consent *per se* voluntary or coerced. Historically, courts are generally prone to find that consents are given voluntarily, in the absence of police misconduct (Sutherland, 2006).

Research on Consent Searches

Even though consent searches are likely occurring on a daily basis (Lichtenberg, 2004a), very little research has examined factors affecting consent to search. Some research on police data regarding actual consent searches provides a sense of how the police and the searchee generally behave in a consent search and whether the search results in the discovery of evidence. Lichtenberg (2000) did a retrospective examination of individuals who had experienced a law enforcement request to search their vehicles. Lichtenberg found that 90–95% of individuals in the study consented to the search. Consistent with previous research on obedience to authority, the participants in the study often reported that they thought the law enforcement officer would have searched the automobile even in the absence of consent or that there would be punishment repercussions if they did not consent to the search. Such retrospective explanations provide unique insights into the minds of people who have consented to a search, but they suffer from the traditional hindsight bias issues that are always at work when asking someone to remember why they behaved a certain way (Lichtenberg, 2000). Importantly, the discovery of illegal contraband appears to occur in very few consent searches (Lichtenberg, 2000; Lichtenberg & Smith, 2001). Review of actual consent searches indicates that illegal items are found in 10% or less of these searches (Lichtenberg & Smith, 2001). This research also indicated that consent search requests are becoming more common over time, and the percentage of searches resulting in the discovery of illegal items is going down over time, potentially calling into question the effectiveness of consent searches as a law enforcement tool (Lichtenberg & Smith, 2001). Overall, this research provides a general picture that consent requests are made frequently by the police, searchees consent to these requests almost all of the time, and illegal evidence is obtained in very few of these searches.

Because there is little research on the behavior and perceptions of the police and of the searchee in actual consent searches, research findings on the voluntariness of confessions provides information on an analogous situation indicating that there may be more coercion present in consent searches than is readily obvious. Assessing the voluntariness of consent to search is analogous to the assessment of the voluntariness of confession because the standards used for the evaluation of consent searches are borrowed from the courts' evaluations of confessions (Simmons, 2005; but see, *Schneckloth v. Bustamonte*, 1973 for the Supreme Court's differentiation of the situations) and because both situations involve relinquishing rights and potentially providing the police with self-incriminating evidence (Simmons, 2005). Providing consent to a search is similar to speaking during an interrogation. In both situations, the person being approached by the police are giving up their

Constitutional rights to either not provide evidence against yourself or to not be searched (Kagehiro, 1990). In a custodial interrogation, *Miranda* rights are triggered. In order to speak with a suspect for whom these rights have been activated, the police must demonstrate – often by a signed form – that the suspect has knowingly and intelligently waived his or her rights. In consent searches, there is no similar requirement of waiver or established rules about how to conduct a consent search.

Much more research has been done on interrogations and confessions, the review of which is beyond the scope of this chapter. However, the confessions literature can be helpful in understanding some of the factors at work in a consent search. The large body of confessions research has demonstrated that false confessions can be coerced and that those false confessions can be very difficult to distinguish from true, voluntary confessions (see Kassin et al., 2009; Kassin & Gudjonsson, 2004; Russano, Meissner, Narchet, & Kassin, 2005). This research has uncovered factors that can increase coercion to confess in an interrogation whose coercive nature is more obvious, such as physical abuse. However, it also has uncovered other factors whose coercive nature was less obvious to courts prior to research indicating their coercive effects, such as the use of minimization techniques. Research on the understanding of *Miranda* warnings indicates that the language of the warnings is poorly understood, that juveniles have less understanding of *Miranda* language, and that the implications of waiving *Miranda* rights are poorly understood (see Kassin et al., 2009 for a review). Just as research on the less apparent sources of coercion in interrogations has assisted courts in assessing the voluntariness and validity of confessions, research on the factors creating coercion in consent searches may assist the courts in assessing the voluntariness of consent under the "totality of the circumstances" standard.

Although it is not plentiful, there is some extant research on consent searches that also could help courts make determinations about voluntariness in consent search situations. Some of that research has focused on the impact of warnings that refusal is an option similar to *Miranda* warnings about the right to remain silent. As stated previously, the freedom to leave, knowledge of rights, and warnings about these rights have been considered by courts in consent search cases. Even though knowledge may be important, the Supreme Court has clearly rejected the requirement of a warning to an individual that she could deny consent, saying such a warning "would, in practice, create serious doubt whether consent searches could continue to be conducted" (*Schneckloth v. Bustamonte,* 1973, p. 227; see also *Ohio v. Robinette*, 1996). The Court was concerned that police would no longer conduct consent searches if required to provide a warning, thus losing a valuable investigative tool. Nonetheless, some states do require warnings (*State (NJ) v. Johnson*, 1975; *State (WA) v. Ferrier*, 1998). For example, Washington State requires that police inform searchees that they can refuse consent, can revoke consent at any time, or limit the scope of consent (*State v. Ferrier*, 1998).

Some research regarding the effects of knowledge of rights and warnings regarding rights during a consent search has been conducted, largely indicating that warnings do not reduce the frequency of consent. Field research comparing the use of consent searches by police with and without warnings in Ohio indicates that police may be even more likely to request consent to search when required to warn (Lichtenberg, 2004a). Other field research demonstrates that people are likely to consent regardless of guilt, warnings do not decrease consent, and people believe police will retaliate or search anyway if consent is denied (Lichtenberg, 2000, 2001). Experimental research indicates that laypersons' knowledge about consent searches might be quite low. Kagehiro (1988) found that over 90% of people claim to understand what a consent search is and that a warrantless search cannot be conducted without consent. However, only half of the participants understood that consent could be withdrawn or limited, and only a quarter of participants knew that the police did not have to warn the consenter about his or her rights in a way similar to a *Miranda* warning (Kagehiro, 1988). Our own research is consistent with these previous results. Our results over several studies indicate that people lack knowledge about consent searches in general and about their own rights within that situation (Wilson, Brank, Groscup, & Marshall, 2015). We also have found that having knowledge and being warned do not reduce consents in an actual search situation (Brank, Groscup, Hoetger, Wiley, & Haby, 2015) or perceptions that a searchee would consent (Groscup, Brank, Roizin, Gold, & Sachs, 2015). However, warnings might increase a consenter's perceptions of the voluntariness of his or her consent (Brank et al., 2015) or the perception that someone else's consent was voluntary (Groscup et al., 2015).

Research also has been conducted on how laypersons believe they would act during a police encounter in the Fourth Amendment arena. Kessler (2009) investigated laypersons' perceptions of how they themselves believed they would feel if approached by the police in the context of a "seizure." Kessler found that the majority of survey respondents believed they would not feel free to leave if asked questions by a police officer either on a sidewalk or on a bus, although actual behavior in a seizure situation was not tested. Individual differences affected respondents' reactions to the seizure situation. Women and younger respondents were less likely to think they would feel free to leave than male and older participants, but no differences in responses were found based on race, income, knowledge of the freedom to leave, or experience with the police (Kessler, 2009). Taken together, these studies indicate that people may be entering the consent search situation feeling little freedom and that knowledge of rights may not change their consent decision regardless of the presence of warnings.

Most of the remaining research on consent searches to date has focused on how laypersons perceive the voluntariness of someone else's consent (Kagehiro, 1988; Kagehiro, 1990; Kagehiro, Taylor, Laufer, & Harland, 1991). Psychological biases existing in other aspects of criminal law decision making have been demonstrated in judgments about consent decisions and perceptions of consent voluntariness, such as the Actor-Observer Effect and Hindsight Bias. Several studies have demonstrated biases in the perceptions of the amount of coercion in a consent search consistent with the Actor-Observer Effect (Kagehiro, 1988; Kagehiro, Taylor, Laufer, & Harland, 1991). In the Actor-Observer Effect, people and situations are theoretically perceived differently from the first-person perspective (the perspective of the person in the situation – the Actor) and from the third-person perspective (the perspective of the person observing the situation – the Observer). The reasons for behavioral choices tend to be attributed to the situation by the Actor, and they tend to be attributed to the characteristics of the person by the Observer. In the consent search situation, this means that the searchee may attribute consent or any coercion in that consent to the actions of the police officer, and the person judging the voluntariness of the consent (the police or the judge) may attribute consent as being the choice of the searchee (Kagehiro, 1988). In other words, perceptions of consent voluntariness may differ dramatically between the person providing consent and the person later judging whether that consent was voluntary or not. Kagehiro (1988) found results consistent with the Actor-Observer Effect. When presented with a vignette about a consent search situation, observers overestimated the likelihood that a consenter would try to request more information from the police, and observers overestimated a consenter's freedom to revoke consent (Kagehiro, 1988). In our own research and across several studies, we presented participants with vignettes of consent search situations and measured participants' perceptions of those situations from the perspective of the Observer and from the perspective of the Actor (Brank et al., 2015; Groscup et al., 2015). Consistent with the Actor-Observer Effect, we found that consent was perceived as less coerced and more voluntary from the Observer's perspective. These findings, taken together, have implications for the legal system because the courts have to determine after the fact whether the consent was voluntary or not if the validity of the search is challenged. As Kagehiro (1988) noted, the individuals in charge of evaluating the voluntariness of consent, judges, are always doing so from an observer's standpoint, which could mean that consent voluntariness is being overestimated by the courts. For example, perspective of the judge could be likened to the perspective taken by cameras filming a suspect providing a confession. As Lassiter, Diamond, Schmidt, and Elek (2007) describe, when a video recorded confession only focuses on suspect rather than other points of view, the confessions are seen as more voluntarily given and the suspects seen as more guilty. This is potentially similar to a consent recorded by a police officer's body camera. The perspective recorded will inevitably be one-sided and focused on the suspect. Further research is obviously needed.

Research has also demonstrated Hindsight Bias in the evaluation of searches. Hindsight Bias, sometimes referred to as the knew-it-all-along effect is the tendency to view actions as predictable after they have occurred (Fischhoff, 1975). For police searches, the level of coercion and misconduct is perceived as less when evidence of guilt is found than compared to when such evidence is not found (Casper, Benedict, & Kelly, 1988; Robbennolt & Sobus, 1997). Casper et al. presented mock jurors with a description of a civil suit resulting from a search in which the evidence found was varied to either indicate guilt, innocence, or be neutral. Knowledge of the search outcome influenced participants' judgments such that lower damages were awarded to plaintiffs for whom incriminating evidence was found. Incriminating evidence also made the police behavior during the search appear better and the violation of the searchee's rights less likely (Casper et al., 1988). Robbennolt and Sobus (1997) conducted a similar study investigating the effect of Hindsight Bias and counterfactual thinking in a lawsuit about a search based on the searchee's similarity to a drug courier profile. The outcome of the search was manipulated as in Casper et al., and the quality of the drug courier profile also was manipulated. Greater compensatory damages were awarded and more sympathy for the searchee was present when no evidence of guilt was uncovered, consistent with the Hindsight Bias (Robbennolt & Sobus, 1997). Although these studies were conducted in a civil context, similar psychological biases may be operating in decisions about search validity in criminal courts.

Even the language used during a consent request could affect how that consent request is perceived. The consent request is supposed to be just that – a request or question. Police generally use requests rather than commands – for example, "Would you mind if I search your car?" However, it is possible that suspects hear the question requesting a search as a demand, and it is possible that the phrasing of the request could impact perceptions of voluntariness. Some scholars have speculated people consent because they are unaware that the police are asking a question rather than demanding that a search take place (Nadler & Trout, 2012), no matter how politely the request is made (Simmons, 2005). After all, many every day "questions" are actually commands (e.g., "Can you pass the salt?" Tiersma & Solan, 2004, p. 235). Research on language use in consent search "requests" indicates that the phrasing of the request can impact perceived consent voluntariness. To evaluate whether consent given by a defendant was perceived as voluntary, Kagehiro (1988) presented vignettes to participants about a search of an apartment in which the phrasing of the request was varied to be either declarative ("I would appreciate it if I could come in and look around") or interrogative ("Would you mind if I came in and looked around?"). When the police used an interrogative phrase versus a declarative phrase, the participants viewed the subject of the search as having more choice in the decision to consent. These results indicate that the way the police word the consent request could affect perceived voluntariness of the consent, such that when the request is actually worded as a question, consenters may be more likely to perceive it as a request, not a command (Kagehiro, 1988). Importantly, the Supreme Court determined that defendants should know these are requests, and not commands, because they are technically phrased as questions (*U.S. v. Drayton*, 2002), meaning that the issue of whether the consent request is actually perceived as a request may not be regularly investigated by courts.

Other research on perceptions of consent searches has investigated the specific situation of third-party consent. Third-party consent occurs when the police request consent to search property that is jointly controlled by the suspect and by a third party. The suspect does not provide consent to search, but the third party does (Lichtenberg, 2004b). The Supreme Court in *U.S. v. Matlock* (1974) considered third-party consent and determined that a third party who is in possession of or in control of property can consent to a search of that property. That consent will be valid if the consenter has legitimate common authority over the property, but it will not be valid if the suspect (not the third party) has exclusive use or control of the property. Anyone entering into a situation in which common authority exists, such as a shared apartment or car, assumes the risk that others who have common use of that property may consent to a search of that property (*U.S. v. Matlock*, 1974). Research indicates that laypersons' perceptions of third-party authority may differ from court decision making (Kagehiro & Taylor, 1991; Kagehiro, Taylor, Laufer, & Harland, 1991). Kagehiro and Taylor (1991) presented a search scenario to laypersons in which the presence of the suspect and the identity of the search requester were varied. Participants correctly understood distinctions between common authority areas of a home and exclusive-use rooms, but this understanding was affected by the presence of the coresident. If the coresident was present and protesting the search, laypersons did not assume there was authority to consent to a search of common-authority areas of the home (Kagehiro & Taylor, 1991). Kagehiro, Taylor, and Harland (1991) tested for the effect of Hindsight Bias in the perceptions of a third-party search. They presented participants with a search vignette in which the presence of the suspect at the third-party search and whether illegal material was found during the search were varied. Consistent with Hindsight Bias, third-party consent was viewed as most valid when illegal materials were found. Consistent with their previous research (Kagehiro & Taylor, 1991), the third-party consenter was perceived as having more rights to consent when the suspect was absent than when the suspect was there and protesting the search (Kagehiro, Taylor, & Harland, 1991). Combined, these studies provide important data on evaluations of third-party consent to search, but they do not address the searchee's perspective. Additionally, third-party consent could become more complicated in the digital age with file-sharing programs and the exchange of electronic information (Couillard, 2011; Watzel, 2014).

In summary, warrantless consent searches are occurring on a daily basis, and searchees consent to requests to search by the police nearly every time. Although we know from reviews of police records that most people consent to these police requests to search, there is not an extensive body of research to date that examines the psychological reasons why almost everyone consents, regardless of guilt or the likelihood of the police discovering illegal material during the search. Similar to the area of interrogations, this raises questions about the voluntariness of these frequent consents. More research is clearly needed to understand the psychological factors that might explain suspect behavior in the consent search situation and whether the police are aware of these underlying factors.

Potential Psychological Explanations for Consent Behavior

When making consent voluntariness determinations, courts often make psychological assumptions about how people view searches and seizures that are not necessarily based on empirical findings, but are based on anecdotal notions and intuition (Blumenthal et al., 2009). Despite the "totality of the circumstances" standard, courts are not particularly sensitive to the possible situational and environmental effects that may make a request to search more or less coercive (Simmons, 2005). For example, the Supreme Court has held that police officers boarding a crowded bus in the middle of the night is not, by itself, so unduly coercive as to render consent to search luggage on the bus involuntary (*Florida v. Bostick*, 1991). Similarly, three police officers on a bus with one blocking the bus entrance is also not unduly coercive in obtaining a consent to search (*U.S. v. Drayton*, 2002). Empirical examination of the factors affecting consent to search will aid in legal decision making in these cases.

Psychological theory and research could assist courts in understanding the potential impact of these environmental, situational, and social factors on consent decision making and voluntariness in a similar way to how it has informed interrogation procedures. We know from both classic and more recent psychological studies that people obey authority (Burger, 2009; Milgram, 1974; but see Twenge, 2009) and that official uniforms make authority stronger (Bickman, 1974); yet, it could be argued that such experiments hold arguably limited value for real-world legal questions such as consenting to a government search (Chanenson, 2004). It also is possible that there are other factors besides obedience to authority impacting decision making in the consent search situation.

Although the consideration of consent by the courts has focused on important factors such as outright coercion, the question of why a person consents to a police search is likely to be influenced by a number of interrelated situational factors. Some of the more obvious factors that could play a part in consent decisions are mentioned above (i.e., obedience to authority, ignorance), but other factors potentially influencing consent decisions are less obvious. For instance, the physical situation may have an effect on why a person would consent. Grounded cognition is the concept that cognition can be affected by various aspects of the situation in which it is made (Barsalou, 2008). How we perceive those situational aspects affects our perceptions of the situation itself. The "grounding" of cognition is the concept that concrete experiences of the body and the environment are cues to how more abstract concepts should be perceived, including social contexts. The label "grounded" cognition is an umbrella term related to and encompassing other theories such as situated cognition or embodied cognition. This form of cognition focuses on the relationship of the body and the environment to cognition (see Smith, 2008; Smith & Collins, 2009; Smith & Semin, 2007; Wilson, 2002). For the current purposes, we use the term situated cognition, which can be thought of as a form of grounded cognition (see Robbins & Aydede, 2009).

Situated cognition holds promise for explaining behavior in legal contexts such as consent searches because it allows consideration of bodily states, the physical environment, and the social context. According to situated cognition theory, the purpose of cognition is for action. Cognition is "situated," meaning that our thoughts are affected by situations. Specifically, situations serve as a resource of information in forming cognitions; cognition is embodied and takes into account sensorimotor experiences (Semin & Smith, 2002; Smith & Semin, 2007). All of these elements can be related to consent searches in that information from the physical and social environment may be used to formulate cognitions about the situation and consent decisions.

Situated cognition research has been conducted on factors relevant to the search situation. For example, researchers examining situated cognition in other settings have investigated a number of factors that are likely to vary in searches and could influence the voluntariness of consents to those searches. These factors include physical aspects of the environment such as space (Tversky, 2009), distance

(Henderson, Wakslak, Fujita, & Rohrbach, 2011; Trope & Liberman, 2010; Williams & Bargh, 2008), lighting (Steidle, Werth, & Hanke, 2011), bodily proximity to property (Chen & Bargh, 1999; Ping, Dhillon, & Beilock, 2009), and ambient temperature (Ijzerman & Semin, 2009). They also include social contexts related to consent and coercion such as social support (Schnall, Harber, Stefanucci, & Proffitt, 2008), which is related to conformity (Asch, 1955), and power relationships (Lakens, Semin, & Foroni, 2011). Although many other situational factors that might affect searches have not yet specifically been investigated under the situated cognition paradigm, research in other related areas of social psychology provides some evidence that they would affect cognition in ways consistent with the theory of situated cognition, such as crowding (Burger, Oakman, & Bullard, 1983; Gochman & Keating, 1980; Stokols, 1972; Webb, Worchel, Riechers, & Wayne, 1986). Under situated cognition, research also indicates that emotion (Griffiths & Scarantino, 2009; Stefanucci, Proffitt, Clore, & Parekh, 2008) and language comprehension (see generally Spivey & Richardson, 2009; and see Scherr & Madon, 2012 for a *Miranda* example) can be affected by the situational context.

In sum, bodily states, the situation, and the social context are all forces that could assert an impact on perceptions, cognitions, and decision making in consent searches according to situated cognition theory. Although concepts related to the body, environment, and cognition have significant implications within the law, these concepts have largely been ignored by legal scholars (Benforado, 2010).

Although there is no published research to date applying situated cognition theory to the consent search situation specifically, our own ongoing research has begun to do so. In our laboratory research using both vignettes and active experiments on actual consent search decisions, we have varied a number of situated cognition relevant factors to determine if they affect consent decisions and consenters' perceptions of consent voluntariness. Some of these factors include the physical search situation (for example, the size of the space, ambient temperature, and lighting) and the relative physical position of the police officer making the search request and the consenter (for example exit blocking and the officer standing over the searchee). Although these situational and social factors have not affected the frequency of consents, they have negatively affected the consenters' perceptions of the situation and perceptions of voluntariness (Brank, Groscup, Haby, & Hoetger, 2016; Groscup, Marshall, & Brank, 2016). Therefore, research indicates that grounded cognition in general may be one of the many explanations for a consenter's feelings about consent searches that could be relevant to court decision making about the voluntariness of consent decisions; however, more research is needed in this area.

Conclusion

The Fourth Amendment has had a rocky history with its broad language and the Supreme Court's seemingly ever-changing standards. Despite a need for empirical insights in the area, there has not been a flood of psychological research on the topic. In the current chapter, we have detailed the historical background highlighting each time the Court made assumptions about human behavior relevant to search or seizure. Sometimes those assumptions were about law enforcement officers and the intended effect of the Exclusionary Rule. Other times those assumptions were about suspects and the public and what they would view and believe to be private. Although some empirical research has examined the public's notions of privacy, technology continues to progress bringing changes to many parts of our lives, but particularly our privacy. As we detailed above, the Supreme Court's recent holdings in cases involving technology-aided searches and surveillance suggest their reservations about allowing too much governmental access even while many individuals are sharing more and more through social media. Of similar concern are the vast majority of people who consent to a search request and the limited research that has addressed why so many people willingly waive their rights. Our own research suggests there may be even subtle situational factors that interfere with the voluntariness of a person's consent. Taken together, the historical background, the puzzle of Court doctrine, the changing world due to technology, and the overwhelming number of people who consent to searches raises an array of both legal and psychological questions. Some of those questions may be answered simply through legal analysis and legislative changes, while others would be well-served in receiving empirical research attention.

References

Amar, A. R. (1994). Fourth Amendment first principles. *Harvard Law Review, 107*(4), 757–819.

Asch, S. E. (1955). Opinions and social pressure. *Scientific American, 193*, 31–35.

Bambauer, J. Y. (2012). How the war on drugs distorts privacy law. *Stanford Law Review Online, 64*, 131–138.

Bambauer, J. Y. (2013). Defending the dog. *Oregon Law Review, 91*, 1203–1211.

Barrett, E. L. (1960). Personal rights, property rights, and the Fourth Amendment. *The Supreme Court Review, 1960*, 46–74.

Barsalou, L. W. (2008). Grounded cognition. *Annual Review of Psychology, 59*, 617–645. https://doi.org/10.1146/annurev.psych.59.103006.093639

Bector, S. (2009). Your laptop, please: The search and seizure of electronic devices at the United States border. *Berkeley Technology Law Journal, 24*, 695–718.

Benforado, A. (2010). The body of the mind: Embodied cognition, law, and justice. *Saint Louis University Law Journal, 54*, 1185–1217.

Bickman, L. (1974). The social power of a uniform. *Journal of Applied Social Psychology, 4*, 47–61.

Blumenthal, J. A., Adya, M., & Mogle, J. (2009). The multiple dimensions of privacy: Testing lay "expectations of privacy." *University of Pennsylvania Journal of Constitutional Law, 11*, 331-373.

Bradley, C. M. (1985). Two models of the Fourth Amendment. *Michigan Law Review Association, 83*(6), 1468–1501.

Brank, E.M., Groscup, J.L., Haby, J.A., & Hoetger, L.A. (2016, March). *I'm cramped and hot: Subtle environmental effects on consents to search.* Paper presented at the annual meeting of the American Psychology-Law Society, Atlanta, GA.

Brank, E.M., Groscup, J.L., Hoetger, L.A., Wiley, L.E., & Haby, J.A. (2015, March). *Even If I know I Shouldn't, I'm Still Going to Consent to a Search: The Impact of Knowledge of Rights and Warnings about Rights on Actual Consent to Search Decisions.* Paper presentation at the annual meeting of the American Psychology-Law Society, San Diego, California.

Brendlin v. California. , 551 U.S. 249 (2007).

Burger, J. M. (2009). Replicating Milgram: Would people still obey today? *American Psychologist, 64*, 1–11. https://doi.org/10.1037/a0010932

Burger, J. M., Oakman, J. A., & Bullard, N. (1983). Desire for control and the perception of crowding. *Personality and Social Psychology Bulletin, 9*, 475–479. https://doi.org/10.1177/0146167283093017

California v. Greenwood, 486 U.S. 35 (1988).

Carbado, D. W. (2002). (E)racing the Fourth Amendment. *Michigan Law Review, 100*(5), 946–1044.

Casper, J. D., Benedict, K., & Kelly, J. R. (1988). Cognitions, attitudes and decision-making in search and seizure cases. *Journal of Applied Social Psychology, 18*, 93–113. https://doi.org/10.1111/j.1559-1816.1988.tb00008.x

Chanenson, S. L. (2004). Get the facts, Jack! Empirical research and the changing constitutional landscape of consent searches. *Tennessee Law Review, 71*, 399–470.

Chen, M., & Bargh, J. A. (1999). Consequences of automatic evaluation: Immediate behavioral predispositions to approach or avoid the stimulus. *Personality and Social Psychology Bulletin, 25*, 215–224. https://doi.org/10.1177/0146167299025002007

Chimel v. California, 395 U.S. 752 (1969).

City of Indianapolis v. Edmond, 531 U.S. 32 (2000).

Couillard, D. A. (2011). Defogging the cloud: Applying the Fourth Amendment to evolving privacy expectations in cloud computing. *Minnesota Law Review, 93*, 101–134.

Davies, T. Y. (1999). Recovering the Original Fourth Amendment. Michigan Law Review, 98, 547-750.

Davies, T. Y. (2008). Correcting search-and-seizure history: Now-forgotten common-law warrantless arrest standards and the original meaning of due process of law. *Mississippi Law Journal, 77*, 1–224.

Dworkin, R. B. (1973). Fact style adjudication and the Fourth Amendment: The limits of lawyering. *Indiana Law Journal, 48*(3), 329–368.

Elkins v. United States, 364 U.S. 206 (1960)

Fischhoff, B. (1975). Hindsight is not equal to foresight: The effect of outcome knowledge on judgment under uncertainty. *Journal of Experimental Psychology: Human Perception and Performance, 1*, 288–299. https://doi.org/10.1037/0096-1523.1.3.288

Florida v. Bostick, 501 U.S. 429 (1991).

Florida v. Harris, 133 S.Ct. 1050 (2013)

Florida v. Jardines, 133 S.Ct. 1409 (2013).

Florida v. J.L., 529 U.S. 266 (2000).

Florida v. Riley, 488 U.S. 445 (1989).

Gochman, I. R., & Keating, J. P. (1980). Misattributions to crowding: Blaming crowding for nondensity-caused events. *Journal of Nonverbal Behavior, 4*, 157–175. https://doi.org/10.1007/BF00986817

Griffiths, P. E., & Scarantino, A. (2009). Emotions in the wild: The situated perspective on emotion. In P. Robbins & M. Aydede (Eds.), *The Cambridge handbook of situated cognition* (pp. 437–453). Cambridge: Cambridge University Press.

Groscup, J.L., Brank, E. M., Roizin, E., Gold, R., & Sachs, L. (2015, March) *Warning me that I can say no will only make me feel better about saying yes: The effects of police warnings and understanding of rights in a consent search.* Paper presentation at the annual meeting of the American Psychology-Law Society, San Diego, CA.

Groscup, J. L., Marshall, E., & Brank, E. M. (2016, March). *Hey officer, don't fence me in! The impact of exit-blocking, physical distance, and relative physical position on perceptions of*

consent searches. Paper presented at the annual meeting of the American Psychology-Law Society, Atlanta, GA.
Groscup, J., Rivera, A., Hoetger, L., & Brank, E. (2014, March). *Give me a home where the drug sniffing dog doesn't roam: Privacy expectations for canine searches.* Paper presented at the American Psychology & Law Association Annual Conference, New Orleans, LA, March, 2014.
Henderson, M., Wakslak, C., Fujita, K., & Rohrbach, J. (2011). Construal level theory and spatial distance: Implications for mental representation, judgment, and behavior. *Social Psychology, 42*, 165–173. https://doi.org/10.1027/1864-9335/a000060
Hinkel, D., & Mahr, J. (2011, January 6). Drug-sniffing dogs in traffic stops often wrong. *The Chicago Tribune.*
Ijzerman, H., & Semin, G. (2009). The thermometer of social relations: Mapping social proximity on temperature. *Psychological Science, 20*, 1214–1220. https://doi.org/10.1111/j.1467-9280.2009.02434.x
Illinois v. Caballes, 543 U.S. 405, 125 S.Ct. 834 (2005).
Illinois v. Gates, 462 U.S. 213 (1983).
Immigration and Naturalization Service (INS) v. Delgado, 466 U.S. 210 (1984).
Kagehiro, D. K. (1988). Perceived voluntariness of consent to warrantless police searches. *Journal of Applied Social Psychology, 18*, 38–49. https://doi.org/10.1111/j.15591816.1988.tb00003.x.
Kagehiro, D. K. (1990). Psycholegal research on the Fourth Amendment. *Psychological Science, 1*, 187–193. https://doi.org/10.1111/j.1467-9280.1990.tb00196.x
Kagehiro, D. K., & Taylor, R. B. (1991). Third-party consent searches: Legal vs. social perceptions of common authority. *Journal of Applied Social Psychology, 18*, 1274–1287. https://doi.org/10.1111/j.1559-1816.1988.tb01206.x
Kagehiro, D. K., Taylor, R. B., & Harland, A. T. (1991). Reasonable expectation of privacy and third-party consent searches. *Law and Human Behavior, 15*, 121–138. https://doi.org/10.1007/BF01044614
Kagehiro, D. K., Taylor, R. B., Laufer, W. S., & Harland, A. T. (1991). Hindsight bias and third-party consentors to warrantless police searches. *Law and Human Behavior, 15*, 305–314. https://doi.org/10.1007/BF01061715
Kassin, S., Drizen, S., Grisso, T., Gudjonsson, G., Leo, R., & Redlich, A. (2009). Police-induced confessions: Risk factors and recommendations. *Law and Human Behavior, 34*, 3–38. https://doi.org/10.1007/s10979-009-9188-6
Kassin, S., & Gudjonsson, G. (2004). The psychology of confessions: A review of the literature and issues. *Psychological Science in the Public Interest, 5*, 33–67. https://doi.org/10.1111/j.1529-1006.2004.00016.x
Katz v. United States. 389 U.S. 347 (1967).
Kerr, O. S. (2007). Four models of Fourth Amendment protection. *Stanford Law Review, 60*, 503–551.
Kerr, O. S. (2010). Applying the Fourth Amendment to the internet: A general approach. *Stanford Law Review, 62*, 1005–1038.
Kerr, O. S. (2012). The mosaic theory of the Fourth Amendment. *Michigan Law Review, 111*, 311–354.
Kessler, D. K. (2009). Free to leave? An empirical look at the Fourth Amendment's seizure standard. *The Journal of Criminal Law and Criminology, 99*, 51–87.
Kyllo v. United States, 533 U.S. 27, 121 S.Ct. 2038 (2001)
LaFave, W., Israel, J., King, N. J., & Kerr, O. S. (2009). *Hornbook on criminal procedure* (5th ed.). St. Paul: West Publishing Co..
Lakens, D., Semin, G., & Foroni, F. (2011). Why your highness needs the people: Comparing the absolute and relative representation of power in vertical space. *Social Psychology, 42*, 205–213. https://doi.org/10.1027/1864-9335/a000064
Lassiter, G. D., Diamond, S. S., Schmidt, H. C., & Elek, J. K. (2007). Evaluating videotaped confessions: Expertise provides no defense against the camera-perspective effect. *Psychological Science, 18*, 224–226. https://doi.org/10.1111/j.1467-9280.2007.01879.x

Lewin, K. (1943). Defining the 'field at a given time.'. *Psychological Review, 50*, 292–310. https://doi.org/10.1037/h0062738
Lichtenberg, I. D. (2000). *Voluntary consent or obedience to authority: An inquiry into the 'consensual' police-citizen encounter.* (Doctoral dissertation). Retrieved from ProQuest. AAT 9947571.
Lichtenberg, I. D. (2001). *Miranda* in Ohio: The effect of *Robinette* on the "voluntary" waiver of Fourth Amendment Rights. *Howard Law Journal, 44*, 349–374.
Lichtenberg, I. D. (2004a). The impact of verbal warning on police consent search practices. *Journal of Criminal Justice, 32*, 85–87. https://doi.org/10.1016/j.jcrimjus.2003.10.008
Lichtenberg, I. D. (2004b). The bus-sweep controversy: Agency, authority, and the unresolved issue of third-party consent. *University of Detroit Mercy Law Review, 81*, 145–173.
Lichtenberg, I. D., & Smith, A. (2001). Testing the effectiveness of consent searches as a law enforcement tool. *The Justice Professional, 14*, 95–111. https://doi.org/10.1080/1478601X.2001.9959612
Loewy, A. (1983). The Fourth Amendment as a Device for Protecting the Innocent. *Michigan Law Review, 81*(5), 1229–1272. https://doi.org/10.2307/1288524
MacLin, T. (1998). Race and the Fourth Amendment. *Vanderbilt Law Review, 51*, 333–393.
Mapp v. Ohio, 367 U.S. 643 (1961).
Milgram, S. (1974). *Obedience to authority: An experimental view*. New York: Harper and Row.
Nadler, J. (2002). No need to shout: Bus sweeps and the psychology of coercion. *Supreme Court Review*, 153–222.
Nadler, J., & Trout, J. D. (2012)). The language of consent in police encounters. In P. Tiersma & L. Solan (Eds.). *Oxford Handbook on Linguistics and the Law.* (326-339). New York: Oxford.
Najdowski, C. J. (2011). Stereotype threat in criminal interrogations: Why innocent black suspects are at risk for confessing falsely. *Psychology, Public Policy, and Law, 17*, 562–591. https://doi.org/10.1037/a0023741
Nardone v. United States, 308 U.S. 338 (1939).
Ohio v. Robinette, 519 U.S. 33 (1996).
Oliver v. U.S., 466 U.S. 170 (1984).
Olmstead v. United States, 277 U.S. 438 (1928).
Ping, R. M., Dhillon, S., & Beilock, S. L. (2009). Reach for what you like: The body's role in shaping preferences. *Emotion Review, 1*(2), 140. https://doi.org/10.1177/1754073908100439
Riley v. California, 134 S. Ct. 2473 (2014).
Rivera, A., & Groscup, J. (2014, March). *Good dog! How the background of law enforcement dogs affects perceptions of canine searches.* Poster presented at the American Psychology & Law Association Annual Conference, New Orleans, LA, March, 2014.
Robbennolt, J. K., & Sobus, M. S. (1997). An integration of hindsight bias and counterfactual thinking: Decision-making and drug courier profiles. *Law and Human Behavior, 21*, 539–560. https://doi.org/10.1023/A:1024879824307
Robbins, P., & Aydede, M. (2009). A short primer on situated cognition. In P. Robbins & M. Aydede (Eds.), *The Cambridge handbook of situated cognition* (pp. 3–10). Cambridge University Press.
Russano, M. B., Meissner, C. A., Narchet, F. M., & Kassin, S. M. (2005). Investigating true and false confessions within a novel experimental paradigm. *Psychological Science, 16*, 481–486.
Scherr, K. C., & Madon, S. (2012). You have the right to understand: The deleterious effect of stress on suspects' ability to comprehend Miranda. *Forthcoming in Law and Human Behavior*. https://doi.org/10.1037/h0093972
Schnall, S., Harber, K. D., Stefanucci, J. K., & Proffitt, D. R. (2008). Social support and the perception of geographical slant. *Journal of Experimental Social Psychology, 44*, 1246–1255. https://doi.org/10.1016/j.jesp.2008.04.011
Schneckloth v. Bustamonte, 412 U.S. 218 (1973)
Semin, G. R., & Smith, E. R. (2002). Interfaces of social psychology with situated and embodied cognition. *Cognitive Systems Research, 1*, 85–97. https://doi.org/10.1016/S1389-0417(02)00049-9
Silverthorne Lumber Co. v. United States (1920)

Simmons, R. (2005). Not "voluntary" but still reasonable: A new paradigm for understanding the consent searches doctrine. *Indiana Law Journal, 80*, 773–824.
Sklansky, D. A. (2000). The Fourth Amendment and common law. *Columbia Law Review, 100*(7), 1739–1814.
Slobogin, C. (1991). The world without a Fourth Amendment. *University of California Los Angeles Law Review, 39*, 1–107.
Slobogin, C., & Schumacher, J. E. (1993). Reasonable expectations of privacy and autonomy in Fourth Amendment cases: An empirical look at "understanding recognized and permitted by society". *Duke Law Journal, 42*, 727–775. https://doi.org/10.2307/1372714
Slobogin, C. (2013). Making the most of *United States v. Jones* in a surveillance society: A statutory implementation of mosaic theory. *Duke Journal of Constitutional Law & Public Policy, 8*, 1-37.
Smith, E. R. (2008). Social relationships and groups: New insights on embodied and distributed cognition. *Cognitive Systems Research, 9*, 24–32. https://doi.org/10.1016/j.cogsys.2007.06.011
Smith, E. R., & Collins, E. C. (2009). Contextualizing person perception: Distributed social cognition. *Psychological Review, 116*, 343–364. https://doi.org/10.1037/a0015072
Smith, E. R., & Semin, G. R. (2007). Situated social cognition. *Current directions in psychological science, 16*(3), 132–135. https://doi.org/10.1111/j.1467-8721.2007.00490.x
Smith v. Maryland, 442 U.S. 735 (1979).
Spivey, M., & Richardson, D. (2009). Language processing embodied and embedded. In P. Robbins & M. Aydede (Eds.), *The Cambridge handbook of situated cognition* (pp. 382–400). Cambridge: Cambridge University Press.
State v. Johnson, 346 A. 2d 66 (N.J. 1975).
State v. Ferrier, 960 P. 2d. 927 (Wash. 1998).
Stefanucci, J. K., Proffitt, D. R., Clore, G., & Parekh, N. (2008). Skating down a steeper slope: Fear influences the perception of geographical slant. *Perception, 37*, 321–323. https://doi.org/10.1068/p5796
Steidle, A., Werth, L., & Hanke, E.-V. (2011). You can't see much in the dark: Darkness affects construal level and psychological distance. *Social Psychology, 42*, 174–184. https://doi.org/10.1027/1864-9335/a000061
Stokols, D. (1972). On the distinction between density and crowding: Some implications for future research. *Psychological Review, 79*, 275–277. https://doi.org/10.1037/h0032706
Stuntz, W. J. (1991). Warrants and Fourth Amendment remedies. *Virginia Law Review, 77*(5), 881–943.
Stuntz, W. J. (1995). The problems with privacy's problem: Reply. *Michigan Law Review, 93*(5), 1102–1104.
Sundby, S. E. (1994). "Everyman"'s Fourth Amendment: Privacy or mutual trust between government and citizen? *Columbia Law Review, 94*(6), 1751–1812.
Sutherland, B. A. (2006). Whether consent to search was given voluntarily: A statistical analysis of factors that predict the suppression ruling of the federal district courts. *New York University Law Review, 81*, 2192–2225.
Taslitz, A. E. (2006). *Reconstructing the Fourth Amendment: A history of search and seizure, 1789-1868*. New York: New York University Press.
Terry v. Ohio, 392 U.S. 1 (1968).
Thompson, A. C. (1999). Stopping the usual suspects: Race and the Fourth Amendment. *New York University Law Review, 74*, 956–1013.
Tiersma, P. M., & Solan, L. M. (2004). Cops and robbers: Selective literalism in American criminal law. *Law and Society Review, 38*, 229–265. https://doi.org/10.1111/j.0023-9216.2004.03802008.x
Trope, Y., & Liberman, N. (2010). Construal-level theory of psychological distance. *Psychological Review, 117*, 440–463. https://doi.org/10.1037/a0018963
Trupiano v. United States, 334 U.S. 699 (1948).
Tversky, B. (2009). Spatial cognition: Embodied and situated. In P. Robbins & M. Aydede (Eds.), *The Cambridge Handbook of Situated Cognition* (pp. 201–216). Cambridge University Press.

Twenge, J. M. (2009). Change over time in obedience: The jury's still out, but it might be decreasing. *American Psychologist, 64*, 28–31. https://doi.org/10.1037/a0014475
U.S. v. Barrows 481 F.3d 1246 (10th Cir. 2007).
U.S. v. David, 756 F. Supp. 1385 (D. Nev. 1991).
U.S. v. Drayton, 536 U.S. 194 (2002).
U.S. v. Jones, Transcript of oral argument at 44. 132S.Ct.945 (2012) (No. 10-1295)
U.S. v. Knotts, 460 U.S. 276 (1983).
U.S. v. Matlock, 415 U.S. 164 (1974)
U.S. v. Miller, 425 U.S. 435 (1976)
U. S. v. Place, 462 U.S. 696 (1983)
U.S. v. Rabinowitz, 339 U.S. 56 (1950)
U.S. v. Rodriguez, 135 S.Ct. 1609 (2014)
U.S. v. White, 401 U.S. 745 (1971).
U.S. v. Wurie, 728 F.3d I (2013)
Watzel, R. (2014). Implications for fourth amendment protection in the cloud. *Yale L. J. F., 124*, 73-79. Retrieved from http://www.yalelawjournal.org/forum/rileys-implications-in-the- cloud
Webb, B., Worchel, S., Riechers, L., & Wayne, W. (1986). The influence of categorization on perceptions of crowding. *Personality and Social Psychology Bulletin, 12*, 539–546. https://doi.org/10.1177/0146167286124017
Weeks v. United States, 232 U.S. 383 (1914).
Williams, L. E., & Bargh, J. A. (2008). Experiencing physical warmth promotes interpersonal warmth. *Science, 332*, 606–607. https://doi.org/10.1126/science.1162548
Wilson, M. (2002). Six views of embodied cognition. *Psychonomic Bulletin and Review, 9(4)*, 625. https://doi.org/10.3758/BF03196322
Wilson, K, Brank, E., Groscup, J., & Marshall, E. (2015, March). *I don't know much, but I know I don't trust you: Knowledge of 4th amendment rights and reactions to police requests to search.* Paper presented at the American Psychology & Law Association Annual Conference, San Diego, CA.
Winn, P. (2009). *Katz* and the origins of the "reasonable expectations of privacy" test. *McGeorge Law Review, 40*, 1–13.
Wylie, L. E., Hazen, K. A., Hoeter, L. A., Haby, J. A., & Brank, E. M. (2018, preprint). *Four decades of psychology and law: An Empirical Review. Scientometrics*. https://doi.org/10.1007/s11192-018-2685-y

The Cognitive and Social Psychological Bases of Bias in Forensic Mental Health Judgments

Tess M. S. Neal, Morgan Hight, Brian C. Howatt, and Cassandra Hamza

This chapter reviews the basic psychological science of bias in human judgment as relevant to judgments and decisions (assessments and recommendations made) by forensic mental health professionals. The legal system itself and many people involved, such as jurors, assume mental health experts can be and typically are "objective" and protected against bias. Moreover, many experts themselves believe they can control their various biases in order to practice objectively. Indeed, psychology ethics codes and guidelines require that practicing psychologists be objective. However, basic psychological science from several branches of the discipline suggests these assumptions about experts' protection from bias are wrong, with empirical studies now showing clear evidence of (unintentional) bias in forensic mental experts' judgments and decisions. This chapter explains how and why human judgments are susceptible to various kinds of bias, with a specific emphasis on expert judgments, particularly, but not exclusively, within the domain of forensic psychology. The implications across these findings are discussed. We close with a discussion of directions for future research and practice.

The Psychology of Bias in Cognitive and Social Judgments

Much of this chapter focuses on cognitive psychological issues of mental functioning, such as perception, reasoning, attention, memory, and decision-making, with coverage of core cognitive psychological literature. However, this chapter also focuses on social psychological issues (particularly, social cognition) involving how

T. M. S. Neal (✉) · M. Hight · B. C. Howatt · C. Hamza
School of Social and Behavioral Sciences, New College of Interdisciplinary Arts & Sciences, Arizona State University, Glendale, AZ, USA
e-mail: Tess.Neal@asu.edu

M. K. Miller, B. H. Bornstein (eds.), *Advances in Psychology and Law*, Advances in Psychology and Law 3,
https://doi.org/10.1007/978-3-319-75859-6_5

other people affect these operations. Some areas in which social cognition can inform the topics discussed in this chapter include attitudes, stereotypes, impression formation, the self, person perception, attribution, persuasion, and conformity (Chaiken & Trope, 1999; Devine, Hamilton, & Ostrom, 1994; Greenwald & Banaji, 1995). The dual-process theoretical foundation of this chapter is inherent in both the cognitive and social-cognitive literatures.

Human cognitive processing abilities are in many ways extraordinary. Our cognitive processing machinery has evolved into an "adaptive toolbox" to help us efficiently process the vast amounts of information we are faced with each day (e.g., Hoffrage & Gigerenzer, 2004). As humans, we literally would not be able to function if we did not have mental "shortcuts" that work well most of the time to help us reduce the complexities of our environment, cope with information overload, and make reasonable judgments and decisions. Haselton et al. (2009) and Gigerenzer (2008) describe how our adaptively rational minds developed based on our ancestors' need for survival, and how mechanisms evolved from the past influence our actions today.

But this very design also makes us susceptible to predictable and systematic errors in judgments and decisions (see e.g., Kahneman, 2011; Kahneman & Klein, 2009). For example, our prior expectations can distort our subsequent processing of new information. Our personal self-interest shapes our interpretation of "objective" data and facts. Other people affect our judgments in ways of which we are unaware. Even random numbers in our environment can act as "anchors" that pull our numeric estimates away from the truth. These biases, one might hope and expect, should be less likely to impact experts—particularly experts making judgments and decisions in their domain of expertise—like forensic psychologists performing forensic psychological evaluations. Yet, experts are indeed human—and evidence suggests their brains work like the rest of ours, for better and for worse. Although experts can be biased by intentional, explicit biases, this chapter focuses on unintentional, "System 1" biases that originate below the level of conscious awareness, as we explain next.

Dual-Process Theories

Evidence from cognitive neuroscience, cognitive psychology, and social cognition is converging on the conclusion that human brain functioning can be characterized by two types of cognition, each with different functions, strengths and weaknesses (Chaiken & Trope, 1999; Greenwald & Banaji, 1995; Kahneman, 2003; Sloman, 1996; Stanovich & West, 2000). These theories propose a cognitive architecture comprised of separable, independent systems. System 1 (sometimes referred to as Type 1—or intuitive) processing occurs automatically, quickly, with little or no effort, and implicitly—that is, below the level of conscious awareness. In contrast, System 2 (Type 2—or reflective) processing is slow, deliberate, effortful, and explicitly conscious. These distinctions are important, because in this chapter we focus on System 1 biases that occur quickly, automatically, and outside of the awareness of experts. Experts are human, and thus it is reasonable and even expected that they should share the cognitive strengths and limitations that other humans possess. Understanding these factors can inform better structuring the decision tasks experts face in order to minimize the chances that System 1 errors and biases can affect their judgments.

While the preceding research has revealed the qualities of dual-*processes* of cognition within a dual-*system* framework, some researchers have argued against this notion. Evans' (2008) review of dual-system models led him to suggest that dual-systems do not necessarily follow from dual-processes, calling this conclusion "oversimplified and misleading" (p. 270). He argues the data show the processes are not mutually exclusive, either structurally or functionally, and that they share conscious and preconscious (unconscious or nonconscious) operations. Instead, he proposes that reflective cognition primarily differs from intuition by requiring access to a central working-memory repository, in which overload or interference can then disrupt its processes—an interactive approach to cognition. We now turn to dual-process models as relevant to bias in cognitive psychology, and later, we will review dual-process models as relevant to bias in social psychology.

Cognitive Psychology: The Heuristics and Biases Literature

The heuristics and biases literature is vast. This brief review provides context for a more focused discussion of how heuristics and biases play out in forensic decision-making. Some researchers have argued that System 1-induced cognitive "biases" are not really biases (Gigerenzer, 1991), but rather illustrate an adaptive rationality (Gigerenzer, 2008; Haselton et al., 2009) that aids an organism's survival by rapidly evaluating environmental data and guiding appropriate behavior. However, these swift processes are nonetheless prone to error in systematic ways. Thus, "bias," as used in the heuristics and biases tradition of cognitive psychology, is a by-product of System 1's mental shortcuts. The framing of System 1 processes as problematic "biases" versus "adaptive strengths" is a longstanding point of contention in the literature (see e.g., Kahneman & Klein, 2009), which is relevant for thinking about experts' decision processes. Although there is disagreement about the types of heuristics and how they are observed, there seems to be a general consensus regarding heuristics as highly serviceable aspects of cognition, though subject to error.

System 1 "heuristics," or mental shortcuts that expedite the time and effort required to process and interpret information, involve a speed/accuracy tradeoff allowing an individual to make judgments and decisions that are "good enough" even though a more maximal outcome might exist. Notable heuristics initially developed by decision researchers include *representativeness* (Kahneman & Tversky, 1972), *availability* (Tversky & Kahneman, 1973), and *anchoring* (Tversky & Kahneman, 1974), with the later addition of *affect* (Slovic, Finucane, Peters, & MacGregor, 2007). Representativeness is a way of identifying and organizing information based upon its similarity to other information, whereas availability affects judgments based on how easy it is to recall other examples of an event in question. Anchoring affects judgments in that initial information encountered is more heavily weighted than subsequent information, especially when making numerical judgments. Finally, affect is an emotion-oriented heuristic in which people pursue pleasure and avoid pain, and it can amplify or dampen perceptions. While these methods are generally sufficient in cuing appropriate behavior, they can distort the likelihood or magnitude of an event, leading to systematic biases in judgments and choices.

Gigerenzer (1991, 1996) has argued against these specific heuristics, calling them merely labels of behavior, and devoid of ecological applicability. Alternatively, he has put forth common misconceptions of heuristics and proposed an "adaptive toolbox" (Gigerenzer, 2008) of behavioral processes, including satisficing, recognition, and default. Satisficing is choosing the first option that meets an acceptable level of criteria; the recognition heuristic places a greater value on options that are recognizable; and the default heuristic prefers the status quo, unless another option is clearly superior. Moreover, he offers conditions under which these adaptive heuristics can outperform objective, mathematical analyses of decision scenarios (e.g., System 2 processes) and calls for research to focus more heavily on the interaction between these strategies and the environments in which they are made. Haselton et al.' (2009) research seems to substantiate Gigerenzer's proposals, suggesting heuristics are not as flawed as previous research posits and that limited environmental information can lead to erroneous conclusions.

It should be noted that Kahneman and Tversky acknowledged the efficacy of heuristics in daily judgments and decisions (e.g., Kahneman & Tversky, 1972; Tversky & Kahneman 1973, 1974), but were more interested in examining how resulting behavior deviated from theories postulating the optimality of statistical intuition (which Gigerenzer also acknowledges can readily happen; e.g., Gigerenzer 2008).

In many ways, experts develop ways of recognizing and diagnosing situations that non-experts cannot—by virtue of both System 1 and System 2 processes. But System 1 can sometimes lead experts astray, even in their own domains of expertise. The reason it is important to recognize how and when this can happen—to identify some common problems—is that people can then develop methodologies to ameliorate their negative influences.

Cognitive Psychological Biases and Forensic Mental Health Judgments

This section considers various cognitive biases that can affect forensic mental health judgments. We also discuss the role of biased behavior in similar expert judgments outside of the forensic mental health field in order to expand this discussion. Neal and Grisso (2014) provide several thought experiments and examples of how heuristics could affect forensic mental health judgments. For example, they provided a vignette about "John P." and his potential mental illness at the time of an alleged crime to illustrate the representativeness heuristic as relevant to forensic mental health judgments, as well as a related real-world example of an internationally recognized forensic psychiatrist neglecting relevant base-rates in the John Hinckley trial (1982 trial of the attempted assassination of President Ronald Reagan). In the Hinckley case, the forensic psychiatrist offered expert testimony about the widened sulci in Mr. Hinckley's brain, opining that he had schizophrenia based on the statistical likelihood of widened sulci in the brains of people with schizophrenia. However, he did not account for the low base rate of schizophrenia in the general population and thus his conclusion was based on erroneous Bayesian statistical reasoning.

To illustrate the availability heuristic, Neal and Grisso discussed the problem of false negatives in sex offender risk assessments, invited readers to attempt an adapted version of the Wason (1968) card task, and described the relevance of Kahneman's (2011) WYSIATI (What You See Is All There Is) concept for forensic mental health assessments. WYSIATI is closely related to the availability heuristic: only ideas that are activated in a person's mind are processed within a given decision task. Finally, to illustrate anchoring, Neal and Grisso described a case in which a mental health professional might encounter one likeable parent versus the other in a child custody evaluation, and they further describe framing and context effects as relevant to forensic decision tasks, to be discussed in more depth in the following section.

Evidence to Date Specifically Relevant to Forensic Mental Health Judgments

Even for experts who are motivated to be unbiased, there is mounting evidence that forensic mental health experts are susceptible to System 1-induced biases. For example, clear evidence of the "self-serving bias," which has been labeled "adversarial allegiance" in the forensic mental health field, has been documented. Adversarial allegiance is an unintentional tendency for experts to find evidence in support of their retaining party's position—an anchoring-like effect—and has been uncovered in forensic mental health judgments (Murrie, Boccaccini, Guarnera, & Rufino, 2013). Confirmation bias, or a tendency for experts to seek evidence in support of an initial hypothesis without seeking disconfirming evidence—another type of System 1 bias—has also been documented in forensic mental health experts' judgments (Neal, MacLean, Morgan, & Murrie, 2017) And hindsight bias, another System 1 bias in which people who know the outcome of an event or situation overestimate what they could have known in foresight (Fischhoff, 1975), has been found in forensic psychiatrists' judgments (LeBourgeois III, Pinals, Williams, & Appelbaum, 2007).

Self-Serving Bias: Affiliations with other people affect one's processing of information. One of the first studies on the power of affiliation documenting the self-serving bias was actually with regard to sports teams. In a classic study, Hastdorf and Cantril (1954) showed that football fans from each team blamed the other team for behaving badly while discounting their own team's behaviors. In a more legally relevant study, Babcock and Loewenstein (1997) showed that even when provided with the same case information, people on opposing sides of a case reached different conclusions based on that evidence—in favor of their own interests. In this study, Babcock and Loewenstein provided pairs of participants with police and medical reports, depositions, and other materials from a lawsuit resulting from a collision between a motorcycle and a car. Participants were randomly assigned to the role of either the motorcyclist plaintiff or car-driving defendant. Participants in the motorcyclist plaintiff role found evidence to support their position and predicted dramatically larger damage awards than participants in the defendant condition.

In the American adversarial legal system, forensic mental health experts are often retained by one side or another in a case. Involvement and affiliation with attorneys influences experts' examination and evaluation of case materials, in that experts end up emphasizing findings and patterns that support "their side." Murrie, Boccaccini and colleagues documented this phenomenon in observational studies in which they found clear patterns of experts scoring standardized psychological tools in favor of their retaining party in sexual offender civil commitment cases (Murrie, Boccaccini, Johnson, & Janke, 2008; Murrie et al., 2009). For example, Murrie et al. (2009) looked at real sexual offender civil commitment cases and measured how experts on each "side" of the case scored three tools that are often used in sex offender risk assessments: the Minnesota Sex Offender Screening Tool-Revised (MnSOST-R; Epperson et al., 1998), Psychopathy Checklist-Revised (PCL-R; Hare, 2003), and the STATIC-99 (Hanson & Thornton, 1999).

Consistent with the self-serving bias/adversarial allegiance hypothesis, Murrie et al. (2009) showed that plaintiff-retained experts scored the offenders on average 3.53 points higher (scoring range is −14 to 30) than respondent-retained experts on the MnSOST-R (Cohen's $d = 0.85$, a large effect size), 5.79 points higher (scoring range is 0 to 40) on the PCL-R (Cohen's $d = 0.78$, a large effect size), and 0.52 points higher (scoring range 0 to 12) on the STATIC-99 (Cohen's $d = 0.34$, a moderately small effect size on a measure with less subjective items). Furthermore, they calculated the proportion of variance in the scores on these tools that were attributable to the offender (which ideally would be 100%), the side of the case (ideally 0%), and other error (ideally 0%). They found that 44% of the variance on the MnSOST-R was attributable to the offender, 26% was attributable to the side of the case (this is the adversarial allegiance effect), and 30% was other error. On the PCL-R, 42% of the variance was attributable to the offender, 23% to the side of the case (adversarial allegiance), and 35% to other error. And for the most structured and least subjective measure, the STATIC-99, 62% of the variance was attributable to the offender, only 4% to the side of the case (adversarial allegiance), and 34% to other error.

The systematic evidence of adversarial allegiance in forensic mental health evaluations led researchers to probe more deeply into potential explanations for the findings. Were forensic mental health evaluators intentionally biased "hired guns?" Or were they unintentionally and unknowingly biased by unconscious System 1 processes? Was it the mere fact of the adversarial hire itself that caused the adversarial allegiance bias, or was it something else (e.g., self-selection factors, like experts choosing which side to work for based on preexisting biases)? Murrie et al. (2013) designed an elegant experiment to explore some of these questions.

In an experimental study of civil commitment proceedings for sex offenders, Murrie et al. (2013) had real forensic mental health experts hired by a referring attorney (randomly assigned to either plaintiff or respondent). That is, the manipulated independent variable was the adversarial "side" for which experts thought they were working (the case and offender materials were held constant, as was the script the attorneys used to hire the experts with the manipulation built directly into the script). The participant-experts were asked to score four offenders on two commonly used and well-researched risk instruments, the PCL-R and the STATIC-99. Importantly, the forensic evaluators were paid $400 for their consultation and were deceived to believe these referrals were real, as opposed to being part of a research study: they did not know they were being studied.

Results revealed a significant bias as a function of the side by which the expert was retained: more evidence of adversarial allegiance. Forensic mental health experts who believed they were working for the plaintiff assigned higher scores on the risk instruments than experts who believed they were working for the respondent. The effect sizes were up to $d = 0.85$ (large effects) for the PCL-R and up to $d = 0.42$ on the STATIC-99 (moderately small effect on this measure with less subjective items). Of course, there is considerable variability in scoring assessment instruments: not every evaluator will produce consistent scores. But here, a large portion of the systematic score differences among opposing experts was explained by adversarial allegiance and not by chance or random error.

The study demonstrated that experts scoring ostensibly objective assessment instruments assigned scores that were systematically biased toward the side that retained them. Given the experimental design of the study, cause can be inferred: the only variable that differed between the two conditions was the hiring party. Participants were unaware that the hiring party influenced their scores, yet there was clear evidence that adversarial allegiance absolutely influenced experts' scores. Thus, Murrie et al. (2013) attributed the adversarial allegiance effect directly to experts' beliefs about for whom they were working, because they controlled for other possible explanations.

The substantive information provided about the offender was constant, so differences in the way the examinee presented could not have explained the findings. Furthermore, they eliminated the overt verbal influence often provided by the referral party in routine forensic practice that contributes to confirmation bias by using a script. This design element is important: their findings show that even when there is no overt framing by a referral party, there is still an insidious, unconscious, and potent effect of adversarial allegiance affecting forensic mental health professionals' judgments and decisions.

McAuliff and Arter (2016) studied the potential influence of adversarial allegiance on different aspects of expert testimony in a simulated child sexual abuse case. Participant-experts were asked by either the prosecution or the defense to read a description of a police officer's low or high suggestive interview with a 5-year-old girl. Experts were more willing to testify if asked by the prosecution when the suggestibility in the police officer interview was low, meaning when the interview was done soundly by the officer and did not raise concerns about the child's accuracy. In contrast, the experts who were asked by the defense were more willing to testify when the suggestibility of the interview was high, meaning the interview between the police officer was unsound and concerns about the child's accuracy were raised. Thus, experts might have perceived their testimony as being more relevant and more helpful to jurors when the evidence favored the party soliciting their testimony—more evidence suggestive of adversarial allegiance and how the adversarial system influences forensic mental health professionals' judgments and decisions.

Confirmation bias: Neal et al. (2017) conducted a recent study of confirmation bias in forensic psychologists' diagnostic reasoning. Confirmation bias is a System-1 type of process in which people tend to seek and rely on information that confirms a "hunch" rather than seeking disconfirmatory information (see Nickerson, 1998). The modern scientific method evolved in part to combat the powerful "confirmatory" bias in hypothesis-testing (Neal & Saks, in preparation; Popper, 1959), yet evidence of confirmation bias persists in many contexts. Some examples include intelligence analysis (Cook & Smallman, 2008), criminal investigations (Ask & Granhag, 2005), radiology diagnostic tasks (Drew, Võ, & Wolfe, 2013), and even in science itself (MacCoun, 1998).

In the Neal et al. (2017) study, a national sample of 118 randomly selected experienced forensic psychologists were invited via an email invitation to participate in the study (17% response rate). Participants provided diagnostic hypotheses for and answer questions about one of four randomly assigned vignettes of people presenting with different sets of symptoms and from different referral contexts. The initial diagnostic question asked participants to rank-order a list of four possible initial diagnostic hypotheses "in order of likelihood that this person might meet DSM-5 diagnostic criteria for each" (the options were the same across vignettes). Next, they received a follow-up question linked to the diagnostic hypothesis they rank-ordered first.

The follow-up question asked "Now, based on your primary diagnostic hypothesis that Mr. G meets criteria for x, what piece of information would you want first in order to effectively test your primary diagnostic hypothesis?" They were provided with a choice between two types of information: one that might *confirm* their initial hypothesis, and one that might *disconfirm* their initial hypothesis. For example, for participants who rank-ordered intellectual disability as their first diagnostic hypothesis, they had the choice between "Did Mr. G show deficits in intellectual functioning on the standardized intelligence tests he took at ages 10 and 14?" (*confirmatory*) and "Does Mr. G have a personality disorder that could explain his symptoms?" (*disconfirmatory*). The authors hypothesized clinicians would be more likely to choose the confirmatory than disconfirmatory information (i.e., engage in confirmation bias).

The survey also included the three-item ($M = 1.41$, SD = 1.17) cognitive reflection task (Frederick 2005), which had good reliability in this sample (alpha = 0.72).

Cognitive reflection is the ability to resist the first "heuristic" response that comes to mind, instead engaging in deliberative thought to reach an answer. The authors predicted clinicians with higher cognitive reflection tendencies would be less likely to engage in confirmatory bias.

Results indicated that forensic clinicians overwhelmingly engaged in confirmation bias: 103 of the 111 people who responded to this question chose the confirmatory information, χ^2 (1) = 81.31, $p < 0.001$. Cognitive reflection had a statistically and theoretically significant association with confirmation bias in the predicted direction. Each unit higher on the three-item cognitive reflection task (representing higher cognitive reflection tendencies) halved the odds of confirmatory bias, B = -0.75, *Wald*(1) = 3.85, $p = 0.050$, *Exp(B)* = 0.473 (logistic regression model χ^2 [1] = 4.67, $p = 0.031$).

These findings demonstrate robust confirmation bias in diagnostic reasoning in a representative sample of licensed psychologists in forensic practice in the USA. Susceptibility to this bias was related to lower cognitive reflection tendencies (i.e., tendency to rely more on System 1 than System 2 thinking). What this study does not tell us is how far confirmation bias persists (i.e., how far beyond the "first piece of information"). Neal and colleagues are currently collecting new data to explore this question.

Hindsight bias: People who know an outcome cannot unknow it—it is like unhearing a bell that was rung—and such knowledge influences people's beliefs about how predictable or foreseeable the outcome actually was (Fischhoff, 1975). This type of judgment is highly relevant for legal cases, because legal decision makers must reason *ex post facto* although they know the outcome of the situation (i.e., the crime in criminal cases or the tort in civil cases). This outcome knowledge can bias decision makers, including jurors (e.g., Labine & Labine, 1996; Robbennolt, 2000) and judges (e.g., Guthrie, Rachlinski, & Wistrich, 2001).

In clinical contexts, previous research has shown that physicians are susceptible to hindsight bias as well (Arkes, Wortmann, Saville, & Harkness, 1981; Caplan, Posner, & Cheney, 1991; Sacchi & Cherubini, 2004). For example, in a study by Caplan et al. (1991), experienced anesthesiologists were provided with a set of clinical case scenarios with set facts and reviewed a previous physician's decisions in the case and rate the standard of care. Importantly, they were randomly assigned to know different outcomes of the cases (i.e., temporary vs. permanent injury). Anesthesiologists who knew the outcome was a permanent injury were more likely to rate the previous physician's care as substandard when compared to knowledge that the injury was just temporary. This finding is significant because the cases themselves were identical, and the outcome of the situation could not have been known at the time of the event itself. Thus, the retrospective judgments of the appropriateness of care delivered by others physicians were, but should not have been, influenced by the outcome of the situation.

Extending this work into the domain of forensic mental health judgments, LeBourgeois and colleagues (2007) exposed psychiatrists to hypothetical cases in which patients with suicidal or homicidal thoughts presented for care. Psychiatrist-participants were randomly assigned to different outcome knowledge conditions:

either that a suicide/homicide occurred shortly after the patients were released from care (hindsight group) or no information about outcome (control group). Psychiatrist-participants estimated the likelihood that suicide or homicide would occur upon the patient's release. Results revealed that forensic psychiatrists were indeed affected by hindsight bias: psychiatrists who knew the outcome of the case rated the patient as at a significantly higher risk of suicide/homicide than those in the control condition who did not know the outcome of the case. LeBourgeois et al. did not ask participants to what degree knowledge of the outcome influenced their judgments. However, given the nature of the hindsight bias and findings from other hindsight bias studies, it is likely that the psychiatrists would not have been aware of how strongly outcome knowledge actually affected their judgments, and they would have overestimated what others actually did know without the outcome knowledge, consistent with a System 1-induced bias (Fischhoff, 1975).

In a recent study of hindsight bias with forensic psychologists as participants, Beltrani, Reed, Zapf, Dror, and Otto (2017) used a method similar to LeBourgeois et al. (2007) and found evidence of hindsight bias in forensic psychologists' decision processes as well. Participants provided with outcome information regarding risk assessment evaluations were more likely to indicate that they would have predicted the outcome than evaluators who were not provided with outcome information, $\chi^2(1) = 4.215$, $p = 0.04$, $\varphi = 0.235$. Furthermore, when asked to provide reasons for their decisions regarding risk, participants in the known-outcome condition provided more risk factors from the initial case information to support their decisions compared to participants in the control condition, who selected more protective factors to support their decisions. These results are consistent with motivated reasoning, a social-cognitive theory proposing that motivation can affect reasoning through biased cognitive processes regarding how information is accessed, constructed, and evaluated (Kunda, 1990). This theory holds that people use the tools of cognition to arrive at desired conclusions, constrained only by one's ability to construct reasonable justifications for that conclusion (Kunda, 1990).

Related Literature on Cognitive Biases in Similar Types of Judgment Tasks

The existence of cognitive biases in similar types of judgment tasks outside of forensic mental health are worth covering briefly. This is because these biases are likely relevant in forensic mental health too, and thus we might generate hypotheses from these studies about how these biases could affect the work of forensic mental health professionals. For example, the judgments and decisions of forensic scientists are subject to the effects of various cognitive biases (e.g., Dror, Charlton, & Péron, 2006; Nakhaeizadeh, Dror, & Morgan, 2014), as have judges (Guthrie et al., 2001; Wistrich, Guthrie, & Rachlinski, 2005), elite arbiters (Helm, Wistrich, & Rachlinski, 2016), and professional accountants (e.g., Moore, Loewenstein, Tanlu, & Bazerman, 2003).

Several studies in the forensic sciences have revealed the power of "context effects" or extraneous information to a case that biases experts' judgments. For instance, Dror et al. (2006) studied whether latent print identification experts were vulnerable to context effects. In an inventive method, they asked experts to make a fingerprint match determination on a set of fingerprints they had previously examined and for which they had made a positive-match decision. The experts were not aware that they were looking at prints they had previously positively identified as a match. Crucially, the experimenters provided contextual information suggesting the prints were a no-match. In the new context, with the biasing contextual information, most of the fingerprint experts made a no-match decision, thus contradicting their own previous match identification decisions.

Nakhaeizadeh et al. (2014) explored whether forensic anthropology experts would be vulnerable to context effects in the assessment of unidentified skeletal remains. They used skeletal remains that had previously been identified as "probable female" but that had some ambiguous morphological features (i.e., pelvis and skull). Sure enough, experts exposed to contextual information about the sex, ancestry, and age at death of the skeletal remains were affected by that information in their interpretation and conclusion of the remains. Compared to experts in a control condition who received no contextual information about the skeletal remains, experts in the contextually biasing information conditions confirmed the extraneous contextual information in their biological profile determinations. For example, only 31% of participants in the control group concluded that the skeletal remains were male. However, among experts in the contextually biasing condition with extraneous information suggesting the remains were male, 72% concluded the remains were male. Among those in the contextually biasing condition with extraneous information suggesting the remains were female, 0% concluded the remains were male. Contextual biases like those described in these studies of forensic scientists are likely present in the work of forensic mental health too.

Like forensic scientists, judges are experienced, well-trained, and typically highly motivated to be accurate and fair. Nevertheless, clear empirical evidence has established the existence of unintentional cognitive biases affecting judges' judgments and decisions. For example, Guthrie et al. (2001) found in a sample of 167 federal magistrate judges that judges were susceptible to anchoring effects, framing effects, hindsight bias, the representativeness heuristic, and egocentric biases on their judicial decision-making. Similarly, Wistrich et al. (2005) showed that judges generally cannot disregard inadmissible information in their legal decisions—even when they were reminded, or they themselves had ruled, that the information was inadmissible. For example, inadmissible information about demands disclosed during settlement conferences, conversations protected by attorney-client privilege, prior sexual history of alleged rape victims, prior criminal convictions of plaintiffs, and information the government had promised not to rely on at sentencing influenced judges' decisions despite their best efforts to ignore them. Like the contextual biases that affect forensic scientists, these various cognitive biases that affect judges do so despite motivation and effort to be unbiased.

Similarly, Helm et al. (2016) found that elite arbitrators are also subject to unintentional System 1-induced biases on their judgments and decisions. Arbitration is an increasingly common type of dispute resolution that provides an alternative to filing a lawsuit and going to court (the traditional method for resolving disputes). Arbitrators resolve thousands of disputes every year, including some high-stakes cases (Helm et al. 2016). Like judges, arbitrators are motivated to be unbiased and fair in their decisions, though judges and arbitrators differ in several ways. Elite arbitrators are highly trained and experienced in specialized areas. Helm et al. studied elite arbitrators specializing in resolving commercial disputes to determine whether these kinds of experts are susceptible to cognitive biases in their work. As might be expected based on the other studies reviewed in this chapter, Helm et al. found that elite arbitrators are subject to the conjunction fallacy, framing effects, confirmation bias, and that their excessive reliance on intuition could exacerbate the effects of System 1 biases on their professional judgments and decisions. These System 1 biases are likely to affect forensic mental health experts too—and they might also over-rely on intuition in problematic ways.

Similar to the training processes and ethics codes in forensic mental health, professional accountants are trained that objectivity is paramount to their work (Moore et al., 2003). Like in forensic mental health, several sources assume that auditor bias is a matter of deliberate choice—that is, auditors are assumed to be able to complete high-quality, objective audits if they so choose (Bazerman, Loewenstein, & Moore, 2002). However, as Moore and colleagues show, the biases that typically affect professional auditors are pervasive, unconscious, and unintentional. Moore et al. showed through three experiments that auditors' judgments are unintentionally biased in favor of their clients (the "self-serving bias"), and that the bias is not easily corrected because auditors are not fully aware of the bias or how it affects their judgments (despite incentives to be objective).

Moore et al. (2003) and Bazerman et al. (2002) make some important points about the conditions that bias professional auditors that are worth mentioning because similar conditions exist in forensic mental health. Bazerman et al. assert that three structural aspects of accounting create substantial opportunities for bias to influence decision makers—two of which in particular are highly relevant to forensic psychology. The first is ambiguity. Bias thrives whenever information can be interpreted in different ways—greater ambiguity leads to more biased information processing and outcomes (Kunda, 1990; Thompson & Loewenstein, 1992). Auditors must accumulate and synthesize a great deal of information to make judgments about client firms—just as forensic psychologists must do to make judgments about case referrals. Like auditing, forensic mental health is an "art" in addition to some science. The imprecision inherent in auditing and forensic mental health allow motivated reasoning to bias experts' judgments. The second condition is attachment, which, as we have already described, breeds the self-interest bias in accountants (Bazerman et al.; Moore et al.) and forensic mental health experts alike (Murrie et al., 2013).

Now that dual-process theories from cognitive psychology and cognitive neuroscience have been reviewed with regard to their potential biasing effects on forensic mental health judgments, we now turn to dual-process theories from social psychology that can help explain these biases as well.

Social Psychology: Explicit and Implicit Social Cognition and Social-Cognitive Biases

Social psychology is a branch of psychology that focuses on how people affect one another's behaviors, and social cognition is an area of social psychology focused on how other people influence a given person's cognitive functions, such as perceptions, reasoning, attention, memory, and decision-making (Devine et al., 1994). Social cognition emerged in the late 1970s (Devine et al., 1994), and dual-process theories in social cognition became increasingly common in the 1980s and 1990s (e.g., Chaiken, 1980; Chaiken & Trope, 1999; Devine, 1989; Greenwald & Banaji, 1995; Petty & Cacioppo, 1986).

Social behavior and judgments were historically assumed to be under conscious control. However, researchers began recognizing that social behavior often is affected by experiences in a manner not known by the actor (Greenwald & Banaji, 1995). Dual-process theories began emerging in social psychology, theorizing that many social-cognitive judgments and behaviors have important implicit (System 1) modes of operation. These dual-process theories in social cognition have attempted to describe implicit, unconscious, heuristic processes (System 1) as separate but certainly related to explicit, conscious, and deliberative processes (System 2) in such areas as attitudes (e.g., Chaiken, 1980; Greenwald & Banaji, 1995; Petty & Cacioppo, 1986), perceptions of the self (e.g., Greenwald & Banaji, 1995), stereotypes (e.g., Devine, 1989; Greenwald & Banaji, 1995), and perception of others (e.g., Chaiken & Trope, 1999), among other areas. In this section, we will review the empirical evidence to date on implicit (System 1) processes including attitudes, perceptions of oneself, and stereotypes as they affect forensic mental health experts' judgments and decisions, as well as experts in fields who face similar judgment tasks.

Social Psychological Biases and Forensic Mental Health Judgments

People's (including experts') perceptions, judgments, and decisions can be influenced by other people, by their expectations about other people's perceptions, by subtle features of the environment, and by their own preexisting attitudes and beliefs (e.g., Devine, 1989; Pronin, Gilovich, & Ross, 2004). Furthermore, people can be biased even when motivated not to be, and when people compare their own biases against others, they have a much harder time seeing their own biases than those of other people (Pronin, Lin, & Ross, 2002). This section examines these kinds of social psychological biases as they might affect forensic mental health judgments and decisions as well as the judgments and decisions of experts in fields who face similar decision tasks. For example, we review evidence about how attitudes toward issues such as capital punishment and gender equality, perceptions of oneself as compared to others, and stereotypes about race and ethnicity unintentionally distort experts' judgments and decisions due to introspective failures. By definition, these implicit processes are below one's level of conscious awareness (Greenwald & Banaji, 1995).

Evidence to Date About Social-Cognitive Biases Relevant to Forensic Mental Health Judgments

Implicit (System 1) social psychological processes affect the judgments and decisions of forensic mental health professionals. Even for experts who are motivated to be unbiased, there is mounting evidence that forensic mental health experts are susceptible to these biases. For example, evidence has emerged that forensic psychologists' capital punishment attitudes affect their judgments and decisions in capital cases (Neal, 2016; Neal & Cramer, in press). Another example is an insidious social-cognitive bias called the "bias blind spot," which refers to an exceedingly common human tendency to recognize bias in others but fail to recognize it in oneself (Pronin et al., 2002), and has been documented in forensic mental health professionals (Commons, Miller, & Gutheil, 2004; Neal & Brodsky, 2016; Neal et al., 2017; Zapf, Kukucka, Kassin, & Dror, 2017). Although we sought to review research on how stereotypes affect forensic mental health professionals' judgments, we could locate no research on this issue to date. The sections that follow review the empirical evidence on attitudes and social perceptions as they affect forensic mental health experts' judgments and decisions.

Attitudes: Neal (2016) sought to determine whether forensic mental health experts' preexisting attitudes might affect their professional judgments and decisions. To investigate this question, Neal focused on death penalty attitudes and decisions relevant to capital cases. She measured the death penalty attitudes of 206 forensic psychologists (using the Death Penalty Attitudes Scale; O'Neil, Patry, & Penrod, 2004) and asked the forensic psychologist respondents whether they would work for the prosecution, defense, and/or court in capital cases. The author hypothesized that evaluators' level of support for capital punishment would systematically influence willingness to accept capital case referrals, such that evaluators with strong support would be more likely to work for the prosecution, and evaluators with low support would be more likely to work for the defense. These hypotheses were partially supported.

As hypothesized, lower support was associated with being willing to work for the defense, as well as a higher likelihood of rejecting any referral from any source (i.e., abstaining completely from capital case evaluations). Stronger support was associated with higher willingness to be involved in capital cases across any referral source. No psychologists reported selective willingness to work only for the prosecution (though several did report selective willingness to work only for the defense—correlated with the strength of their opposition to the death penalty). Neal asserted these findings raise the specter of systematically biased involvement of forensic psychologists in capital case evaluations based on their death penalty attitudes. She also suggested these findings provide a partial explanation for the "allegiance effect," such that evaluators' preexisting attitudes could influence their selective participation in the legal process via "filtering" effects. Future research is needed to further explore the effect of experts' preexisting attitudes and whether these attitudes transfer to biased decision-making in the cases themselves. In this study, attitudes were measured explicitly rather than implicitly—future work must measure the effects of implicit attitudes on judgments.

Neal and Cramer (in press) studied forensic psychologists' death penalty attitudes again, this time studying whether these attitudes were systematically related to forensic psychologists' willingness to conduct the most ethically questionable clinical task in the criminal justice system: competence for execution evaluations. Although there was no direct effect of death penalty attitudes on willingness to accept competence for execution referrals, that relationship was fully mediated by moral disengagement. Moral disengagement is a social-cognitive process through which people reason their way toward harming others (Bandura, 2015). Thus, moral disengagement served as a theoretical "bridge" between forensic psychologists' attitudes and judgments, an interesting finding for helping clarify how psychologists decide to engage in competence for execution evaluations. Here again, the measures were explicit rather than implicit, and studies of implicit attitudes are needed.

The Self: Bias Blind Spot: The bias blind spot occurs across many social groups: college students believe they are less biased than their fellow students, airline passengers think they are less biased than other passengers, car drivers on average believe themselves to be above-average drivers, and so forth. Pronin et al. (2002) conducted a series of studies looking at multiple biases by having participants self-report various biases, and then indicate how much the average American was biased. Participants overwhelmingly reported that they personally were less biased than the average American across many different types of biasing situations, showing the generalizability of this concept.

The bias blind spot is theorized to arise from the interplay of two phenomena: the introspection illusion and naive realism. People tend to self-evaluate the extent of bias in their own behavior through introspection. Because introspection is unlikely to reveal biased thought processes (due to these implicit processes occurring below the level of conscious awareness), they typically go unnoticed and uncorrected. Naive realism is the conviction that oneself interacts with the world objectively and therefore one's behavior sufficiently reflects a rational response to the environment, while others respond in ways that are not grounded in reality (Pronin et al., 2004; Scopelliti et al., 2015). A few studies investigate the phenomenon of the bias blind spot in forensic mental health professionals' judgments.

Commons et al. (2004) asked forensic psychiatrists to rate their potential bias in a number of situations, including recent cases in which they had served as an expert witness. They asked participants to rate 26 potentially biasing factors, such as money, prestige, and amount of public attention attracted by cases, including how often "opposing experts" showed these biases and how often they themselves were affected by such biases. They concluded that forensic psychiatrists markedly underestimate their own biases compared to their peers, consistent with the bias blind spot. Moreover, some situations were perceived as more biasing than others, and participants underestimated the biasing effects of conflicts of interest for both themselves and opposing experts.

Neal and Brodsky (2016) found evidence suggestive of a bias blind spot in forensic psychologists. Using deep narrative interviews in a qualitative study with board-certified forensic psychologists, they found that forensic evaluators perceived themselves as less vulnerable to bias compared to their colleagues. Participants had no trouble identifying bias in their colleagues (100% of the sample discussed ways in which they had observed bias in their colleagues), but fewer reported any concern about bias in themselves (60% mentioned any concern). Some even reported that they take over cases that might be considered a challenge for others because they believe they are able to control themselves in a way that their colleagues cannot. This finding was theorized to be a result of bias blind spot-induced overconfidence in one's own judgments, a negative consequence that could lead to risky decision-making and rejecting aid that might reduce bias and improve validity.

In a recent study of 1,099 forensic mental health professionals across 39 different countries, Zapf et al. (2017) also found evidence of the bias blind spot. In their sample, the mean accuracy rating that forensic mental health professionals provided for forensic evaluations was 78.5%, yet the experts estimated their own accuracy in forensic evaluations at 81.85% (a statistically significant difference with a medium effect size). Furthermore, they rated other forensic mental health professionals as more susceptible to cognitive bias in their forensic evaluations (78.1%) than themselves (52.2%).

In the Neal et al. (2017) study of confirmation bias in forensic mental health diagnostic judgments described earlier in this chapter, participants rated the extent to which their own forensic work is influenced by bias as well as the extent to which work by other forensic psychologists is influenced by bias, each on a 1 (never) to 9 (always) point Likert-scale. These questions were designed to measure the bias blind spot. They calculated the size of an expert's bias blind spot by subtracting self-rating from other rating. They hypothesized the size of participants' bias blind spot would be positively related to confirmatory bias. They also hypothesized that cognitive reflection tendencies (the ability to resist incorrect heuristic responses in favor of deliberative thought) would be inversely related to the size of the bias blind spot.

The bias blind spot hypothesis yielded a meaningful effect size (i.e., theoretically significant) in the predicted direction, but was not statistically significant. Each additional unit of discrepancy between self and other ratings of bias (i.e., increasing bias blind spot) more than doubled the odds of forensic clinicians engaging in confirmation bias. The prediction that cognitive reflection tendencies would be inversely related to the bias blind spot emerged with a small effect size in the predicted direction, but the trend did not reach statistical significance. Forensic clinicians with higher cognitive reflection tendencies had somewhat smaller bias blind spots.

Related Literature on Social-Cognitive Biases in Similar Types of Judgment Tasks

Outside of the forensic mental health contexts, the influence of implicit (System 1) attitudes, self-perceptions, and stereotypes on related types of expert judgment tasks are reviewed here. These findings are relevant to forensic mental health, because it is likely that many of these same implicit social-psychological processes affect the judgments of forensic mental health professionals in similar ways. For example, judges' (Segal & Spaetch 2002), professional arbitrators' (Girvan, Deason, & Borgida 2015), and law students' (Braman & Nelson, 2007) legal decisions are systematically affected by their attitudes. Further, the bias blind spot has been documented in forensic scientists (Kukucka, Kassin, Dror, & Zapf, 2017); and both judges and physicians show evidence of implicit racial biases in their legal and medical decisions (Green et al., 2007; Rachlinski, Johnson, Wistrich, & Guthrie, 2009). The sections that follow review the empirical evidence on attitudes and social perceptions as they affect other legal experts' judgments and decisions.

Attitudes: Segal and Spaetch (2002) present systematic evidence of what they call the "attitudinal model" that explains and predicts judicial decision-making. This model holds that judges' decisions and behaviors are largely determined by their attitudes and policy preferences—including Supreme Court Justices. This model conflicts with the traditional rational choice model in which people assume that judges make decisions independent of their attitudes.

In a study with professional arbitrators who work in the area of labor arbitration, Girvan et al. (2015) measured the experts' explicit and implicit gender attitudes. In the first part of their study, an experimental lab-based study, they did not find evidence that the experts' gender attitudes affected their decisions in two mock arbitration cases in which the gender of the employee-grievants was manipulated (though non-expert undergraduate students did show the expected gender biases in their decisions). However, in a second study, arbitrators' explicit and implicit gender attitudes did predict their decisions in actual published labor arbitration cases. Girvan et al. concluded that implicit and explicit attitudes are important to understand as they affect experts' legal decisions, but that laboratory experiments might not capture the nature of these attitudes' effects on real decisions—an important insight for continued research in this area.

The effect of attitudes about civil rights (gay rights in this case) on legally relevant perceptions and judgments by law students was studied by Braman and Nelson (2007). These researchers had participants (both law students and undergraduate students) participate in an experiment in which they studied motivated reasoning in legal judgments (see Kunda, 1990). Specifically, they asked participants to make legally relevant decisions about the similarity and applicability of previous case law on the target case in the study. In the law, legal precedents (previous case decisions) are used as a guide for deciding future similar cases (known by the legal term *stare decisis*). But judges have some flexibility in determining which cases are most similar and whether or not a given case is analogous enough to a target case to cite as legal precedent.

The target case used in Braman and Nelson's (2007) study was the *Boy Scouts of the United States of American v. Dale* (2000) case, in which a gay male claimed unlawful discrimination by the Boy Scouts after having been removed as a youth leader and dismissed from the organization based on his sexual orientation. The researchers varied some aspects of the case in an experimental design, including the outcome of source cases, such that some participants saw a source case (potential legal precedent) in which unlawful discrimination had been found, or a source case in which the defendant had been found to be acting within his rights. Participants were asked to rate how similar the source case was to the target case on a four-point scale (i.e., how analogous the source case was to cite as legal precedent for deciding the target case). They also measured participants' support on a six-point scale on a question about how acceptable it is for a gay man to serve as a Boy Scout.

Results revealed that participants' attitudes influenced their legal judgments by affecting the perceived similarity between the source cases and the target case. Participants found the source cases that supported their policy views in the target case as more relevant to that litigation. Braman and Nelson (2007) found that legal training did not seem to attenuate motivated perceptions: the law students' attitudes influenced their judgments just as much as undergraduate students' attitudes influenced their judgments.

This question about whether legal training attenuates bias is more complicated than this, however. Kahan et al. (2016) found that legal training did protect judges' and lawyers' statutory interpretations from their cultural values compared to general public participants making the same legal interpretations. They noted that law students' interpretations, however, were somewhat biased by their cultural values. Girvan (2016) showed through an elegant experimental design that not all legal professionals' judgments are protected from bias by virtue of their legal training. The distinction between legal rules and legal standards is important in this regard. Legal rules are rigid and remove subjectivity and discretion from judgment, whereas legal standards are more flexible and allow for some subjectivity and discretion in judgment. Girvan showed that learning and applying legal *rules* (i.e., removes discretion) does protect legal experts from stereotype-induced bias compared to novices, but that learning and applying legal *standards* (i.e., discretion allowed) does not protect legal experts.

The Self: Bias Blind Spot: Similar to results that have emerged in forensic mental health, recent findings of the bias blind spot in forensic scientists' perceptions of themselves has also emerged. Kukucka et al. (2017) conducted a recent study of 403 forensic scientists across various domains (e.g., latent prints, questioned documents, toxicology, biology/serology/DNA, crime scene investigation, bitemarks, and firearms/toolmarks) from 21 countries. The mean accuracy rating that forensic scientists provided for their field was 94.41%, yet the experts estimated their own accuracy at 96.25% (a statistically significant difference with a small effect size). Furthermore, consistent with the bias blind spot, they rated other forensic scientists as much more susceptible to cognitive bias in their work (70.1%) than themselves (25.7%).

Stereotypes: Although we could not locate any studies of how stereotypes affect forensic mental health professionals' judgments, there are provocative studies of how implicit racial biases affect judicial (Rachlinski et al., 2009) and physician (Green et al., 2007) decision-making that are likely relevant for forensic psychology. In both of these studies, the researchers used a tool called the Implicit Association Test (IAT) to measure participants' implicit attitudes about race. The IAT was developed through decades of research on bias and stereotypes, and is typically administered via computer through a sorting task in which participants pair words and faces (Greenwald & Banaji, 1995; Greenwald, McGhee, & Schwartz, 1998). These researchers found that experts typically do not endorse or exhibit explicit (System 2) stereotype-based biases that affect their professional judgments and decisions. But in both studies, implicit (System 1) stereotype-based biases unintentionally affected the judges' and doctors' judgments and decisions.

For example, Rachlinski et al. (2009) asked judge-participants to complete the computer-based IAT first, and then respond to hypothetical vignettes and make decisions about them. In some vignettes, the race of the defendant was subliminally primed but not identified explicitly, whereas in the final vignette the race of the defendant was made explicit. Results from this study, first, showed that judges hold implicit racial biases that mirror the general public's implicit attitudes about race (in this IAT's case, a systematic white over black preference). Second, the results showed that judges are not explicitly biased—race-related primes did not directly affect their judgments.

However, the implicit racial attitudes of judges did affect their legal judgments (Rachlinski et al., 2009). Judges' scores on the race IAT had a consistent, marginally significant influence on their judgments across two different vignettes. Judges with stronger white preferences on the IAT gave harsher sentences to defendants when they had been primed with black-associated words (e.g., graffiti, Harlem, homeboy, jerricurl, rap, segregation, basketball, gospel, afro, reggae, athlete) compared to judges who were primed with neutral words (e.g., baby, heaven, coffin, summer, truth, accident, mosquito, virus, toothache, rainbow, paralysis). And judges who exhibited a black preference on the IAT gave less harsh sentences to defendants when they had been primed with black-associated words compared to judges primed with neutral words.

Green et al. (2007) studied how implicit racial biases affect physicians' clinical decision-making. They asked physician-participants to respond to a clinical vignette of a patient presenting to an emergency room with an acute heart problem and to make a decision about whether or not to use thrombolysis, a treatment to dissolve blood clots. Physician-participants were randomly assigned to either a black or white patient vignette. They were asked to complete the race IAT to measure their implicit racial attitudes as well as respond to questions about perceptions of patient cooperativeness, attribution of symptoms to coronary artery disease, and respond to a questionnaire about their explicit racial attitudes.

Results indicated that physicians did not endorse explicitly racial attitudes (Green et al., 2007). However, like judges and the general public, physicians exhibited an implicit racial preference favoring white people over black people, and they endorsed implicit stereotypes of black people as less cooperative in general, and with medical procedures specifically. Furthermore, these implicit attitudes affected their clinical decision-making. As the strength of physicians' implicit pro-white bias increased, their likelihood of treating white patients with thrombolysis and not treating black patients with thrombolysis increased. These results demonstrate the disconnect between implicit and explicit attitudes, and the predictive validity of implicit attitudes for experts' judgments—here in a clinical context not dissimilar from what forensic psychologists are typically asked to do. Results suggest physicians' implicit racial biases might contribute to the minority health disparities present in this country.

Conclusions and Future Directions

In this chapter, we have reviewed evidence of unintentional biases in experts' judgments. We have focused specifically on forensic mental health experts, but we have also described relevant findings from other professional arenas in which experts face similar decision tasks. We started with foundational background from cognitive and social psychology, explaining dual-process theories of cognition in both subfields of psychology to ground our discussion of bias. By "bias" in this chapter, we focus exclusively on System 1-induced cognitive and social-cognitive biases; and unintentional, understandable, predictable, systematic errors that even experts make. When the contexts and situations in which these types of biases emerge are understood, these contexts and situations can be changed so as to minimize the likelihood of biases exerting negative effects on experts' judgments. In reviewing this literature, we have identified several gaps that future research can address. There are serious implications for biased judgments in forensic mental health for people involved in the legal system, such as missed or misdiagnoses that could lead to death in the most extreme circumstances (e.g., capital cases). Thus, the need for research in this area is critical.

Most of the empirical evidence of cognitive and social-cognitive biases in experts' judgments is outside of the forensic mental health domain. We reviewed the burgeoning body of evidence regarding cognitive biases in forensic mental health judgments, but a lot of this work has not yet gone through the peer-review system and is not yet published. Most of the evidence about how cognitive biases influence experts' judgments is in other areas (e.g., forensic science, medicine, law). Thus, there is a need for researchers to conduct methodologically strong, ecologically valid experimental research in forensic mental health domains to further clarify how and when cognitive biases affect forensic mental health experts' judgments and decisions. Perhaps there are some forces that make forensic psychologists less susceptible to these biases than experts in other domains (e.g., motivation to be objective by virtue of the gravity of forensic work), but perhaps other forces make forensic psychologists more susceptible to the biases (e.g., the insidious adversarial pressure).

Similarly, very little of the evidence on implicit social-cognitive biases is in the domain of forensic mental health. In fact, only emerging information about the "bias blind spot" is in the forensic mental health domain. We did review some studies of how forensic mental health professionals' attitudes influence their judgments; however, these attitudes have only been measured explicitly to date and it is not clear whether implicit attitudes would also affect forensic mental health judgments. It is highly likely, given findings from law (e.g., Girvan et al., 2015), but as of yet remains unstudied in forensic mental health.

We were unable to find a single study of how implicit stereotypes affect the judgments and decisions of forensic mental health experts. There is compelling evidence from law (Rachlinski et al., 2009) and medicine (Green et al., 2007) that implicit racial stereotypes will likely influence forensic mental health professionals' judgments too, but as of yet there appear to be no studies of this issue. This issue is especially important in light of the gross racial disparities in the American justice system—especially in the criminal justice system (Cole, 1999). Furthermore, there is a need for studying how other kinds of implicit stereotypes (not just race) affect professionals' decisions—both in forensic mental health and in other domains. This area is ripe for future research.

In sum, there are strong theoretical reasons to suspect that forensic mental health professionals are subject to the effects of unintentional System 1-induced cognitive and social-cognitive biases in their judgments and decisions. Emerging research from the forensic mental health domain supports these theoretical predictions, but much work remains to be done to better understand the boundary conditions of when and how these particular kinds of experts are biased in the particular environmental contexts in which they work. As more research in this area emerges, it will flesh out the unique ways in which the contextual environments of forensic mental health affect our judgments. It will also inform solutions to mitigate the effects of these unintentional and unwanted biases in forensic mental health professionals' judgments and decisions.

References

Arkes, H. R., Wortmann, R. L., Saville, P. D., & Harkness, A. R. (1981). Hindsight bias among physicians weighing the likelihood of diagnoses. *Journal of Applied Psychology, 66*, 252–254.

Ask, K., & Granhag, P. A. (2005). Motivational sources of confirmation bias in criminal investigations: The need for cognitive closure. *Journal of Investigative Psychology and Offender Profiling, 2*, 43–63.

Babcock, L., & Loewenstein, G. (1997). Explaining bargaining impasse: The role of self-serving biases. *Journal of Economic Perspectives, 11*, 109–126.

Bandura, A. (2015). *Moral disengagement: How people do harm and live with themselves*. New York: Worth Publishing.

Bazerman, M. H., Loewenstein, G., & Moore, D. A. (2002). Why good accountants do bad audits. *Harvard Business Review, 80*, 96–103.

Beltrani, A., Reed, A., Zapf, P. A., Dror, I. E., & Otto, R. K. (2017, March). *Is hindsight really 20/20? The impact of outcomes on the decision making process*. Paper presented at the annual conference of the American Psychology-Law Society, Seattle, WA.

Braman, E., & Nelson, T. E. (2007). Mechanism of motivated reasoning? Analogical perception in discrimination disputes. *American Journal of Political Science, 51*, 940–956. https://doi.org/10.1111/j.1540-5907.2007.00290.x

Boy Scouts of the United States of American v. Dale, 530 US 640 (2000).

Caplan, R. A., Posner, K. L., & Cheney, F. W. (1991). Effect of outcome on physician judgments of appropriateness of care. *Journal of the American Medical Association, 265*, 1957–1960.

Chaiken, S. (1980). Heuristic versus systematic information processing and the use of source versus message cues in persuasion. *Journal of Personality and Social Psychology, 39*, 752–766. https://doi.org/10.1037/0022-3514.39.5.752

Chaiken, S., & Trope, Y. (Eds.). (1999). *Dual-process theories in social psychology*. New York: Guilford.

Cole, D. (1999). *No equal justice: Race and class in the American criminal justice system* (Vol. 1). New York: New Press.

Commons, M. L., Miller, P. M., & Gutheil, T. G. (2004). Expert witness perceptions of bias in experts. *The Journal of the American Academy of Psychiatry and the Law, 32*(1), 70–75.

Cook, M. B., & Smallman, H. S. (2008). Human factors of the confirmation bias in intelligence analysis: Decision support from graphical evidence landscapes. *Human Factors: The Journal of the Human Factors and Ergonomics Society, 50*, 745–754.

Devine, P. G. (1989). Stereotypes and prejudice: Their automatic and controlled components. *Journal of Personality and Social Psychology, 56*, 5–18. https://doi.org/10.1037/0022-3514.56.1.5

Devine, P. G., Hamilton, D. L. E., & Ostrom, T. M. (Eds.). (1994). *Social cognition: Impact on social psychology*. Cambridge, MA: Academic Press.

Drew, T., Võ, M. L. H., & Wolfe, J. M. (2013). The invisible gorilla strikes again sustained inattentional blindness in expert observers. *Psychological Science, 24*, 1848–1853.

Dror, I. E., Charlton, D., & Péron, A. E. (2006). Contextual information renders experts vulnerable to making erroneous identifications. *Forensic Science International, 156*, 74–78. https://doi.org/10.1016/j.forsciint.2005.10.017

Epperson, D. L., Kaul, J. D., Goldman, R., Hout, S., Hesselton, D., & Alexander, W. (1998). *Minnesota Sex Offender Screening Tool—Revised (MnSOST-R)*. St. Paul: Minnesota Department of Corrections. Available online at. http://www.psychology.iastate.edu

Evans, J. S. (2008). Dual-processing accounts of reasoning, judgment, and social cognition. *Annual Review of Psychology, 59*, 255–278. https://doi.org/10.1146/annurev.psych.59.103006.093629

Fischhoff, B. (1975). Hindsight is not equal to foresight: The effect of outcome knowledge on judgment under uncertainty. *Journal of Experimental Psychology: Human Perception and Performance, 1*, 288–299. https://doi.org/10.1037/0096-1523.1.3.288

Frederick, S. (2005). Cognitive reflection and decision making. *Journal of Economic Perspectives, 19*, 25–42. https://doi.org/10.1257/089533005775196732

Gigerenzer, G. (1991). How to make cognitive illusions disappear: beyond "heuristics and biases". *European Review of Social Psychology, 2*, 83–115. https://doi.org/10.1080/14792779143000033

Gigerenzer, G. (1996). On narrow norms and vague heuristics: A reply to Kahneman and Tversky. *Psychological Review, 103*, 592–596. https://doi.org/10.1037/0033-295X.103.3.592

Gigerenzer, G. (2008). Why heuristics work. *Perspectives on Psychological Science, 3*, 20–29.

Girvan, E. J. (2016). Wise restraints?: Learning legal rules, not standards, reduces the effects of stereotypes in legal decision-making. *Psychology, Public Policy, and Law, 22*, 31–45. https://doi.org/10.1037/law0000068

Girvan, E. J., Deason, G., & Borgida, E. (2015). The generalizability of gender bias: Testing the effects of contextual, explicit, and implicit sexism on labor arbitration decisions. *Law and Human Behavior, 39*, 525–537. https://doi.org/10.1037/lhb0000139

Green, A. R., Carney, D. R., Pallin, D. J., Ngo, L. H., Raymond, K. L., Iezzoni, L. I., et al. (2007). Implicit bias among physicians and its prediction of thrombolysis decisions for black and white patients. *Journal of General Internal Medicine, 22*, 1231–1238. https://doi.org/10.1007/s11606-007-0258-5

Greenwald, A. G., & Banaji, M. R. (1995). Implicit social cognition: attitudes, self-esteem, and stereotypes. *Psychological Review, 102*, 4–27. https://doi.org/10.1037/0033-295X.102.1.4
Greenwald, A. G., McGhee, D. E., & Schwartz, J. L. K. (1998). Measuring individual differences in implicit cognition: The implicit association test. *Journal of Personality and Social Psychology, 74*, 1464–1480. https://doi.org/10.1037/0022-3514.74.6.1464
Guthrie, C., Rachlinski, J. J., & Wistrich, A. J. (2001). Inside the judicial mind. *Cornell Law Review, 86*, 777–778.
Hanson, R. K., & Thornton, D. (1999). *Static-99: Improving actuarial risk assessments for sex offenders (User Report 99–02)*. Ottawa, Ontario, Canada: Department of the Solicitor General of Canada.
Hare, R. D. (2003). *The Hare Psychopathy Checklist—Revised* (2nd ed.). Toronto, Ontario, Canada: Multi-Health Systems.
Haselton, M., Bryant, G. A., Wilke, A., Frederick, D., & Galperin, A. (2009). Adaptive rationality: An evolutionary perspective on cognitive bias. *Social Cognition, 27*, 733–763.
Hastdorf, A. H., & Cantril, H. (1954). They saw a game: A case study. *Journal of Abnormal and Social Psychology, 49*, 129–134.
Helm, R. K., Wistrich, A. J., & Rachlinski, J. J. (2016). Are arbitrators human? *Journal of Empirical Legal Studies, 13*, 666–692. https://doi.org/10.1111/jels.12129
Hoffrage, U., & Gigerenzer, G. (2004). How to improve the diagnostic inferences of medical experts. In E. Kurz-Milcke & G. Gigerenzer (Eds.), *Experts in science and society* (pp. 249–268). Heidelberg: Springer.
Kahan, D. M., Hoffman, D., Evans, D., Devins, N., Lucci, E., & Cheng, K. (2016). 'Ideology' or 'situation sense'? An experimental investigation of motivated reasoning and professional judgment. *University of Pennsylvania Law Review, 2*, 394.
Kahneman, D. (2003). A perspective on judgment and choice—Mapping bounded rationality. *American Psychologist, 58*, 697–720. https://doi.org/10.1037/0003-066x.58.9.697
Kahneman, D. (2011). Thinking, fast and slow. New York: Farrar, Straus and Giroux.
Kahneman, D., & Klein, G. (2009). Conditions for intuitive expertise: A failure to disagree. *American Psychologist, 64*, 515–526. https://doi.org/10.1037/a0016755
Kahneman, D., & Tversky, A. (1972). Subjective probability: A judgment of representativeness. *Cognitive Psychology, 3*, 430–454. https://doi.org/10.1016/0010-0285(72)90016-3
Kukucka, J., Kassin, S. M., Dror, I. E., & Zapf, P. A. (2017, March). *Cognitive bias: A survey of forensic examiners*. Paper presented at the annual conference of the American Psychology-Law Society, Seattle, WA.
Kunda, Z. (1990). The case for motivated reasoning. *Psychological Bulletin, 108*, 480–498. https://doi.org/10.1037/0033-2909.108.3.480
LaBine, S. J., & LaBine, G. (1996). Determinations of negligence and the hindsight bias. *Law and Human Behavior, 20*, 501–516.
LeBourgeois, H. W., III, Pinals, D. A., Williams, V., & Appelbaum, P. S. (2007). Hindsight bias among psychiatrists. *The Journal of the American Academy of Psychiatry and the Law, 35*, 67–73.
MacCoun, R. J. (1998). Biases in the interpretation and use of research results. *Annual Review of Psychology, 49*, 259–287. https://doi.org/10.1146/annurev.psych.49.1.259
McAuliff, B. D., & Arter, J. L. (2016). Adversarial allegiance: The devil is in the evidence details, not just on the witness stand. *Law and Human Behavior, 40*, 524–535. https://doi.org/10.1037/lhb0000198
Moore, D. A., Loewenstein, G., Tanlu, L., & Bazerman, M. H. (2003). Auditor independence, conflict of interest, and the unconscious intrusion of bias. *Harvard Business School Working Paper No 03-116*. Retrieved from http://citeseerx.ist.psu.edu/viewdoc/download?doi=10.1.1.9.2829&rep=rep1&type=pdf
Murrie, D. C., Boccaccini, M. T., Guarnera, L. A., & Rufino, K. A. (2013). Are forensic experts biased by the side that retained them? *Psychological Science, 24*, 1889–1897. https://doi.org/10.1177/0956797613481812

Murrie, D. C., Boccaccini, M., Johnson, J., & Janke, C. (2008). Does interrater (dis)agreement on psychopathy checklist scores in sexually violent predator trials suggest partisan allegiance in forensic evaluation? *Law and Human Behavior, 32*, 352–362. https://doi.org/10.1007/s10979-007-9097-5

Murrie, D. C., Boccaccini, M. T., Turner, D. B., Meeks, M., Woods, C., & Tussey, C. (2009). Rater (dis)agreement on risk assessment measures in sexually violent predator proceedings: Evidence of adversarial allegiance in forensic evaluation? *Psychology, Public Policy, and Law, 15*, 19–53. https://doi.org/10.1037/a0014897

Nakhaeizadeh, S., Dror, I. E., & Morgan, R. M. (2014). Cognitive bias in forensic anthropology: Visual assessment of skeletal remains is susceptible to confirmation bias. *Science and Justice, 54*, 208–214. https://doi.org/10.1016/j.scijus.2013.11.003

Neal, T. M. S. (2016). Are forensic experts already biased before adversarial legal parties hire them? *PLoS ONE, 11*(4), e0154434. https://doi.org/10.1371/journal.pone.0154434

Neal, T. M. S., & Brodsky, S. L. (2016). Forensic psychologists' perceptions of bias and potential correction strategies in forensic mental health evaluations. *Psychology, Public Policy, and Law, 22*, 58–76. https://doi.org/10.1037/law0000077

Neal, T. M. S. & Cramer, R. J. (in press). Moral disengagement in legal judgments. *Journal of Empirical Legal Studies.*

Neal, T. M. S., & Grisso, T. (2014). The cognitive underpinnings of bias in forensic mental health evaluations. *Psychology, Public Policy, and Law, 20*, 200–211. https://doi.org/10.1037/a0035824

Neal, T. M. S., MacLean, N., Morgan, R. D., & Murrie, D. C. (2017, March). *Robust evidence of confirmation bias in forensic psychologists' diagnostic reasoning.* Paper presented at the annual conference of the American Psychology-Law Society, Seattle, WA.

Neal, T. M. S. & Saks, M.J. (in preparation). *Context effects in forensic mental health science: A review and application of the science of science to the practice of forensic mental health evaluations.*

Nickerson, R. S. (1998). Confirmation bias: A ubiquitous phenomenon in many guises. *Review of General Psychology, 2*, 175–220.

O'Neil, K. M., Patry, M. W., & Penrod, S. D. (2004). Exploring the effects of attitudes toward the death penalty on capital sentencing verdicts. *Psychology, Public Policy, and Law, 10*, 443–470.

Petty, R. E., & Cacioppo, J. T. (1986). The elaboration likelihood model of persuasion. *Advances in Experimental Social Psychology, 19*, 123–205.

Popper, K. R. (1959). *The logic of scientific discovery*. London: Hutchinson.

Pronin, E., Gilovich, T., & Ross, L. (2004). Objectivity in the eye of the beholder: Divergent perceptions of bias in self versus others. *Psychological Review, 111*, 781–799. https://doi.org/10.1037/0033-295X.111.3.781

Pronin, E., Lin, D. L., & Ross, L. (2002). The bias blind spot: Perceptions of bias in self versus other. *Personality and Social Psychology Bulletin, 28*, 369–381. https://doi.org/10.1177/0146167202286008

Rachlinski, J. J., Johnson, S. L., Wistrich, A. J., & Guthrie, C. (2009). Does unconscious racial bias affect trial judges? *Notre Dame Law Review, 84*, 1195–1246.

Robbennolt, J. K. (2000). Outcome severity and judgments of "responsibility": A meta-analytic review. *Journal of Applied Social Psychology, 30*, 2575–2609. https://doi.org/10.1111/j.1559-1816.2000.tb02451.x

Sacchi, S., & Cherubini, P. (2004). The effect of outcome information on doctors' evaluations of their own diagnostic decisions. *Medical Education, 38*, 1025–1027.

Scopelliti, I., Morewedge, C. K., McCormick, E., Min, L. H., Lebrecht, S., & Kassam, K. S. (2015). Bias blind spot: Structure, measurement, and consequences. *Management Science, 61*, 2468–2486.

Segal, J. A., & Spaetch, H. J. (2002). *The Supreme Court and the attitudinal model revisited.* Cambridge, UK: Cambridge University Press.

Sloman, S. A. (1996). The empirical case for two systems of reasoning. *Psychological Bulletin, 119*, 3–22. https://doi.org/10.1037/0033-2909.119.1.3
Slovic, P., Finucane, M. L., Peters, E., & MacGregor, D. G. (2007). The affect heuristic. *European Journal of Operational Research, 177*, 1333–1352. https://doi.org/10.1016/j.ejor.2005.04.006
Stanovich, K. E., & West, R. F. (2000). Individual differences in reasoning: implications for the rationality debate? *The Behavioral and Brain Sciences, 23*, 645–726. https://doi.org/10.1017/S0140525X00003435
Thompson, L., & Loewenstein, G. (1992). Egocentric interpretation of fairness and interpersonal conflict. *Organizational Behavior and Human Decision Processes, 51*, 176–197.
Tversky, A., & Kahneman, D. (1973). Availability: A heuristic for judging frequency and probability. *Cognitive Psychology, 5*, 207–232.
Tversky, A., & Kahneman, D. (1974). Judgment under uncertainty: Heuristics and biases. *Science, 185*, 1124–1131. https://doi.org/10.1126/science.185.4157.1124
Wason, P. C. (1968). Reasoning about a rule. *Quarterly Journal of Experimental Psychology, 20*, 273–281. https://doi.org/10.1080/14640746808400161
Wistrich, A. J., Guthrie, C., & Rachlinski, J. J. (2005). Can judges ignore inadmissible information? The difficulty of deliberately disregarding. *University of Pennsylvania Law Review, 153*, 1251–1345.
Zapf, P. A., Kukucka, J., Kassin, S. M., & Dror, I. E. (2017, March). *Cognitive bias: A survey of forensic evaluators*. Paper presented at the annual conference of the American Psychology-Law Society, Seattle, WA.

Restorative Justice: Reflections and the Retributive Impulse

Alana Saulnier and Diane Sivasubramaniam

In this chapter, we review the literature surrounding restorative justice as a response to crime. While originally introduced in the form of an alternative dispute resolution process, only loosely incorporated into the formal criminal justice system, restorative justice is now a vital feature of justice processes in many jurisdictions. Here, we offer a thorough introduction to the theoretical foundations and empirical realities associated with restorative procedures. Our goal is to provide a wide-ranging review of what is currently known about restorative interventions in the psychological literature and what remains unclear.

We begin with an in-depth introduction to restorative justice, comparing it with the formal criminal justice system in terms of philosophical foundations, structural applications, and outcomes. From here, we move to a review of recent empirical evidence. We reflect on the findings of program evaluations (in particular, those related to stakeholders' perceptions and recidivism reduction), evaluating the empirical support for reintegrative shaming and procedural justice as central theoretical explanations for the effects seen in restorative justice. In this section of the chapter, we summarize what is well-known about restorative justice in the psychological literature, highlighting the importance of continuing to better understand factors driving the effectiveness of restorative interventions.

Finally, we emphasize the need to investigate public perceptions of appropriate justice; we argue these are key to identifying the conditions under which restorative interventions will be evaluated as an acceptable justice response and, therefore, they

A. Saulnier (✉)
Department of Interdisciplinary Studies, Lakehead University, Orillia, ON, Canada
e-mail: alana.saulnier@lakeheadu.ca

D. Sivasubramaniam
Faculty of Health, Arts and Design, Department of Psychological Sciences, Swinburne University of Technology, Hawthorn, VIC, Australia
e-mail: dsivasubramaniam@swin.edu.au

M. K. Miller, B. H. Bornstein (eds.), *Advances in Psychology and Law*,
Advances in Psychology and Law 3,
https://doi.org/10.1007/978-3-319-75859-6_6

will greatly affect the long-term viability of restorative justice. We dedicate the latter part of the chapter to addressing an underdeveloped area in relation to restorative justice: dual-process models of cognitive processing. Ultimately, we argue that the *success* of restorative justice is as dependent on public perceptions of the *appropriateness* of restorative interventions as it is on demonstrations of the *effectiveness* of such interventions in evaluative research. We draw attention to the discrepancy between legal and lay notions of justice, on the basis that legal notions of justice revolve around deliberative cognitive processing, whereas lay notions of justice stem from heuristic cognitive processing and are often dominated by a retributive impulse. We speculate about the effect of this discrepancy on the long-term viability of restorative practices, arguing that retributive motivations present an inherent challenge to the widespread use of restorative justice, but that psychological research on dual-process models will be useful in overcoming this challenge.

We conclude by suggesting more focused research directions that would advance the current state of knowledge in restorative justice, highlighting the value of experimental methods in building support for restorative interventions. We argue that such research would better equip scholars to overcome the challenges presented by the retributive impulse in ways that encourage the long-term viability of restorative justice.

What Is Restorative Justice?

The formal criminal justice system is characterized by distinctive features, including an adversarial process, adjudication by unbiased third parties (such as judges and juries), and punitive outcomes (most notably, incarceration). The court-based model associated with this system is likely the most well-recognized means of responding to criminal behavior among citizens of Western democracies such as Australia, Canada, and the USA. Despite several decades of application alongside or as an alternative to the formal criminal justice system (Braithwaite, 1999; Strang & Sherman, 2015), restorative justice is undoubtedly less well recognized as a means of responding to crime. While both the traditional and restorative justice models prioritize the provision of an efficient and effective response to crime as their ultimate purpose, there are notable differences between the two in terms of philosophical foundations, structural applications, and outcomes.

Philosophically, the formal criminal justice system and restorative justice differ in the extent to which they prioritize retribution. The two models are founded on distinct justice motivations that differentially prioritize retribution (i.e., punishment) and restoration (i.e., reconciliation of harm caused by a transgression; Wenzel, Okimoto, Feather, & Platow, 2008). Formal models of criminal justice in Western democracies have historically been grounded in the retributive philosophy. This orientation is linked closely with the dominance of rational choice sensibilities in Western nations. Central to the rational choice position are matters of individual culpability and calculated decision-making. From this perspective, consequences are recognized as very important to deterring secondary offending behavior generally, and primary offending behavior specifically (Zehr, 1997). A retributive philosophy naturally complements rational choice sensibilities, prioritizing punishment as the most effective response to criminal behavior. Punishment reprimands the individual criminal, while also conveying a message of the consequences of engaging in criminal behavior to would-be offenders in the broader population. Formal models of criminal justice embody the punitive orientation that accompanies a retributive philosophy of justice. However, retribution is but one justice motivation, and an alternative motivation—that of restoration—is generally not well represented in responses to crime that prioritize retribution (Braithwaite, 1989, 2000).

The fundamental orientation of restorative justice models is identifying and resolving the harm produced by criminal behavior, rather than simply punishing the offender. This involves recognizing that criminal acts produce harm for a range of parties, and that a central objective of responding to crime should be reconciling the harm that has been caused for all stakeholders. Restoration of the victim(s) and community to their pre-transgression states is a key priority of restorative justice, but comprehensive restoration also involves engaging with the harms suffered by the offender (Bergseth & Bouffard, 2007). Returning the offender to his pre-transgression state, in addition to providing him with opportunities for self-improvement, is key to a restorative philosophy. The philosophical starting points of justice models prioritizing retributive versus restorative motivations therefore vary considerably, highlighting distinct objectives. Their fundamentally different frames of reference lead to fundamentally different processes and outcomes.

The retributive philosophy guiding the formal criminal justice system in Western democracies lays the foundation for an adversarial process, in which the focus is the behavior and culpability of the accused. The procedure is characterized by pitting two parties (the defense and the state) against each other, who do not agree on a shared understanding of the accused's behavior. The very language foundations of this model (e.g., guilty/not guilty, defense/prosecution) are indicative of the level of confrontation inherent in this approach; undoubtedly, there will be parties who are dissatisfied with the outcome. To minimize the financial costs associated with the process of the formal criminal justice system, plea agreements—which require offenders to admit to a crime (typically of lesser severity than the crime with which they were initially charged)—are often used to establish a form of negotiated consensus at the expense of the state's desired conviction. However, when a shared understanding of offender culpability cannot be reached between the defense and prosecution, the full adversarial process is engaged. The offender is presumed innocent and represented by a defense attorney, while the state carries the burden of proof and is represented by a prosecuting attorney. Both parties have the opportunity to present relevant evidence to a designated third party (i.e., a judge, panel of judges, or jury) tasked with reaching a determination regarding the accused's guilt. Victims are most typically incorporated into this process as witnesses, having very limited opportunity to share information that is not specifically asked of them or which is not directly relevant to the accused's culpability—amounting to very restricted opportunities to have a voice in the process. All parties to the procedure have clearly defined roles in the process, which creates very formal, structured interactions, generally with the victim and accused not directly interacting at all, and with less directly affected victims (e.g., family members of the primary victim/s) having very little to no involvement in the procedure. If a determination of guilt is reached, the potential outcomes are focused on offender punishment and tend to be narrowly constructed (e.g., probation, incarceration, fines); these outcomes are capable of being administered to a broad offender population but do not necessarily speak well to individual offenders' needs and largely fail to consider the needs of other stakeholders. Ultimately, the consequence imposed is intended to be the result of a sober calculation of proportional punishment that draws from existing formal guidelines and legal precedents (Bazemore & Umbreit, 1995).

In contrast, restorative procedures are relatively informal when compared with court procedures. There is not a single formula for conducting a restorative procedure as there is with court. Restorative practices have been recognized as taking a variety of forms, with victim-offender mediation, family-group conferencing, and peacemaking circles being recognized as some of the most prevalent strategies (Bouffard, Cooper, & Bergseth, 2016; Latimer, Dowden, & Muise, 2005; Zehr, 2002).

In general, restorative justice procedures can be characterized by a broad set of basic features which are fundamentally different from court. For instance, although restorative approaches tend to have a "leader" guiding the procedure—in the same way that a judge might be described as the leader in court-based procedures—this leadership is much less rigid and formal. Facilitators (as they are called in restorative conferencing) guide participants through the procedure (e.g., encouraging reflection on specific topics such as harm incurred and ideal restoration, as well as ensuring that all participants have adequate opportunities for voice), but they do not govern the procedure in the same way that a judge does (Wenzel et al., 2008). Instead, conference participants have substantial ownership over the workings of the process. Restorative justice procedures require the participation of an offender who acknowledges commission of an offence—very different from the role the accused adopts in court-based procedures. Additional participants in restorative justice ideally include victim(s), support persons for both offenders and victims, and, in some cases, community members more generally. Conference participants are substantially more engaged in restorative justice than court participants are in court procedures. For instance, while the state represents the victim in the formal criminal justice system, victims are given much greater latitude to choose the manner in which they represent themselves and play an active, decisive role in the restorative model (Zehr, 1997). Restorative justice advocates argue that this does not imply the offender is disenfranchised relative to the victim in restorative procedures (Braithwaite, 2000). Instead, the shared starting point that restorative justice begins with (i.e., acknowledgment by all parties of the harm caused and an effort to resolve that harm) is intended to level perceptions of hierarchy in the procedure, between participants as well as facilitators. In these ways, responses to crime founded on both restorative and retributive philosophies result in consequences for criminal behavior, but there is immense procedural variability between the two.

While the consequences prioritized in the formal criminal justice system emphasize punishment, this does not mean that the consequences of retributive oriented justice models are inherently cruel, harsh, or unfair; rather, retributive models of criminal justice aim to swiftly, proportionally, and fairly administer a punitive consequence to a particular offender while also conveying a message of general deterrence to the public more broadly (Bazemore & Umbreit, 1995). While addressing punitive concerns, models of justice prioritizing a retributive orientation tend to be criticized for being inattentive to a broader range of post-crime concerns, such as restoration of harm. In this regard, a restorative orientation to justice has proven particularly valuable, as a complementary as well as an alternative model to the formal criminal justice system.

Consequences are conceptualized differently in restorative justice, with the terminology of *sanctions* preferred to *punishments*, underscoring that restorative outcomes are not primarily punitive in orientation. Sanctions are the tangible outcomes of restorative procedures for offenders. The principles of specific and general deterrence are still communicated through sanctions; however, rather than prioritizing punishment, sanctions prioritize the restoration of stakeholders both materially and in terms of relationships following a transgression (Van Ness, 1993). A fundamental difference between retributive and restorative philosophies of justice is observable through sanctions. Specifically, restorative justice emphasizes the redemption of the offender; while an act worthy of condemnation has been committed, the individual offender is socially recognized as redeemable. Sanctions are still directed at the offender in restorative interventions—as punishments are in retributive models of justice—but restorative justice sanctions strive to assist the offender in returning specific victims, the community more broadly, and themselves, to their pre-transgression states. Just as participants are granted greater ownership over the procedure in restorative justice, they are also granted considerably more control over the crafting of outcomes (Braithwaite, 2000; Latimer et al., 2005). Consequently, restorative sanctions tend to be much more responsive to the needs of particular situations and stakeholders than the consequences of the formal criminal justice system (Bazemore & Umbreit, 1995). While there is considerable flexibility in the specific sanctions developed in any given scenario, sanctions are not inherently inconsistent. Two underlying motivations are intended to guide the development of all sanctions: stakeholder restoration and the personal growth of offenders (Zehr, 1997). Through these more diversified outcomes, restorative justice is argued to more reflexively and successfully respond to the needs of victims, offenders, and communities.

More specific examples of sanctions in restorative justice would include personal growth opportunities (e.g., completion of programs or tasks), victim compensation (e.g., personal service or financial remuneration), and community compensation (e.g., community service or fines), which would be selected based on offender, victim, and community needs. Take the instance of a case where a 16-year-old youth (John) is engaged in a restorative conference because he has vandalized a neighbor's property. John (offender), the neighbor (victim), John's parents (supporters), and the local neighborhood watch leader (community member) are all present for the conference along with the trained conference facilitator. During the conference, John reveals that he has a difficult time coping with anger and committed the vandalism as a random act of destruction in frustration after his parents told him they could not afford to give him money to go out to the movies with his friends. All of the conference participants agree that John has behaved inappropriately, but that steps can be taken to rectify the situation. The neighbor requests that he be compensated for the $100 of damage that John caused, but recognizes John's parents' strained financial situation and suggests that it would be best for John to be responsible for the reimbursement. John agrees, but says he has no money to compensate his neighbor and does not know how to get it. The neighbor suggests a local office that offers classes in résumé building as well as an employment service that helps connect potential employees with employers. John accepts these suggestions and three sanctions are established; John is expected to: (1) complete a résumé within 2 weeks at the local office, (2) submit his résumé to the employment office and apply to at least three available part-time job opportunities within 3 weeks, and (3) reimburse his neighbor financially or through personal assistance if he cannot secure the money within 3 months. Furthermore, John's parents draw attention to the need for John to better control his emotions. The neighborhood watch leader describes an emotion management program in the community that helps youth develop patience, stress management, and accomplishment through gardening. John is interested in this program and the rest of the conference participants agree that John and the community would benefit from him learning to better control his emotions. As such, a fourth sanction, that John must join a program oriented towards emotion management and attend regular sessions for a minimum of 2 months, is also established. As the example illustrates, the victim, offender, and community more broadly participated in the determination of meaningful sanctions that aim to restore the victim to his pre-transgression state alongside restoring, or even improving, the pre-transgression states of the offender and community more generally.

The preceding review has now established an understanding of the philosophy, procedure, and outcomes of restorative justice, relative to the more dominant retributive justice model. Restorative justice has been described as offering a response to crime that is less punitive and stigmatizing than retributive justice, providing the offender with greater opportunities for personal growth and community reintegration while also responding to the harms of crime more broadly (i.e., victim and community concerns; Bazemore & Umbreit, 1995). However, the conceptual overview provided thus far largely centers on the intentions of the restorative justice approach, engaging very little with the empirical realities associated with the use of restorative procedures. Although restorative procedures conceptually promote a more holistic, empathetic response to wrongdoing, we cannot assume that these approaches to crime are inherently better or, indeed, that they do not cause harm to stakeholders (Strang & Sherman, 2015). Evidence-based policy is key to the development and administration of responses to crime; reflecting on the findings of program evaluations, theoretical explanations of effects, and links between theory and practice are all central in this regard.

The heterogeneity of restorative justice programs is both a strength and a challenge of restorative responses to crime. Flexibility in program design and administration allows individual programs to be geared towards community needs, as well as allowing individual conferences to be responsive to the realities of specific victims and offenders. Embracing diverse tactics is a quality of restorative justice that contributes to its success in some ways; however, this strength also presents a challenge to evaluating and replicating the achievements of restorative programs. This has been, and will surely remain, a reality that makes it difficult to be confident in reaching definitive conclusions in evaluative research. Despite this caveat, a number of high quality evaluations and meta-analyses have illuminated the value of restorative responses to crime. Through these empirical projects, there is an accumulation of evidence supportive of some of the central optimistic promises associated with restorative justice; in particular, its capacity for stakeholder restoration and satisfaction, as well as reductions in recidivism (Braithwaite, 1999). These findings are demonstrated across a number of research projects engaging a variety of methodological approaches and exploring a diverse range of restorative procedures, but they are generally consistent with regard to stakeholders' perceptions and rates of recidivism.

Stakeholder Perceptions

Restorative justice has long been argued to foster more positive sentiments among both victims and offenders than the formal criminal justice system (Braithwaite, 1999). These positive outcomes are observable in stakeholders' perceptions of each other as well as of the justice process more generally. Most notably, both victims and offenders report greater perceptions of satisfaction with restorative relative to retributive procedures. This effect has a substantial history of empirical validation in a number of high quality meta-analyses (e.g., Latimer et al., 2005; Mazerolle, Antrobus, Bennett, & Tyler, 2013; Sherman & Strang, 2007). More recent program evaluations continue to support these findings. For instance, Bouffard et al. (2016) examined a variety of restorative interventions for youth (incorporating varied degrees of direct contact between offenders and victims) and concluded that "participants in RJ programs often report high degrees of satisfaction with the intervention" (p. 14). Researchers tend to attribute these effects on satisfaction to the highly engaging nature of restorative justice relative to court-based procedures. In particular, opportunities for voice during restorative procedures help establish a shared sense of process control between parties, while the joint crafting of sanctions promotes the understanding that outcomes are a collaborative effort between parties. The ability of all parties to actively contribute to both the process and outcomes of the procedure enhances perceptions of fairness and satisfaction from the perspective of both victims and offenders.

Restorative justice practices are also associated with other positive perceptions for stakeholders. For instance, offenders participating in restorative processes report higher levels of engagement in the proceedings as well as enhanced perceptions of ethical treatment relative to court-based procedures (Barnes, Hyatt, Angel, Strang, & Sherman, 2013). Much of the research has focused on victims' experiences, producing findings that participation in restorative conferencing leaves victims feeling less fearful of offenders (Strang, 2002), less angry with offenders Sherman & Strang, 2007), and less likely to experience the symptoms of post-traumatic stress disorder (Angel et al., 2014). Overall, a substantial body of evidence suggests that restorative procedures leave victims and offenders feeling more satisfied with their encounter, and more positive in general, than does the formal criminal justice system. While stakeholder perceptions have long been of interest to researchers, rates of recidivism are the most broadly recognized measure of the success of restorative interventions.

Recidivism

The measurement of recidivism is quite challenging. One key issue is establishing an operational time period over which recidivism will be assessed; however, clarity and transparency in operationalization have allowed researchers to demonstrate relatively consistent findings. For instance, Sherman, Strang, Mayo-Wilson, Woods and Ariel (2014) adopted a 2-year operational definition of recidivism and found that offenders who completed restorative procedures were less likely to reoffend than offenders who completed non-restorative procedures. Many program evaluations have produced similar findings, demonstrating a reduction in recidivism for offenders engaged in restorative justice within relatively short follow-up periods (e.g., Bergseth & Bouffard, 2007, 2012; Bradshaw, Roseborough, & Umbreit, 2006; Braithwaite, 2007). A number of meta-analyses support similar conclusions across offender types. For instance, restorative procedures perform at least as well as, if not better than, retributive justice responses with regard to recidivism rates among both juvenile and adult offenders (e.g., Latimer et al., 2005; MacKenzie & Farrington, 2015; Sherman & Strang, 2007). Most recently, a meta-analysis of 21 studies exploring the effect of restorative procedures on juvenile recidivism rates concluded that restorative programs have a beneficial effect for youth, as evidenced through longer desistance periods between reoffending than youths directed to traditional court procedures (Wong, Bouchard, Gravel, Bouchard, & Morselli, 2016). Particularly interesting is that even restorative procedures that involve very minimal or indirect contact between victims and offenders were more effective at reducing recidivism than court-based procedures (suggesting that the success of restorative procedures might not hinge on the direct interaction between offenders and victims—allowing greater opportunities for restorative procedures to be engaged). Overall, these evaluations provide substantial evidence in support of the association between offender participation in restorative procedures and recidivism reduction.

Limitations of existing research: While the findings highlighted above have concentrated on the optimistic outcomes of restorative justice, empirical work also demonstrates limitations of existing research. For instance, returning to the importance of the operational definition of recidivism adopted, the observed effects of restorative relative to retributive models dissipate when a longer time frame for recidivism is considered. In particular, Bergseth and Bouffard (2007) found that when recidivism was assessed over a 4-year follow-up period, differences between restorative and court-based interventions were no longer significant.

Likewise, Tyler, Sherman, Strang, Barnes, and Woods (2007) demonstrate that differences between restorative and court-based procedures are not statistically significant so long as key mechanisms (i.e., reintegrative shaming and procedural justice) are incorporated into the design of each; this casts doubt on longstanding assumptions that retributive and restorative orientations produce fundamentally different outcomes. Instead, this finding suggests that procedural treatment makes all the difference in outcome effects. While a substantial body of accumulated research suggests that restorative justice is, in many ways, superior to the formal criminal justice system in responding to crime, it is important to remain critical of the actual nature of these effects.

A particularly important consideration is the existence of a self-selection bias, which might strongly skew the results of restorative justice research. Victims and offenders who take part in restorative procedures *choose* to do so, suggesting that these persons could be fundamentally different than victims and offenders engaged with court-based procedures. The voluntary nature of restorative procedures coupled with the fundamentally different starting point of offender acknowledgment of harm might set the stage for participants in restorative procedures to interpret justice quite differently from those in court-based procedures (Latimer et al., 2005). In particular, stakeholders in restorative justice might simply be more motivated to reach a resolution to the criminal act, providing baseline conditions that promote the realization of the intended effects of restorative procedures (Braithwaite, 2016). As opposed to the formal criminal justice system, which is primarily engaged with imposing corrections upon offenders, restorative justice strives to seize opportunities to encourage an existing desire for desistance in offenders (Robinson & Shapland, 2008).

It is imperative that scholars scrutinize the methodology of research that demonstrates the effectiveness of restorative relative to court-based procedures. Doing so will allow researchers to more comprehensively understand and, ultimately, to better predict the outcomes of specific justice processes for specific persons. Theoretical explanations are essential to developing these better understandings, and two dominate the restorative justice literature: reintegrative shaming and procedural justice.

Explaining the Effects of Restorative Justice: Theoretical Foundations

Alongside research evaluating restorative justice programming, a considerable body of work has been dedicated to explaining the effects observed. Given that both restorative and retributive justice aim to produce meaningful consequences to crime, the focus for most researchers has been the procedural differences associated with their application. While court-based procedures can be somewhat dismissive of the perspectives of both victims and offenders, restorative programs have been recognized as more adequately attending to stakeholders' perspectives through the theoretical principles of reintegrative shaming and procedural justice. At their core, both of these theories advocate for the importance of process, maintaining that critical outcomes of justice responses (e.g., participant perceptions of satisfaction and legitimacy, as well as reoffending behavior) are highly dependent on the *means* used to administer justice.

Reintegrative Shaming

Although the formal criminal justice system operates on principles of proportional retributive justice, criminological theory suggests that this model might be detrimental to the offender. In particular, it has been argued that offenders experience harmful stigmatization as a result of encounters with the criminal justice system—particularly those which result in the administration of punishment—through a process of *labelling*. In other words, to be labelled as a "criminal" prompts society to reject offenders, identifying them as different and treating them accordingly (Becker, 1963; Links, Cullen, Frank, & Wozniak, 1987).

The origins of reintegrative shaming theory lie in the recognition that retributive responses to crime can be detrimental to offenders specifically, and to society more generally. In particular, a harmful form of stigmatization results from determinations of guilt levied in the formal criminal justice system, and this stigmatization can make reintegration into mainstream society difficult by way of a labelling effect (Braithwaite, 2000; Braithwaite & Mugford, 1994; Maruna, LeBel, Mitchell, & Naples, 2004). A function of stigmatization in retributive justice models is to connect the commission of a criminal act with feelings of shame—feelings which are seen as essential to foster future desistance from crime. However, the effects of shame are argued to be dependent on the structure of its administration, with stigmatizing shaming actually increasing subsequent offending (Braithwaite, 1989, 2000). Shame that is stigmatizing is grounded in messages of degradation, humiliation, and a lack of forgiveness; the offender is recognized as a bad person as indicated by his bad behavior. Consequently, the offender's social reintegration is made more challenging as the individual is likely to perceive, as well as actually experience, exclusion on the basis of the criminal label (Braithwaite, 2000; Braithwaite &

Mugford, 1994; Maruna et al., 2004). By contrast, restorative procedures recognize the value of shame but avoid engaging it through stigmatization by employing a model of reintegrative shaming.

Reintegrative shaming seeks to communicate shame for the harmful act while maintaining a position that is respectful to the offender and demonstrative of a willingness to forgive him (Braithwaite, 1989, 2000; Braithwaite & Mugford, 1994). As opposed to producing damaging consequences, shame incurred through a reintegrative process aims to encourage self-improvement, relationship restoration with those harmed by their actions, and inclusion with rather than exclusion from the community. Reintegrative shaming requires a different perspective from the offender—namely, that she is willing to accept responsibility for her behavior and acknowledge it as harmful—but also involves a fundamentally different structure of shaming, during which the offender (along with other stakeholders) is empowered with process control (Braithwaite & Mugford, 1994; Tyler et al., 2007). Reintegrative shaming is not an isolated component of the restorative justice conference; rather, it is an underlying philosophy that guides the procedure. This structure of shame is argued to work because it draws together people respected by the offender to disapprove of her behavior constructively, allowing the offender to recognize that, while her action was wrong, she is still valued (Braithwaite, 2000). Reintegrative shaming is a core foundation of the practice of restorative justice.

Restorative justice procedures endeavor to foster future desistance from crime by constructively conveying the harmful implications of a specific criminal act. This process ideally engages feelings of shame, but not stigmatizing shame. Instead, the various consequences of a crime (e.g., emotional, physical, material) are conveyed by stakeholders civilly in a way that is intended to genuinely compel the offender to avoid repeating the behavior in question. In these procedures, personal denunciation is ideally avoided; constructive disapproval of the offender's *behavior*, rather than the offender on the whole, is the objective (Braithwaite, 1989). Communicating the harmful consequences of behavior is intended to prompt feelings of shame on the part of the offender, but the communication of this information also ideally conveys care and support for the offender (Braithwaite, 2000). In these ways, restorative procedures embody the essence of reintegrative shaming and, as such, have been hypothesized to produce positive outcomes for offenders (Johnstone, 2002).

Empirical investigations have validated reintegrative shaming as a promising technique for responding to crime. Barnes et al. (2013) suggest that incorporating a reintegrative shaming philosophy into restorative procedures enhances the overall effectiveness of the response to crime, particularly with regard to participants' perceptions of satisfaction with the justice process. A key aspect of this satisfaction from the perspective of the offender is the extent to which procedures utilizing reintegrative shaming articulate respect for the offender. Procedures that promote the communication of respect for offenders foster positive relationship development for conference stakeholders (Ahmed, Harris, Braithwaite, & Braithwaite, 2001). Tyler et al.'s (2007) work provides a further test of this relationship. Adopting the starting point that reintegrative shaming strengthens the offender's relational ties to significant others, the authors hypothesized that offenders taking part in restorative procedures would be less likely to reoffend than those in court-based procedures because offenders in restorative programs would be more concerned with negatively affecting the relational bonds they had established as a result of the process. Using longitudinal data drawn from a portion of the Reintegrative Shaming Experiments (RISE) program in Australia that focused on offenders involved in drunk driving incidents, recidivism rates for offenders who were directed to court-based procedures were compared against those who were diverted to restorative programming after 4 years. The results provided evidence in favor of the use of reintegrative shaming practices; specifically, that the use of reintegrative shaming techniques in justice responses reduced recidivism rates (Tyler et al., 2007). Regardless of whether an offender was assigned to restorative or court-based procedures, if the procedure incorporated reintegrative shaming, lower rates of reoffending were observed than if the procedure did not incorporate reintegrative shaming.

It might be the case that reintegrative shaming promotes the development of social bonds that encourage abstaining from crime. Alternatively, the effectiveness of reintegrative shaming in reducing offending might be due to the enhanced perceptions of respect and fairness reported by participants in such procedures (Mazerolle et al., 2013). The role of fairness perceptions in restorative justice can be better understood by turning to the procedural justice literature.

Procedural Justice

While reintegrative shaming theory is directly linked to the restorative justice literature, procedural justice theory has a broader history. In the legal context, procedural justice is concerned with evaluations of the application of law; specifically, the extent to which a *procedure*, as opposed to an *outcome*, is perceived as fair and satisfying (emphasizing the subjective interpretations that define perceptions of justice; Tyler, 1989). Procedural justice theory rests on the assertion that perceptions of the extent to which an outcome (e.g., consequences for criminal behavior) is evaluated as fair and satisfying rest heavily on the procedure used to determine the outcome. This is demonstrated through a wealth of psychological literature exploring the relationships between processes and outcomes (e.g., Lind & Tyler, 1988; Thibaut & Walker, 1975; Tyler, 1989).

Relational models of procedural justice contend that procedural features such as "voice" (i.e., the opportunity to express one's opinion) are influential because they imply that the participant is a valued member of the group overseeing the procedure (i.e., she is asked to provide input because she has an important contribution to offer; Lind, Tyler, & Huo, 1997). Relational interpretations of procedural justice provide an explanation for a consistent finding in the literature: Even when individuals know that the voice they are permitted during a procedure will have *no* effect on the outcome reached, ratings of fairness and satisfaction associated with the procedure and outcome are still greater than when there is no opportunity for voice incorporated into the procedure. In fact, even *post*-decision opportunities for voice lead to higher fairness evaluations than no voice (Lind, Kanfer, & Earley, 1990). This finding necessitates an explanation grounded in non-instrumental, or relational, concerns. Fundamentally, relational models posit that treatment is a way of conveying messages of status in social groups. When treatment by authorities demonstrates attention to relational concerns, subordinates' feelings of in-group membership and value to the group are fostered, which in turn increases their fairness perceptions. Conversely, when treatment demonstrates disregard for relational concerns, this can lead to perceptions of exclusion, and consequently, decreased fairness perceptions (Bradford, 2014; Lind & Tyler, 1988).

Voice is not the only relational concern; it is one indicator among several process-oriented concerns that affect the extent to which a procedure, as well as its outcome, is determined to be fair and satisfactory (Lind et al., 1990, 1997; Platow et al., 2013). Although multiple relational models have now been developed to explain procedural justice effects (e.g., the Relational Model of Authority, Tyler & Lind, 1992; the Group Engagement Model, Tyler & Blader, 2000), these iterations all maintain the same core tenets outlined in the first model developed, the Group Value Model (Lind & Tyler, 1988), which still serves as the dominant relational explanation in the procedural justice literature.

Lind and Tyler (1988) posited that the extent to which a procedure appeals to central relational concerns dictates evaluations of fairness and satisfaction with not only the procedure, but its outcomes as well. In particular, three relational concerns were identified: (1) neutral and consistent treatment, (2) trust in administrator benevolence, and (3) interactions demonstrative of respect and dignity. All three variables independently affect procedural justice perceptions, and demonstrate procedural concerns that go beyond desires to wield control over outcomes (Tyler, 1989).

Perceptions of respect are derived from interpersonal interactions that are perceived as polite, dignifying and considerate of personal rights (Tyler, 1989, 1994; Tyler & Lind, 1992). Ultimately, disrespectful treatment conveys to the individual that he is a person of low status within the group in question, and can also imply the social standing of groups in relation to one another (Heuer & Stroessner, 2011; Tyler, 1989). Likewise, relational models of procedural justice have always incorporated "trust," understood as the extent to which the decision-making authority is perceived as trustworthy. This aspect of procedural justice concerns involves evaluating the perceived intentions of the administering authority, specifically, the extent to which the authority is perceived as reasonable (Tyler, 1989, 1994). Perceptions of trust are based on evaluations of the benevolence of the authority's treatment (Tyler & Lind, 1992), and are particularly influential in shaping perceptions of legitimacy because the inference of a benevolent disposition fosters the belief that an authority can be trusted in the long term (Hough, Jackson, Bradford, Myhill, & Quinton, 2010; Tyler, 1994). Finally, "neutrality" broadly refers to the "even-handedness" of a procedure (Lind & Tyler, 1988; Tyler, 1989, 1994). This concern is based on the extent to which treatment by an administering authority is perceived as unbiased, objective and administered with equality (Tyler, 1994; Tyler & Lind, 1992). Together, these *relational* variables shape procedural justice judgments.

The consequences of procedural justice perceptions underscore the need for procedural concerns to be taken very seriously in legal contexts. A plethora of research has demonstrated that when people feel that the relational concerns described above are acknowledged and implemented in a procedure, the procedure's outcome is likely to be described as more acceptable (Mazerolle et al., 2013; Tyler & Degoey, 1995), more satisfying (Mazerolle, Bennett, Antrobus, & Eggins, 2012; Mossholder, Bennett, & Martin, 1998), and more legitimate (Sunshine & Tyler, 2003; Tyler, Degoey, & Smith, 1996; Tyler & Wakslak, 2004). Likewise, the administrator of the procedure also tends to be evaluated as more legitimate, and these legitimacy perceptions are of particular significance in legal contexts. Legitimacy engenders behavioral compliance to the specific outcome in question as well as to the future instructions of the administrator of the procedure more generally (Gibson, 1989; Sunshine & Tyler, 2003). In other words, responses to criminal behavior that are perceived by the offender as fair and legitimate are more likely to promote future desistance from criminality. For these reasons, procedural justice theory in general, and the Group Value Model in particular, have been explored as offering explanatory power in relation to the effects of restorative procedures.

Restorative justice models cater well to relational concerns. In particular, they allow the opportunity for respect, trust, and neutrality to feature prominently in the procedure (Morrison, 2006; Tyler, 2006). The underlying philosophy of the model—disapproving of criminal acts but recognizing offenders as worthy of redemption—lays the foundation for inclusive treatment that helps convey to offenders that they will be treated without bias, with respect, and that they can trust in the process. Although they are being sanctioned, this treatment demonstrates care for the offender rather than simply control, and recognizes the offender as a valued member of the community, which serves to affirm value consensus and shared group membership (Gromet & Darley, 2009; Okimoto, Wenzel, & Feather, 2009; Wenzel et al., 2008). Finally, restorative procedures bestow a good deal of process control on participants, establishing substantial opportunities for voice (Braithwaite, 1998; Tyler, 2006; Zehr, 1997), which, in turn, enhances procedural justice evaluations (Lind et al., 1990; Tyler et al., 1996). Cumulatively, procedures adhering to a restorative justice philosophy should be guided by foundations that are likely to enhance perceptions of procedural justice, and that are attentive to relational concerns in particular.

Translating Theory into Practice: When Is Restorative Justice Effective?

Reintegrative shaming and procedural justice offer sound theoretical explanations for the success and effectiveness of restorative justice models. Before proceeding further, however, we must note that the notion of "restorative justice models" suggests a dichotomous understanding of restorative justice: That justice interventions either are, or are not, restorative, and, depending on that label, are, or are not, successful. Some restorative justice scholars have argued that their findings are better interpreted through the realization that responses to crime exist along a continuum of "restorativeness" (Bolitho, 2012). The manner in which justice responses are enacted affects the positioning of any intervention on the restorativeness continuum as well as the attributes of success being prioritized. For instance, the restorativeness of a justice intervention is enhanced by the procedural inclusion of practices indicative of reintegrative shaming and stakeholder relationship restoration (Ahmed & Braithwaite, 2012); the provision and nature of opportunities for empowerment, community restoration and remorse (Braithwaite, 2002); and "other values such as storytelling, respectful listening, victim and support attendance, and apology" (Bolitho, 2012, p. 61). In terms of effectiveness, empirical findings support the prediction that justice interventions falling along the restorative end of the continuum reduce subsequent offending (Hipple, Gruenewald, & McGarrell, 2014).

It is worth noting that, while identifying and incorporating effective procedural aspects in restorative interventions is important, rigidly prescriptive procedures that reduce the flexibility associated with restorative responses to crime should be avoided. Procedural flexibility is a hallmark of restorative justice that cannot be eliminated (Ahmed & Braithwaite, 2012; Bolitho, 2012); it is this flexibility that will allow restorative interventions to remain relevant and satisfying to the greatest possible range of offenders, victims, and offence types. The valuable notion that restorativeness is not measured dichotomously, but instead, along a continuum is highly relevant here. In this sense, a procedure is not "restorative" as a result of adherence to a strict procedure; rather, a variety of flexible qualities (such as stakeholder participation and collaborative decision-making) contribute to the relative restorativeness of procedures, and flexibility helps ensure that the intervention appropriately addresses the transgression and the needs of the stakeholders in question. Although restorativeness can be encouraged by striving for the inclusion of general components (e.g., empowerment, community restoration, remorse), it is not ideal to mandate them (Bolitho, 2012). Our objective is not to advocate for a singular restorative solution.

To demarcate justice interventions as either restorative or not fails to take into consideration the variety of components that would be undesirable to specifically mandate in a restorative justice procedure but that, nonetheless, might influence the overall restorativeness of the intervention. For instance, victim presence is assumed to be essential to a procedure being identified as restorative. However, interestingly, both experimental work (Saulnier & Sivasubramaniam, 2015a) and field work (Bouffard et al., 2016) have provided evidence that it might be viable to use less intensive forms of victim presence (i.e., presence of a victim representative or indirect mediation) and still attain positive outcomes for offenders in terms of their subjective evaluations of the procedure as well as reoffending behavior. Conceptualizing victim presence in alternative forms is an example of a procedural aspect of restorative interventions that complicates a singular notion of restorative justice, drawing attention to the value of a continuum of restorativeness.

Several other procedural features problematize a singular understanding of restorative justice. For instance, restorative interventions generally encourage communications conveying apology from the offender to the victim, and forgiveness from the victim to the offender. While the inclusion of these characteristics is highly flexible in every restorative procedure, empirical evidence has associated positive outcomes with these features. For instance, the issuance of apology has been associated with subjective benefits for conference participants in field research, including greater outcome satisfaction for victims (Dhami, 2012). Likewise, experimental laboratory work has demonstrated that offers of apology improve victims' perceptions of offenders and diminish victims' punishment recommendations (Jehle, Miller, & Maskaly, 2012). However, that does not mean mandating an offer of apology in a procedure would make it restorative. For instance, while Jehle et al. (2012) found that offenders who offered apologies were reacted to more favorably by victims than offenders who did not offer apologies, they also found that victims were sensitive to whether apologies were coerced or voluntary, with voluntary apologies producing the most favorable reactions to offenders. Further, experimental work has suggested that coercing offenders to offer an apology negatively affects the quality of the apology offered as well as offenders' subjective evaluations of the procedure (Saulnier & Sivasubramaniam, 2015a).

Victims' attitudes towards offenders will also determine the restorativeness of a procedure, and these attitudes are closely tied to offenders' behavior and the structure of the decision-making process. For instance, offers of apology by offenders foster victims' feelings of forgiveness and reduce desire for revenge in some circumstances (Fehr, Gelfand, & Nag, 2010; Jehle et al., 2012). Empirical work has demonstrated that the means of justice—whether the orientation of a procedure is fundamentally about punishment or consensus-seeking—strongly drives the achievement of forgiveness, with more restorative procedures more effectively engaging forgiveness (Wenzel & Okimoto, 2014). However, again, classifying a procedure as restorative on the basis of whether forgiveness was achieved is not appropriate. A restorative procedure that failed to foster the communication of forgiveness is not inherently non-restorative; rather, a procedure that incorporated the communication of forgiveness simply speaks to achieving some aspects of restorativeness.

In sum, restorative procedures must be recognized as multifaceted; even "core" aspects of restorative justice such as victim presence, apology, and forgiveness are better understood as positioning justice interventions along a continuum of restorativeness, rather than simply restorative or not. According to this logic, evaluations of the success of restorative justice would be more valid if they focused on evaluating the effectiveness of various, core procedural features that locate a process at one end or another of the restorativeness spectrum, rather than comparing the effectiveness of "restorative" versus "non-restorative" procedures, per se. Further attention should be devoted to identifying the procedural elements of restorative interventions that translate theory into effective action and evaluating the effectiveness of those procedural elements. However, the *effectiveness* of restorative justice in producing socially desirable outcomes in response to crime does not inherently align with *success* in terms of public support for restorative responses to crime.

Effectiveness Versus Acceptability: The Restorative Justice Dilemma

The notion of "success" is already complicated in justice interventions by the variety of ways in which effectiveness can be operationalized and the relative weight assigned to those outcomes (e.g., producing positive subjective perceptions of the experience for offenders and victims, reducing recidivism, punishing offenders). Restorative justice tends to fare better than the formal criminal justice system in terms of its effects on stakeholders' subjective perceptions, such as respectful treatment (Braithwaite, 2002), procedural fairness (Umbreit, Coates, & Vos, 2001), procedural and outcome satisfaction (Latimer et al., 2005), process finality (Strang & Sherman, 2006), accountability (Regehr & Gutheil, 2002), value consensus between parties (Okimoto & Wenzel, 2009), remorse, and empathy (Choi & Severson, 2009). While these potential outcomes of restorative interventions are key to understanding the effectiveness and, thereby, success of restorative justice, equally important to the viability of such procedures are public perceptions of the appropriateness of restorative responses to crime.

Developing a better understanding of how support for various justice procedures is constructed, produced, or maintained requires recognizing dominant lay philosophical justice orientations. Retributive motivations are generally recognized as being the dominant philosophy engaged by laypersons in response to crime (Carlsmith & Darley, 2008; Cullen, Fisher, & Applegate, 2000; van Prooijen, 2010). Empirical research suggests that retributive motivations are simply a default standard among average members of the public responding to observed transgressions in Western nations. For instance, van Prooijen (2010) concluded that unbiased third party decision makers default to retributive motivations in response to crime, on the basis of two findings. First, that participants assigned greater financial penalties to hypothetical offenders when the payment was described as a punishment for their crime rather than as compensation for the victim; and, second, that participants were more attentive to information pertinent to offender punishment relative to victim compensation when asked to relay key details of a vignette describing a hypothetical justice intervention.

Researchers have explored the factors that might drive this general tendency towards retributive motives. Evidence suggests that certain characteristics associated with the offence can affect justice motivations. For example, offences committed by youth as well as transgressions that are non-violent are associated with greater desires for restorative oriented responses (Cullen et al., 2000). Alternatively, relationship bias—specifically, greater emotional proximity to a victim—produces the opposite effect, enhancing punitive oriented responses (van Prooijen, 2010).

Third party perceptions of appropriate justice responses are also associated with more symbolic concerns, such as perceptions of group membership, transgression meaning, and offender deservingness (Feather, 2006; Wenzel et al., 2008; Wenzel, Okimoto, & Cameron, 2012). Perceptions of group membership refer to an identification that a target person is an in- versus out-group member relative to oneself. Although the exact criteria used to make this judgment vary considerably depending on context (e.g., race, religious orientation, family membership), research suggests that when third parties to a transgression identify the offender as an in-group member, they are more likely to adopt a restorative response to crime (Wenzel et al., 2008). Alternatively, identifying the offender as an out-group member promotes retributive responses. Similarly, the symbolic meaning of the transgression itself influences perceptions of appropriate justice. Retributive motivations tend to be engaged when a transgression is seen as a violation of status/power expectations, whereas restorative motivations are more likely to be engaged when a transgression is seen as a violation of values (Wenzel et al., 2012).

Finally, and fundamentally, justice motivations are driven by the treatment the offender is judged to deserve. Perceptions of deservingness are a product of the relative accord between actions and outcomes (Feather, 1996, 2006; Lerner, 1980); in other words, in the context of criminal behavior, a variety of characteristics associated with the criminal act come to influence perceptions of the way in which the offender should be treated. Evaluations of intent, harm caused, and provocation are all key criteria used to evaluate offender behavior (Saulnier, Lutchman, & Sivasubramaniam, 2012). When offender behavior is recognized as particularly egregious (e.g., deliberate, harmful, and/or unprovoked), third parties do not see the offender as deserving respectful treatment (Heuer, Blumenthal, Douglas, & Weinblatt, 1999). Given that conveying respect for the offender is a core aspect of restorative justice, this finding suggests that members of the public might not see many offenders as deserving of a restorative intervention. Justice responses of a fundamentally retributive or restorative orientation prioritize different justice goals (Gromet & Darley, 2009), but neither response will be recognized as adequately satisfying the goal of justice when the offender is not seen as deserving the treatment received (regardless of the reason for that lack of congruence).

As noted earlier, differences in outcome measures between restorative conferences and court-based procedures were negligible, so long as the approach that was employed incorporated reintegrative shaming and demonstrated attention to procedural justice concerns (Tyler et al., 2007). Recognizing that the theoretical foundations of restorative justice have a place in primarily retributive procedures prompts reflection on whether there is a place for punishment in primarily restorative procedures. Philosophical starting points of restorative and retributive responses to crime suggest that the models are driven by fundamentally conflicting goals; however, it could be the case that striking a balance between the two is the best way to appeal to public justice motivations while also producing socially desirable outcomes. For example, empirical research demonstrates that the incorporation of *opportunities* for retributive outcomes in restorative procedures enhances third party perceptions of the appropriateness of restorative interventions as a response to serious crime

(Gromet & Darley, 2006). Here, again, it is important to remember that restorative justice is not best understood dichotomously, but instead, along a continuum of restorativeness. Including the possibility for punishment does not inherently negate the restorative potential of a justice response (Gromet, 2012). Conceptualizing justice responses as simultaneously capable of serving restorative functions while also appealing to retributive motivations through the possibility of punishment substantially broadens the scope of restorative interventions by appealing to a wider, lay audience.

Public support for restorative justice is based on a variety of factors independent of the *effectiveness* of restorative justice. Advancing the *success* of restorative justice involves not only implementing restorative interventions that are empirically demonstrated to be successful on various important outcome measures; it also involves engaging with public perceptions of acceptability. This requires a more complex approach to making restorative justice viable in the long term. One way to achieve this viability is to accommodate widespread public notions of deservingness and retribution within restorative procedures through the inclusion of opportunities for offender punishment. Another way to achieve this viability is to investigate those public notions of retributive justice with the goal of amending them to be more amenable to restorative interventions. This requires being attentive to people's preferences for "just deserts" (Carlsmith & Darley, 2008) and the cognitive processes engaged during justice-oriented decision-making.

Cognitive Processing, Justice Reasoning, and Restorative Justice

Although outcomes such as stakeholder satisfaction and offender recidivism should be the key factors guiding the implementation of justice interventions, public perceptions of appropriate justice might, in fact, be among the most influential factors affecting the widespread application and long-term viability of restorative justice. Justice motivations shape satisfaction with justice interventions (Gromet, 2012; Okimoto & Wenzel, 2011; Wenzel et al., 2012). However, research has demonstrated that the justice motive comes in different forms, capable of producing quite different understandings of just outcomes.

The Justice Motive

We have already described the importance of procedural concerns as drivers of justice perceptions, but it is also important to consider research on distributive justice in order to understand perceptions of just outcomes among the public more broadly. In particular, the cognitive processing of responses to criminal behavior is divided into two streams; one relying on intuitive, heuristic processing, and the other on systematic, deliberative processing (Chaiken & Trope, 1999; Lerner, 2003; Sivasubramaniam, forthcoming). Though punishment is often central to both lay and legal notions of justice, the reasoning driving punishment decisions tends to be initiated through distinct cognitive processing mechanisms (heuristic versus deliberative processing, respectively; Chaiken & Trope, 1999; Gigerenzer & Gaissmaier, 2011; Lerner, 2003) that produce different renditions of justice.

Dual-process theories of cognition describe the processes underlying immediate, intuitive reactions to scenarios versus judgments based on some extended deliberation. Heuristic processing is an initial reaction, involving a more automated response (Chaiken & Trope, 1999; Lerner, 2003). In the justice context, this typically involves identifying a person directly responsible for causing a harm and desiring a consequence (most frequently punishment) for that wrongdoing. Systematic processing involves a more thorough review of available evidence. In the justice context, this typically involves overriding the reaction produced through heuristic processing to arrive at a more tempered outcome than that which was immediately desired. A fundamental difference between these systems is the extent to which they are automatically versus consciously engaged. Decisions reached as a result of heuristic processing are the product of scripted associations that reside within the individual (though these can be influenced by external factors such as cultural norms); whereas decisions reached as a result of systematic processing are the product of a conscious decision-makingeffort that involves considering a wider variety of variables, as well as determining the varied importance of those variables (Richetin, Perugini, Adjali, & Hurling, 2007). This fundamental variation in the rendering of judgments is essential to understanding how and why perceptions of appropriate justice are established, the ways in which legal and lay notions of justice vary, and finally, how support for restorative justice might be affected.

Legal notions of justice: Although the desire to restore a sense of justice following the commission of an offence is a goal of both the legal system and lay people, the processes the two groups employ prompt what actually constitutes a just outcome to be construed quite differently. Legal notions of justice are the product of complex and deliberative processing of information guided by procedural law (Krasnostein & Freiberg, 2013). This is a highly systematic means of determining just outcomes that fosters careful, sober and reflective second thought, actively striving to avoid the inclusion of emotional impulses. In practice, this involves a legal professional carefully considering a number of key factors that guide the legal production of just outcomes, such as ensuring adherence to sentencing principles and statutory law (i.e., abiding by legislated definitions of criminal offences including minimum and maximum consequences), as well as considering case-specific aggravating or mitigating factors alongside more generally prescriptive legal precedents. These factors are considered independently and in combination by persons specially *educated* and *trained* for this complex decision-making task: normally, judges.

The means by which sanctions are determined in restorative procedures are quite different from those employed in the formal criminal justice system, but they do share the fundamental feature of clearly involving deliberative, systematic reasoning. For example, participants in restorative interventions are encouraged to be reflective and think outside of their isolated position in the conflict when determining the harms that have been caused and how they should best be resolved, and they are guided by experienced facilitators in this process.

Lay notions of justice: The deliberative decision-making invoked in legal responses to crime involves a process of reasoning and reflection; by contrast, the intuitive decision-making process—which tends to be the first, if not the only, way in which lay notions of justice are rendered—is more akin to perception (i.e., not engaging with reasoning and reflection but, instead, more compulsory reactions; Haidt, 2001). The process is simple: A person learns of an offence and heuristic processing takes over, quickly establishing a sense of who is at fault in the interest of determining how the injustice can be rectified, with little regard for other relevant data such as contextual information. Without active attention to engaging in systematic processing, it is the heuristic system—and therefore, in the context of criminal behavior, retributive impulses—that dominate.

Heuristics function by actively ignoring substantial portions of relevant information (Gigerenzer & Gaissmaier, 2011), and while the judgments produced through this process might be accessible, the process itself is not (Haidt, 2001). Intuitive processing produces an outcome judgment by way of a process that is entirely opaque. Perhaps most troubling about judgments reached through heuristic processing is that perceptions associated with intuitive judgments are particularly difficult to challenge or reverse. These are visceral reactions, and although people tend to not be able to explain them well, they do tend to be highly invested in their accuracy (Haidt, Koller, & Dias, 1993; Haidt & Hersh, 2001).

Furthermore, intuitive reactions to descriptions of harm—particularly direct acts of harm between people—tend to frame justice responses primarily in terms of punishment (Carlsmith & Darley, 2008; Vidmar & Miller, 1980). Heuristic processing involves the production of a simple script in which emotions drive cognitive reactions to offending, prompting a tendency towards anger and the prioritizing of punishment. Several explanations exist for this effect: ideological preferences, instrumental motivations, and relational motivations (Gerber & Jackson, 2016). The first, ideological preferences, simply suggests that different people view the world differently; in particular, that persons who rank highly on scales of authoritarianism and conservatism are more likely to support punitive justice responses (Gerber & Jackson, 2013, 2016; Tyler & Boeckmann, 1997). The second, instrumental concerns, suggests that the fear of victimization drives more punitive responses as a strategy to reduce future exposure to harm by incapacitating known offenders as well as generally deterring others from engaging in crime (King & Maruna, 2009; Tyler & Boeckmann, 1997). Finally, the third explanation is grounded in relational concerns associated with interpersonal bonds. This explanation suggests that more punitive responses are a strategy of maintaining moral boundaries in response to community breakdowns (Carlsmith, Darley, & Robinson, 2002; Darley, Carlsmith, & Robinson, 2000; Tyler, 2006). Through this lens, the offender is fundamentally seen as someone who *deserves* to be punished. This sentiment is much more in line with the retributive orientation and stigmatizing structure of shame common to the formal criminal justice system than to the broader scope of harm response and the reintegrative structure of shame common to restorative procedures.

While explanations for the retributive impulse vary, the impulse is recognized as widespread and fundamental. It appears to be a product of a basic human response that is unlikely to vary considerably across persons on the basis of characteristics such as demographic variables. However, there is a need to continue to explore factors associated with variations in this impulse. For instance, actual victims of crime are more satisfied with responses to crime that are less punitive than more removed observers, demonstrating that we tend to react more punitively to observed, rather than personally experienced, harm (FeldmanHall, Sokol-Hessner, Van Bavel, & Phelps, 2014). Developing a greater understanding of the individual and situational variables that influence the retributive impulse is necessary to continue advancing understanding of this impulse, which can be usefully applied to improving subjective and objective outcomes of responses to crime.

While heuristic processing tends to be fundamental in establishing lay notions of justice, it must also be acknowledged that members of the general public are capable of engaging in deliberative processing, particularly when the emotions that initially compelled intuitive responses dissipate. Deliberative processing simply involves a more thoughtful evaluation of information relevant to the decision-making process (such as deservingness, culpability, and considering multiple forms of recourse), all in the interest of establishing the most appropriate justice response possible. Importantly, engaging deliberative processing can lead to different outcome judgments than those initial responses produced through heuristic processing (Haidt, 2001). In the context of evaluating criminal behavior, engagement solely with intuitive reasoning tends to be associated with a retributive impulse to punish the offender. Engaging with more reasoned, deliberative processing fosters a sober-second thought to retributive impulses, making it more likely that responses to criminal behavior will consider a broader range of socially desirable outcomes; notably, adherence to the principle of due process, but potentially more restorative responses to crime as well.

Unfortunately, the cognitive resources required to move beyond simple heuristic processing mean that transitioning to deliberative processing does not automatically follow initial, intuitive responses. Characteristics unique to the individual (e.g., personal cognitive capacities or tendencies to avoid deliberative reasoning) as well as the situation (e.g., limited time or resources) will influence one's ability and likelihood of engaging in deliberative processing (Sivasubramaniam, forthcoming). As such, while judges responsible for formal decision-making in legal contexts are required to engage in deliberative processing that overcomes their initial heuristic response, there are no guarantees that laypersons will find themselves in a situation, or with the skills, to do the same.

The dominance of the retributive impulse among lay people might seem somewhat inconsequential; after all, it is judges and not laypersons who determine the consequences levied on offenders (though laypersons do determine consequences in some situations, such as capital punishment and some serious felonies in the USA).

However, while a reasoned, deliberate approach to decision-making dominates responses to crime in the formal criminal justice system, public opinion is still highly influential in shaping the parameters within which legal decision makers operate (e.g., in shaping the legislation governing judges' determinations; for a broader discussion of the importance and pitfalls of relying on community sentiment in lawmaking, see Miller & Chamberlain, 2015). To the extent that public opinion is driven by intuitive, heuristic (and therefore retributive) approaches, formal legal responses will tend to adopt a fundamentally retributive orientation. This retributive impulse among lay people also poses a serious and specific challenge to advocates of restorative justice: restorative responses to crime adopt a much more divergent position from lay notions of justice than the formal criminal justice system and, therefore, will be less likely to receive the public approval necessary to become a widely deployed justice response. However, advocates of restorative justice might find productive paths in psychological research addressing ways to either override or amend the retributive impulse.

Restorative Justice and the Retributive Impulse

The key question we are left considering is: "Can restorative justice serve a sense of justice if it does not centralize the imposition of punishment on the offender?" (Sivasubramaniam, forthcoming, p. 151). We believe the answer is "yes," but that achieving this sense of justice requires careful attention to the relationship between cognitive processing mechanisms and the retributive impulse. Support for restorative justice can be increased in two distinct ways that take advantage of this relationship. The first path would be to encourage deliberative rather than heuristic processing; and the second would be to amend the scripts contained in people's justice-related heuristics, so that when heuristic processing is engaged, restorative (rather than retributive) responses to transgressions are primed.

First, increases in the use of deliberative processing by the public can be encouraged. Research suggests that people will default to heuristic processing unless encouraged to engage in deliberative processing (Simon, 1967). Therefore, ways to prompt deliberative processing of justice-related information need to be explored. In a very general sense, this is something that should be advocated for as central to the learning process; in other words, children, from a very young age, should learn about decision-making in emotionally complex situations through school-based curricula that differentiate between "fast" and "slow" thinking (Kahneman, 2012) and provide a series of steps, akin to the scientific method, for encouraging deliberative processing when faced with such situations. In the more specific sense of encouraging systematic reasoning once a person is exposed to a justice scenario, research programs that address the question of how to generate deliberative processing in emotional, justice-related scenarios that would normally evoke intuitive, heuristic responding need to be developed.

Without centralizing punishment, it might be assumed that restorative justice cannot achieve a sense of justice that satisfies lay notions of justice. However, research demonstrates that a variety of factors influence support for restorative justice, indicating that if deliberative cognitive processing can be engaged, then a desire for punishment is only one factor among several that people will consider when establishing their support for restorative interventions. When systematic processing is engaged and a wider variety of relevant information is taken into consideration, restorative justice tends to be acknowledged as meeting a wider array of desirable justice outcomes than justice responses with a primarily retributive orientation. In particular, other dimensions of success, such as greater opportunities for stakeholder inclusion (Moore, 2012), enhanced victim restoration and satisfaction (Bazemore, 1998; Latimer et al., 2005; Strang et al., 2006), and more successful offender reintegration into the community as well as reduced recidivism rates (Ahmed & Braithwaite, 2012; Braithwaite, 2002), become more central in determining people's support for restorative interventions. The existing evidence certainly suggests that victims' and observers' perceptions of the appropriateness of restorative responses to crime are improved when this wider array of factors is taken into consideration (Gromet, 2012), an outcome which can be partially credited to their own engagement with deliberative processing. However, it should be noted that systematic processing does not necessarily, or wholly, negate a desire for punishment; and research has demonstrated that restorative interventions tend to be evaluated more favorably when they include opportunities for retribution as a possibility (Carlsmith et al., 2002; Gromet & Darley, 2006). As such, designing restorative interventions that permit the possibility of retributive outcomes but foster deliberative processing could simultaneously appeal to retributive impulses, while not necessarily seeing the retributive impulses realized.

Second, heuristic processing can be harnessed to garner support for restorative justice. Specifically, better understanding the intuitive reasoning process associated with crime and justice responses might make it possible to alter the heuristic that tends to produce a retributive impulse. Essentially, this would involve reprogramming the basic scripts/associations that people hold so that heuristic processing no longer leads to the retributive impulse but, instead, leads to support for restorative responses to crime. To understand how to achieve this goal, we turn to the social psychology research on stereotypes.

In the social cognition literature (e.g., Schneider, Hastorf, & Ellsworth, 1979), stereotypes are employed to minimize the use of cognitive resources. In this sense, stereotypes are a form of heuristic processing reliant on simple associations to quickly reach decisions (Kahneman & Tversky, 1972). In the context of crime and justice responses, the simple association is: crime equals punishment. Punishment is an automatic association with crime and, so, it is overweighted in responses to justice produced through intuitive processing. As a result, we propose that the problem of heuristic processing producing retributive impulses can gradually be overcome by rescripting automatic responses to crime to: crime equals resolving harm.

There is some direction in the literature for rescripting heuristic processing. Bordalo, Coffman, Gennaioli, and Shleifer (2016) present empirical findings demonstrating that perceptions of greater representativeness foster the creation of stereotypes (in other words, the more commonly associations are seen, the more likely stereotypes based on those associations will be formed). This presents a difficult problem, as this finding suggests that retributive legal justice responses beget punitive lay notions of justice—bearing in mind that fundamental changes to the criminal justice system (such as a transition away from a primarily retributive orientation) require public support, thus producing a catch-22. However, social and economic circumstances can be leveraged in this regard. For example, nations adopting highly punitive justice responses, such as the United States, now find themselves driven to urgently change their punitive incarceration policies out of financial necessity. The monetary burden of sustaining large numbers of prisoners for extended periods of time is simply too great for the economy to bear (Shannon, 2015). As such, there is a window of opportunity to put forward a restorative agenda that can appeal to the general public through lowered relative cost, and which promotes alternatives to simply punishing offenders through extended incarceration. Research has demonstrated that justice concerns are, in part, influenced by people's perceptions that they will also be negatively affected by the decision (e.g., losing desired resources; Greenberg & Cohen, 1982; Lerner, 2003; Steensma & Vermunt, 1991). Therefore, cognitive rescripting that effectively associates administering punishment to others with harmful consequences for oneself (such as diminished resources) could be useful in diverting the association between criminal acts and retributive impulses. On a broader level, this would equate to an incremental, implicit change in the norms of society.

Advancing the Science: The Value of Psychological Research

Developing a more meaningful understanding of restorative justice necessitates continued research. In particular, investigations adopting a psychological approach would be highly valuable (Sivasubramaniam, 2012). Psychological research is highly useful for identifying variables relevant to the initiation, workings, and outcomes of restorative procedures, all of which are valuable in establishing when and why restorative justice is a viable response to crime. Psychological investigations advocate for the systematic exploration of variables associated with restorative justice, which is particularly suitable for better understanding how support for restorative interventions can be established and maintained. To this end, attention to cognitive processing is an essential and underdeveloped area.

There are a variety of methods that can be used to gain a more thorough understanding of the psychological mechanisms underlying restorative justice processes, but experimental work is particularly lacking in the restorative justice field. Experimental designs prioritize the isolation and manipulation of variables in a controlled setting, in the interest of determining their effects. This is an especially useful strategy for developing understandings of the existence, direction, and strength of relationships between variables in restorative procedures (Ahmed & Braithwaite,

2012; Dhami, 2012; Saulnier & Sivasubramaniam, 2015b). Experimental designs offer a means to test hypotheses while striving to eliminate the influence of confounding variables. As such, experimental methods are capable of generating knowledge of causal relationships between variables (Cosby, 1977; Salkind, 2006), which can be particularly compelling when results are replicated in both laboratory-based and field-based tests. Experimental investigations of justice-related cognitive processing mechanisms would be a valuable new direction for restorative justice researchers to pursue, offering considerable practical value in terms of better aligning restorative justice with lay notions of justice (either by amending the characteristics of restorative justice or by amending the architecture of lay notions of justice). In preparation for experimental field research, we suggest beginning with simple experimental laboratory work exploring cognitive processing that would allow relevant factors of interest surrounding restorative interventions to be controlled, isolated, and manipulated.

For instance, above we suggested exploring whether heuristic cognitive processing can be rescripted. A simple experimental laboratory design might invite participants to read a short vignette detailing a criminal transgression in the interest of subsequently assessing retributive impulses through questionnaire items, manipulating participants' pre-experiment intuitive associations (and, thereby, their heuristic processing). Specifically, participants could be assigned to one of three conditions (restorative, retributive, control) in which they are given details of, and encouraged to imagine, justice responses that are either primarily restorative or retributive, depending on their condition. (The control condition would provide a comparison to assess the general effect of priming.) Significant reductions in retributive impulses following exposure to the restorative condition would suggest that heuristic processing is capable of being reprogrammed in the short term (mirroring work suggesting that heuristic processing associated with stereotypes can be rescripted; Blair, Ma, & Lenton, 2001), and on the basis of such initial investigations, larger scale research programs could investigate the reprogramming of heuristic scripts in the longer term.

We also suggested exploring whether deliberative processing can be encouraged among lay people, to decrease retributive impulses. A simple, laboratory-based experimental paradigm could measure retributive impulses after manipulating the extent to which participants were permitted to "rush to judgment." Imposing different time limits and other criteria associated with the participant's decision-making process would allow for different styles of cognitive processing (i.e., heuristic versus deliberative) to be prompted. For example, participants could be randomly assigned to one of three conditions (heuristic, deliberative, control), given a short vignette to read detailing a criminal transgression, and asked to offer their decision about the most appropriate justice response from pre-crafted options (ranging from highly retributive to highly restorative in orientation). In this case, significant reductions in retributive impulses following exposure to the deliberative condition would suggest that actively encouraging deliberative processing is a means of influencing lay notions of justice to be less retributive.

In general, research on dual-process models of justice reasoning will allow us to better understand variations in support for justice interventions, and how support for restorative interventions can be increased. However, further work is also needed to improve understanding of the mechanisms at work *within* restorative procedures. While it is generally established that primarily restorative procedures are more successful than primarily retributive procedures across a variety of measures, advancing the current state of knowledge requires dissecting the success of restorative procedures at the operational level—what works, when, and for whom? A prime example of a procedural feature that requires further operational investigation is the issuance of an apology by the offender to the victim. Although apology has long been recognized as central to successful restorative procedures, empirical work exploring the actual effect of apology on desirable outcomes of restorative justice has been limited. The evidence that does exist suggests that apologies are associated with beneficial outcomes of restorative procedures, such as victim satisfaction (Dhami, 2012), perceptions of offenders and inclination towards punitive responses (Jehle et al., 2012), as well as offender perceptions of process finality (Saulnier & Sivasubramaniam, 2015a), but further research is needed to establish the conditions under which apology is a beneficial procedural feature.

Conclusion

In this chapter, we provided an up-to-date review of key information pertaining to the psychological study of restorative justice, closing with important future directions for researchers to pursue in this domain. We identified distinct philosophical foundations, structural applications, and outcomes of restorative justice models and the formal criminal justice system. We then discussed evidence-based policy as it pertains to restorative interventions—recognizing this as key to the development and administration of any successful response to crime. We reflected on the findings of program evaluations, theoretical explanations of effects, and linkages between theory and practice. We established the need to be clear about the multifaceted nature of restorative justice, as well as the multiple dimensions of *success* in such interventions. Crucially, we also noted that *effectiveness* in producing desirable outcomes in response to crime does not inherently align with *success* in terms of public perceptions of support for restorative responses to crime.

We discussed the crucial role of public perceptions of justice in shaping the viability of restorative justice, noting that the widespread retributive impulse dominates lay notions of justice. We argued that restorative justice can serve a sense of justice without prioritizing the punishment of offenders, but we reached two key conclusions in this regard: (1) that heuristic processing leads to retributive impulses, which does not promote a favorable response to restorative justice; and (2) that deliberative processing tends to temper retributive impulses, encouraging greater consideration of a wider variety of information, including more restorative responses to rectifying harm. Heuristic processing, therefore, should be associated with diminished support for restorative justice, and deliberative processing should be associated with enhanced support for restorative justice.

We considered two ways in which we might draw on the psychological literature to amend the retributive impulse: first, encouraging increases in the use of deliberative processing by the public in justice-related scenarios; and second, harnessing heuristic processing to garner support for restorative justice by disrupting the retribution-oriented script and replacing it with a restoration-oriented script. Finally, we advocated for continued research adopting a psychological orientation as key to advancing the science, noting experimental designs as particularly valuable in establishing a better understanding of causal effects and particularly well suited to investigating cognitive processing mechanisms and how they relate to the justice motive.

In conclusion, we note that we are undergoing an important, new stage in the development of restorative justice research. Early work in this field drew attention to the promises of restorative justice and laid the foundation for theoretical explanations of differences between restorative and retributive responses to crime. A second wave of research built on this groundwork through data-driven contributions offering empirical evidence of the distinctions between the mechanisms and outcomes of restorative interventions and court-based procedures. Researchers are now moving beyond replicating what is already fairly well established in the restorative literature, and are focusing on producing research that will continue to foster reform in the formal criminal justice system via *more restorative* procedures; however, regardless of the *effectiveness* of restorative justice, the *success* of restorative justice might be limited by its alignment (or lack of alignment) with the justice notions of the general public. The new wave of restorative justice research must not only improve the effectiveness of restorative justice; it must also enhance the success of restorative justice (in terms of public support for its expansion across the justice system and its long-term viability), through understanding, appealing to, and managing public notions of justice.

References

Ahmed, E., & Braithwaite, V. (2012). Learning to manage shame in school bullying: Lessons for restorative justice interventions. *Critical Criminology, 20*(1), 79–97. https://doi.org/10.1007/s10612-011-9151-y

Ahmed, E., Harris, N., Braithwaite, J., & Braithwaite, V. (2001). *Shame management through reintegration*. Cambridge: Cambridge University Press.

Angel, C. M., Sherman, L. W., Strang, H., Ariel, B., Bennett, S., Inkpen, N., & Richmond, T. S. (2014). Short-term effects of restorative justice conferences on post-traumatic stress symptoms among robbery and burglary victims: A randomized controlled trial. *Journal of Experimental Criminology, 10*(3), 291–307. https://doi.org/10.1007/s11292-014-9200-0

Barnes, G. C., Hyatt, J. M., Angel, C. M., Strang, H., & Sherman, L. W. (2013). Are restorative justice conferences more fair than criminal courts? Comparing levels of observed procedural justice in the reintegrative shaming experiments (RISE). *Criminal Justice Policy Review, 26*, 1–28. https://doi.org/10.1177/0887403413512671

Bazemore, G. (1998). Restorative justice and earned redemption communities, victims, and offender reintegration. *American Behavioral Scientist, 41*(6), 768–813. https://doi.org/10.1177/0002764298041006003

Bazemore, G., & Umbreit, M. (1995). Rethinking the sanctioning function in juvenile court: Retributive or restorative responses to youth crime. *Crime and Delinquency, 41*(3), 296–316. https://doi.org/10.1177/0011128795041003002

Becker, H. (1963). *Outsiders: Studies in the sociology of deviance*. New York, NY: Free Press.

Bergseth, K., & Bouffard, J. (2007). The long term impact of restorative justice programming for juvenile offenders. *Journal of Criminal Justice, 35*(4), 433–451. https://doi.org/10.1016/j.jcrimjus.2007.05.006

Bergseth, K. J., & Bouffard, J. (2012). Examining the effectiveness of a restorative justice program for various types of juvenile offenders. *International Journal of Offender Therapy and Comparative Criminology, 57*(9), 1054–1075. https://doi.org/10.1177/0306624X12453551

Blair, I. V., Ma, J. E., & Lenton, A. P. (2001). Imagining stereotypes away: The moderation of implicit stereotypes through mental imagery. *Journal of Personality and Social Psychology, 81*(5), 828–841. https://doi.org/10.1037/0022-3514.81.5.828

Bolitho, J. J. (2012). Restorative justice: The ideals and realities of conferencing for young people. *Critical Criminology, 20*(1), 61–78. https://doi.org/10.1007/s10612-011-9150-z

Bordalo, P., Coffman, K., Gennaioli, N., & Shleifer, A. (2016). Stereotypes. *The Quarterly Journal of Economics, 131*(4), 1753–1794. https://doi.org/10.1093/qje/qjw029

Bouffard, J., Cooper, M., & Bergseth, K. (2016). The effectiveness of various restorative justice interventions on recidivism outcomes among juvenile offenders. *Youth Violence and Juvenile Justice, 1*(1), 1–16. https://doi.org/10.1177/1541204016647428

Bradford, B. (2014). Policing and social identity: Procedural justice, inclusion and cooperation between police and public. *Policing & Society, 24*(1), 22–43. https://doi.org/10.1080/10439463.2012.724068

Bradshaw, W., Roseborough, D., & Umbreit, M. S. (2006). The effect of victim offender mediation on juvenile offender recidivism: A meta-analysis. *Conflict Resolution Quarterly, 24*(1), 87–98. https://doi.org/10.1002/crq.159

Braithwaite, J. (1989). *Crime, shame and reintegration*. Melbourne: Cambridge University Press.

Braithwaite, J. (1998). A future where punishment is marginalized: Realistic or utopian. *UCLA Law Review, 46*, 1727–1750.

Braithwaite, J. (1999). Restorative justice: Assessing optimistic and pessimistic accounts. *Crime and Justice Canadian, 25*, 1–127. https://doi.org/10.1086/449287

Braithwaite, J. (2000). Shame and criminal justice. *Canadian Journal of Criminology, 42*(2), 281–298.

Braithwaite, J. (2002). Setting standards for restorative justice. *British Journal of Criminology, 42*(3), 563–577. https://doi.org/10.1093/bjc/42.3.563

Braithwaite, J. (2007). Encourage restorative justice. *Criminology & Public Policy, 6*(4), 689–696. https://doi.org/10.1111/j.1745-9133.2007.00459.x

Braithwaite, J., & Mugford, S. (1994). Conditions of successful reintegration ceremonies: Dealing with juvenile offenders. *British Journal of Criminology, 34*(4), 139–172.

Braithwaite, J. B. (2016). Restorative justice and responsive regulation: The question of evidence.

Carlsmith, K. M., & Darley, J. M. (2008). Psychological aspects of retributive justice. *Advances in Experimental Social Psychology, 40*, 193–236. https://doi.org/10.1016/S0065-2601(07)00004-4

Carlsmith, K. M., Darley, J. M., & Robinson, P. H. (2002). Why do we punish? Deterrence and just deserts as motives for punishment. *Journal of Personality and Social Psychology, 83*(2), 284–299. https://doi.org/10.1037/0022-3514.83.2.284

Chaiken, S., & Trope, Y. (Eds.). (1999). *Dual-process theories in social psychology*. New York: Guilford Press.

Choi, J., & Severson, M. (2009). What! What kind of apology is this?: The nature of apology in victim offender mediation. *Children and Youth Services Review, 31*(7), 813–820. https://doi.org/10.1016/j.childyouth.2009.03.003

Cosby, P. C. (1977). *Methods in behavioral research* (3rd ed.). Palo Alto, CS: Mayfield.

Cullen, F. T., Fisher, B. S., & Applegate, B. K. (2000). Public opinion about punishment and corrections. *Crime and Justice, 27*, 1–79. https://doi.org/10.1086/652198

Darley, J. M., Carlsmith, K. M., & Robinson, P. H. (2000). Incapacitation and just deserts as motives for punishment. *Law and Human Behavior, 24*(6), 659–683. https://doi.org/10.1023/A:1005552203727

Dhami, M. K. (2012). Offer and acceptance of apology in victim-offender mediation. *Critical Criminology, 20*(1), 45–60. https://doi.org/10.1007/s10612-011-9149-5

Feather, N. T. (1996). Reactions to penalties for an offense in relation to authoritarianism, values, perceived responsibility, perceived seriousness, and deservingness. *Journal of Personality and Social Psychology, 71*(3), 571–587. https://doi.org/10.1037/0022-3514.71.3.571

Feather, N. T. (2006). Deservingness and emotions: Applying the structural model of deservingness to the analysis of affective reactions to outcomes. *European Review of Social Psychology, 17*(1), 38–73. https://doi.org/10.1080/10463280600662321

Fehr, R., Gelfand, M. J., & Nag, M. (2010). The road to forgiveness: A meta-analytic synthesis of its situational and dispositional correlates. *Psychological Bulletin, 136*(5), 894–914. https://doi.org/10.1037/a0019993

FeldmanHall, O., Sokol-Hessner, P., Van Bavel, J. J., & Phelps, E. A. (2014). Fairness violations elicit greater punishment on behalf of another than oneself. *Nature Communications, 5*, 1–25. https://doi.org/10.1038/ncomms6306

Gerber, M. M., & Jackson, J. (2013). Retribution as revenge and retribution as just deserts. *Social Justice Research, 26*(1), 61–80. https://doi.org/10.1007/s11211-012-0174-7

Gerber, M. M., & Jackson, J. (2016). Authority and punishment: On the ideological basis of punitive attitudes towards criminals. *Psychiatry, Psychology and Law, 23*(1), 113–134. https://doi.org/10.1007/s11211-012-0174-7

Gibson, J. L. (1989). Understandings of justice: Institutional legitimacy, procedural justice, and political tolerance. *Law and Society and Review, 23*(3), 469–496.

Gigerenzer, G., & Gaissmaier, W. (2011). Heuristic decision making. *Annual Review of Psychology, 62*, 451–482. https://doi.org/10.1146/annurev-psych-120709-145346

Greenberg, J., & Cohen, R. L. (1982). The justice concept in social psychology. In J. Greenberg & R. L. Cohen (Eds.), *Equity and Justice in Social Behavior* (pp. 1–47). New York, NY: Academic Press.

Gromet, D. M. (2012). Restoring the victim: Emotional reactions, justice belief, and support for reparation and punishment. *Critical Criminology, 20*(1), 9–23. https://doi.org/10.1007/s10612-011-9146-8

Gromet, D. M., & Darley, J. M. (2006). Restoration and retribution: How including retributive components affects the acceptability of restorative justice procedures. *Social Justice Research, 19*(4), 395–442. https://doi.org/10.1007/s11211-006-0023-7

Gromet, D. M., & Darley, J. M. (2009). Punishment and beyond: Achieving justice through the satisfaction of multiple goals. *Law and Society Review, 43*(1), 1–38. https://doi.org/10.1111/j.1540-5893.2009.00365.x

Haidt, J. (2001). The emotional dog and its rational tail: A social intuitionist approach to moral judgment. *Psychological Review, 108*(4), 1024–1057. https://doi.org/10.1037/0033-295X.108.4.814

Haidt, J., & Hersh, M. A. (2001). Sexual morality: The cultures and emotions of conservatives and liberals. *Journal of Applied Social Psychology, 31*(1), 191–221. https://doi.org/10.1111/j.1559-1816.2001.tb02489.x

Haidt, J., Koller, S. H., & Dias, M. G. (1993). Affect, culture, and morality, or is it wrong to eat your dog? *Journal of Personality and Social Psychology, 65*(4), 613–628. https://doi.org/10.1037/0022-3514.65.4.613

Heuer, L., Blumenthal, E., Douglas, A., & Weinblatt, T. (1999). A deservingness approach to respect as a relationally based fairness judgement. *Personality and Social Psychology Bulletin, 25*(10), 1279–1292. https://doi.org/10.1177/0146167299258009

Heuer, L., & Stroessner, S. J. (2011). The multi-value basis of procedural justice. *Journal of Experimental Social Psychology, 47*(3), 541–553. https://doi.org/10.1016/j.jesp.2011.01.007
Hipple, N. K., Gruenewald, J., & McGarrell, E. F. (2014). Restorativeness, procedural justice, and defiance as predictors of reoffending of participants in family group conferences. *Crime & Delinquency, 60*(8), 1131–1157. https://doi.org/10.1177/0011128711428556
Hough, M., Jackson, J., Bradford, B., Myhill, A., & Quinton, P. (2010). Procedural justice, trust and institutional legitimacy. *Policing: A Journal of Policy and Practice, 4*(3), 203–210. https://doi.org/10.1093/police/paq027
Jehle, A., Miller, M. K., & Maskaly, J. (2012). How voluntariness of apologies affects actual and hypothetical victims' perceptions of the offender. *The Journal of Social Psychology, 152*(6), 727–745.
Johnstone, G. (2002). *Restorative justice: Ideas, values*. Debates: Willan Publishing.
Kahneman, D. (2012). A proposal to deal with questions about priming effects. *Nature, 490*.
Kahneman, D., & Tversky, A. (1972). Subjective probability: A judgment of representativeness. In C.-A. Staël von Holstein (Ed.), *The concept of probability in psychological experiments* (pp. 25–48). Netherlands: Springer.
King, A., & Maruna, S. (2009). Is a conservative just a liberal who has been mugged? Exploring the origins of punitive views. *Punishment & Society, 11*(2), 147–169. https://doi.org/10.1177/1462474508101490
Krasnostein, S., & Freiberg, A. (2013). Pursuing consistency in an individualistic sentencing framework: If you know where you're going, how do you know when you've got there. *Law and Contemporary Problems, 76*, 265.
Latimer, J., Dowden, C., & Muise, D. (2005). The effectiveness of restorative justice practices: A meta-analysis. *The Prison Journal, 85*(2), 127–144. https://doi.org/10.1177/0032885505276969
Lerner, M. (1980). *The belief in a just world: A fundamental delusion*. NY: Plenum Press.
Lerner, M. J. (2003). The justice motive: Where social psychologists found it, how they lost it, and why they may not find it again. *Personality and Social Psychology Review, 7*(4), 388–399. https://doi.org/10.1207/S15327957PSPR0704_10
Lind, E. A., Kanfer, R., & Earley, C. P. (1990). Voice, control, and procedural justice: Instrumental and noninstrumental concerns in fairness judgments. *Journal of Personality and Social Psychology, 59*(5), 952–959. https://doi.org/10.1037/0022-3514.59.5.952
Lind, E. A., & Tyler, T. R. (1988). *The social psychology of procedural justice*. New York, NY: Plenum Press.
Lind, E. A., Tyler, T. R., & Huo, Y. J. (1997). Procedural context and culture: Variation in the antecedents of procedural justice judgments. *Journal of Personality and Social Psychology, 73*(4), 767–780. https://doi.org/10.1037/0022-3514.73.4.767
Links, B., Cullen, F. T., Frank, J., & Wozniak, J. F. (1987). The social rejection of former mental patients: Understanding why labels matter. *American Sociological Review, 92*, 1461–1500. https://doi.org/10.1086/228672
MacKenzie, D. L., & Farrington, D. P. (2015). Preventing future offending of delinquents and offenders: What have we learned from experiments and meta-analyses? *Journal of Experimental Criminology, 11*(4), 565–595. https://doi.org/10.1007/s11292-015-9244-9
Maruna, S., LeBel, T. P., Mitchell, N., & Naples, M. (2004). Pygmalion in the reintegration process: Desistance from crime through the looking glass. *Psychology, Crime and Law, 10*(3), 271–281. https://doi.org/10.1080/10683160410001662762
Mazerolle, L., Antrobus, E., Bennett, S., & Tyler, T. R. (2013). Shaping citizenship perceptions of police legitimacy: A randomized field trial of procedural justice shaping citizens perceptions of police. *Criminology, 51*(1), 33–63. https://doi.org/10.1111/j.1745-9125.2012.00289.x
Mazerolle, L., Bennett, S., Antrobus, E., & Eggins, E. (2012). Procedural justice, routine encounters and citizens perceptions of police: Main findings from the Queensland Community Engagement Trial (QCET). *Journal of Experimental Criminology, 8*(3), 343–367. https://doi.org/10.1007/s11292-012-9160-1

Miller, M. K., & Chamberlain, J. (2015). "There ought to be a law!": Understanding community sentiment. In M. K. Miller, J. A. Blumenthal, & J. Chamberlain (Eds.), *Handbook of community sentiment*. New York, NY: Springer.

Moore, R. (2012). Beyond the prison walls: Some thoughts on prisoner 'resettlement' in England and Wales. *Criminology & Criminal Justice, 12*(2), 129–147. https://doi.org/10.1177/1748895811425445

Morrison, B. (2006). School bullying and restorative justice: Toward a theoretical understanding of the role of respect, pride, and shame. *Journal of Social Issues, 62*(2), 371–392. https://doi.org/10.1111/j.1540-4560.2006.00455.x

Mossholder, K. W., Bennett, N., & Martin, C. L. (1998). A multilevel analysis of procedural justice context. *Journal of Organizational Behavior, 19*(1), 131–141.

Okimoto, T. G., & Wenzel, M. (2009). Punishment as restoration of group and offender values following a transgression: Value consensus through symbolic labelling and offender reform. *European Journal of Social Psychology, 39*(3), 346–367. https://doi.org/10.1002/ejsp.537

Okimoto, T. G., & Wenzel, M. (2011). Third-party punishment and symbolic intragroup status. *Journal of Experimental Social Psychology, 47*(4), 709–718. https://doi.org/10.1016/j.jesp.2011.02.001

Okimoto, T. G., Wenzel, M., & Feather, N. T. (2009). Beyond retribution: Conceptualizing restorative justice and exploring its detriments. *Social Justice Research, 22*(1), 156–180. https://doi.org/10.1007/s11211-009-0092-5

Platow, M. J., Eggins, R. A., Chattopadhyay, R., Brewer, G., Hardwick, L., Milsom, L., … Welsh, J. (2013). Two experimental tests of relational models of procedural justice: Non-instrumental voice and authority group membership. *British Journal of Social Psychology, 52*(3), 361–376. https://doi.org/10.1111/j.2044-8309.2011.02083.x

Regehr, C., & Gutheil, T. (2002). Apology, justice, and trauma recovery. *Journal of American Academy of Psychiatry and Law, 30*(3), 425–430.

Richetin, J., Perugini, M., Adjali, I., & Hurling, R. (2007). The moderator role of intuitive versus deliberative decision making for the predictive validity of implicit and explicit measures. *European Journal of Personality, 21*(4), 529–546. https://doi.org/10.1002/per.625

Robinson, G., & Shapland, J. (2008). Reducing recidivism: A task for restorative justice? *British Journal of Criminology, 48*(3), 337–358. https://doi.org/10.1093/bjc/azn002

Salkind, N. (2006). *Exploring research* (6th ed.). Upper Saddle River, NJ: Pearson/Prentice Hall.

Saulnier, A., Lutchman, K., & Sivasubramaniam, D. (2012). Laboratory experiments: A meaningful contribution to restorative justice research? *Critical Criminology, 20*(2), 99–115. https://doi.org/10.1007/s10612-011-9152-x

Saulnier, A., & Sivasubramaniam, D. (2015a). Restorative justice: Underlying mechanisms and future directions. *New Criminal Law Review, 18*(4), 510–536. https://doi.org/10.1525/nclr.2015.150014

Saulnier, A., & Sivasubramaniam, D. (2015b). The effects of victim presence and coercion in restorative justice: An experimental paradigm. *Law and Human Behavior, 39*(4), 378–387. https://doi.org/10.1037/lhb0000130

Schneider, D. J., Hastorf, A. H., & Ellsworth, P. (1979). *Person perception*. New York: Random House.

Shannon, C. (2015). The smarter sentencing act: Achieving fairness through financially responsible federal sentencing policies. *The John Marshall Law Review, 48*(3), 909–930.

Sherman, L., Strang, H., Mayo-Wilson, E., Woods, D., & Ariel, B. (2014). Are restorative justice conferences effective in reducing repeat offending? Findings from a Campbell systematic review. *Journal of Quantitative Criminology, 31*, 1–24. https://doi.org/10.1007/s10940-014-9222-9

Sherman, L. W., & Strang, H. (2007). *Restorative justice: The evidence*. London: Smith Institute.

Simon, H. A. (1967). Motivational and emotional controls of cognition. *Psychological Review, 74*(1), 29. https://doi.org/10.1037/h0024127

Sivasubramaniam, D. (2012). A special issue on restorative justice: Unravelling the mystery. *Critical Criminology, 20*(1), 1–7. https://doi.org/10.1007/s10612-011-9148-6
Sivasubramaniam, D. (forthcoming). The justice motive: Psychological research on perceptions of justice in criminal law. In R. Levy (Ed.), *New directions for law in Australia: Essays in contemporary law reform* (pp. 147–153). Canberra, ACT: ANU Press.
Steensma, H., & Vermunt, R. (1991). Future trends in the study of social justice. In H. Steensma & R. Vermunt (Eds.), *Social justice in human relations* (pp. 269–278). New York: Springer.
Strang, H. (2002). *Repair or revenge: Victims and restorative justice*. Oxford, UK: Oxford University Press.
Strang, H., & Sherman, L. (2015). The morality of evidence: The second annual lecture for restorative justice: An international journal. *Restorative Justice, 3*(1), 6–27. https://doi.org/10.1080/20504721.2015.1049869
Strang, H., Sherman, L., Angel, C., Woods, D., Bennett, S., Newbury-Birch, D., & Inkpen, N. (2006). Victim evaluations of face-to-face restorative justice conferences: A quasi-experimental analysis. *Journal of Social Sciences, 62*(2), 281–306. https://doi.org/10.1111/j.1540-4560.2006.00451.x
Strang, H., & Sherman, L. W. (2006). *Restorative justice to reduce victimization. Preventing crime*. New York, NY: Springer.
Sunshine, J., & Tyler, T. (2003). The role of procedural justice and legitimacy in shaping public support for policing. *Law and Society Review, 37*(3), 513–548. https://doi.org/10.1111/1540-5893.3703002
Thibaut, J. W., & Walker, L. (1975). *Procedural justice: A psychological analysis*. Hillside, NJ: Erlbaum.
Tyler, T. R. (1989). The psychology of procedural justice: A test of the group-value model. *Journal of Personality and Social Psychology, 57*(5), 830–838. https://doi.org/10.1037/0022-3514.57.5.830
Tyler, T. R. (1994). Psychological models of the justice motive: Antecedents of distributive and procedural justice. *Journal of Personality and Social Psychology, 67*(5), 850–863. https://doi.org/10.1037/0022-3514.67.5.850
Tyler, T. R. (2006). Restorative justice and procedural justice: Dealing with rule breaking. *Journal of Social Issues, 62*(2), 305–323. https://doi.org/10.1111/j.1540-4560.2006.00452.x
Tyler, T. R., & Blader, S. L. (2000). *Cooperation in groups: Procedural justice, social identity, and behavioral engagement*. Philadelphia, PA: Psychology Press.
Tyler, T. R., & Boeckmann, R. J. (1997). Three strikes and you are out, but why? The psychology of public support for punishing rule breakers. *Law and Society Review, 31*, 237–265. https://doi.org/10.2307/3053926
Tyler, T. R., & Degoey, P. (1995). Collective restraint in social dilemmas: Procedural justice and social identification effects on support for authorities. *Journal of Personality and Social Psychology, 69*(3), 482–497. https://doi.org/10.1037/0022-3514.69.3.482
Tyler, T. R., Degoey, P., & Smith, H. (1996). Understanding why the justice of group procedures matter: A test of the psychological dynamics of the group-value model. *Journal of Personality and Social Psychology, 70*(5), 913–930. https://doi.org/10.1037/0022-3514.70.5.913
Tyler, T. R., & Lind, E. A. (1992). A relational model of authority in groups. *Advances in Experimental Social Psychology, 25*, 115–191. https://doi.org/10.1016/S0065-2601(08)60283-X
Tyler, T. R., Sherman, H., Strang, L., Barnes, G. C., & Woods, D. (2007). Reintegrative shaming, procedural justice, and recidivism: The engagement of offenders' psychological mechanisms in the Canberra RISE drinking-and-driving experiment. *Law and Society Review, 41*(3), 553–586. https://doi.org/10.1111/j.1540-5893.2007.00314.x
Tyler, T. R., & Wakslak, C. J. (2004). Profiling and police legitimacy: Procedural justice, attributions of motive, and acceptance of police authority. *Criminology, 42*(2), 253–281. https://doi.org/10.1111/j.1745-9125.2004.tb00520.x
Umbreit, M., Coates, R., & Vos, B. (2001). *Juvenile victim offender mediation in six Oregon counties*. Retrieved from http://www.rjp.umn.edu

Van Ness, D. W. (1993). New wine and wineskins: Four challenges of restorative justice. *Criminal Law Forum, 4*(2), 251–276. https://doi.org/10.1007/BF01096074

van Prooijen, J. W. (2010). Retributive versus compensatory justice: Observers' preferences for punishing in response to criminal offences. *European Journal of Social Psychology, 40*(1), 72–85. https://doi.org/10.1002/ejsp.611

Vidmar, N., & Miller, D. T. (1980). Socialpsychological processes underlying attitudes toward legal punishment. *Law & Society Review, 14*(3), 565–602. https://doi.org/10.2307/3053193

Wenzel, M., & Okimoto, T. G. (2014). On the relationship between justice and forgiveness: Are all forms of justice made equal? *British Journal of Social Psychology, 53*(3), 463–483. https://doi.org/10.1111/bjso.12040

Wenzel, M., Okimoto, T. G., & Cameron, K. (2012). Do retributive and restorative justice processes address different symbolic concerns? *Critical Criminology, 20*(1), 25–44. https://doi.org/10.1007/s10612-011-9147-7

Wenzel, M., Okimoto, T. G., Feather, N. T., & Platow, M. J. (2008). Retributive and restorative justice. *Law and Human Behavior, 32*(5), 375–389. https://doi.org/10.1007/s10979-007-9116-6

Wong, J. S., Bouchard, J., Gravel, J., Bouchard, M., & Morselli, C. (2016). Can at-risk youth be diverted from crime? A meta-analysis of restorative diversion programs. *Criminal Justice and Behavior, 43*(10), 1310–1329. https://doi.org/10.1177/0093854816640835

Zehr, H. (1997). Restorative justice: The concept. *Corrections Today, 59*(7), 68–70.

Zehr, H. (2002). Journey to belonging. In E. G. M. Weitekamp & H. J. Kemer (Eds.), *Restorative justice: Theoretical foundations*. Cullompton, UK: Willan Publishing.

Examining the Presenting Characteristics, Short-Term Effects, and Long-Term Outcomes Associated with System-Involved Youths

Melanie Taylor, Philip Mulvey, Kristan Russell, and Brice Terpstra

Examining the Presenting Characteristics, Short-Term Effects, and Long-Term Outcomes Associated with System-Involved Youths

Contact with the juvenile justice system has long been recognized as detrimental to juveniles' life outcomes. Although the number of juveniles informally and formally processed in the United States has decreased in recent years, high numbers of juveniles still come into contact with the juvenile justice system annually. In 2012, over 1.3 million juveniles were arrested (Puzzanchera & Kang, 2014), while in 2013 over 200,000 juveniles were adjudicated delinquent (Sickmund, Sladky, & Kang, 2015), 36,000 were committed to a detention facility (Sickmund, Sladky, Kang, & Puzzanchera, 2015), and nearly 400,000 juveniles were placed on probation (Sickmund, Sladky, & Kang, 2015). As sizeable numbers of juveniles still make contact with the system each year, it is important to consider how system-involved delinquents differ from nondelinquents and delinquents who were diverted out of the system.

The juvenile justice system was founded on ideals of rehabilitation and treatment of juvenile delinquents; however, the reality is that mere contact with the juvenile

M. Taylor (✉)
Department of Criminal Justice, University of Nevada, Reno, Reno, NV, USA
e-mail: melanietaylor@unr.edu

P. Mulvey · B. Terpstra
Department of Criminal Justice Sciences, Illinois State University, Normal, IL, USA
e-mail: pwmulve@ilstu.edu; bjterps@ilstu.edu

K. Russell
Interdisciplinary Social Psychology PhD Program, University of Nevada, Reno, Reno, NV, USA
e-mail: kristanr@nevada.unr.edu

M. K. Miller, B. H. Bornstein (eds.), *Advances in Psychology and Law*, Advances in Psychology and Law 3,
https://doi.org/10.1007/978-3-319-75859-6_7

justice system oftentimes leads to poor outcomes for juveniles in both adolescence and later when these adolescents enter adulthood (Emanuel, 2013; Gilman, Hill, & Hawkins, 2015). In some cases, formal and informal criminal labels placed upon juveniles can lead to the internalization and eventual expression of these labels long after system contact. Furthermore, juvenile justice policies increasingly fail to consider developmental processes experienced in adolescence, even though most juvenile delinquents mature and age out of delinquent behaviors. Nevertheless, punishments delinquent youths experience during the short period of adolescence can haunt these youths well into adulthood. It is also critically important to recognize that many delinquent youths present unique challenges in the system due to prior mental health and substance abuse problems—issues that are often exacerbated by system contact.

This chapter explores some of the most notable consequences that system-involved juveniles face. Foremost among these is the finding that these youths are more likely to reoffend in the future than juveniles who were diverted out of the system (Whitehead & Lab, 1989). Growing evidence also suggests that there is a direct link between dropping out of high school and incarceration in adulthood (Hjalmarsson, 2008). There are also several less considered outcomes of juvenile system involvement that we examine in the present chapter. For example, formerly delinquent youths face challenges in obtaining employment and limited wage growth in comparison to their nondelinquent counterparts. There is also growing evidence that delinquent youths confront challenges in establishing successful romantic relationships in similar ways to the marital struggles experienced by adults with felony records. Examinations of the outcomes of delinquent youths in both the short- and long-term are critical, as significant life events that impact successful reintegration could be stunted because of juvenile system contact.

The focal goal of this chapter is to investigate the initial characteristics and outcomes of those who are processed through the juvenile justice system, as well as later life outcomes in adulthood for these individuals. First, theoretical explanations of both short- and long-term delinquent behaviors are briefly examined, including internalization of delinquent labels, disruption of the life course, and adolescent development. Second, unique problems experienced by delinquent youths in comparison to nondelinquents are considered, with a specific focus on mental disorders; alcohol and drug abuse; and suicidal behaviors of system-involved youths. Finally, the focus of the chapter then shifts to the outcomes of former delinquents as they emerge into adulthood. This section examines high school graduation and college attendance of delinquent youths; linkages between dropping out of school and adult incarceration; recidivism following system contact; the impact of publicized delinquent records on employment; and long-term mental health outcomes of formerly delinquent youths, with a focus on the persistence of mental illness and increased likelihood of suicidal behavior following detention. The chapter concludes with some thoughts on future research and policy implications using the empirical evidence discussed in the chapter as a catalyst for consideration.

Theoretical Explanations of Delinquent Behaviors

Several sociological and criminological theories attempt to explain delinquent behaviors, including the impact of delinquent peer associations (Akers, 1998), informal social controls (Hirschi, 1969), and general strains in life (Agnew, 1992). While many delinquency theories focus upon conditions surrounding the juvenile, a few theories explain how delinquency is shaped by system contact. The most notable of these theories is labeling theory, which posits that contact with the juvenile system is actually harmful and nonrehabilitative for juveniles. In contrast, the life course theory approaches delinquency from the perspective that system contact shapes the life events of delinquents, oftentimes preventing them from entering into conventional social institutions (e.g., marriage, employment). A final emerging thesis is that the juvenile justice system fails to account for the developmental nature of adolescence, where juveniles are maturing over time, and most will eventually mature out of delinquency. These theories are explored below to establish a foundation for the rest of the chapter.

Labeling Theory

Contact with the juvenile justice system contributes to higher rates of continued deviancy (Bernburg & Krohn, 2003). One explanation for this relationship is the impact of formal criminal labels on delinquents. Labeling theory posits that placing a negative social label (e.g., deviant) on a person is psychologically and socially detrimental (Becker, 1963). Official interventions (e.g., arrest, juvenile detention), therefore, result in delinquent labels (Bernburg & Krohn, 2003). Society subsequently views those with deviant labels as having undesirable traits. To further complicate this, the stigmatizing nature of deviant labeling can then perpetuate a long-lasting pattern of deviancy (Sampson & Laub, 1997).

There are two primary routes through which deviant labeling could place a person on a trajectory toward future deviancy. First, labeling could alter a person's self-concept by supporting deviant self-meanings (i.e., sentiments people hold toward themselves that are associated with their deviant labels) (Kroska, Lee, & Carr, 2017). The stigmatization and change in self-concept might influence the person to withdraw from society (Bernburg, 2009). Consequently, after adopting a deviant identity, a juvenile might engage in subsequent deviant behavior (Liska & Messner, 1999). Labeling that occurs through contact with the juvenile justice system results in higher rates of criminal offending in adulthood (Lee, Courtney, Harachi, & Tajima, 2015). Second, social exclusion can also contribute to subsequent offending. In other words, labeling people as deviants restricts their access to structured opportunities (e.g., education) (Sampson & Laub, 1997) and reduces opportunities for fulfilling conventional norms (Bernburg & Krohn, 2003). Deviant labeling can result in exclusion from educational opportunities (Bernburg & Krohn,

2003), lack of stable employment, and exposure to deviant peers (Sweeten, 2006). This exclusion is exceptionally detrimental, as these educational and employment opportunities typically act as protective factors against future deviancy.

Labeling theory also suggests that offending and arrest rates are not necessarily consistent with one another. For example, first arrest and subsequent labeling could increase the scrutiny of former delinquents by police and other authority figures (Liberman, Kirk, & Kim, 2014). Juveniles who begin this cycle from an already disadvantaged stance due to race or social class are the most affected by deviant labels (Sampson & Laub, 1997). Ultimately, youths could experience dual stigmatization due to negative stereotypes associated with their social disadvantages and system labeling, further limiting future opportunities for these adolescents. Adding additional disadvantages to deviant labeling might then further contribute to the cycle of criminal offending into adulthood.

Life Course Theory

Scholars who examine the prevalence and impact of crime across the life course normally focus on the notions of "timing" and "age" (Slocum, 2016). Life course theorists consider the dynamic processes across the lifespan and consider how continuity, change, and other developmental progressions, especially in childhood and adolescence, can affect offending (for examples and reviews, see: Lilly, Cullen, & Ball, 2015; Laub & Lauritsen, 1993; Laub & Sampson, 1993; Moffitt, 1993; Sampson & Laub, 1990). Central to the notion of the theory are the concepts known as *trajectories* and *transitions* that shape one's developmental processes across the life course (Elder, 1985, 1998).

Trajectories are the life course pathways (or unique future options) a person is propelled into by specific life transitions. These transitions are typically nominal life course events that develop into something more substantial. For instance, a healthy romantic relationship or a new employment opportunity can serve as a catalyst to a larger event, or *turning point,* in the process of desistance from crime (Sampson & Laub, 1993). When turning points occur, they often inspire more significant change within the person and lead to different developmental trajectories (Elder, 1985). Informal social controls are important in life course theory, as poor family bonding or weak interpersonal conditions can lead an adolescent to transition to delinquency in the same way that strong informal social controls can lead people away from crime. The stronger the social bonds, the greater the likelihood for desistance from crime for the person (Giordano, Cernkovich, & Holland, 2003).

Other scholars have examined longitudinal developmental processes to explore the varying patterns of desistance from crime across the life course through more neuropsychological progressions. Moffitt (1993) found that there are two primary groups of adolescent offenders. One group, referred to as *adolescent-limited offenders,* encompasses most people who commit crime. This group's deviance normally begins and ends during adolescence and is largely considered a normative developmental process—a time in the life course when immense biological and social change for most youths occurs. However, as these offenders age, more conventional life paths normally present themselves (e.g., stable romantic relationships or opportunities for employment) and deviance subsequently subsides.

The other group of offenders is referred to as *life-course-persistent offenders* (Moffitt, 1993). This group's deviance begins at an earlier age; they usually show nonnormative development early in the life course, with markers like maladaptive temperament, poor self-control, decreased verbal ability, and other neuropsychological deficits (Moffitt & Caspi, 2001). Although this group makes up only 5–10% of all adolescent offenders, their delinquency is more chronic, as well as more pathological across the life course, with their offending behavior beginning before, and extending well beyond, adolescence.

Maturation of Juveniles

Another theory prominent in developmental science focuses on psychosocial maturity. This perspective posits that adolescents make decisions differently than adults, and suggests that juveniles are especially vulnerable to impulsivity and risky decision-making (Cauffman & Steinberg, 2000; Leshem, 2016). Developmental scientists also argue that during this transitional phase in the life course, maturation in the brain is occurring, but also "during adolescence, the brain is more plastic than it will ever be again" (Leshem, 2016, p. 2). These formative brain processes function in concert with the social pressures of peer influence, elevated risk taking, judgment, and impulsivity during this time. As a result, decision-making processes are often quite different for juveniles in comparison to adults (Cauffman & Steinberg, 2000; Scott, 2000). Steinberg (2005) argued that it is critical that these developmental processes are weighed heavily in the juvenile justice system, as "adolescence is often a period of especially heightened vulnerability as a consequence of potential disjunctions between developing brain, behavioral and cognitive systems that mature along different timetables" (p. 69). In other words, delinquent behaviors oftentimes stem from immaturity, the inability of adolescents to effectively regulate behaviors, and the inability to recognize risks of behaviors.

Over the past decade, policymakers have begun to recognize the psychosocial immaturity of delinquents, resulting in significant changes in the arrest practices and court processing of delinquents. Most notable of these are Supreme Court decisions that eliminated the juvenile death penalty in 2005 (*Roper v. Simmons*, 2005), life without parole sentences for nonhomicide offenders in 2010 (*Graham v. Florida*, 2010), and life without parole sentences for homicide offenders in 2012 (*Miller v. Alabama*, 2012). Limited cognition and impulsivity of adolescents have also been reconsidered in the admissibility of confessions due to limited comprehension of legal rights and the likelihood of making false confessions. Following the *Miranda v. Arizona* (1966) decision, officers were required to notify suspects who were in custody (i.e., not free to leave) of their legal rights prior to interrogations; however, the age of the suspect was not considered in the determination of custody. In other words, an officer might not perceive that a juvenile is in custody, but the immaturity and lack of judgment of a juvenile could cause the juvenile to perceive that he or she is in custody. Drawing upon a developmental science perspective, the U.S. Supreme Court ruled in the 2011 case of *J.D.B. v. North Carolina* that officers must consider the age of the juvenile in making the determination of custody, as juveniles could "lack the capacity to exercise mature judgment and possess only an incomplete ability to understand the world around them" (p. 10).

While the aforementioned cases signal a growing recognition in the juvenile and adult courts that juveniles are different based upon their evolving brain development, most justice system-related policies remain unchanged. Despite the temporary nature of adolescent immaturity, delinquents are processed in a system with punishments that are largely based upon the notion that juveniles make rational decisions and are deserving of harsh punishments. Consequently, juveniles are placed into a system that poses both short- and long-term harms, ultimately resulting in worsened outcomes, even though they would have likely matured out of their delinquent behaviors in time.

Presenting Problems of System-Involved Youths

Juveniles who have contact with the justice system tend to experience adolescence in unique ways in comparison to juveniles who avoid system exposure. Notably, delinquent juveniles have disproportionately higher rates of mental health disorders (Grisso, 2004), rates of substance abuse (White, Loeber, Stouthamer-Loeber, & Farrington, 1999), and rates of suicidal behavior (Hayes, 2009). These problems are exacerbated when juveniles are placed into adult correctional facilities (Abram et al., 2008), but are rarely treated for system-involved youth (Sukhodolsky & Ruchkin, 2006).

Mental Health Disorders in System-Involved Youths

Prior to the 1990s, there was generally little focus on how juveniles coped with confinement or subsequent recidivism (Shufelt & Cocozza, 2006), while children with psychological and behavioral problems were largely ignored (Knitzer, 1982). Furthermore, mental health evaluations of delinquent youths lacked methodological rigor, and mental health classifications were inconsistent, essentially crippling the juvenile justice system's ability to respond to these issues (Otto, Greenstein, Johnson, & Friedman, 1992).

Estimates vary in the overall prevalence of youths with mental health disorders in the community. It is estimated that between 15 and 25% of youths have a diagnosable mental health disorder (Grisso, 2004), while 12% of children and adolescents have mental health disorders with associated functional impairment (Costello, Egger, & Angold, 2005). System-involved youths exhibit rates of mental health disorders that are "two to three times higher than the prevalence for youth in general in the community" (Grisso, 2004, p. 13). Estimates of the prevalence of mental health disorders among delinquent juveniles vary widely and generally range from 40 to 90% (Abram, Teplin, McClelland, & Dulcan, 2003; Fazel, Doll, & Långström, 2008; Teplin, Abram, McClelland, Dulcan, & Mericle, 2002). Considering the variation in prevalence rates, it is critical that sound psychometrics with valid and reliable instrumentation are used to assess prevalence rates of mental health disorders (Wasserman, Ko, & McReynolds, 2004). One meta-analysis examining mental health disorders among thousands of delinquents in confinement found "mental disorders [were] substantially more common in adolescents in detention than among age-equivalent individuals in the general population" (Fazel et al., 2008, p. 1016). This suggests that there is an association between some mental disorders and juvenile justice involvement "either directly or indirectly" (p. 1016).

The most empirically rigorous epidemiological studies suggest that system-involved youths have higher rates of mental health disorders. For example, in a study of 1829 randomly sampled youths in Cook County, Illinois, Teplin et al. (2002) found that two-thirds of males and almost three-fourths of females in detainment met diagnostic criteria for at least one mental health disorder. Even when excluding conduct disorder, most males and females in the study met diagnostic criteria for a mental health disorder. The study also found a noteworthy racial effect, as non-Hispanic whites possessed higher rates of mental health disorder in detention than their minority counterparts (Teplin et al., 2002). The authors noted that this finding supports the widely held notion that white youths, without significant impairment, have greater opportunities for diversion away from the juvenile justice system than their minority counterparts.

Although the vast majority of research examining mental health disorders has been conducted on incarcerated youths, juveniles on probation make up the bulk of system-involved youths (Sickmund, Sladky, Kang, & Puzzanchera, 2015). While research is limited in this vein, one notable exception is a study of counties in Texas that found a prevalence rate of mental health disorder at approximately 50% for females and 45% for males (Wasserman, McReynolds, Ko, Katz, & Carpenter, 2005). They also found that females and males experienced similar rates of disruptive and substance use disorders, but that females were afflicted with affective and anxiety disorders more often. Furthermore, females were more likely to suffer from co-occurring disorders (Wasserman et al., 2005).

Interestingly, one critique of the concern over mental health disorders in juvenile justice settings has surrounded the notion that the mental health issues of youths largely encompass only the symptomatology of conduct disorder (Grisso, 2004). Grisso noted that many people consider the mental health issues of system-involved youths as not "real mental disorders" (p. 34). As a result, this viewpoint has historically been used as justification to take the mental health needs of system-involved youths less seriously and to argue against mental health treatment for these youths. To be sure, conduct disorder is prevalent in system-involved youths. Thirty-three percent of the adolescent males in the Wasserman and colleagues' (2002) study and 38% of males and 41% of females in the Teplin et al. (2002) study had a diagnosable conduct disorder. Overall, however, the rates of other disorders were also major concerns for these youths (e.g., anxiety, affective, and substance use disorders).

The potential gendered prevalence of mental health disorder in system-involved youths is also noteworthy. As discussed above in the review of Teplin et al. (2002) and Abram et al. (2003), females generally have higher rates of disorder in detained populations than males. The prevalence rates of internalizing disorders (e.g., anxiety and depression) are substantially higher for females in comparison to males—a finding that has also been supported in a variety of settings and systematic reviews (Abram et al., 2003; Fazel et al., 2008; Teplin et al., 2002; Wasserman et al., 2005). Other research has explored gender differences in involvement in both the mental health and juvenile justice systems. Graves, Frabutt, and Shelton (2007) found that males were more likely to be involved in both systems and were generally more delinquent, while dually involved females had greater functional impairment and more significant mental health problems. They also noted higher rates of anxiety and depression in females; however, they found these factors were associated, with females being less likely to be dually involved in the mental health and criminal justice systems—not more likely as one might initially hypothesize. Generally, there is some evidence that female youths with mental disorders (except substance use disorders) are less often placed in secure settings (e.g., incarceration) than their male counterparts (Kempker, Schmidt, & Espinosa, 2016). It could be that females are considered less dangerous than males; however, female youths who have particularly complex psychosocial histories and functional impairment could warrant secure confinement.

There is also evidence that the prevalence rates of mental disorders for system-involved youths who are adjudicated in juvenile court, as opposed to youths who are transferred to adult criminal court, possess mental health disorders at similar rates. In a relatively small sample, Beyer (2006) found no difference in psychiatric illnesses between youths tried in juvenile and adult courts. A later study of 1715 youths (275 who were processed in adult court) found similar rates of mental health disorders between youths processed in the juvenile and adult criminal justice systems—64% versus 62% (although both groups had substantially larger prevalence rates than youths in the general public) (Washburn et al., 2008).

Overall, it is apparent that system-involved juveniles present with relatively high rates of mental health disorders and are in need of treatment.

Substance Abuse in System-Involved Youths

Similar to the disproportionate rates of mental health disorders exhibited when comparing delinquent and nondelinquent populations, delinquents are also more likely to abuse substances in comparison to nondelinquents. Typically, delinquent behavior and drug use are closely linked (White et al., 1999). In illustration of this problem, scholars have noted that the vast majority of youths have engaged in illegal drug use (Dembo, Wareham, & Schmeidler, 2007). Furthermore, Grisso (2004) noted that the rates of drug use are nearly five times greater for offenders in the juvenile justice system in comparison to their non-offending counterparts. Researchers have also suggested that youths who become involved in the juvenile justice system have a higher likelihood of meeting the criteria for alcohol abuse or dependency (Gilman et al., 2015). Over half of males (50.7%) and nearly half of females (46.8%) met criteria for a substance-related disorder in juvenile detention (Teplin et al., 2002). A follow-up study found that over 21% of males and over 22% of females possessed multiple co-occurring substance use disorders in detention (McClelland, Elkington, Teplin, & Abram, 2004). This is of particular concern for adolescent males as they are more likely to use substances in comparison to their female counterparts; males also have increased lifetime prevalence of substance-related disorders (Sickmund & Puzzanchera, 2014; Welty et al., 2016).

When considering incarceration rates for drug crimes, minority youths are incarcerated at disproportionate rates in comparison to their white counterparts (Sickmund, Sladky, Kang, & Puzzanchera, 2015). These elevated rates of detention are especially troubling as researchers have shown that in actuality, it is less common for nonwhites to use drugs and/or alcohol in relation to non-Hispanic whites (Sickmund & Puzzanchera, 2014; Welty et al., 2016). Additionally, non-Hispanic white youths in detention are more likely to possess any type of substance use disorder in comparison to detained African American youths (Teplin et al., 2002). These findings suggest that delinquent juveniles are more likely to abuse substances in comparison to nondelinquents, but minority youths are more likely to experience harsh treatment in the juvenile system.

Suicide and System-Involved Youths

In addition to substance abuse, there is ample evidence that system-involved youths are at a substantially elevated risk for suicide in comparison to juveniles in the general population (Gray et al., 2002; Hayes, 2009). In a systematic review of the literature on suicidal ideation and behavior, Stokes, McCoy, Abram, Byck, and Teplin (2015) found that system-involved youths are often at significant risk for suicidal ideation and attempts before, during, and after their involvement in the juvenile justice system. This same analysis estimated that suicidal ideation rates for system-involved youths vary between 19 and 32%, and between 12 and 15.5% for a past suicide attempt. Gender, race, mental health disorders, and substance abuse are also recognized as relevant predictors for youths who are at risk for suicidal ideation and/or attempts (Stokes et al., 2015).

In one study of 1829 youths detained in Chicago, roughly 1 in 10 youths had at least thought about suicide at some point in the six months prior to the interview (Abram et al., 2008). Abram and colleagues further noted that almost 6% of the sample had a specific suicide plan at some point in the past six months. In this study,

11% of detained youths had at least one suicide attempt in their lifetime, with 3% attempting suicide in the six months leading up to the interview. In both instances, the rates for females were significantly larger than those for males (Abram et al., 2008). Others studies have also noted that gender could play an important role with suicidal behavior of youths in detention. For instance, Rohde, Seeley, and Mace (1997) found that, beyond the standard elevated risk of suicidal behavior for youths in detention, it was "especially elevated" for females and that depression played a significant role for both males and females (p. 172).

Studies completed for youths on probation largely mirror the findings of those of detained youths in the juvenile justice system. For example, Wasserman and McReynolds (2006) discovered that for youths on probation, suicide attempts were more common in females; those with a major depressive disorder or substance use disorder (both a recent and lifetime attempt); and those youths who had committed a violent offense (recent attempt). Another study completed with females who had been required to receive community care after a criminal referral, found that participants who had experienced prior sexual victimization were more likely to attempt a subsequent suicide (Rabinovitch, Kerr, Leve, & Chamberlain, 2015).

Experts have argued for a series of policy considerations to assist with the alarming problem of suicidal behavior in system-involved youths (Hayes, 2000). There is evidence that facilities where suicide screenings are performed at intake have lower rates of suicide attempts. Hayes also suggested that staff training, ongoing assessments, communicating with youths, and proper supervision of youths in detention could all assist with reducing suicidal ideation and behavior for confined youths. Furthermore, Stokes et al. (2015) advocated for improvements in how suicide is reported among youths to better understand prevalence rates regarding the problem, in addition to better exploration of risk and protective factors for system-involved youths, and better evaluation techniques of intervention programs for youths in confinement. The above findings highlight the increased suicide risk that is present among delinquent youths and offer suggestions for responding to suicidal youths in correctional facilities.

Dangers of Incarcerating Juveniles with Adults

Risks of adolescent suicide are particularly high when detaining juveniles in adult correctional facilities (Abram et al., 2008). Juveniles who are prosecuted as adults lose many protections that are standard in the juvenile justice system, including the right to remain sight and sound separated from adult offenders in jails and prisons (Sickmund, Snyder, & Poe-Yamagata, 1997). This often results in significant placement challenges for correctional administrators. For instance, placement of juveniles in the general population makes them vulnerable to physical and sexual victimization, and protection is typically only possible through solitary confinement (Arya, 2007). Both solitary confinement and victimization while incarcerated are detrimental to the mental functioning of young juveniles, exacerbating already existing mental health issues and increasing suicide risks (American Civil Liberties Union, 2014). In comparison to similarly situated young adults, juveniles in adult facilities are also more likely to be housed in a higher custody level, less likely to have a work assignment, and have a longer delinquency history (McShane & Williams, 1989).

While juveniles could be subject to harmful and abusive conditions in adult institutions, many transferred juveniles do not end up serving long prison sentences. For example, one study of sentence dispositions found that over 50% of *statutorily* waived juveniles (i.e., placed in criminal court via a statute based upon type of offense and/or age of juvenile) were either not convicted or were reverse waived back into the juvenile system (Arya, 2007). In contrast, over 80% of *judicially* waived juveniles were convicted in criminal court. Oftentimes juveniles received nonprison sentences following their pretrial detention in jail. For example, 74% of juveniles who received probation and 77% of juveniles who were placed in a juvenile facility were detained in an adult jail. As a result of this placement, transferred juveniles who were detained in adult jails were potentially exposed to dangerous conditions and criminal labeling, but after their detention in these adult facilities, they received relatively minor sentences. These findings highlight the extreme dangers present when incarcerating juveniles with adults despite the rarity of final placement in adult facilities.

Treatment of Mental Health and Substance Use Disorder for System-Involved Youths

Youths in the justice system present with alarming rates of mental health disorders. These youths bring significant histories of neglect, trauma, and both sexual and physical abuse (Gover & MacKenzie, 2003; Mason, Zimmerman, & Evans, 1998). Although estimates vary, one sample of nearly 900 detained youths found that practically the entire sample (92.5%) had experienced at least one traumatic event in their lifetime (Abram et al., 2004). Furthermore, over half of the detained youths had experienced six or more traumatic events in their lifetime, and over 11% met criteria for post-traumatic stress disorder (PTSD). These rates were generally larger than the prevalence of PTSD for youths in the general public. Scholars have also demonstrated empirically that incarcerated youths who were once abused or neglected (a key traumatic event) also have higher rates of mental health disorders, and those rates of abuse and neglect are higher than youths in the general population (King et al., 2011). This was especially true for sexual assault, in which "nearly all youths who were sexually abused with force had a psychiatric disorder" (p. 1430).

Despite the significant need for mental health care in system-involved juvenile populations, some experts have noted that the majority of youths have not traditionally received mental health care while incarcerated, and treatments are often not available (e.g., for a review see Sukhodolsky & Ruchkin, 2006). For example,

Novins, Duclos, Martin, Jewett, and Manson (1999) noted in one sample that fewer than 40% of juveniles with a substance use or mental health disorder had received services for those behavioral health needs. In their review of mental health care in the United States, Desai et al. (2006) found that mental health services in general have increased in number and quality. They also stated, however, that "many detained juveniles in need of care do not receive services, and with both overcrowding and a large number of mentally ill youths in detention centers, episodes of injuries, suicides, and other adverse health effects are increasing" (p. 204).

When considering substance use disorders, services for juveniles in detention with these problems are also limited (McClelland et al., 2004). This is especially concerning as researchers have found that youths with lower levels of supervision in general are at an increased risk of continued substance abuse. Offenders with high levels of supervision as youths, however, showed no increase in substance abuse across time (Mauricio et al., 2009). These results highlight the importance of early substance abuse treatment options for system-involved youths. The findings of the current section highlight the immense differences that exist between delinquents and nondelinquents. Delinquents have high rates of mental health conditions, substance abuse, and suicide, all of which are exacerbated by juvenile justice contact. Emerging research suggests that these differences will continue into adulthood and can have deleterious impacts on reentry.

Long-Term Outcomes of System-Involved Juveniles

In most states, juvenile court jurisdiction typically ends at the age of 17, at which time criminal behavior becomes the responsibility of criminal courts (Juvenile Justice Geography, Policy, Practice & Statistics, 2017). However, the impact of juvenile system contact persists long after juvenile courts relinquish control. Delinquents face several consequences that are commonly recognized as barriers to reentry for adult felons, yet are seldom considered for delinquents. The following section examines several aspects of reentry that have been particularly challenging for former delinquents. First, the relationship between dropping out of or being removed from school (i.e., suspension or expulsion) and entering prison in adulthood, often termed the school-to-prison pipeline, is briefly examined. Second, the educational outcomes of former delinquents are considered. Next, several aspects of recidivism are examined, including recidivism outcomes for various types of delinquents and factors that contribute to desistance from delinquency. The section then explores the increased accessibility of juveniles' records. As a result of these changes, former delinquents now face significant challenges upon entry into adulthood, including obtaining employment and earning a livable wage. Relatedly, romantic partners may perceive former delinquents in a negative light and may be less likely to engage in a relationship. Finally, the chapter concludes by considering potential long-term physical and mental health issues exhibited by former delinquents.

School-to-Prison Pipeline

In the 1990s, schools adopted "zero-tolerance" policies to combat weapons on campuses, which resulted in more punitive responses to delinquency (Monohan, VenDerhei, Bechtold, & Cauffman, 2014; Wald & Losen, 2003), increased police presence, and reduced procedural protections within schools (Kim, 2012). This approach simultaneously contributed to the criminalization of student misbehavior and to stark increases in the number of students suspended or expelled from schools (Wald & Losen, 2003). The empirical evidence has also supported clear racial disparities, as African American and Hispanic youths are more often affected by these "get tough"-era policies than white youths, suggesting that zero-tolerance policies are worsening the disproportionate criminal justice system contact of nonwhites.

Zero-tolerance approaches have contributed to the *"school-to-prison pipeline."* This pipeline is the path through which youths experience increasingly punitive and isolating obstacles. For example, in comparison to nondelinquents, delinquent youths are more likely to take classes taught by unqualified teachers, be held back in school, be placed in restrictive programs (e.g., special education), and experience punitive measures (e.g., suspension or alternative schooling) (Wald & Losen, 2003). Consequently, these juveniles have an increased likelihood of encountering the criminal justice system (Monohan et al., 2014; Wald & Losen, 2003). Researchers have recently explored which factors could disrupt or redirect the pipeline, such as school engagement (Monohan et al., 2014), mental health services (Garcia, Greeson, Kim, Thompson, & DeNard, 2015), mentoring (Wald & Losen, 2003), and other protective and risk factors (Garcia et al., 2015; Wald & Losen, 2003). To date, however, an agreed upon solution to disrupting the school-to-prison pipeline is elusive.

Educational Outcomes Following System-Involvement

Formal social controls are recognized as detrimental to the educational outcomes of delinquents (De Li, 1999). One of the immediate consequences of system involvement experienced by delinquents is the reduced likelihood of high school graduation. High school graduation is a critical life event that contributes to crime desistance and general life success (Natsuaki, Ge, & Wenk, 2008), highlighting the importance of completion for delinquent youths. More generally, dropping out has severe financial costs nationally. For example, in California it is estimated that "$1.1 billion of the costs of juvenile crime are a result of having large numbers of high school dropouts" in the population (Belfield & Levin, 2009, p. 38).

Most notable of the stages of juvenile system contact is arrest, as arrested juveniles are more likely to drop out of high school than their non-arrested peers, especially when arrests occur early in their high school careers (Hirschfield, 2009). When arrest is coupled with a court appearance, the impact on dropping out of school is more salient, suggesting that court involvement is stigmatizing for juveniles (Sweeten, 2006). While unobservable characteristics in the lives of delinquents (e.g., poor decision-making practices, school policies) shape the likelihood of high school graduation, there does not appear to be a causal link between arrest and dropping out (Hjalmarsson, 2008). However, the impact of incarceration remains a significant predictor of dropping out even after controlling for unobservable life characteristics, indicating that adolescent incarceration reduces the likelihood of graduation. In other words, more formal responses to delinquents could result in a higher degree of labeling, ultimately preventing successful reintegration in school.

One less-considered outcome of juvenile justice contact is college attendance and graduation. Limited research indicates that system-involved juveniles are less likely to be enrolled in college (Emanuel, 2013; Kirk & Sampson, 2013) or obtain a college degree (Tanner, Davies, & O'Grady, 1999). There are several reasons why former delinquents could be less likely to attend college. First, having certain types of criminal charges (e.g., drug, sexual offense) excludes former offenders from obtaining federal student aid (Students with Criminal Convictions, 2017). Second, many colleges ask about a criminal record on admissions applications (Ambrose & Millikan, 2013), potentially preventing those with a delinquent record from being admitted. Finally, former delinquents could self-select out of college attendance due to perceptions of lack of acceptance and stereotyping by students and teachers (Strayhorn, Johnson, & Barrett, 2013). While the educational outcomes of system-involved youths have been less studied in comparison to other aspects of juvenile reentry, limited research suggests that delinquents have poor educational outcomes in comparison to nondelinquents.

Recidivism Patterns of System-Involved Youths

Over three-fourths of detained youths return to the community within 12 months of their detainment (Sickmund & Puzzanchera, 2014). For those youths who are not properly rehabilitated and continue to offend (60–80%), a multitude of negative outcomes exist (Tarolla, Wagner, Rabinowitz, & Tubman, 2002). These include criminal recidivism, poor social functioning, and poor physical health.

For system-involved youths there are multiple factors associated with recidivism. These youths could have poor social support, lack adult guidance, have poor academic outcomes, use alcohol and/or drugs, and lack cognitive resources—each of which can lead to an inordinate risk of poor life outcomes as adults (Laub & Sampson, 1993; Myner, Santman, Cappelletty, & Perlmutter, 1998). Gender is also considered an important risk factor for recidivism in youths, as males are more likely to recidivate than females (Cottle, Lee, & Heilbrun, 2001). However, for both males and females, age of onset of offending is an important risk factor for recidivism. Youths who are early-onset offenders (i.e., prior to the age of 13) are more likely to have adult convictions than those who engage in offending at later ages

(Myner et al., 1998; White & Piquero, 2004). It could be that early age offenders are particularly vulnerable to more negative outcomes because these are largely the life course persistent offenders as described by Moffitt (1993), who begin deviant acts earlier as a result of nonnormative neurophysiological development during childhood. Other factors that can shape recidivism include the type of offense committed by the juvenile, specifically sexual offenses, and the transfer of the juvenile into criminal court.

Recidivism of juvenile sex offenders. Juveniles commit a substantial share of sexual offenses that are committed annually in the United States (Ryan & Otonichar, 2016). In 2015, juveniles comprised 16% of rape offenders, 1.5% of prostitution offenders, and 17.5% of all other sex offenders (United States Department of Justice, 2015). However, of all juvenile offenses, sex-related offenses comprise just 1% of total arrests (Sickmund & Puzzanchera, 2014). In comparison to other offender groups, sex offenders in general are the least likely to reoffend (Petteruti & Walsh, 2008). A 10-year follow-up of juvenile offenders found that sex offenders were less likely to be rearrested in comparison to nonsex offenders (Waite et al., 2005). Recidivism rates for incarcerated juvenile sex offenders were low (4.7%), regardless of treatment intensity. Juvenile sex offenders are like other nonsexual juvenile offenders, in that they tend to mature out of their deviant behaviors and typically do not reoffend in adulthood (Ryan & Otonichar, 2016). Furthermore, adolescent sex offending is not empirically predictive of sex offending in adulthood (Zimring, Piquero, & Jennings, 2007).

Researchers have identified several adolescent risk factors that could help predict sexual reoffending in adulthood. For example, recidivism is predicted by having sexual interest in children (Worling & Curwen, 2000); scoring high on impulsivity/antisocial behavior on the Juvenile Sex Offender Assessment Protocol II and on antisocial factors of the Psychopathy Checklist: Youth Version (Parks & Bard, 2006); and having static and historical factors (e.g., having multiple victims or stranger victims) (Gerhold, Browne, & Beckett, 2007).

Recidivism of transferred juveniles: Juveniles transferred to criminal court have different recidivism patterns in comparison to juveniles retained in juvenile court. Research examining transferred juveniles suggests that they are more likely to recidivate than nontransferred juveniles in both the short-term (Bishop, Frazier, Lanza-Kaduce, & Winner, 1996) and long-term (Winner, Lanza-Kaduce, Bishop, & Frazier, 1997). While property offenders do not vary based upon transfer status, juveniles transferred for all other types of offenses commit more crimes and are arrested sooner in contrast to nontransferred juveniles. In addition to rearrest, other research has considered related outcomes of transferred juveniles. For example, most transferred juveniles continue engaging in antisocial behaviors and are reincarcerated following release (Schubert et al., 2010).

Explanations as to why juveniles have worse outcomes as compared to nontransferred juveniles after transfer include internalization of criminal labels, learned criminal behaviors, and lack of rehabilitative services in adult facilities (Bazemore & Umbriet, 1995; Thomas & Bishop, 1984). One alternative explanation for the relationship between transfer and recidivism is that there are selection effects in which only the most serious and violent juveniles are transferred out of the system, thus they would be expected to be the most likely to recidivate (Myers, 2003). By comparing a large sample of serious and violent juveniles who were retained in the juvenile system, Myers found that the deleterious impact of transfer on recidivism still held, suggesting that transfer directly affects subsequent offending.

One argument in support of the use of transfer is that some juveniles could be deterred from offending because they know they will be transferred into criminal court (Feld, 1987). However, studies on the deterrent effect of transfer indicate that delinquents are undeterred by policy changes, as juvenile violent crime rates were unaffected by the imposition of national transfer policies (Jensen & Metsger, 1994). Surveys of juveniles indicate that they are unaware of transfer policies, but they report that if they had known the degree of punishment they would face, they would have been less likely to offend (Redding & Fuller, 2004).

Desistance from delinquency: Not all juvenile offenders, however, have long-lasting negative outcomes as adults. The vast majority of juveniles eventually desist from offending behavior before adulthood (Laub & Sampson, 2003; Moffitt, 1993). Reasons for desistance from crime vary widely across delinquents, although there is ample evidence that positive life transitions (e.g., employment, positive social and/or romantic relationships) can serve as turning points to shift one's life course away from criminal trajectories (Giordano et al., 2003; Laub & Sampson, 1993, 2003; Schubert, Mulvey, & Pitzer, 2016). Other predictors of desistance include psychological development within a person, prosocial integration, and shifts in offender attitudes about the law (Mulvey et al., 2004; Schubert et al., 2016).

Prosocial integration could also serve as a tool for producing more positive traits in juvenile offenders (Laub & Sampson, 1993, 2003). As juveniles grow older, they normally become more invested in the positive social roles they start to take on. As overviewed in the discussion of life course theory, examples of these positive social roles are marriage, education, employment, and military service. For example, employment can promote a prosocial lifestyle. Schubert et al. (2016) found that legitimate income was one of the most effective prosocial variables that led to criminal desistance. Without the need to make money from an illegal source, the propensity to engage in criminal behavior was reduced substantially. These conventional social roles require people to make investments and commit to law-abiding lifestyles (Mulvey et al., 2004). The more invested in these roles people become, the less likely they are to offend so they can maintain their attachments to these prosocial roles. The fear of losing these roles, as a result of reoffending, often outweighs any desire to recidivate. An additional factor associated with juvenile desistance is a change in the views of the legitimacy of the law. During the transition from adolescence to adulthood, perceptions, beliefs, and attitudes change significantly, particularly surrounding the criminal justice system (Mulvey et al., 2004), and people often perceive this agent of formalized social control as more legitimate than they might have as a youth.

Eroding Protections of Former Delinquents

Entrance into positive social institutions (e.g., employment, relationships, education) significantly reduces recidivism of former delinquents (Sampson & Laub, 2003). Recent changes nationwide, however, are making it more difficult for juveniles to transition into these positive life situations (Shah, Fine, & Gullen, 2014). The following section examines the increasing loss of record protections for delinquents, the impact that a juvenile record can have on adult convictions, hiring practices of former delinquents, and wage outcomes of former delinquents.

Nationwide expungement policies: Historically, juveniles' delinquency records were sealed (i.e., publicly inaccessible) or expunged (i.e., destroyed) to protect them from the stigma of a record (Shah et al., 2014). Nevertheless, many states now allow schools, employers, criminal justice agencies, and the public to access delinquent records. Only nine states fully protect records from public access, while 33 states and the District of Columbia allow for some public access; and nine states allow for full public access. Of those that allow some access, 33 states and the District of Columbia allow for school access; 33 states allow for government agency (e.g., social services) access; and 27 states and the District of Columbia allow for victim access. These policies are typically shaped by the type of offense committed, prior criminal history, and age of the juvenile at the time of the offense. While most states require the juvenile to apply for an expungement or sealing, 14 states automatically expunge delinquent records after specific criteria are met (Litwok, 2014).

In some cases, juveniles could request to have public access to their record restricted or to have their record deleted entirely once they have reached a certain age (typically 18 years) (Ambrose & Millikan, 2013). This process does not remove the record from existence, but rather, it restricts the public's access to viewing the record. While public access is restricted, criminal justice workers, such as prosecutors and sentencing judges, could still access these records (Shah et al., 2014). In fact, every state provides a process through which prosecutors or the courts can access juvenile records for adult defendants, which can then be used to enhance sentencing (discussed further in the following section; see Miller & McEwen, 1996).

Evidence suggests that juveniles now rarely have records expunged or sealed (Shah et al., 2014). For example, only three out of every 100 juvenile arrests in Illinois result in an expungement (Illinois Juvenile Justice Commission, 2016). Similarly, in Washington, only 6% of delinquency records are sealed (Calero, 2013). The lack of expungements is attributed to the high cost (e.g., up to $320 per expungement in Illinois), burdensome process (e.g., contacting all agencies with records), and eligibility constraints (e.g., committing a new offense prior to expungement) associated with protecting delinquents. In recognition of the barriers faced by those with delinquent records, the "Record Expungement Designed to Enhance Employment Act of 2014" was proposed to the U.S. House of Representatives (H.R. 5158). This legislation proposed the automatic sealing of nonviolent delinquency records and early sealing of nonviolent delinquency records (i.e., 3 years after adjudication decision). Although the bill ultimately failed, it signaled a recognition of the harms of publicizing delinquent records.

Juvenile record and impact on adult convictions: Juvenile records can affect sentencing for criminal convictions, either through enforcing higher penalties or mandating sentences for first-time offenders in adulthood. State laws differ in how defendants' juvenile records are used in sentencing (Miller & McEwen, 1996). Twenty-four states provide a structured method through which defendants' juvenile records are used in determining sentences. For example, 14 of these states calculate a "criminal history score" from factors within the juvenile record. This score is then matched with the seriousness of the crime the juvenile is being charged with, yielding a recommendation for what sentence should be imposed.

Other states (e.g., Wisconsin) consider a juvenile record an aggravating factor that can be used to implement maximum penalties (Miller & McEwen, 1996). It is not routine practice to utilize juvenile records in adult court cases in every state. However, when these records are used, they can result in harsher penalties for adult offenders. For example, juvenile records are counted toward the "three strikes" rule in California and toward the habitual offender law in Louisiana (Miller & McEwen, 1996). These variations highlight the inconsistency across states in how juvenile records are used in adult courts.

Hiring job applicants with a delinquent history: Ease of accessibility and increased publicity of delinquent records are raising concerns about the reentry of former delinquents and the long-term ramifications of public records. One specific aspect of reentry that could be affected by publicity of delinquent records is employer callbacks. Pager (2003) examined how employers perceive applicants with a felony on their record by submitting fictitious employment applications of felons and nonfelons to employers, finding that felons face stigmas that reduce the likelihood of employer callbacks. Limited replications with juvenile applications indicate that juvenile delinquents experience stigmas similar to adult felons (Baert & Verhofstadt, 2015; Taylor & Spang, 2017). In response to awareness of the harms of a juvenile record, the aforementioned H.R. 5158 was proposed in order to "protect children and adults against damage stemming from their juvenile acts and subsequent delinquency records" (H.R. 5158, p. 20).

Related to the challenges faced in obtaining employment, former delinquents fare worse in the labor market in comparison to their nondelinquent counterparts. For example, arrested juveniles are more likely to be unemployed in adulthood (Wiesner, Kim, & Capaldi, 2010). One longitudinal study of formerly incarcerated delinquents found that, after 5 years, only 40% were employed and/or in school (Emanuel, 2013). However, the relationship between juvenile system contact and likelihood of employment could be mediated by the amount of time a juvenile is in a community (Sharlein, 2016). More specifically, juveniles processed in juvenile court typically receive community placements in which they are able to work and are more successful in obtaining employment in comparison to juveniles prosecuted in criminal courts in which they are formally detained and unable to work.

Wages of former delinquents: System-involved juveniles also have lower incomes and wages than nondelinquent juveniles, a finding that exists at several points of juvenile justice contact. For example, arrested juveniles earn up to 26% less than non-arrested juveniles, while continued system-involvement further worsens incomes in adulthood (Joseph, 2003). One longitudinal study of wages for formerly delinquent youths showed that adjudication resulted in a 28% wage reduction in comparison to nondelinquents (Allgood, Mustard, & Warren Jr., 1999). Adolescent incarceration and transfer to criminal courts similarly damper wages in adulthood, findings that remain significant even after controlling for relevant factors like education and work history (Jung, 2015; Taylor, 2015).

Although system-involvement is associated with lower incomes and wages, this relationship appears to be temporary for young adults (Grogger, 1995). Furthermore, some young offenders actually have higher incomes than their noncriminal counterparts (Nagin & Waldfogel, 1995). One explanation is that delinquents frequently enter into temporary, albeit lucrative, "spot-market jobs." Comparatively, nondelinquents could have a delay in earned income while obtaining an education, but they will eventually have greater financial success. Despite research indicating that system-involved juveniles have worse employment outcomes, it appears that some types of delinquent juveniles still fare well in the labor market (Bullis & Yovanoff, 2006). For example, non-gang members and those who completed programming during detention were more likely to be successfully employed in adulthood.

There are several reasons why system-involved juveniles could experience worsened job outcomes in adulthood. First, just as employers could be less inclined to hire former delinquents, the applicants themselves could self-select into less successful careers. Those with delinquent records typically have low career aspirations that are short-sighted, including "labor and trades work, the military, pursuing community college, and the music industry" (Bartlett & Domene, 2015, p. 229). Second, "young [formerly incarcerated] adults may have few, if any, marketable skills [and] minimal work experience in legitimate settings" (Shannon, 2013, p. 135). Finally, former delinquents' long-term wages are directly tied to expungement policies, as former delinquents' wages are higher in states with automatic expungement policies in comparison to states where they have to apply for an expungement (Litwok, 2014).

Researchers have linked juvenile delinquency with difficulty securing employment (Baert & Verhofstadt, 2015), having reduced incomes (Allgood et al., 1999), and having worse educational outcomes (Schubert et al., 2010; Sweeten, 2006). Consequently, former delinquents could have difficulty in relationship formation as their potential partners could perceive them as being a less marriageable partner due to financial instability and difficulties securing stable employment (Apel, Blockland, Nieuwbeerta, & Van Schellen, 2009; Western, 2002).

Relationship Prospects of Former Delinquents

Certain factors in adulthood could serve a protective purpose against continued criminal reoffending. One such factor is marriage (Laub, Nagin, & Sampson, 1998; Warr, 1998). However, contact with the juvenile justice system could impact relationship formation in adulthood and entry into marriage. If youths' contact with the justice system decreases the likelihood of entering marriage in adulthood, these former delinquents could have lowered rates of desistance from criminal offending (Sampson & Laub, 2003). Essentially, contact with the juvenile justice system could contribute to the cycle of reoffending on a long-term basis by creating a barrier to needed protective factors.

Researchers have provided several explanations for how juvenile justice contact can create a barrier in adult relationships. It is possible that the labeling of a delinquent as deviant and subsequent stigmatization could signal to others that the person is not marriageable (Apel et al., 2009). Especially in cases in which the previous crimes committed were violent in nature, potential spouses could perceive those with deviant labels as having the potential to put them at a higher risk of victimization (Cherlin, Burton, Hurt, & Purvin, 2004). Thus, their perception of the former delinquent's marriageability can be greatly reduced.

One of the few empirical studies to examine relationship formation among a delinquent sample found that men who had no juvenile justice system contact were more likely to marry than those who had prior contact (Mack, 2012). Males who had been detained in adolescence had higher rates of cohabitating with partners in comparison to those who had no previous contact or whose only contact was through arrest. This finding is concerning, as marriage is known to be a key factor in the desistance process (Laub & Sampson, 2003). It appears that the experience of juvenile justice contact could have unique consequences in relationship formation for former delinquents as they enter adulthood.

Long-Term Physical and Mental Health Outcomes of Former Delinquents

In addition to weakened social outcomes, poor health outcomes can be associated with juvenile delinquency (Piquero, Daigle, Gibson, Piquero, & Tibbetts, 2007). Persistent offenders are more likely to suffer negative physical health outcomes such as heart problems, kidney issues, and diabetes. Furthermore, system-involved youths (both male and female) are significantly more likely to die in late adolescence or early adulthood (up to 29 years old) in comparison to the general population (Teplin et al., 2014). Perhaps, most alarming, delinquent youths are especially likely to die violently (90% by gun violence) and African Americans were most affected by early violent death (Teplin et al., 2014, 2015).

Scholars have also illustrated the important need to better understand the dynamic relationship between mental health disorders and their effects on the longer-term outcomes for system-involved youths. For instance, there is some evidence that youths with multiple co-occurring mental health and/or substance use disorders are at increased risk of recidivism (Cottle et al., 2001; Hoeve, McReynolds, & Wasserman, 2013). Furthermore, a common assumption among experts is that many mental health and substance use disorders will persist over time for previously delinquent youths (Wareham & Dembo, 2007). Other scholars have found that delinquent youths with mental health and substance use disorders are at greater risk of violence (Elkington et al., 2015) than those without a disorder, and co-occurring disorders in youths are associated with increased risk of violent offenses in adulthood (Copeland, Miller-Johnson, Keeler, Angold, & Costello, 2007).

In exploring the longer-term prevalence of mental health disorders, Teplin, Welty, Abram, Dulcan, and Washburn (2012) examined longitudinal data on 1829 youths 5 years after detention. The prevalence rates of most mental health disorders in this group declined over time, but they were still substantial; approximately 47% of males and 30% of females still met diagnostic criteria for a mental health disorder. Substance use and behavioral disorders, especially for men, remained the most common mental health disorders (see also, Teplin et al., 2015). A more recent analysis, utilizing the same longitudinal data set, but 12 years after detention, found that nearly a quarter of formerly detained youths still had a substance use disorder (Welty et al., 2017). In sum, there is ample evidence that many youths with diagnosable mental health and substance use disorders continue to struggle with these problems as they emerge into adulthood.

Discussion

The goal of this chapter was to provide an overview of presenting problems of system-involved youths and their subsequent outcomes after juvenile justice system contact. Overall, it is evident that these youths are confronted with a multitude of disadvantages that are also closely associated with maladaptive short-term and long-term consequences. Coupled with "get tough" criminal justice policies for juveniles, this ultimately has exacerbated the obstacles that system-involved youths encounter. In general, the empirical studies reviewed in this chapter provide ample evidence that youths who enter the system possess a variety of risk factors including past histories of trauma, greater prevalence of mental disorders, increased substance use disorders, elevated functional impairment and more suicidal behaviors (Grisso, 2004; Hayes, 2009; White et al., 1999). Furthermore, while confined in detention these youths confront inauspicious challenges regarding their safety, and many develop mental health disorders while in confinement (or become more symptomatic with already diagnosed disorders) (Fazel et al., 2008). Additionally, for many youths, being transferred to adult court and adult incarceration are sizeable concerns, especially given this adult treatment is for offenses these youths committed *as children* (Arya, 2007). Post-detention, these same persons face increased risks for recidivism (Myner et al., 1998); substantial barriers to finding stable employment and quality education (Taylor, 2015; Wiesner et al., 2010); difficulty entering into prosocial relationships (Mack, 2012); increased prevalence of long-term mental health disorders (Teplin et al., 2012); physical health illnesses (Piquero et al., 2007); and elevated risk for early violent death (Teplin et al., 2014). In sum, it is unmistakable that the complex difficulties that youths bring to the juvenile justice system, their poor short-term outcomes, and their problematic longer-term life course trajectories, far too commonly present vexing problems for a system that was founded on the notion of rehabilitating wayward children and teens—but frequently falls short of that foundational goal.

It is also important to note that findings of studies completed with system-involved youths described in this chapter reveal several demographic disparities. First, there are noteworthy dissimilarities between minority and white youths who enter the juvenile system. For example, minority youths show fewer symptoms of mental health disorders, yet often fare worse after detention than their white counterparts (Teplin et al., 2002). In considering these findings, some scholars have hypothesized this could be a result of the over-criminalization of youths of color in the juvenile justice system and that white youths benefit from enhanced opportunity structures to divert them away from the system prior to juvenile arrest or detention (Bishop & Frazier, 1996). Thus, only the most clinically ill and functionally impaired white youths are detained. Similarly, there are also important gender disparities in system-involved samples of youths summarized in this chapter. The literature illustrates that, although females are much less likely to come into contact with the justice system than males, when they do, females often present with significantly more mental disorders. Additionally, those mental health disorders are more likely to be recognized (or diagnosed) by correctional staff, and females are also more likely to be provided services than males for mental health disorders while in confinement. It could be that the juvenile justice system overly pathologizes female deviance and inversely criminalizes male deviance, labeling females "mentally ill" as a reason for entering the system and males simply as "criminal." Perhaps, the studies examined in this chapter could also serve as evidence that females have greater opportunities to be diverted away from the criminal justice system than males (paternalism of the system), and only those females with the most significant histories of trauma and pathology, and greater functional impairment due to mental health disorders, ever become system-involved.

Policy Implications

Juvenile justice policies grew punitive toward delinquents in the 1980s and 1990s, but several policy changes in the 2000s signaled a revival of the rehabilitative ideal that was once the primary goal of juvenile justice (Liles & Moak, 2015). A growing understanding of developmental science, coupled with public outcry that juveniles were being punished unnecessarily harshly, has shifted the response to juveniles. Despite these positive changes, further steps still need to be taken to fully move the pendulum away from crime control to rehabilitation for the juvenile justice system. The following section examines several of these policy implications, including increased prevention programs and treatment for delinquents; reconsideration of developmental science among policymakers; improvements in data collection; changes in confinement practices; and increased protections of juveniles' records.

The value of prevention and treatment for justice involved youths: Prevention and treatment are essential for system-involved youths. Given what is known about outcomes for these juveniles, better prevention programming to assist children before they ever enter the system is necessary. As noted earlier, Grisso (2004) reported that anywhere from 15 to 25% of youths in the general public have a mental health problem, but these rates double or triple for youths in the criminal justice system. Youths typically only receive attention after they commit offenses serious enough to warrant detention. By providing more frequent and more significant social service assistance to these youths in the community, their chances of never entering the system at all could improve. There are specific risk factors for criminal involvement that are almost universal for justice involved youths. For instance, Abram et al. (2004) found that nearly all detained youths in their sample had experienced a significant trauma in their lifetime, and many had multiple traumas before ever entering the justice system. By completing more research on how those traumas specifically impact later confinement, and also providing more opportunities for preventative treatment, far more youths might be able to be diverted from the criminal justice system. Beyond just providing preventative programming, however, comprehensive outcome evaluations to better understand what works and for which at-risk youths are necessary. For example, some prevention programs for youths are politically popular (e.g., D.A.R.E.), but have not produced their intended outcomes (Harmon, 1993).

It is also important to consider which youths make contact with the juvenile justice system and the types of services they receive upon contact. One notable issue across the United States is that nonwhite juveniles are disproportionately processed in the juvenile justice system and often receive more punitive treatment than white juveniles (Pope, Lovell, & Hsia, 2002). While many states have struggled to meet requirements outlined in the Juvenile Justice and Delinquency Prevention Act to identify and respond to disproportionate minority contact, several states have experienced tremendous success in ensuring that nonwhite youths are treated fairly in juvenile justice processing (Spinney et al., 2014). Several strategies that have contributed to this success, including shifting away from punitive treatment of youths, developing long-term plans to reduce minority contact with the system, and improving data collection, should all be considered by states nationwide. Females also face significant challenges that need to be addressed during juvenile justice processing and treatment. Notably, females enter the juvenile system with significantly worse issues than males, including increased rates of mental health disorders (Teplin et al., 2002), co-occurring disorders (Wasserman et al., 2005), and suicide attempts (Abram et al., 2008). While females typically receive greater mental health treatment in comparison to males, the reality is that treatment overall is deficient in the juvenile system (Grisso, 2004).

Once youths enter the system, the mental health and behavioral services that are provided to them are often lacking in quantity and quality (Grisso, 2004). Epidemiological studies discussed throughout this chapter have illustrated that approximately one-half of youths entering detention possess a diagnosable major mental disorder or substance use disorder, and many of those youths have co-occurring disorders (Teplin et al., 2002). The problem, however, is that these youths are too frequently considered to not possess "legitimate" disorders, but instead are believed to simply have behavioral problems. Overall, quality mental health treatment is often not provided at all, or to the extent that it could benefit detained youths. If mandatory screenings for mental health disorders at intake were more readily available in all facilities, as well as more opportunity for mental health care for justice involved youths across the system, the justice system would come closer to fulfilling its foundational goal of rehabilitation.

It is particularly important to consider policies for youths who are currently suicidal or who have had past suicide attempts. Abram et al. (2008) found that over 10% of detained youths have tried to commit suicide at some point in their lives. Experts have considered a multitude of policy considerations to assist with the alarming rates at which justice involved youths attempt suicide. Included in these are increased staff education and training, intake assessment and ongoing assessments, and greater supervision of youths in detention, among others (Hayes, 2000; Stokes et al., 2015). Given the frequency with which justice involved youths either consider or attempt suicide, these are reasonable policies to consider for these youths.

Remember that children are children: Policymakers must better appreciate that the best developmental science has demonstrated that juveniles are generally inept in making decisions in the same capacity as adults, and this has important ramifications regarding culpability. Developmental scientists, employing rigorous empirical evidence, have played an important role in overturning capital punishment for persons under the age of 18 in 2005 (*Roper v. Simmons*) and in ending life in prison without parole sentences in 2010 and 2012 (*Graham v. Florida; Miller v. Alabama*). Other legislation has also recently been passed around the country to lower draconian sentencing policies for youths. This, however, should serve as the beginning for sentencing policy reform with youths and not the end. Ultimately, no matter how heinous the crime, the best developmental science has illustrated that youths and adults are different in cognition, decision-making, and impulsivity (Scott, 2000). Harsher sentences for more youths, at younger ages, and for less serious crimes do not change the likelihood that youths make decisions in a different capacity than adults, and certain brain regions are still developing well into a person's twenties. Likewise, most young offenders will eventually mature and desist from offending as they take on more prosocial roles (Moffitt, 1993). Scholars must continue to promote these empirical findings to legislators, policy makers, and the general public who have often supported the notion that youths should be treated like adults for some crimes.

Improve data collection of transferred juveniles: In recent years, it has been widely reported that judicial waivers of juvenile delinquents have decreased significantly (Sickmund & Puzzanchera, 2014). In the 1980s, approximately 6000 juveniles were waived each year and the frequency of transfer increased to a peak of approximately 13,000 in 1994, but decreased to fewer than 6000 judicially waived youths annually in recent years. These changes have largely paralleled the drop in adolescent offending. These shifts are a positive sign, but they only tell a portion of the story. While juveniles could enter the criminal justice system through a judicial waiver, they could also be moved with a direct file by a prosecutor or a statutory exclusion. Currently data are systematically collected on a national level for judicial waivers, but not for direct files and statutory exclusions.

Transference in frequency from judicial waivers to direct files and statutory exclusions would be expected, as states expanded the usage of the latter two transfer mechanisms in the 1990s. Considering that both direct files and statutory exclusions would place a juvenile into criminal court prior to encountering a judge would suggest fewer juveniles would be eligible for a judicial transfer, thus decreasing their usage. One study of 40 counties in the United States found that only 24% of cases were moved to criminal court through a judicial waiver, while the remaining transfers were the result of a prosecutorial direct file or statutory exclusion (Rainville & Smith, 2003). Only six states currently report detailed transfer statistics based upon all transfer forms (Juvenile Justice Geography, Policy, Practice & Statistics, 2017). Just as data is currently collected on the prevalence of judicial transfers, data now needs to be collect on a national scale on the prevalence of statutory exclusions, direct files, reverse waivers, and "once and adult, always an adult" cases.

Stop confining juveniles with adults in jails under any circumstance: Every year, thousands of juveniles are confined in adult jails prior to being convicted of any crime (Arya, 2007). While some of these are juveniles who have committed violent crimes that will result in lengthy prison sentences, many of the juveniles confined in adult jails are not convicted of any crime or are reverse waived back into the juvenile justice system. In other words, juveniles who are ultimately deemed unacceptable for the adult system are initially subject to contact with adult offenders. During confinement, jailers often must make difficult placement decisions. In some cases, juveniles are allowed to remain in the general population where they are at increased risk of physical or sexual victimization. In others, juveniles are held in solitary confinement for their own protection, but are then at risk for psychological harm. Juveniles retained in the juvenile justice system must be sight and sound separated from adults, but there is currently a loophole that juveniles placed into adult courts do not have these protections. Despite several attempts to remedy this issue through reauthorizations of the Juvenile Justice and Delinquency Prevention Reauthorization Act (JJDPA), currently this practice remains. Future reauthorizations of the JJDPA should require that these juveniles remain temporarily in juvenile correctional facilities until they have been convicted in criminal court to avoid unnecessary adult contact.

Protect juvenile delinquents' records: Historically, the juvenile justice system was designed to protect juveniles from the harms of the criminal justice system. These protections extended beyond standard crime control measures by also protecting the records of delinquents from future employers, the military, schools, and the public. In recent years, these protections have deteriorated, as nearly all states allow for increased publicity of delinquency records (Shah et al., 2014). As protections are now being lost, it is critical to remember why these policies were initially created. Most juvenile delinquents offend for a short period of time and then age out of crime. Upon reintegration, it is critical that these former delinquents enter back into school or begin a career. However, it is well documented that a criminal record serves as a barrier to education and employment when that record is accessible (Illinois Juvenile Justice Commission, 2016). At this point, little is known about the potential ramifications of a delinquency record on later life outcomes, which is why it is important to explore these outcomes before putting policies in place that could steer delinquents toward becoming career criminals.

Future Research

In recent years, much attention has been devoted to exploring the root causes of juvenile delinquency, processing patterns of juvenile delinquents, and recidivism outcomes after juveniles have made system contact (Bishop & Frazier, 1996; Cottle et al., 2001; Hoeve et al., 2013; Myner et al., 1998). Research has also been increasingly devoted to developmental science, which in turn has dramatically shaped recent juvenile justice policies (Scott, 2000). To extend this research, scholars need to continue to study the effectiveness of different mental health, substance use, and behavioral interventions for youth (both prevention and treatment) in order to better understand what programs work and are evidenced based so that stronger treatments and prevention programs can be created. Further research is also needed on nuances on how youth make decisions differently than adults and how their culpability differs. Scholars are beginning to understand these differences, but much additional empirical analysis is needed.

While juvenile justice system processing has received much attention in recent years, some areas are in need of further investigation. For example, the prevalence of juveniles waived by a prosecutor or statue remains unclear. Better data must be collected on these two methods of placing juveniles into the criminal justice system because at this point, it still remains unclear how many juveniles make contact with the adult system each year. A second area in need of future research is the use of screening tools for juvenile delinquents upon intake. Research should examine the difficulty in implementing a universal screening tool for mental health problems and suicidality in justice involved youth.

Finally, further research should focus on the long-term outcomes of delinquents. Extensive research has found that an adult felony charge has a deleterious impact on several life outcomes, including chances of obtaining employment (Baert & Verhofstadt, 2015), income (Jung, 2015), education (Taylor, 2015), and relationship formation (Mack, 2012). As juvenile records are increasingly publicized, with some states now providing little protections for delinquency records (Shah et al., 2014), researchers now need to consider how a delinquency record could also shape the later life outcomes of former delinquents. For example, a limited body of research suggests that employers might be less likely to hire applicants with a delinquency record (Taylor & Spang, 2017), but this needs to be tested experimentally, as has been done for adult applicants with a criminal record. These issues need to be informed by longitudinal research focused on the long-term collateral consequences of system contact.

Conclusion

The vast majority of literature involving system-involved youths has pointed to multiple negative outcomes (Altschuler & Brash, 2004). As touched upon, however, most youths do eventually stop offending and, in time, establish prosocial life course trajectories after delinquency (Moffitt, 1993). It is imperative that policy makers continue to attempt to understand what drives the juxtaposition between positive and negative outcomes for youths in the system. As well, prevention and treatment are essential for system-involved youths. Given what is known about outcomes for these juveniles, better prevention programming must be provided to assist children before they ever enter the system. For those who are arrested and detained, policy makers must seek to better appreciate that the best developmental science available has demonstrated that juveniles are generally incapable of making decisions in the same capacity as adults, and this has important ramifications regarding culpability. Additionally, quality mental health, substance abuse, and suicide screenings are vital for system-involved youths, as are quality treatment interventions and services for those youths deemed to have behavioral health problems in confinement. Finally, quality post-detainment programming is needed to help formerly system-involved youths gain employment and educational opportunities, in addition to engaging in prosocial relationships to help reduce recidivism and foster more positive life course outcomes. Such steps will help protect juveniles and assist the juvenile justice system reach the intended purpose of rehabilitation.

References

Abram, K. M., Choe, J. Y., Washburn, J. J., Teplin, L. A., King, D. C., & Dulcan, M. K. (2008). Suicidal ideation and behaviors among youths in juvenile detention. *Journal of the American Academy of Child & Adolescent Psychiatry, 47*(3), 291–300. https://doi.org/10.1097/CHI.0b013e318160b3ce

Abram, K. M., Teplin, L. A., Charles, D. R., Longworth, S. L., McClelland, G. M., & Dulcan, M. K. (2004). Posttraumatic stress disorder and trauma in youth in juvenile detention. *Archives of General Psychiatry, 61*(4), 403–410. https://doi.org/10.1001/archpsyc.61.4.403

Abram, K. M., Teplin, L. A., McClelland, G. M., & Dulcan, M. K. (2003). Comorbid psychiatric disorders in youth in juvenile detention. *Archives of General Psychiatry, 60*(11), 1097–1108. https://doi.org/10.1001/archpsyc.60.11.1097

Agnew, R. (1992). Foundation for a general strain theory of crime and delinquency. *Criminology, 30*, 47–87. https://doi.org/10.1111/j.1745-9125.1992.tb01093.x

Akers, R. (1998). *Social learning and social structure: A general theory of crime and deviance*. Boston: Northeastern University Press.

Allgood, S., Mustard, D. B., & Warren Jr., R. S. (1999). *The impact of youth criminal behavior on adult earnings*. Working paper, University of Georgia.

Altschuler, D. M., & Brash, R. (2004). Adolescent and teenage offenders confronting the challenges and opportunities of reentry. *Youth Violence and Juvenile Justice, 2*(1), 72–87. https://doi.org/10.1177/1541204003260048

Ambrose, K., & Millikan, A. (2013). Beyond juvenile court: Long-term impact of a juvenile record. Washington Defender Association. Retrieved from http://www.defensenet.org/resources/publications-1/beyond-juvenile-court/Beyond%20Juvenile%20Court.pdf

American Civil Liberties Union. (2014). Alone & afraid: Children held in solitary confinement and isolation in juvenile detention and correctional facilities. Retrieved from http://www.stopsolitaryforkids.org/wp-content/uploads/2016/04/Alone-and-Afraid-COMPLETE-FINAL.pdf

Apel, R., Blockland, A. J., Nieuwbeerta, P., & Van Schellen, M. (2009). The impact of imprisonment on marriage and divorce: A risk set matching approach. *Journal of Quantitative Criminology, 26*, 269–300. https://doi.org/10.1007/s10940-009-9087-5

Arya, N. (2007). Jailing juveniles: The dangers of incarcerating youth in adult jails in America. A campaign for youth justice report. Retrieved from http://www.campaignforyouthjustice.org/Downloads/NationalReportsArticles/CFYJ-Jailing_Juveniles_Report_2007-11-15.pdf

Baert, S., & Verhofstadt, E. (2015). Labour market discrimination against former juvenile delinquents: Evidence from a field experiment. *Applied Economics, 47*, 1067–1072. https://doi.org/10.1080/00036846.2014.990620

Bartlett, J., & Domene, J. F. (2015). The vocational goals and career development of criminally involved youth: Experiences that help and hinder. *Journal of Career Development, 42*(3), 229–243. https://doi.org/10.1177/0894845314547269

Bazemore, G., & Umbriet, M. (1995). Rethinking the sanctioning function in juvenile court: Retributive or restorative responses to youth crime. *Crime and Delinquency, 41*, 296–316.

Becker, H. S. (1963). *Outsiders: Studies in the sociology of deviance*. New York, NY: Free Press.

Belfield, C. R., & Levin, H. M. (2009). High school dropouts and the economic losses from juvenile crime in California. *California Dropout Research Project Report, 16*, 1–55.

Bernburg, J. D. (2009). Labeling theory. In M. D. Krohn, A. J. Lizotte, & G. Hall (Eds.), *Handbook on crime and deviance*. New York, NY: Springer.

Bernburg, J. G., & Krohn, M. D. (2003). Labeling, life chances, and adult crime: The direct and indirect effects of official intervention in adolescence on crime in early adulthood. *Criminology, 41*(4), 1287–1318. https://doi.org/10.1111/j.1745-9125.2003.tb01020.x

Beyer, M. (2006). Fifty delinquents in juvenile and adult court. *American Journal of Orthopsychiatry, 76*(2), 206–214. https://doi.org/10.1037/0002-9432.76.2.206

Bishop, D. M., & Frazier, C. E. (1996). Race effects in juvenile justice decision-making: Findings of a statewide analysis. *Journal of Criminal Law & Criminology, 86*(2), 392–414.

Bishop, D. M., Frazier, C. E., Lanza-Kaduce, L., & Winner, L. (1996). The transfer of juveniles to criminal court: Does it make a difference? *Crime & Delinquency, 42*(2), 171–191. https://doi.org/10.1177/0011128796042002001

Bullis, M., & Yovanoff, P. (2006). Idle hands: Community employment experiences of formerly incarcerated youth. *Journal of Emotional and Behavioral Disorders, 14*(2), 71–85. https://doi.org/10.1177/10634266060140020401

Calero, T. (2013). *Open juvenile records in Washington state: Process, effects, and costs of protective mechanisms* (Doctoral dissertation, University of Washington).

Cauffman, E., & Steinberg, L. (2000). (Im) maturity of judgment in adolescence: Why adolescents may be less culpable than adults. *Behavioral Sciences & the Law, 18*(6), 741–760.

Cherlin, A. J., Burton, L. M., Hurt, T. R., & Purvin, D. M. (2004). The influence of physical and sexual abuse on marriage and cohabitation. *American Sociological Review, 69*, 768–789. https://doi.org/10.1177/000312240406900602

Copeland, W. E., Miller-Johnson, S., Keeler, G., Angold, A., & Costello, E. J. (2007). Childhood psychiatric disorders and young adult crime: A prospective, population-based study. *American Journal of Psychiatry, 164*, 1668–1675. https://doi.org/10.1176/appi.ajp.2007.06122026

Costello, E. J., Egger, H., & Angold, A. (2005). 10-year research update review: The epidemiology of child and adolescent psychiatric disorders: I. Methods and public health burden. *Journal of the American Academy of Child & Adolescent Psychiatry, 44*(10), 972–986. https://doi.org/10.1097/01.chi.0000172552.41596.6f

Cottle, C. C., Lee, R. J., & Heilbrun, K. (2001). The prediction of criminal recidivism in juveniles: A meta-analysis. *Criminal Justice and Behavior, 28*(3), 367–394.

De Li, S. (1999). Legal sanctions and youths' status achievement: A longitudinal study. *Justice Quarterly, 16*(2), 377–401. https://doi.org/10.1080/07418829900094181

Dembo, R., Wareham, J., & Schmeidler, J. (2007). Drug use and delinquent behavior: A growth model of parallel processes among high-risk youths. *Criminal Justice and Behavior, 34*(5), 680–696.

Desai, R. A., Goulet, J. L., Robbins, J., Chapman, J. F., Migdole, S. J., & Hoge, M. A. (2006). Mental health care in juvenile detention facilities: A review. *The Journal of the American Academy of Psychiatry and the Law, 34*(2), 204–214.

Elder, G. H. (1985). Perspectives on the life course. In G. H. Elder (Ed.), *Life course dynamics* (pp. 23–49). Ithaca, NY: Cornell University Press.

Elder, G. H. (1998). The life course as developmental theory. *Child Development, 69*(1), 1–12. https://doi.org/10.1111/j.1467-8624.1998.tb06128.x

Elkington, K. S., Teplin, L. A., Abram, K. M., Jakubowski, J. A., Dulcan, M. K., & Welty, L. J. (2015). Psychiatric disorders and violence: A study of delinquent youth after detention. *Journal of the American Academy of Child & Adolescent Psychiatry, 54*(4), 302–312.

Emanuel, K. (2013). *Positive outcomes of delinquent youth: Who is doing well 5 years later?* (Doctoral dissertation). Retrieved from ProQuest LLC. (3508259).

Fazel, S., Doll, H., & Långström, N. (2008). Mental disorders among adolescents in juvenile detention and correctional facilities: A systematic review and metaregression analysis of 25 surveys. *Journal of the American Academy of Child & Adolescent Psychiatry, 47*(9), 1010–1019. https://doi.org/10.1097/CHI.ObO13e31817eecf3

Feld, B. C. (1987). The juvenile court meets the principle of the offense: Legislative changes in juvenile waiver statutes. *The Journal of Criminal Law and Criminology, 78*(3), 471–533. https://doi.org/10.2307/1143567

Garcia, A., Greeson, J., Kim, M., Thompson, A., & DeNard, C. (2015). From placement to prison revisited: Do mental health services disrupt the delinquency pipeline among Latino, African American and Caucasian youth in the child welfare system? *Journal of Adolescence, 45*, 263–273. https://doi.org/10.1016/j.adolescence.2015.10.008

Gerhold, C. K., Browne, K. D., & Beckett, R. (2007). Predicting recidivism in adolescent sexual offenders. *Aggression and Violent Behavior, 12*(4), 427–438. https://doi.org/10.1016/j.avb.2006.10.004

Gilman, A. B., Hill, K. G., & Hawkins, J. D. (2015). When is a youth's debt to society paid? Examining the long-term consequences of juvenile incarceration for adult functioning. *Journal of Developmental and Life-Course Criminology, 1*(1), 33–47. https://doi.org/10.1007/s40865-015-0002-5

Giordano, P. C., Cernkovich, S. A., & Holland, D. D. (2003). Changes in friendship relations over the life course: Implications for desistance from crime. *Criminology, 41*(2), 293–328. https://doi.org/10.1111/j.1745-9125.2003.tb00989.x

Gover, A. R., & MacKenzie, D. L. (2003). Child maltreatment and adjustment to juvenile correctional institutions. *Criminal Justice and Behavior, 30*(3), 374–396. https://doi.org/10.1177/0093854803030003006

Graham v. Florida, 560 U.S. 48 (2010).

Graves, K. N., Frabutt, J. M., & Shelton, T. L. (2007). Factors associated with mental health and juvenile justice involvement among children with severe emotional disturbance. *Youth Violence and Juvenile Justice, 5*(2), 147–167. https://doi.org/10.1177/1541204006292870

Gray, D., Achilles, J., Keller, T., Tate, D., Haggard, L., Rolfs, R., … McMahon, W. M. (2002). Utah youth suicide study, phase I: Government agency contact before death. *Journal of the American Academy of Child & Adolescent Psychiatry, 41*(4), 427–434. https://doi.org/10.1097/00004583-200204000-00015

Grisso, T. (2004). *Double jeopardy: Adolescent offenders with mental disorders*. Chicago, IL: University of Chicago Press.

Grogger, J. (1995). The effect of arrests on the employment and earnings of young men. *Quarterly Journal of Economics, 110*(1), 51–71. https://doi.org/10.2307/2118510

Harmon, M. A. (1993). Reducing the risk of drug involvement among early adolescents: An evaluation of drug abuse resistance education. *Evaluation Review, 17*(2), 221–239.

Hayes, L. M. (2000). Suicide prevention in juvenile facilities. *Juvenile Justice, 7*(1), 2–10.

Hayes, L. M. (2009). *Juvenile suicide in confinement: A national survey*. Collingdale, PA: Diane Publishing.

Hirschfield, P. (2009). Another way out: The impact of juvenile arrests on high school dropout. *Sociology of Education, 82*(4), 368–393. https://doi.org/10.1177/003804070908200404

Hirschi, T. (1969). *Causes of delinquency*. Berkeley, CA: University of California Press.

Hjalmarsson, R. (2008). Criminal justice involvement and high school completion. *Journal of Urban Economics, 63*(2), 613–630. https://doi.org/10.1016/j.jue.2007.04.003

Hoeve, M., McReynolds, L. S., & Wasserman, G. A. (2013). The influence of adolescent psychiatric disorder on young adult recidivism. *Criminal Justice and Behavior, 40*(12), 1368–1382. https://doi.org/10.1177/0093854813488106

Illinois Juvenile Justice Commission. (2016). *Burdened for life: The myth of record confidentiality and expungement in Illinois*. Illinois Juvenile Justice Commission. Retrieved from http://www.law.northwestern.edu/legalclinic/cfjc/documents/Commission-Report-4-27-16-web.pdf

J.D.B. v. North Carolina, 564 U.S. 261 (2011).

Jensen, E. L., & Metsger, L. K. (1994). A test of the deterrent effect of legislative waiver on violent juvenile crime. *Crime & Delinquency, 40*(1), 96–104. https://doi.org/10.1177/0011128794040001007

Joseph, M. (2003). The effect of arrests on the earnings of young men: Evidence from the National Survey of youth. *Chicago Policy Review, 7*(1), 47–60.

Jung, H. (2015). The long-term impact of incarceration during the teens and 20s on the wages and employment of men. *Journal of Offender Rehabilitation, 54*(5), 317–337. https://doi.org/10.1080/10509674.2015.1043480

Juvenile Justice Geography, Policy, Practice & Statistics (2017). National Center for Juvenile Justice (NCJJ). Retrieved from http://www.jjgps.org/jurisdictional-boundaries#transfer-trends?&state=52

Kempker, S. M., Schmidt, A. T., & Espinosa, E. M. (2016). Understanding the influence of mental health diagnosis and gender on placement decisions for justice-involved youth. *Journal of Youth and Adolescence, 46*, 1562–1581. https://doi.org/10.1007/s10964-016-0572-5

Kim, C. Y. (2012). Policing school discipline. *Brooklyn Law Review, 77*, 861–903.

King, D. C., Abram, K. M., Romero, E. G., Washburn, J. J., Welty, L. J., & Teplin, L. A. (2011). Childhood maltreatment and psychiatric disorders among detained youths. *Psychiatric Services, 62*(12), 1430–1438. https://doi.org/10.1176/appi.ps.004412010

Kirk, D. S., & Sampson, R. J. (2013). Juvenile arrest and collateral educational damage in the transition to adulthood. *Sociology of Education, 86*(1), 36–62. https://doi.org/10.1177/0038040712448862

Knitzer, J. (1982). *Unclaimed children*. Washington, D.C.: Children's Defense Fund.

Kroska, A., Lee, J. D., & Carr, N. T. (2017). Juvenile delinquency and self-sentiments: Exploring a labeling theory proposition. *Social Science Quarterly, 98*(1), 73–88. https://doi.org/10.1111/ssqu.12307

Laub, J. H., & Lauritsen, J. L. (1993). Violent criminal behavior over the life course: A review of the longitudinal and comparative research. *Violence and Victims, 8*(3), 235–252.

Laub, J. H., Nagin, D. S., & Sampson, R. J. (1998). Trajectories of change in criminal offending: Good marriages and the desistance process. *American Sociological Review, 63*(2), 225–238. https://doi.org/10.2307/2657324

Laub, J. H., & Sampson, R. J. (1993). Turning points in the life course: Why change matters to the study of crime. *Criminology, 31*(3), 301–325. https://doi.org/10.1111/j.17459125.1993.tb01132.x

Laub, J. H., & Sampson, R. J. (2003). *Shared beginnings, divergent lives: Delinquent boys to age 70*. Cambridge, MA: Harvard University Press.

Lee, J. S., Courtney, M. E., Harachi, T. W., & Tajima, E. A. (2015). Labeling and the effect of adolescent legal system involvement on adult outcomes for foster youth aging out of care. *American Journal of Orthopsychiatry, 85*(5), 441. https://doi.org/10.1037/ort0000090

Leshem, R. (2016). Brain development, impulsivity, risky decision-making, and cognitive control: Integrating cognitive and socioemotional processes during adolescence. *Developmental Neuropsychology, 41*(1–2), 1–5. https://doi.org/10.1080/87565641.2016.1187033

Liberman, A. M., Kirk, D. S., & Kim, K. (2014). Labeling effects of first juvenile arrests: Secondary deviance and secondary sanctioning. *Criminology, 52*, 345–370. https://doi.org/10.1111/1745-9125.12039

Liles, A., & Moak, S. C. (2015). Changing juvenile justice policy in response to the US Supreme Court: Implementing Miller v. Alabama. *Youth Justice, 15*(1), 76–92.

Lilly, J., Cullen, F., & Ball, R. (2015). *Criminological theory: Context and consequences* (6th ed.). Los Angeles, CA: Sage.

Liska, A. E., & Messner, S. F. (1999). *Perspectives on crime and deviance* (3rd ed.). Upper Saddle River, NJ: Prentice Hall.

Litwok, D. (2014). Have you ever been convicted of a crime? The effects of juvenile expungement on crime, educational, and labor market outcomes (Doctoral dissertation, Michigan State University, East Lansing).

Mack, J. (2012). Union formation and maturation of juvenile delinquents: A new look at development and desistance in early adulthood (Doctoral dissertation, Bowling Green State University).

Mason, W. A., Zimmerman, L., & Evans, W. (1998). Sexual and physical abuse among incarcerated youth: Implications for sexual behavior, contraceptive use, and teenage pregnancy. *Child Abuse & Neglect, 22*(10), 987–995. https://doi.org/10.1016/S0145-2134(98)00080-5

Mauricio, A. M., Little, M., Chassin, L., Knight, G. P., Piquero, A. R., Losoya, S. H., & Vargas-Chanes, D. (2009). Juvenile offenders' alcohol and marijuana trajectories: Risk and protective factor effects in the context of time in a supervised facility. *Journal of Youth and Adolescence, 38*(3), 440.

McClelland, G. M., Elkington, K. S., Teplin, L. A., & Abram, K. M. (2004). Multiple substance use disorders in juvenile detainees. *Journal of the American Academy of Child & Adolescent Psychiatry, 43*(10), 1215–1224. https://doi.org/10.1097/01.chi.0000134489.58054.9c

McShane, M. D., & Williams, F. P. (1989). The prison adjustment of juvenile offenders. *Crime & Delinquency, 35*(2), 254–269. https://doi.org/10.1177/0011128789035002005

Miller, N., & McEwen, T. (1996). Prosecutor and criminal court use of juvenile court records: A national study. *Institute of Law and Justice, Office of Justice Programs, National Institute of Justice*, 1–58.

Miller v. Alabama, 567 U.S. 460 (2012).

Miranda v. Arizona, 384 U.S. 436 (1966).

Moffitt, T. E. (1993). Adolescence-limited and life-course-persistent antisocial behavior: A developmental taxonomy. *Psychological Review, 100*(4), 674–701. https://doi.org/10.1037/0033-295X.100.4.674

Moffitt, T. E., & Caspi, A. (2001). Childhood predictors differentiate life-course persistent and adolescence-limited antisocial pathways among males and females. *Development and Psychopathology, 13*(2), 355–375.

Monohan, K. C., VenDerhei, S., Bechtold, J., & Cauffman, E. (2014). From the school yard to the squad car: School discipline, truancy, and arrest. *Journal of Youth and Adolescence, 43*(7), 1110–1122. https://doi.org/10.1007/s10964-014-0103-1

Mulvey, E., Steinberg, L., Fagan, J., Cauffman, E., Piquero, A., Chassin, L., ... Losoya, S. (2004). Theory and research on desistance from antisocial activity among serious adolescent offenders. *Youth Violence and Juvenile Justice, 2*(3), 1–23. https://doi.org/10.1177/1541204004265864

Myers, D. L. (2003). The recidivism of violent youths in juvenile and adult court: A consideration of selection bias. *Youth Violence and Juvenile Justice, 1*(1), 79–101. https://doi.org/10.1177/1541204002238365

Myner, J., Santman, J., Cappelletty, G. G., & Perlmutter, B. F. (1998). Variables related to recidivism among juvenile offenders. *International Journal of Offender Therapy and Comparative Criminology, 42*(1), 65–80. https://doi.org/10.1177/0306624X98421006

Nagin, D., & Waldfogel, J. (1995). The effects of criminality and conviction on the labor market status of young British offenders. *International Review of Law & Economics, 15*(1), 109–126. https://doi.org/10.1016/0144-8188(94)00004-E

Natsuaki, M. N., Ge, X., & Wenk, E. (2008). Continuity and changes in the developmental trajectories of criminal career: Examining the roles of timing of first arrest and high school graduation. *Journal of Youth and Adolescence, 37*(4), 431–444. https://doi.org/10.1007/s10964-006-9156-0

Novins, D. K., Duclos, C. W., Martin, C., Jewett, C. S., & Manson, S. M. (1999). Utilization of alcohol, drug, and mental health treatment services among American Indian adolescent detainees. *Journal of the American Academy of Child & Adolescent Psychiatry, 38*(9), 1102–1108. https://doi.org/10.1097/00004583-199909000-00013

Otto, R. K., Greenstein, J. J., Johnson, M. K., & Friedman, R. M. (1992). Prevalence of mental disorder among youth in the juvenile justice system. In J. J. Cocozza (Ed.), *Responding to the mental health needs of youth in the juvenile justice system* (pp. 7–48). Seattle: The National Coalition for the Mentally Ill in the Criminal Justice System.

Pager, D. (2003). The mark of a criminal record. *American Journal of Sociology, 108*(5), 937–975. https://doi.org/10.1086/374403

Parks, G. A., & Bard, D. E. (2006). Risk factors for adolescent sex offender recidivism: Evaluation of predictive factors and comparison of three groups based upon victim type. *Sexual Abuse: A Journal of Research and Treatment, 18*(4), 319–342. https://doi.org/10.1007/s11194-006-9028-x

Petteruti, A., & Walsh, N. (2008). Registering harm: How sex offense registries fail youth communities. Justice Policy Institute. Retrieved from http://www.justicepolicy.org/uploads/justicepolicy/documents/walsh_act.pdf

Piquero, A. R., Daigle, L. E., Gibson, C., Piquero, N. L., & Tibbetts, S. G. (2007). Research note: Are life-course-persistent offenders at risk for adverse health outcomes? *Journal of Research in Crime and Delinquency, 44*(2), 185–207. https://doi.org/10.1177/0022427806297739

Pope, C. E., Lovell, R. D., & Hsia, H. M. (2002). *Disproportionate minority confinement: A review of the research literature from 1989 through 2001*. Washington, DC: US Department of Justice, Office of Justice Programs, Office of Juvenile Justice and Delinquency Prevention.

Puzzanchera, C., & Kang, W. (2014). Easy access to FBI arrest statistics 1994–2012. Retrieved from http://www.ojjdp.gov/ojstatbb/ezaucr/

Rabinovitch, S. M., Kerr, D. C., Leve, L. D., & Chamberlain, P. (2015). Suicidal behavior outcomes of childhood sexual abuse: Longitudinal study of adjudicated girls. *Suicide and Life-threatening Behavior, 45*(4), 431–447. https://doi.org/10.1111/sltb.12141

Rainville, G., & Smith, S. (2003). *Juvenile felony defendants in criminal courts: Survey of 40 counties, 1998*. Washington, DC: US Department of Justice, Office of Justice Programs, Bureau of Justice Statistics.

Record Expungement Designed to Enhance Employment Act of 2014, H.R. 5158, 114th Cong. (2014).

Redding, R., & Fuller, E. (2004). What do juvenile offenders know about being tried as adults? Implications for deterrence. *Juvenile and Family Court Journal, 55*(3), 35–44. https://doi.org/10.1111/j.1755-6988.2004.tb00167.x

Rohde, P., Seeley, J. R., & Mace, D. E. (1997). Correlates of suicidal behavior in a juvenile detention population. *Suicide and Life-threatening Behavior, 27*(2), 164–175. https://doi.org/10.1111/j.1943-278X.1997.tb00288.x

Roper v. Simmons, 543 U.S. 551 (2005).

Ryan, E. P., & Otonichar, J. M. (2016). Juvenile sex offenders. *Current Psychiatry Reports, 18*(7), 1–10. https://doi.org/10.1007/s11920-016-0706-1

Sampson, R. J., & Laub, J. H. (1990). Crime and deviance over the life course: The salience of adult social bonds. *American Sociological Review, 55*(5), 609–627.

Sampson, R. J., & Laub, J. H. (1993). Structural variations in juvenile court processing: Inequality, the underclass, and social control. *Law and Society Review, 27*(2), 285–311. https://doi.org/10.2307/3053938

Sampson, R. J., & Laub, J. H. (1997). A life-course theory of cumulative disadvantage and the stability of delinquency. *Developmental Theories of Crime and Delinquency, 7*, 133–161.

Sampson, R. J., & Laub, J. H. (2003). Life-course desisters? Trajectories of crime among delinquent boys followed to age 70. *Criminology, 41*(3), 555–592. https://doi.org/10.1111/j.1745-9125.2003.tb00997.x

Schubert, C. A., Mulvey, E. P., Loughran, T. A., Fagan, J., Chassin, L. A., Piquero, A. R., ... Cauffman, E. (2010). Predicting outcomes for youth transferred to adult court. *Law and Human Behavior, 34*(6), 460–475. https://doi.org/10.1007/s10979-009-9209-5

Schubert, C. A., Mulvey, E. P., & Pitzer, L. (2016). Differentiating serious adolescent offenders who exit the justice system from those who do not. *Criminology, 54*(1), 56–85. https://doi.org/10.1111/1745-9125.12098

Scott, E. S. (2000). Criminal responsibility in adolescence: Lessons from developmental psychology. In T. Grisso & R. Schwarz (Eds.), *Youth on trial: A developmental perspective on juvenile justice* (pp. 291–324). Chicago, IL: University of Chicago Press.

Shah, R. S., Fine, L., & Gullen, J. (2014). *Juvenile records: A national review of state laws on confidentiality, sealing and expungement*. Philadelphia, PA: Juvenile Law Center and Community Legal Services of Philadelphia. Retrieved from http://juvenilerecords.jlc.org/juvenilerecords/documents/publications/national-review.pdf

Shannon, C. R. (2013). *Juvenile incarceration and reentry: A photovoice study*. El Paso, TX: LFB Scholarly Publishing LLC.

Sharlein, J. (2016). Beyond recidivism investigating comparative educational and employment outcomes for adolescents in the juvenile and criminal justice systems. *Crime & Delinquency*, 1–27. https://doi.org/10.1177/0011128716678193.

Shufelt, J. L., & Cocozza, J. J. (2006). *Youth with mental health disorders in the juvenile justice system: Results from a multi-state prevalence study* (pp. 1–6). Delmar, NY: National Center for Mental Health and Juvenile Justice.

Sickmund, M., & Puzzanchera, C. (2014). Juvenile offenders and victims: 2014 national report. National Center for Juvenile Justice. Retrieved from https://www.ojjdp.gov/ojstatbb/nr2014/downloads/NR2014.pdf

Sickmund, M., Sladky, A., & Kang, W. (2015). *Easy access to juvenile court statistics: 1985–2013*. Office of Juvenile Justice and Delinquency Prevention. Retrieved from http://www.ojjdp.gov/ojstatbb/ezajcs/

Sickmund, M., Sladky, A., Kang, W., & Puzzanchera, C. (2015). *Easy access to the census of juveniles in residential placement*. Retrieved from http://www.ojjdp.gov/ojstatbb/ezacjrp/

Sickmund, M., Snyder, H. N., & Poe-Yamagata, E. (1997). Juvenile offenders and victims: 1997 update on violence. Office of Juvenile Justice and Delinquency Prevention. Retrieved from https://www.ojjdp.gov/pubs/juvoff/contents.html

Slocum, L. A. (2016). Crime and the life course. In T. S. Bynum & B. M. Huebner (Eds.), *The handbook of measurement issues in criminology and criminal justice* (pp. 496–534). Chichester, UK: Wiley.

Spinney, E., Cohen, M., Feyerherm, W., Stephenson, R., Yeide, M., & Hopps, M. (2014). *Case studies of nine jurisdictions that reduced disproportionate minority contact in their juvenile justice systems*. Office of Juvenile Justice and Delinquency Prevention. Retrieved from https://www.ncjrs.gov/pdffiles1/ojjdp/grants/250301.pdf

Steinberg, L. (2005). Cognitive and affective development in adolescence. *Trends in Cognitive Sciences, 9*(2), 69–74. https://doi.org/10.1016/j.tics.2004.12.005

Stokes, M. L., McCoy, K. P., Abram, K. M., Byck, G. R., & Teplin, L. A. (2015). Suicidal ideation and behavior in youth in the juvenile justice system: A review of the literature. *Journal of Correctional Health Care, 21*(3), 222–242. https://doi.org/10.1177/1078345815587001

Strayhorn, T. L., Johnson, R. M., & Barrett, B. A. (2013). Investigating the college adjustment and transition experiences of formerly incarcerated black male collegians at predominantly white institutions. *Spectrum: A Journal on Black Men, 2*(1), 73–98. https://doi.org/10.2979/spectrum.2.1.73

Students with Criminal Convictions (2017). Federal student aid. Retrieved from https://studentaid.ed.gov/sa/eligibility/criminal-convictions

Sukhodolsky, D. G., & Ruchkin, V. (2006). Evidence-based psychosocial treatments in the juvenile justice system. *Child and Adolescent Psychiatric Clinics of North America, 15*(2), 501–516. https://doi.org/10.1016/j.chc.2005.11.005

Sweeten, G. (2006). Who will graduate? Disruption of high school education by arrest and court involvement. *Justice Quarterly, 23*, 462–480. https://doi.org/10.1080/07418820600985313

Tanner, J., Davies, S., & O'Grady, B. (1999). Whatever happened to yesterday's rebels? Longitudinal effects of youth delinquency on education and employment. *Social Problems, 46*(2), 250–274. https://doi.org/10.1525/sp.1999.46.2.03x0188f

Tarolla, S. M., Wagner, E. F., Rabinowitz, J., & Tubman, J. G. (2002). Understanding and treating juvenile offenders: A review of current knowledge and future directions. *Aggression and Violent Behavior, 7*(2), 125–143. https://doi.org/10.1016/S1359-1789(00)00041-0

Taylor, M. (2015). Juvenile transfers to adult court: An examination of the long-term outcomes of transferred and non-transferred juveniles. *Juvenile and Family Court Journal, 66*, 29–47. https://doi.org/10.1111/jfcj.12050

Taylor, M. T., & Spang, T. (2017). I'd prefer an applicant who doesn't have a delinquent history: Delinquents in the labor market. *Journal of Juvenile Justice, 6*(1), 48–62.

Teplin, L. A., Abram, K. M., McClelland, G. M., Dulcan, M. K., & Mericle, A. A. (2002). Psychiatric disorders in youth in juvenile detention. *Archives of General Psychiatry, 59*(12), 1133–1143. https://doi.org/10.1001/archpsyc.59.12.1133

Teplin, L. A., Jakubowski, J. A., Abram, K. M., Olson, N. D., Stokes, M. L., & Welty, L. J. (2014). Firearm homicide and other causes of death in delinquents: A 16-year prospective study. *Pediatrics, 134*(1), 63–73. https://doi.org/10.1542/peds.2013-3966

Teplin, L. A., Welty, L. J., Abram, K. M., Dulcan, M. K., & Washburn, J. J. (2012). Prevalence and persistence of psychiatric disorders in youth after detention: A prospective longitudinal study. *Archives of General Psychiatry, 69*(10), 1031–1043. https://doi.org/10.1001/archgenpsychiatry.2011.2062

Teplin, L. A., Welty, L. J., Abram, K. M., Dulcan, M. K., Washburn, J. J., McCoy, K., & Stokes, M. L. (2015). *Psychiatric disorders in youth after detention*. Washington, DC: US Department of Justice, Office of Justice Programs, Office of Juvenile Justice and Delinquency Prevention.

Thomas, C. W., & Bishop, D. M. (1984). The impact of legal sanctions on delinquency: A longitudinal comparison of labeling and deterrence theories. *Journal of Criminal Law and Criminology, 75*, 1222–1245.

United States Department of Justice. (2015). Uniform crime reporting: Crime in the United States. Retrieved from https://ucr.fbi.gov/crime-in-the-u.s/2015/crime-in-the-u.s.-2015

Waite, D., Keller, A., McGarvey, E. L., Wieckowski, E., Pinkerton, R., & Brown, G. L. (2005). Juvenile sex offender re-arrest rates for sexual, violent nonsexual and property crimes: A 10-year follow-up. *Sexual Abuse: A Journal of Research and Treatment, 17*(3), 313–331. https://doi.org/10.1007/s11194-005-5061-4

Wald, J., & Losen, D. J. (2003). Defining and redirecting a school-to-prison pipeline. *New Directions for Youth Development, 2003*(99), 9–15. https://doi.org/10.1002/yd.51

Wareham, J., & Dembo, R. (2007). A longitudinal study of psychological functioning among juvenile offenders: A latent growth model analysis. *Criminal Justice and Behavior, 34*(2), 259–273. https://doi.org/10.1177/0093854806289828

Warr, M. (1998). Life-course transitions and desistance from crime. *Criminology, 36*, 183–216. https://doi.org/10.1111/j.1745-9125.1998.tb01246.x

Washburn, J., Teplin, L., Voss, L., Simon, C., Abram, K., & McClelland, G. (2008). Psychiatric disorders among detained youths: A comparison of youths processed in juvenile court and adult criminal court. *Psychiatric Services, 59*(9), 965–973.

Wasserman, G. A., Ko, S. J., & McReynolds, L. S. (2004). *Assessing the mental health status of youth in juvenile justice settings*. Office of Juvenile Justice and Delinquency Prevention: Juvenile Justice Bulletin.

Wasserman, G. A., & McReynolds, L. S. (2006). Suicide risk at juvenile justice intake. *Suicide and Life-threatening Behavior, 36*(2), 239–249. https://doi.org/10.1521/suli.2006.36.2.239

Wasserman, G. A., McReynolds, L. S., Ko, S. J., Katz, L., & Carpenter, J. R. (2005). Gender difference in psychiatric disorders at juvenile probation intake. *American Journal of Public Health, 95*(1), 131–137.

Wasserman, G. A., McReynolds, L. S., Lucas, C. P., Fisher, P., & Santos, L. (2002). The voice DISC-IV with incarcerated male youths: Prevalence of disorder. *Journal of the American Academy of Child & Adolescent Psychiatry, 41*(3), 314–321. https://doi.org/10.1097/00004583-200203000-00011

Welty, L. J., Harrison, A. J., Abram, K. M., Abram, K. M., Olson, N. D., Aaby, D. A., … Teplin, L. A. (2016). Health disparities in drug- and alcohol-use disorders: A 12-year longitudinal study of youths after detention. *American Journal of Public Health, 106*(5), 872–880.

Welty, L. J., Hershfield, J. A., Abram, K. M., Han, H., Byck, G. R., & Teplin, L. A. (2017). Trajectories of substance use disorder in youth after detention: A 12-year longitudinal study. *Journal of the American Academy of Child & Adolescent Psychiatry, 56*(2), 140–148. https://doi.org/10.1016/j.jaac.2016.10.018

Western, B. (2002). The impact of incarceration on wage mobility and inequality. *American Sociological Review, 67*(4), 526–546.

White, H. R., Loeber, R., Stouthamer-Loeber, M. B., & Farrington, D. P. (1999). Developmental associations between substance use and violence. *Development and Psychopathology, 11*, 785–803.

White, N. A., & Piquero, A. R. (2004). A preliminary empirical test of Silverthorn and Frick's delayed-onset pathway in girls using an urban, African-American, U.S.-based sample. *Criminal Behavior and Mental Health, 14*, 291–309. https://doi.org/10.1002/cbm.595

Whitehead, J. T., & Lab, S. P. (1989). A meta-analysis of juvenile correctional treatment. *Journal of Research in Crime and Delinquency, 26*(3), 276–295.

Wiesner, M., Kim, H. K., & Capaldi, D. M. (2010). History of juvenile arrests and vocational career outcomes for at-risk young men. *Journal of Research in Crime and Delinquency, 47*(1), 91–117. https://doi.org/10.1177/0022427809348906

Winner, L., Lanza-Kaduce, L., Bishop, D. M., & Frazier, C. E. (1997). The transfer of juveniles to criminal court: Reexamining recidivism over the long term. *Crime & Delinquency, 43*(4), 548–563. https://doi.org/10.1177/0011128797043004009

Worling, J., & Curwen, T. (2000). Adolescent sexual offender recidivism: Success of specialized treatment and implications for risk prediction. *Child Abuse & Neglect, 24*(7), 965–982. https://doi.org/10.1016/S0145-2134(00)00147-2

Zimring, F. E., Piquero, A. R., & Jennings, W. G. (2007). Sexual delinquency in racine: Does early sex offending predict later sex offending in youth and young adulthood? *Criminology & Public Policy, 6*(3), 507–534. https://doi.org/10.1111/j.1745-9133.2007.00451.x

Indigenous Youth Crime: An International Perspective

Jeffrey E. Pfeifer, John Winterdyk, Fiona Hutton, Sarah Monod de Froideville, Cyndi Banks, and Justin S. Trounson

"No study of adolescence can be complete without some study of nearly one-third of the human race, occupying two-fifths of the land surface of the globe, now included in the one hundred and thirty-six colonies and dependencies of the world, that are in a relation of greater or less subjection to a few civilized nations." G. Stanley Hall (1904, p. 561).

Although this quote from G. Stanley Hall is somewhat dated, it is important to acknowledge the fact that one of the earliest foundational contributors to modern psychology highlighted the importance of including the experiences of Indigenous people[1] as part of any comprehensive assessment of human behavior, especially as it related to an understanding of adolescence. Among other things, Hall suggested that the negative effects of colonization had resulted in a number of hardships for Indigenous adolescents throughout the world and that these experiences culminated in a variety of challenges including poverty, educational difficulties, racism, and crime. Given this situation, he suggested that any research aimed at positively

[1] For the purposes of this chapter, "Indigenous" refers to the original inhabitants of Australia, Canada, New Zealand, and the United States.

J. E. Pfeifer (✉) · J. S. Trounson
Department of Psychological Sciences, Centre for Forensic Behavioural Science, Swinburne University of Technology, Melbourne, VIC, Australia
e-mail: jpfeifer@swin.edu.au

J. Winterdyk
Department of Economics, Justice, and Policy Studies, Mount Royal University, Calgary, AB, Canada

F. Hutton · S. Monod de Froideville
Institute of Criminology, Victoria University, Victoria University Institute of Criminology, School of Social and Cultural Studies, Wellington, New Zealand

C. Banks
Capilano University, North Vancouver, BC, Canada

M. K. Miller, B. H. Bornstein (eds.), *Advances in Psychology and Law*, Advances in Psychology and Law 3,
https://doi.org/10.1007/978-3-319-75859-6_8

affecting the lives of adolescents would be incomplete if it did not also include an understanding of the specific experiences of Indigenous youth.

Despite the fact that Hall's words represent an early recognition by psychology and other social sciences that the study of Indigenous youth is an essential inclusion in any scientific examination of adolescence, a review of the literature indicates that this philosophy has not been vigorously embraced with regard to the issue of youth crime[2] (Colenutt & Toye, 2012). More specifically, although it is clear that empirical interest into the causes and treatment of youth crime has a long history in the fields of criminology (see e.g., Sahin & Maier, 2011), penology (see e.g., Shoham, Beck, & Kett, 2008), and forensic psychology (see e.g., Grigorenko, 2012), it is equally clear that there is an identifiable gap in the literature with regard to a comprehensive analysis on the relationship of this knowledge to Indigenous youth (Colenutt & Toye, 2012; Martin, 2014; Perry, 2009).

The overarching purpose of this chapter therefore is to apply a systematic and comprehensive approach for identifying, reviewing, and commenting on the available literature regarding Indigenous youth crime across four countries (Australia, Canada, New Zealand, and the United States).[3] To accomplish this, the chapter begins with an examination of systematic reviews on the issue of Indigenous youth crime. This section will be followed by an overview of the current context relating to Indigenous youth crime for each of the countries, including statistics relating to the issue as well as identifying any important jurisdictional factors (e.g., distinct Indigenous judicial systems, constitutional issues). The chapter then summarizes the specific studies that have been conducted on Indigenous youth crime and identifies a set of systemic and individual factors that have been empirically linked to this issue. Following this, an overview of the various interventions aimed at meeting the challenges related to this issue are presented in terms of system-based interventions (i.e., those aimed at addressing political, cultural, and social policies and practices) as well as targeted frontline interventions (i.e., those aimed at directly assisting Indigenous youth who are engaging in criminal activities). Finally, the chapter identifies a number of significant gaps in the scientific study of Indigenous youth crime and provides suggestions for future research and intervention.

[2] Although there are a variety of terms employed throughout the literature for describing the concept of criminal activity by young people (e.g., juvenile delinquency, teen crime, adolescent offending), the term "youth crime" will be employed throughout the chapter.

[3] Although it is acknowledged that many other countries and jurisdictions also include Indigenous people as part of their community, the bulk of research and scientific investigation into Indigenous youth crime to date emanates from the four identified countries.

Existing Literature Reviews

Despite the fact that a myriad of systematic reviews have been published on the contributing factors to youth crime, comparatively few of these attempt to identify the extent to which these factors relate to Indigenous youth (see e.g., Harris, 2015). This is a noteworthy omission in the literature given that the relatively few studies that have been conducted with regard to Indigenous youth crime indicate significant differences when compared to the experiences of non-Indigenous youth (see e.g., Lynch, Buckman, & Krenske, 2003). For example, a study conducted by Homel, Lincoln, and Herd (1999) identified several unique risk and protective factors among Australian Indigenous youth and subsequently argued that these factors should be employed to develop a culturally responsive resiliency paradigm aimed at reducing the risk of Indigenous youth turning to a life of crime.

In addition to the dearth of specific research on Indigenous youth crime, there is also a distinct lack of a comprehensive systematic review of the area, especially from an international perspective.[4] In short, although a number of systematic reviews have been published on various aspects of youth crime, there appears to be no such examination specifically aimed at Indigenous youth crime, nor do the existing reviews appear to comment on the applicability/relatedness of their content to an Indigenous population (see e.g., Carney & Myers, 2012). Interestingly, although a number of these systematic reviews on youth crime include analyses of race or culture as part of the design, few include a formalized assessment of Indigenous youth (see e.g., Redding, 2010).

The absence of a comprehensive review of the issue is especially surprising given continual academic, judicial, and governmental recognition of the need for such an endeavor. In New Zealand, for example, academic discourse on youth justice and offending often includes critical commentary on the lack of research attention given to the challenges faced by Indigenous youth (see e.g., Tauri, 2012). Similar calls for increased research on the issue of Indigenous youth crime have been made in Australia (see e.g., Australian Institute of Health and Welfare, 2012; Standing Committee on Aboriginal and Torres Strait Islander Affairs, 2011; Troth & Grainger, 2000), Canada (see e.g., Monchalin, 2016), and the United States (see e.g., Rodriguez, 2008).

The need for a systematic review on this issue is especially significant given the overrepresentation of Indigenous youth in the criminal justice systems of Australia, Canada, New Zealand, and the United States (see e.g., Cunneen, 2006; Hartney, 2008). A recent study in Australia, for example, found that "[a]lthough only 5% of young Australians are Indigenous… 39% of those under juvenile justice supervision on an average day were Indigenous" (Australian Institute of Health and Welfare, 2012, p. 1). This situation has culminated in the Australian Medical Association and

[4] In terms of Indigenous issues more broadly, the literature indicates a clear trend toward international analyses and comparisons between Australia, Canada, New Zealand, and the United States (see e.g., Galaway & Hudson, 1996; Goran, 2001; Hudson, Morris, Maxwell, & Galaway, 1996; Winterdyk, 2015).

other organizations recommending that a national strategy be introduced to respond to the health and welfare needs of Indigenous people, including the overrepresentation of Indigenous adults and youth in the justice system (Holland, 2015). The overrepresentation of Indigenous youth in the Australian justice system is paralleled in Canada (Greenberg, Grekul, & Nelson, 2016), New Zealand (Ministry of Justice, 2013), and the United States (Hartney, 2008).

Given the above, there are a number of reasons why a comprehensive review of this issue is not only timely and germane but could also provide valuable assistance to researchers, policy makers, and a variety of agencies (e.g., Departments of Corrections and Justice, Juvenile Justice Agencies). First, although there is a small but growing research literature on Indigenous youth and crime, there has been no attempt to review and integrate this literature from an international perspective in order to provide commentary and potential direction.[5]

Second, in addition to the research literature, there is a fairly substantial compendium of instructive gray literature (e.g., program evaluations, agency research, government reports) which has not been formally reviewed from an international perspective nor been effectively integrated with the existing research literature. Third, although much of the literature relating to Indigenous youth crime provides important empirical information, few of these publications identify gaps in the literature nor formalized proposals for moving forward. Finally, it is clear from a variety of recent publications that the issue of Indigenous youth crime is one which has been identified as a priority for a number of countries seeking to develop effective policies and practices (see e.g., Holland, 2015). As such, in addition to providing an assessment of the literature, this chapter might also be of assistance to policy-makers, government and nongovernment agencies, and professionals (e.g., correctional facility administrators, justice workers, community corrections staff) who wish to meet the challenges currently faced by Indigenous youth.

Indigenous Youth Crime: Numbers and Jurisdictional Context

In order to gain a more comprehensive perspective on Indigenous youth crime, it is important to first provide contextual information from across the four countries. The following section provides an overview of the various jurisdictional aspects that play a significant role in the issue of Indigenous youth crime for each country as well as the related statistical information.

[5]Although there have been a limited number of publications examining specific issues related to Indigenous youth crime from an international perspective (see e.g., Hudson et al., 1996; Shoemaker, 1996), few if any have provided a more comprehensive overview of the issue across four countries with substantial Indigenous populations.

Australia

Despite a considerable level of congruence across Australia in relation to general youth justice practices, each state and territory of Australia implements its own youth justice legislation, policies, and practices (AIHW, 2016). Young people can be charged with a criminal offense in Australia if they are 10 years or older and are considered under the jurisdiction of the youth justice system while under the age of 18 (17 years of age in Queensland). The common law in Australia presumes, however, that children between the ages of 10 and 14 do not possess the necessary knowledge to have criminal intention (i.e., *doli incapax*; ALRC, 1997). Despite the provision of *doli incapax* across all jurisdictions, concern has been raised regarding the low age of criminal responsibility in Australia and its bearing on Indigenous youth (Amnesty International Australia, 2015).

In addition to the above, there has been an emergence of formalized Indigenous sentencing courts across Australia (Marchetti & Daly, 2004). The first of these courts was established in Port Adelaide on the 1st of June 1999, and there are now over 50 adult and children's Indigenous sentencing courts operating across Australia, including the New South Wales Youth Koori Court (Children's Court of NSW, 2016), Queensland's Murri Court (Westcott, 2006), and the Children's Koori Court in Victoria (Grant, 2009). These courts utilize the Australian criminal law framework and procedures to sentence Indigenous offenders who plead guilty or have been found guilty. Despite the formalization of these courts, the number of Indigenous offenders sentenced by these courts is still quite low compared to mainstream courts (Marchetti & Daly, 2004).

Like other countries, Indigenous youth are overrepresented within the Australian criminal justice system (AIHW, 2012). It is estimated that on an average day there are 5629 young people under youth justice supervision in Australia and that approximately half are Indigenous (AIHW, 2014, 2016). In addition, Indigenous young people aged 10–17 are 15 times more likely to be under supervision than non-Indigenous young people (AIHW, 2016). Research in this area indicates Indigenous youth enter the juvenile justice system at younger ages, have more contacts, and experience more periods of supervision compared to non-Indigenous youth (AIHW, 2012; Carrington & Pereira, 2009; Snowball, 2008). The most common types of offenses Indigenous youth engage in include burglary, break and enter, theft, public order and violence-related offenses (see e.g., Brame, Mazerolle, & Piquero, 2010; Carrington & Pereira, 2009; Cunneen & White, 2007). Research also indicates that even though 5% of young people aged 10–17 in Australia are Indigenous, it has been estimated that 39% of young people under supervision and more than half of those in detention identify as being Indigenous (Australian Institute of Health and Welfare, 2012). It has been suggested that these figures have important implications for a variety of issues including criminal career trajectories (see e.g., Livingston, Stewart, Allard, & Ogilvie, 2008; Yessine & Bonta, 2009) and psychological health (see e.g., Troth & Grainger, 2000).

Canada

In Canada, the Youth Criminal Justice Act (YCJA) details the legal framework for all youth between the ages of 12 and 18. Although the YCJA is federal legislation, it is the responsibility of the ten provinces and three territories to administer the Act (Green, 2016). The current youth justice model is best described as a system which places an emphasis on due process and criminal offense bifurcation (Winterdyk, 2015). For example, the Act includes provisions to transfer serious juvenile offenders to adult court and includes other provisions that avail the use of alternative measures or alternative sanctions for less serious offenses. The Act also includes special provisions that allow the provinces and territories to respond to the special needs of certain young offenders. Therefore, depending on resources, demographics, and regional needs, there are some variations in how young offenders are processed (see e.g., Peters & Corrado, 2016).

Both federal and provincial governments across Canada have begun to initiate various strategies to address Indigenous youth crime and the criminal justice system (Monchalin, 2016). For example, the YCJA acknowledges the status of Indigenous youth and includes special provisions to help respond to their specific risks and needs (see e.g., Greenberg et al., 2016). Sections 4 and 5 of the Act provide for alternative interventions which, although not specifically intended for Indigenous youth, have been subsequently employed by several provinces as a basis for establishing Indigenous-specific programs.

As with the Australian Indigenous community, First Nations people (including the Inuit, Innu, and Métis[6]) are also overrepresented in the Canadian criminal justice system (Boyce, 2016; Latimer & Foss, 2005). The incarceration rate for Indigenous youth in Canada is 64.5 per 10,000 and 8.2 per 10,000 for non-Indigenous youth (Perreault, 2014). There is also a clear disconnect regarding the percentage of resource allocation to Indigenous youth relative to their overrepresentation in the justice system in Canada. For example, between 2008/09 and 2010/11 less than 10% of Indigenous youth received court worker services despite having had previous convictions (Aboriginal Courtwork Program Evaluation, 2015). The picture is further complicated as there are regional variations. Although Indigenous youth are overrepresented in all regions of the country, the trend becomes more pronounced as one moves from east to west and from south to north (see e.g., Malekieh, 2017).

[6]The Inuit generally inhabit the far northern regions of the country, while the Innu, who were formerly known as the Naskapi-Montagnais, reside on the eastern portion of the Quebec-Labrador peninsula in eastern Canada, and the Métis are generally considered to be persons of mixed European and Indigenous ancestry and aretypically found in western Canada.

New Zealand

The New Zealand youth justice system focuses on restorative justice through family group conferences and emphasizes diversion for young offenders (Cleland & Quince, 2014; Lynch, 2012a). The principles of restorative justice and diversion were included in the Children, Young Persons and their Families Act of 1989, which encourages a hybrid justice/welfare approach to young offenders in which communities would be involved in taking responsibility for offending (Ludbrook, 2009). Section 208 of the Act states that criminal proceedings should be used as a last resort in order to curb a tendency on behalf of the police to use powers of arrest (Watt, 2003). Given that it is the police who are critical in ensuring that this principle is put into practice, the New Zealand Police Service includes a specialist division to whom young offenders are referred by frontline officers if the offending in question requires more than an initial warning. This Youth Aid Division has the discretion to deal with the young person in an informal way by employing alternative resolutions (e.g., meeting with the family; requiring the young person to write an apology letter to his or her victim; requiring the young person to attend a drug and alcohol program; applying a curfew) or by referring the matter to a family group conference with an intention to charge or lay a charge directly in the Youth Court (Cleland, 2016; Lynch, 2012a).

Analysis of national statistics indicates that Māori[7] people are overrepresented in the New Zealand criminal justice system (Ioane, Lambie, & Percival, 2016; Statistics New Zealand, 2016). Māori are more likely to be apprehended for a criminal offense, more likely to be prosecuted and more likely to receive a punitive sentence for the same offense type when compared with non-Māori (Ministry of Justice, 2015; Quince, 2007a, 2007b; Workman, 2016; Workman & McIntosh, 2013). In terms of Māori youth, like the other countries examined in this chapter, there is a clear and disturbing trend toward overrepresentation across the youth justice system. For example, in the period between 1992 and 2008, Māori child (those aged 10–13)[8] apprehensions were more than five times that of Pacific[9] or New Zealand European youth, and Māori youth apprehensions (those aged 14–16) were three times that of Pacific or New Zealand European youth (Ministry of Justice, 2010).

---

[7] Māori are the indigenous people of New Zealand. They are a diverse population affiliated with different Iwi (tribes/tribal group). Māori make up 14.9% of the NZ population (Statistics New Zealand, 2013).

[8] The New Zealand youth justice system separates out "children" aged 10–13 years and "youth" aged 14–16 years. The New Zealand government has recently agreed to include 17-year-olds in the YJS beginning in 2018.

[9] The term "Pacific" is commonly used in New Zealand to refer to people who self-affiliate with one or more of the Island nations in the Pacific: Samoa, Tonga, Fiji, Cook Islands, Niue, Tokelu, Tuvalu and Tahiti (Suaalii-Sauni, Samu, Dunbar, Pulford, & Wheeler, 2012). Pacific peoples are a diverse population that make up 7.4% of the New Zealand population (Statistics New Zealand, 2013).

In 2014, despite only accounting for 20% of the youth population, 60% of total youth apprehended were of Māori descent (Statistics New Zealand, 2016). Research also indicates that Māori youth are not only more likely to enter the youth justice system having committed a less severe offense than non-Māori but also more likely to receive a supervision order than non-Māori, and more likely to be formally dealt with than are non-Māori (Workman, 2016). Moreover, as young Māori appear disproportionately at every stage of the criminal justice process, the effects they experience are cumulative and may be difficult to address at any one single point (Cleland, 2016; Fergusson, Swain-Campbell, & Horwood, 2003).

It has been argued that get-tough approaches have a significant implementation bias with regard to Māori, potentially contributing to their overrepresentation in criminal justice statistics (Workman, 2016). Prior to 2010, children aged between 10 and 14 could only be prosecuted for murder or manslaughter (Lynch, 2012b). An amendment to the 1989 CYPF Act in 2010 meant that children aged 12 and 13 are now prosecutable for offenses that carry a maximum sentence of at least 14 years. Children aged 12 and 13 who have previously offended are prosecutable for offenses that carry a maximum sentence of 10 years (but less than 14 years). Lynch (2012b) argues that these changes mark a move towards using criminal justice proceedings to deal with *social* problems. Nevertheless, despite these problematic issues, there are some initiatives underway to address the overrepresentation of young Māori in the youth justice system.

United States

The Indigenous population in the United States is comprised of two major groupings, American Indians and Alaskan Natives.[10] According to the 2010 Census, 5.2 million (1.7% of the total U.S. population) identified as Indigenous. Most of this population report that they reside outside American Indian and Alaskan Native areas (i.e., American Indian Reservations and Alaskan Native Villages). In terms of identifying regional areas of interest, the 2010 Census also indicates that five states (Alaska, Montana, New Mexico, Oklahoma, and South Dakota) had juvenile populations with more than 10% American Indians or Alaskan Natives (Sickmund & Puzzanchera, 2014).

It is estimated that 22% of Native Americans reside on "Indian Country" (i.e., Native American reservation and trust lands) (U.S Census, 2010). Although those living in Indian Country are subject to tribal, state, and federal jurisdictions, the authority exercising jurisdiction depends on the exact location of the crime and type of crime as well as the status of the perpetrator and victim (Development Services Group, 2016). Those living off reservation are subject to state and federal law only. In general, all federal crimes (i.e., serious crimes such as murder and manslaughter)

[10] In the United States the racial category "Native Americans" refers to American Indians and Alaskan Natives.

committed on Indian Country fall under the jurisdiction of the federal justice system, regardless of the status of the perpetrator and victim. If the offense is not a crime under federal law, jurisdiction might fall under tribal or state law. Interestingly, since 1953 six states allow both the state and the tribe jurisdictional authority and as such, even when a state decides to prosecute an Indigenous youth, the tribe might also prosecute for the same crime. In comparison, when a non-Indigenous youth commits a crime, only the state has jurisdiction (Development Services Group, 2016).

Studies of Indigenous youth crime since the 1960s indicate a clear trend toward disproportionality at key stages across the juvenile justice system. For example, a 1963 study of an Idaho reservation showed rates of youth crime increasing threefold between 1955 and 1960. In 1968, a study of the Pine Ridge Reservation reported a youth crime rate four times higher than the national average. By 2001, however, Indigenous youth (aged 17 or under) across the United States had an alcohol violation arrest rate of 681 per 100,000, nearly double that of all other racial groupings assessed (Perry, 2004). By 2008, analyses indicated that Indigenous youth comprised almost half of the young people processed by the federal court system and about 72% of tribal youth were investigated for violent crimes (Motivans & Snyder, 2011). Further analysis indicated that, of the Indigenous youth admitted to federal prisons and juvenile facilities between 1999 and 2008, most were admitted for assault, burglary and sexual abuse (Motivans & Snyder, 2011).

The extent of the trend toward overrepresentation is perhaps best illustrated in the 2010 National Relative Rate Index (measuring racial disparity in state justice systems), which revealed that Indigenous young people were more likely to be referred to juvenile court, detained while awaiting trial, and found guilty than youths of other cultural backgrounds. Similarly, Sickmund and Puzzanchera (2014) found that Indigenous youth were less likely to be diverted than white youth and more likely than both Black and White youth to be waived from juvenile court to criminal court. These authors also found that, in terms of status offenses (i.e., violations of the law that could only be committed by youth such as running away from home and truancy) between 1995 and 2010, the total status offense case rate for Indigenous youth in the United States was higher than that found for any other racial category. Finally, research on referrals by law enforcement for alleged youth offenses in Alaska between 2003 and 2013 indicates that referrals of Indigenous young people increased by 16.4%, whereas referrals of white youth declined by 19.1% (Parker & Myrstol, 2013).

Contributing Factors

Although a variety of jurisdictional differences exist across the four countries, there is a clear parallel with regard to the issue of Indigenous overrepresentation and youth crime. Interestingly, despite the consistent international evidence, relatively little empirical attention has been paid to identifying and assessing the specific contributing factors to this situation. In addition to the lack of research on the specific factors related to this issue, there is also an absence of any overarching theoretical model which attempts to collate and assess the limited knowledge in this area within a framework aimed at positively responding to this challenge (see e.g., Totten, 2012, 2014).

A review of the above jurisdictional and statistical information across the four countries suggests that, despite a number of important differences, it might be possible to put forward a theoretical framework for assessing the current research (as well as guiding future research). Specifically, it is clear from a review of the literature that studies examining Indigenous youth crime have identified a number of contributing factors that can be divided into those which might be defined as systemic and those which are individual in nature. This fairly clear division is not surprising given that the bulk of research on this area tends to emanate from the disciplines of psychology, sociology, and criminology—disciplines that tend to vary in terms of a social (systemic) paradigm versus a more individual-based paradigm. Given this situation, it is suggested that a more integrated and comprehensive vision of Indigenous youth crime might be attained through a framework which distinguishes the systemic from the individual contributing factors.

Systemic Factors

A review of the literature on Indigenous youth crime appears to indicate that a number of the contributing factors to this issue could be defined as systemic in nature. These factors include colonization, cultural differences, discrimination, and poverty.

Colonization: Research examining the myriad of challenges facing Indigenous people throughout the world indicates that, for many, the issue of colonization is an important and salient contributing factor (Chenhall & Senior, 2009). Colonization has been directly linked to a number of the current challenges confronting Indigenous communities, including those related to physical health (see e.g., Sherwood, 2013), mental health (see e.g., Chenhall & Senior, 2009), alcohol and drug dependency (see e.g., Stewart, 1997), and the disintegration of family and community (see e.g., Browne, 1988).

Although research examining the effects of colonization on Indigenous people has been conducted in a number of countries, there is only a very limited amount of literature directly identifying the implications of colonization on Indigenous people and crime (see e.g., Cull & Wehner, 1998) and even less attention on Indigenous youth crime (see e.g., Monchalin, 2016; Troth & Grainger, 2000). Despite the lack of research on how colonization might be directly linked to Indigenous youth crime, some indications of an indirect link have been put forward. For example, a number of studies (see e.g., Cunneen, 2007; Nielsen & Robyn, 2003) suggest that the association between colonization and Indigenous youth crime could be a by-product of a variety of factors such as: destabilization of traditional cultural practices (including beliefs regarding justice) (see e.g., Bourke & Cox, 1994), implementation of foreign teaching practices (e.g., Monchalin, 2016; Munro-Harrison, Trounson, & Ironfield, 2016), and exploitation (e.g., Totten, 2012).

In Australia, a complex and interrelated set of factors contribute to the overrepresentation of Indigenous Australians in the criminal justice system (Senate Select Committee, 2010), and these factors can be traced back to colonization (Homel et al., 1999). Although highly diverse in dialect, social structures, and cultural practices, prior to colonization Indigenous communities across Australia were self-governing groups with well-established systems of law and order (Bourke & Cox, 1994). As part of the colonization process, Westernized justice systems were adopted leaving Indigenous Australians in the difficult position of being expected to abide by the newly imported foreign laws and practices despite having limited understanding of their parameters and having never agreed to be bound by them.

As is the case with Australia and most other countries that were colonized by the Europeans, Indigenous peoples in Canada had a rich and varied history dating to well before the arrival of European settlers. Although Indigenous peoples in Canada were nomadic and their methods of addressing crime were thought to be nonexistent by the early settlers, Monchalin (2016, p. 53) argues that they "had very advanced laws and spiritual practices" which were simply quite different from those of the European colonizers. Although the practices varied among Indigenous peoples, their legal practices and customs tended to focus on communal values and peoples' relationships to their world.

Commentators in New Zealand also recognize the effect of colonization on Indigenous people and the relationship this has to a variety of challenges including youth crime (Quince, 2007a, 2007b; Tauri & Webb, 2012; Workman, 2011). One explanation for Māori overrepresentation is that there are differential patterns of offending by young Māori (Marie, 2010) and that such patterns stem from the ongoing effects of colonization, structural disadvantage, and cultural alienation (Cleland & Quince, 2014; Workman & McIntosh, 2013; Poa & Wright, 2016). According to some researchers, the effects of colonization were far reaching for Māori and they continue to affect contemporary Indigenous experiences in both the adult and youth justice systems (Bull, 2004; Tauri, 1999; Tauri & Webb, 2012).

In the United States, colonization is central to any account of Native American criminology,[11] as it has positioned Indigenous people within a framework of discrimination, extreme violence, and victimization based on European ideas of "civilized" peoples (see e.g., Monchalin, 2016; Neilsen, 1996). According to Neilsen (1996) the implementation of this framework criminalized local traditional practices, denied Indigenous culture through imposed alien practices and procedures, and sanctioned the forcible dispossession of ancestral lands.

[11] In the 1830s, the U.S Supreme Court declared that the relationship between the U.S. government and Native Americans was that the latter were dependent, domestic nations. They possessed only a right of occupancy to land, not a right of ownership. The Indian Removal Act 1830 mandated that the tribes would exchange their land in the east for land west of the Mississippi and relocate there (Kidwell & Velie, 2005).

Cultural Differences: Research indicates that many of the current challenges related to Indigenous youth crime could also be linked to traditional cultural differences, especially with regard to beliefs about justice (see e.g., Pennell & Burford, 1996). Although the process of colonization included the implementation of foreign laws, many Indigenous people retain their original beliefs regarding a variety of issues such as definitions of offending, perceptions of justice, and conceptualizations of rehabilitation (see e.g., Hart-Mitchell & Pfeifer, 2003). As such, when these traditional beliefs lead to practices and behaviors that are antithetical to colonial-based laws, it results in additional conflict with the various justice agencies such as police, courts, and youth protection. Dawes (2002), for example, has applied this approach to the act of "joyriding" by Australian Indigenous youth and suggested that it is more easily understood as a cultural act aimed at resisting forms of governance rather than simply a crime.

Although undoubtedly an important factor for consideration, a review of the literature also indicates that there is a significant gap regarding identifying how these cultural differences on perceptions of justice relate specifically to the overrepresentation of Indigenous youth across the four countries. Despite the fact that a number of publications refer to the importance of ensuring that general cultural differences between Indigenous and non-Indigenous people are recognized within the context of justice and crime (see e.g., Blagg, 2012; Memmott, Nash, & Pasi, 2015; Silverstein, 2005), very few articles have attempted to delineate the specific cultural differences linked to youth crime (see e.g., Kenny & Lennings, 2007).

Discrimination: When reviewing the international literature on Indigenous youth crime, one area which has received a significant amount of attention relates to the role which discrimination is playing in terms of explaining the overrepresentation of young Indigenous people across the justice system (see e.g., McRae, Nettheim, & Beacroft, 1997). The impact of discriminatory practices and policies has been noted across a variety of the justice agencies including police, courts, and youth justice organizations.

Given that the police are often the first point of contact for Indigenous youth who have been identified as engaging in offending behavior, it is not surprising that this sector has received a substantial share of attention from researchers seeking to identify the degree to which bias might be incorporated into the decision-making of frontline officers. Interestingly, a review of the literature indicates that, in terms of Indigenous people, indications of discrimination by policing agencies tend to be descriptive in nature (i.e., general trends and statistics) rather than specific (i.e., controlled studies identifying direct indications of bias on decision-making and behaviors). In Canada, for example, research indicates that Indigenous people may receive additional levels of arbitrary stops, searches, arrests, and unnecessary use of force (Perry, 2006). Similar trends have been identified in Australia (Blagg, Morgan, Cunneen, & Ferrante, 2005), New Zealand (Andrae, McIntosh, & Coster, 2017; Quince, 2007a, 2007b; Webb, 2009), and the United States (Perry, 2006).

Though informative, the above research is somewhat limited in that it only presents a cumulative picture of systematic bias with regard to Indigenous youth and policing, but does little to increase our knowledge about the underlying factors that lead to this finding. It might be argued however that any effective intervention relating to this situation could be enhanced by gaining a clearer vision of how and why racially disparate decisions are made with regard to policing and Indigenous youth. For example, McKillop and Pfeifer (2004) examined the decision-making of serving police officers in Australia and found that the decisions of officers were influenced by the combination of a number of variables rather than one single factor. Specifically, these authors found that an officer's decision to arrest or caution a youth was directly related to the amount of discretion the officer had as well as the combination of a variety of aspects related to the youth such as age, race, intoxication, and the reaction of the youth to police questioning.

In addition to the police, a variety of other sectors of the criminal justice system have been identified as explanatory sources for issues of overrepresentation. In the United States, for example, a review of 11 studies on racial disparities in juvenile justice systems conducted between 2002 and 2010 reported that race had a negative effect in over half of the case outcomes (Cohen, Feyerherm, Spinny, Stephenson, & Yeide, 2013). In addition, studies have found that Indigenous young people in Arizona are more likely to be detained (Rodriguez, 2008) and less likely to be diverted out of the juvenile justice system when compared to white young people (Leiber, Johnson, & Fox, 2006). Reports of Indigenous youth referrals in Alaska for the period 2003–2013 show that the number of charges of individual offenses declined by 51.7%. Over the period, about 70% of referrals were male. The proportion of Indigenous youth referrals increased over the period by 16.4%, while the number of referrals for non-Indigenous youth decreased. In an analysis of all juvenile case referrals to juvenile courts in Alaska between July 1, 2002 and June 30, 2003, researchers found that "race still mattered at four decision making outcomes even after controlling for legal criteria. Race directly influenced decision making" (Leiber et al., 2006, p. 6).

The literature indicates a similar pattern in New Zealand, where the practices of direct and indirect discrimination within the criminal justice system have been identified as contributing factors for the overrepresentation of Māori in the youth justice system (Jackson, 1988; Tauri, 2005; Workman, 2011, 2016). Latu and Lucas (2008), for example, argue that Māori are under-referred to restorative justice programs compared to non-Māori, and therefore benefit less from diversionary practices. Disparity in sentencing between ethnic groups has also been observed in a New Zealand context. An early study found that young Māori are 1.6–1.8 times more likely to be convicted than non-Māori of the same socio-economic background and self-reported offending record (Fergusson et al., 2003). This bias might have been compounded by a political shift toward more punitive youth justice practices in 2010 (Lynch, 2012b). Finally, it is important to note that government agencies as well as the police themselves have identified the importance of addressing discrimination with regard to Indigenous youth and, as a result, there has been an increased movement toward the development of programs and initiatives aimed at eradicating this bias (see e.g., Blandford & Sarre, 2009).

Poverty (Community Hardship): Another systemic factor which has been identified as contributing to the overrepresentation of Indigenous youth in the criminal justice system is poverty and community hardship (La Prairie, 2002). Research from all four of the countries included in this chapter indicates that exceptional rates of poverty are experienced by Indigenous people and that this situation has a direct relationship to the hardships experienced by both individuals as well as communities (see e.g., Doolan, Najman, Mills, Cherney, & Strathearn, 2013; Eitle & McNulty-Eitle, 2016). According to Statistics Canada, for example, in 2005 the median income for Indigenous peoples aged 24–54 was just over $22,000 (CDN), compared to over $33,000 (CDN) for the same age group of non-Indigenous peoples (Aboriginal Statistics, 2015). In the United States, about one in four Indigenous people live in poverty (Pew Research Center, 2012) and suffers the highest national poverty rate of 27.0% compared to a rate of 11.6% for whites (U.S. Census Bureau, 2010). The importance of the poverty rates experienced by Indigenous people is highlighted by the research literature identifying a consistent relationship between economic hardship and crime (see e.g., Bushway, 2010; Sampson, 2009).

Individual Factors

Although the above review of the systemic factors is an important inclusion, the utility of these factors is limited in terms of providing a remedy to the situation. Specifically, though contributory, these factors are, by definition, infused within social constructions and contexts which will take a significant amount of effort to alter. As such, it is also important to assess the literature relating to the more individual factors associated with Indigenous youth crime. The identification of these factors will allow for the development and implementation of empirically grounded responses to the issue of Indigenous youth crime.

Education: Education has been identified as a key factor that might be associated with the overrepresentation of Indigenous youth in criminal justice systems (Greenberg et al., 2016; Skues, Pfeifer, Oliva, & Wise, in press). For example, according to Statistics Canada, in 2011 just under half of Indigenous people between the ages of 25–64 had a postsecondary qualification compared to almost 65% of the non-Indigenous population. Drawing on data from the 2004 General Social Survey, Brzozowski, Taylor-Butts, and Johnson (2006) suggest that there is a strong association between a lack of education among Indigenous youth and their offending behavior.

Research from Australia indicates a similar pattern with regard to education and Indigenous youth crime (Cunneen, 2006; Higgins & Davis, 2014; Homel et al., 1999). In Australia, Indigenous people remain the most educationally disadvantaged group in the country (Mahuteau, Karmel, Mavromaras, & Zhu, 2015). Despite a high school retention rate increasing from 38.0% in 2002 to 51.1% in 2012, Indigenous Australians continue to be less likely than non-Indigenous Australians to complete secondary education (Karmel et al., 2014). Level of academic performance also continues to differ substantially between Indigenous and non-Indigenous Australian youth, with half of Indigenous Australian students categorized as low performers in mathematics (50% compared to 18% for non-Indigenous students), science (37% compared to 13% for non-Indigenous students), and reading (39% compared to 14% for non-Indigenous students) (Thomson, De Bortoli, & Buckley, 2013). Similarly, in New Zealand, Māori school leavers have the lowest rates of achievement of the National Certificate of Achievement (NCEA) when compared with other ethnic groups (Education Counts, 2017), a disparity which has been linked with the overrepresentation of young Māori in New Zealand's youth justice system (see e.g., Poa & Monod, 2016).

In the United States, the high school dropout rate for Indigenous youth is 11%, compared to 5% for non-Indigenous youth. Moreover, only 17% of Indigenous people hold a college degree compared to 33% of non-Indigenous (Pew Research Center, 2012). As with other jurisdictions, these figures have been identified as having a direct relationship with Indigenous youth crime (Faircloth & Tippeconnic III, 2010).

Drug and Alcohol Use: A review of the literature indicates that although drug and alcohol use are significant contributing factors for youth and crime regardless of cultural background, the issue is especially prevalent for Indigenous youth (see e.g., Armstrong, Guilfoyle, & Melton, 1996a, 1996b). Data from the United States on Indigenous youth crime suggest that alcohol abuse is a major causal factor in offending (Feldstein, Venner & May, 2006). Studies conducted during the 1970s suggest that higher rates of youth crime on reservations in the United States corresponded with alcohol-related offenses. One study on youth crime revealed that Indigenous youth were arrested more often than non-Indigenous youth for less serious crimes and at much higher rates for alcohol and drug-related offenses (Armstrong et al., 1996a, 1996b).

Similar findings have been reported in Australia, Canada and New Zealand (see e.g., Sittner-Hartshorn, Whitbeck, & Prentice, 2015). Stewart (1997), for example, reviewed the consequences of increased alcohol consumption within Indigenous communities in both New Zealand and Australia and found that the rates of usage aligned with a number of community challenges including crime. More recently, Kenny and Lennings (2007) examined 242 incarcerated young offenders in New South Wales (Australia) and found that Indigenous youths were more likely to commit crimes under the influence of alcohol or drugs when compared to non-Indigenous youths. Indigenous youths were also more likely to commit crimes to obtain alcohol or drugs than were their non-Indigenous counterparts.

Importantly, a number of studies have also illustrated the extreme challenges faced by Indigenous youth in remote communities with regard to crime and drug/alcohol use (Armstrong et al., 1996a, 1996b). Senior, Chenhall, and Daniels (2006), for example, identified the significant effect that petrol (i.e., gas) sniffing has had on the health and behaviors of Indigenous people residing in remote communities of Australia. Among other things, the authors note the negative consequences that this behavior has on the youth in the communities, including their criminal behavior.

Mental Health/Intellectual Disability: Over the past 15 years there has been an increased level of attention paid to the relationship between mental health, intellectual ability, and criminal behavior (see e.g., Frize, Kenny, & Lennings, 2008;

Ogloff, Pfeifer, Shepherd, & Ciorciari, 2017; Shepherd, Ogloff, Pfeifer, & Paradies, 2017; Shepherd, Ogloff, Shea, Pfeifer, & Paradies, 2017). Although this area of investigation continues to grow, there has only been a limited amount of research conducted regarding its relationship to Indigenous youth (see e.g., Moore, Gaskin, & Indig, 2015). The lack of empirical attention is puzzling given research indicating the clear challenges faced by this population. In Canada, for example, Indigenous youth face a variety of mental health-related issues including higher levels of drug and/or substance abuse, poorer health, higher death rates due to unintentional injuries, and higher suicide rates than non-Indigenous youth (Joseph, 2012). A 1994 study reported that suicide rates among Indigenous people between the ages of 10 and 29 was 5–6 times higher than among non-Indigenous people; a 2000 report from the Canadian Institute of Health found little improvement, as the suicide rate among Indigenous youth aged 15–24 remained approximately 5–6times higher than that of non-Indigenous youth in Canada (Kirmayer, Brass, Paul, Simpson, & Tait, 2007).

A review of the limited literature produced to date indicates three distinct areas of study regarding the issue of Indigenous youth crime and mental health. First, there appears to be an identified interest in examining what role intellectual disabilities play in Indigenous youth crime. Frize et al. (2008), for example, examined data relating to the interaction between intellectual disability, age, and Indigenous status in a sample of youth on supervised community orders in New South Wales. They identified a relationship between intellectual disability and Indigenous status in terms of risk of re-offending and highlighted the need for additional research in order to more effectively respond to the needs of Indigenous youth with intellectual disabilities. Similar studies have been conducted elsewhere and have also found relationships between Indigenous status and intellectual disabilities (see e.g., Rojas & Gretton, 2007).

Of note is the research in this area which identifies Fetal Alcohol Spectrum Disorders (FASD) as a contributing factor to intellectual disabilities in Indigenous youth (see e.g., Greenberg et al., 2016; Hughes, Clasby, Chitsabesan, & Williams, 2016). Although somewhat difficult to diagnose, Canadian studies suggest that the rates of FASD are notably higher among Indigenous youth than non-Indigenous youth and that FASD can impair intellect, attention, memory, and language and social communication skills, thereby placing affected Indigenous youth at greater risk of making poor life choices (see e.g., Adler, Mueller, Laufer, & Gerkul, 2009).

A second area which appears to be gaining research attention relates to gaining a better understanding of the relationship between mental health and crime with regard to Indigenous youth. Jones and Day (2011), for example, conducted a review of the mental health needs of Indigenous Australian males and females in the criminal justice system and concluded that there was a need for additional research and collaboration across agencies in order to address this situation. The authors also highlighted the need for these initiatives to be implemented within culturally based definitions and perceptions of mental health. Additional areas of empirical investigation include the study of crime and Indigenous youth presenting with attention deficit hyperactivity disorder (Silva, Colvin, Glauert, & Bower, 2014), alexithymia

(Snow, Woodward, Mathis, & Powell, 2016) and childhood trauma (Gover, 2005; Malvaso, Day, Casey, & Corrado, 2017).

A third and final area that appears to be emerging in the literature relates to how the various systemic factors experienced by Indigenous youth (as described above) relate to mental health and criminal behavior. Chenhall and Senior (2009), for example, suggest that the combination of colonization and poverty has resulted in an increased rate of mental health issues for Indigenous youth (e.g., depression, suicide ideation, anxiety) and that this has implications for a variety of issues including crime.

Peers/Associates: Attention has also been given to the empirical examination of how peers/associates influence the behaviors of Indigenous youth with regard to engaging in criminal activity (see e.g., Totten, 2012). Not surprisingly, the bulk of research has revolved around gang affiliation and research on gang affiliation and Indigenous youth across the four countries indicates that the number of young Indigenous people joining these gangs is increasing (see e.g., Caputo & Kelly, 2015; Grant & Feimer, 2007; Hailer & Hart, 1999; Joseph & Taylor, 2003; Totten, 2014).

Some indicators of the relationship between Indigenous youth crime and gang affiliation might be gleaned from studies conducted in Canada (see e.g., Totten, 2014, 2016). Among other things, this research suggests that Indigenous gang involvement can best be addressed through community-wide programs which build on traditional values and beliefs (see e.g., Chettleburgh, 2008; Totten, 2012, 2014). Other research indicates that this trend is attributable to several factors, including: a need for belonging (see e.g., Goldsmith & Halsey, 2013), notoriety (Totten, 2014), and an expression of Indigenous pride (see e.g., Koch & Scherer, 2016).

Criminogenic Needs: There appears to be a very small but important literature developing in relation to the concept of Indigenous youth crime, criminogenic needs, and risk assessment (see e.g., Shepherd, Luebbers, Ferguson, Ogloff, & Dolan, 2014; Thompson & Pope, 2005). Despite the fact that criminogenic needs, and the related risk assessment instruments employed to identify these needs, have received considerable empirical attention, it is only recently that these concepts have been questioned in terms of their applicability to Indigenous samples (Olver, Stockdale, & Wormith, 2009; Samra-Grewa, Pfeifer, & Ogloff, 2000) as well as Indigenous youth samples (Shepherd et al., 2014; Stathis et al., 2008; Thompson & McGrath, 2012).

A review of the literature to date, however, suggests that there has been a limited attempt to assess the degree to which the standard risk assessment model relates to the risk of Indigenous youth engaging in criminal activities based on their criminogenic needs. For example, in a meta-analysis of the predictive accuracy of three well-established risk assessment measures (i.e., the Level of Service Inventory—LSI, Psychopathy Checklist—PCL, and Structured Assessment of Violence Risk in Youth—SAVRY) with young offenders, Olver et al. (2009) commented on the lack of peer-reviewed research examining the predictive utility of such risk assessment measures with Indigenous youth. This was further evidenced within their meta-analysis as predictive validity information was only available for the youth adaptation of the LSI, meaning that the predictive ability of the PCL or SAVRY could not be assessed. It should be noted, however, that results supported the predictive ability of the youth-adapted LSI with Aboriginal youth.

Programs and Interventions

Despite a clear deficit in the empirical research related to Indigenous youth crime, a large number of programs and interventions have been developed and implemented across all four countries. Although empirical examinations of the various culturally based initiatives aimed at curbing Indigenous youth crime are limited, there are a number of promising system-based and targeted frontline initiatives that warrant review. These system-based initiatives may be defined as culturally aligned interventions grounded in the traditions, beliefs, and practices of a defined Indigenous population and implemented across a relevant jurisdiction. In contrast, targeted frontline initiatives may be defined as culturally aligned interventions grounded in the traditions, beliefs, and practices of a defined Indigenous population and targeting a specific population or agency.

System-Based Initiatives

A review of the literature across Australia, Canada, New Zealand, and the United States indicates that the majority of system-based programs appear to have been developed through the combined efforts of Indigenous communities and various agencies within the criminal and/or youth justice sectors. It is also apparent that the descriptions for the majority of these programs are to be found in the gray literature and that very few published empirical studies seem to have been conducted with relation to these programs. A review of the various system-based programs is provided below for each country.

Australia: There are a number of system-based initiatives that have been implemented across Australia that have specific relevance to Indigenous young people. The broadest of these is the establishment of the Children's Courts (Spiranovic, Clare, Clare, & Clare, 2013). These courts are specifically designed to cater to the unique needs of young Australians with a focus on diversion rather than incarceration. The Koori Children's Court is one example of a more culturally responsive, system-based effort to curb the issue of Indigenous youth crime in Australia. The Court aims to increase Indigenous participation in sentencing by integrating Elders into the sentencing process. Although there have been some promising findings reported in relation to the benefits of this initiative, with one study reporting a reduction in recidivism (Harris, 2015), there is still little clear consensus in relation to the courts' overall effectiveness (Marchetti & Daly, 2004). In a recent review of the Victorian Koori Children's Court, however, Borowski (2011) found that the court did foster increased positive participation by Koori youth, their families and their community. Furthermore, it was found that the court increased accountability of the Koori community for Koori youth, promoted community awareness of community codes of conduct, and that it was implemented in accord with its design. Additional research is needed to gain a deeper understanding of the effectiveness of such system-based initiatives.

Youth justice conferencing is another system-based initiative that has been firmly established within the Australian youth justice system (see e.g., Blagg, 1997; Stewart, Hayes, Livingston, & Palk, 2008). Unlike warnings, cautions or court, youth justice conferencing helps young offenders to take steps toward directly repairing the harm they have caused to their victims and the community. Despite being widely implemented across Australia, there is some evidence to suggest that actively involving young Indigenous people and their families in the process has proven challenging (Blagg, 1997). In addition, Weatherburn et al. (2003) have suggested that system-based approaches such as youth justice conferencing and other diversionary schemes can unintentionally overemphasise criminal justice responses and that more progress might be made by exploring and addressing the underlying causes of Indigenous crime.

Community-based supervision is another form of system-based initiatives aimed at reducing the high rate of incarceration of young Indigenous Australians. However, for community-based supervision to be successful with young Indigenous offenders, there are several good-practice principles that should be upheld. According to Trotter, Baidawi, and Evans (2015), a good practice model for community-based supervision of Indigenous youth should recognize the value of culturally informed communications, Indigenous knowledge, the significance of family, and recognition of strengths and achievements.

Canada: Referring to evidence from other countries with similar issues, Corrado et al. (2014, p. 57) suggest that future initiatives should consider developing specialized early intervention programs that focus on "the empowerment and expressed needs of Aboriginal families" as well as expanding the use of restorative justice programs which align with many of the traditional values of Indigenous peoples. Despite the positive initiatives being undertaken, it must be recognized that there is no one type of Indigenous culture, nor one type of issue confronting Indigenous youth. As such, it has been suggested that any proposed responses to issues such as crime should be multi-faceted and should reflect the cultural complexity and historical legacy of Indigenous people (Corrado et al., 2014; Greenberg et al., 2016).

One initiative which acknowledges the unique social and cultural heritage of Indigenous youth has been the recent establishment of Aboriginal Youth Courts. Although the introduction of the First Nations Court opened in Alberta in 2000 (see e.g., Johnson, 2014), it was not until around 2010 that Aboriginal Youth Courts began to appear across the country. In one of the first comprehensive studies of these courts, Clark (2016) reports the courts were meeting their main objectives in supporting Indigenous youth, their families, the larger Indigenous community, and in providing critically important services to Indigenous youth. Related initiatives that have been introduced to honor Indigenous social and cultural values include Healing

Courts, Gladue courts,[12] and tribal courts, all of which are established to help address the issue of Indigenous overrepresentation in the criminal justice system. Another recent notable initiative is found in the *First Nations Community Justice Handbook* which was produced by the Restorative Justice Unit in the province of Saskatchewan in 2010 (Restorative Justice, 2010).

New Zealand: In New Zealand, the family group conference (FGC) process builds on the Māori practice of consensual decision-making to resolve disputes and allows for the inclusion of Māori customs and protocols (Becroft, 2012). Section 208 of the *Children, Young Persons and Their Families Act of 1989* states that measures should enable family groups to find and enact their own solutions to deal with offending by a young person and that sanctions should be the least restrictive available and promote the development of the young person in question.[13] It is on this principle that the FGC process was developed for practice. The FGC process provides a forum for informing primary decisions such as the development of a plan to address the offending by the young person and the inclusion of apologies to the victim or some form of reparation. If the FGC plan is carried out then proceedings are usually withdrawn, and the young person is not charged and does not receive a criminal record. If the plan breaks down, a further FGC is convened or the matter is dealt with by the youth court.

While designed to be culturally appropriate, empowering, and participatory (see e.g., Becroft, 2006), research into Māori experiences of FGCs has found the conferences lack cultural responsiveness and the capability to incorporate a Māori worldview (Moyle & Tauri, 2016; Tauri & Webb, 2012). Becroft (2006) argues that FGCs modify the Western approach to justice by incorporating the family and the victims into the decision-making process, but some elements, such as the presence of state representatives, are at odds with an Indigenous approach to justice. Moreover, the primary aim of the forum is not to restore relationships (which would be concomitant with an Indigenous approach), but to hold the young offender *accountable* for his or her actions (Doolan, 2003; Moyle & Tauri, 2016). Māori are also concerned the FGC process has resulted in a number of removals of Māori children from their families and placement in non-Māori households (Moyle & Tauri, 2016).

In 2008, the Nga Kooti Rangatahi courts initiative was developed in recognition that New Zealand's Youth Justice System was not meeting the needs of young Māori. The philosophy underpinning the courts is that offending is a result of a loss of identity and self-worth, and so the as aim is to reestablish these for the young

[12] Based on a decision by the Supreme Court of Canada on a ruling involving the Gladue case, an amendment was made to the Criminal Code [i.e., section 718.2(e)] allowing the courts to consider an alternative sentence that is culturally more sensitive and appropriate for Aboriginal offenders who are charged with less serious crimes.

[13] Cleland (2016) notes that for young Māori, this meant that they were to be seen in the context of whanau (family), hapu (sub-tribe) and iwi (tribe), and then responded to in a holistic way that took account of their physical and spiritual well-being. The links between families are critically important to the structure of Māori society and are the foundation from which a Māori worldview stems (Durie, 1994).

person in question. Proceedings are held on the Marae[14] where traditional protocols must be respected and adhered to. There are now 14 Rangatahi courts, as well as 2 Pasifika courts, in New Zealand. Rangatahi courts also reconnect young Māori with aspects of their culture including Te Reo (Māori language) (Taumaunu, 2014). An evaluation of the courts in 2012 noted that young Māori appearing there felt welcome and respected, understood the court process, perceived the monitoring process as legitimate, and had positive relationships with youth justice professionals and the Marae community. It is important to note that the Nga Kooti Rangatahi, like the Koori court system in nearby Australia, does not address the structural reasons for offending such as poverty and systemic disadvantage (see e.g., Poa & Wright, 2016; Toki, 2014). It is also unclear whether the courts can address recidivism amongst young Māori (Toki, 2014).

United States: A 2014 report by the *Attorney-General's Advisory Committee on American Indian and Alaska Native Children Exposed to Violence* reviewed the juvenile justice systems across Indigenous communities and made important recommendations for reform. According to Dorgan et al. (2014), even though many Indigenous people regard the juvenile justice system as inappropriate, Tribal Councils have tended to copy juvenile justice codes from non-Indigenous sources.[15] These authors also suggest that tribal juvenile justice systems rely on federal funding which is limited to 3 years for each funding grant, and even where tribes have income streams that provide funding, training is inadequate.

The majority of Indigenous youth go through state juvenile justice systems, but states are not required to notify tribes or involve tribes in such proceedings. It is contended that state juvenile justice programming fails to meet juvenile needs and that states ought to provide funding to tribes so that tribal programs become alternatives to state programs (Dorgan et al., 2014).

Targeted Frontline Initiatives

A review of the literature relating to targeted frontline initiatives aimed at positively responding to the challenges related to Indigenous youth and crime indicates two interesting trends. First, unlike the system-based initiatives, these initiatives tend to be more often represented in the standard academic literature (i.e., peer-reviewed journals) rather than the gray literature. Second, although the below review indicates that a number of these initiatives have been implemented, there seems to be very little coordination relating to their implementation, suggesting a clear need for an overarching framework to guide these types of programs.

---

[14] Traditional meeting grounds of Māori communities.

[15] The Tribal Law and Policy Institute has developed a Tribal Juvenile Justice Code that is intended to assist tribes in developing laws that align with cultural practices and de-institutionalize status offenses (Coalition for Juvenile Justice, 2008/2009).

Australia: Cameron and Telfer (2004) argue that cognitive-behavioral group-based approaches are not as effective with Indigenous Australians as they are with mainstream offenders (see e.g., Blandford & Sarre, 2009). In contrast, these authors argue that more localized and creative approaches are necessary in order to cater to the unique needs of young Indigenous Australians. As such, more options should be made available to divert young Indigenous Australians who commit offenses away from the justice system and toward culturally relevant treatment services (see e.g., Dawes, 2011).

The move toward diversionary programming has led to the empirical examination of several frontline programs (see e.g., Clough, Kim San Lee, & Conigrave, 2008). For example, Clough et al. (2008) describe one such diversionary program implemented in the Northern Territory involving local police identifying appropriate candidates for diversion and referring them to case managers. Once referred, diversion program components were provided locally and included the provision of counseling services, community work or activities, training and education, and restitution-based components. Of the 32 young Indigenous offenders tracked through the diversionary program process, 25 completed the program, 4 were continuing participation, 3 had breached and only one client had reoffended after completion of the diversion program.

Blandford and Sarre (2009) detailed a diversionary program for young Indigenous offenders implemented in two remote communities in South Australia. As part of this initiative, officers must consider diversionary options prior to interviewing young Indigenous Australians suspected of crime in case the allegation is admitted. According to the authors, preliminary outcomes indicate that youth crime in these areas reduced since the implementation of this program and the frequency of re-offending has fallen for those engaged in diversionary services. Finally, Barrett and Baker (2012) detail the potential benefits of a music program implemented within a youth detention setting aimed at encouraging Indigenous residents to engage in music and learning. According to their study findings, these benefits included increased positive social behaviors, confidence and self-esteem, and capacity to engage in and persist with learning tasks.

Canada: In addition to the initiatives aimed at positively impacting the overrepresentation of Indigenous people in the justice system (see e.g., Hart-Mitchell & Pfeifer, 2003), there have also been several notable initiatives that have shown promise in addressing the social and psychological needs of young Indigenous people (see e.g., Grekul & Sanderson, 2011). For example, in 2005 the LEVELS NGO program was started by a group of lawyers whose goal was "to engage the Canadian legal community to positively change lives in Canada and abroad" (LEVEL, 2017). One of their programs (i.e., "Dare to Dream") specifically targets Indigenous youth and offers participants an innovative justice education program that is designed to break down the existing barrier between Indigenous communities and the justice sector.

Another frontline initiative is the Save the Children Foundation which, through the Relationship Framework, draws on Indigenous culture and practices to create a range of programs aimed at assisting young people to deal with some of the social and emotional challenges they are confronted with. One notable initiative that confirms positive steps are being taken is found in the *First Nations Community Justice Handbook* which was produced by the Restorative Justice Unit in the province of Saskatchewan in 2010 (Restorative Justice, 2010). The Handbook was produced with input from local Indigenous groups to ensure ownership and authenticity. Given that most of these initiatives are quite recent, there are no substantive data currently available on the relative effectiveness of individual programs. Collectively, however, they serve to illustrate that a shift is taking place to address the plight of young incarcerated Indigenous peoples.

New Zealand: Outside of the justice system, several initiatives funded by the Ministry of Māori Development through Te Puni Kōkiri[16] have been implemented to continue supporting local, community-based initiatives to address Māori overrepresentation in the youth justice system (Te Puni Kōkiri, 2011a, 2011b). Bicultural programs such as "Te Hurihanga" have also proven to be effective in intervening in young Māori offending (Lynch, 2012b). Nathan (2009a, 2009b) notes the success of this program and argues that these kinds of interventions and holistic approaches are effective with young Māori (as well as other offenders).

Reviews of effective interventions for Indigenous youth offending also note that successful programs include the following components: (1) including a whānau family approach, (2) acknowledging the importance of identity, cultural knowledge and connectivity, (3) addressing educational and vocational needs, (4) ensuring social and economic well-being, and (5) employing people (preferably Māori) who have mana[17] that young people can identify with (Cleland & Quince, 2014; Poa & Wright, 2016; Singh & White, 2000; Youth Justice Advisory Group, 2009). For example, it has been suggested that effective interventions are those that respond to the important community/familial aspects of Indigenous youth rather than focusing on "get tough" approaches such as boot camps, shock probation, scared straight, and para-military training (McLauren, 2000 p. 13). Commentators have also noted the value of program evaluations for future planning, as well as the need for in-depth research into what works to prevent offending by young Māori and how criminal justice agencies respond and react to young Māori who do offend (Workman, 2016).

United States: Numerous initiatives and programs that apply forms of "traditional" justice in Indigenous communities have been supported by states and by the federal government. These programs commonly divert youth, such as first offenders or those with issues of drug or alcohol abuse, out of the formal justice system into alternative systems which apply restorative justice-type solutions. Foremost among these initiatives is the long-established Navaho Peacemaking Program, which began with the establishment of Peacemaker Courts in 1982 and was intended to operate

[16] Te Puni Kōkiri is a Department within the Ministry of Māori Development that leads Māori Public Policy initiatives and advises on policy affecting Māori well-being. They are the principal advisor on Government-Māori relationships, monitoring policy and legislation, and providing government with policy advice.

[17] Respect and status.

as a parallel track to regular western-style criminal courts. Peacemaker Courts provide a forum for parties seeking dispute resolution and utilize the assistance of tribal elders who apply traditional values and concepts. The Peacemaker programs have multiplied over time and more recent iterations have sought to resolve tensions between traditional and western conceptions of justice.

In 2011, the Lower Brule Sioux Tribal community introduced Talking Circles, which provide an alternative to detention for girls adjudicated delinquent, offer a site for their voices to be heard, and provide programs through which youth in conflict with the law can access community mentors and address issues such as drug abuse (Jweied, 2014). Drug and alcohol abuse are similarly addressed within the Ojibwe Tribe through a multijurisdictional Wellness Court, which links state and tribal resources and to which youth eligible for diversion can be referred (Jweied, 2014).

The Office of Juvenile Justice and Delinquency Prevention has evaluated a number of tribal programs for youth which have shown mixed outcomes. An example is the Cherokee Talking Circle (CTC), which targets substance use among Cherokee youth in Oklahoma and applies Cherokee values and concepts of self-reliance. The evaluation found that the program was significantly more effective in reducing substance use and other related problem behaviors among Indigenous youth compared with nonculturally specific substance abuse programs (OJJDP, 2016).

Knowledge Gaps and Future Research

Even the briefest review of the research literature on Indigenous youth crime reveals two very clear trends. First, it is exceptionally obvious that the totality of research into this issue is woefully low when compared to the magnitude of the challenge. Specifically, the accumulated research base on this issue pales in comparison to the overwhelming empirical evidence regarding the overrepresentation of Indigenous youth across the criminal justice system in every country that has been studied. Despite a recent increase in studies examining Indigenous youth crime, it is still abundantly clear that the level of empirical need continues to be significantly greater than the empirical responses from researchers.

A review of the existing literature indicates a second interesting trend. Ironically, most of the scientific attention paid to this issue revolves almost solely around empirically documenting the unacceptable levels of overrepresentation of Indigenous youth in the criminal justice system. As indicated earlier in the chapter, there is clear evidence from all four countries that Indigenous youth receive more punitive treatment across all sectors of youth justice systems when compared to non-Indigenous samples. Although this literature forms a very important function with regard to the demonstration of the gravity of the issue, it is clear that the required level of empirical response to this issue has not been met.

In order to assist with the acceleration of research and empirical examination of this issue, the following gaps have been identified across the existing literature.

Research on Overrepresentation: As noted above, the documentation of overrepresentation of Indigenous youth in the criminal justice system has received the majority of empirical attention to date. The existing literature indicates that Indigenous youth are clearly overrepresented across the justice systems of Australia, Canada, New Zealand, and the United States. Although the data present clear evidence that there is an empirical need to address this challenge, additional research must be conducted regarding aligning the issue with specific identified touchpoints across the youth justice systems. Specifically, it would be helpful to have a clear overview of the specific key aspects of the youth justice system (e.g., police contact, arrest, diversion, adjudication, sentencing, confinement) for each country and then map on the empirical data relating to overrepresentation in order to provide a more formal model regarding where the issue is greatest as well as inter-related connections between touchpoints.

Research on Contributing Factors: Although the research conducted to date appears to cover a broad range of both systemic and individual factors, it is also abundantly clear that each of the identified factors requires additional empirical attention. In addition, a review of the research suggests an interesting trend with regard to the nature of the identified factors. That is, the individual factors studied to date reflect a bias in that they appear to represent the factors one might expect to be present in non-Indigenous youth (e.g., peers, drug, and alcohol use). Although there might be some credence regarding including these factors when examining Indigenous youth crime, the identification of what the contributing factors are should be informed from an Indigenous perspective.

Specifically, it might be that Indigenous people, if asked, would identify a number of additional or different contributing factors than those which have been identified along more traditional criminogenic lines. Evidence for this possibility is found in a recent study by Pfeifer (2017) who asked a sample of Indigenous youth in Canada to identify their reasons for not seeking employment as a police officer. Although several reasons aligned with the literature from other ethnic groups (e.g., perceived discrimination, peer influence), a number of unique reasons were also identified which had previously been absent in the literature (e.g., a belief that any type of criminal record precluded employment as a police officer, advice from family members who were officers not to join).

In addition to the above, future research on the contributing factors related to Indigenous youth crime should attempt to ensure that the issue is investigated within a more integrated framework which looks at the cumulative effect that these factors have as opposed to examining them within a silo. Certainly, there is at least some indication that Indigenous youth who are in contact with the criminal justice system are experiencing several challenges and, as such, a more integrated view is warranted. For example, in their study on incarcerated Indigenous youth in Australia, Kenny and Lennings (2007) found that a significant segment of their sample were experiencing a number of systemic and individual contributing factors, including family hardship, poverty, social disadvantage, substance use and conduct disorder. These findings emphasize that future research should not only empirically identify the individual contributing factors related to Indigenous youth crime but also empirically examine how these factors combine and integrate.

Research on Programming: As indicated above, while a review of the research to date on the various system-based and focused programs aimed at Indigenous youth crime provides a sense of how this issue might be positively addressed, it also highlights several gaps in the literature. First and foremost, this issue requires additional empirical evidence. Even though a number of successful programs have been developed across the four countries, there remains a clear need for additional research. Second, there is also a clear need for ensuring these programs are culturally grounded, theoretically sound, and empirically supported. These three factors form the foundation of successful programming and as such, additional attention must be given to ensure this triad of factors is included in the research and practice related to Indigenous youth programs. Achieving this goal will of course be contingent upon the call for additional empirical assessment of the contributing factors identified above. Finally, as indicated above, there is a need to develop a framework for the development of effective programming.

Cultural Responsivity: Although there is a genuine need to gain an empirical understanding of the issue of Indigenous youth crime, an assessment of the research conducted to date remains woefully inadequate given the overrepresentation figures (see e.g., Greenberg et al., 2016). Importantly, a review of the limited number of studies conducted to date provides strong evidence for the importance of cultural responsivity with regard to the study of Indigenous youth crime (see e.g., Homel et al., 1999; Pavkov, Travis, Fox, Bear-King, & Cross, 2010). In a review of the research, Banks (2000, p. 15) highlights the need for cultural specificity and suggests it might be attained by articulating a "holistic and contextual ethnography" of a society. Here, a culturally specific criminology would explain how traditional social controls were affected by the colonial project and how they have persisted, suggesting a need for justice constructs among Native American groups to be culturally specific (Dumont, 1996). Like Banks, Marenin (1992) argues for an approach that focuses more on the lived experience of specific Native American communities, identifying factors in villages such as tensions between the dominant culture and Native American culture and "social and personal identities and conflicts."

Future research should continue to highlight the importance of engaging in studies that are both culturally responsive and culturally sensitive (see e.g., Goodwill & Giannone, 2017; Melander, Sittner-Hartshorn, & Whitbeck, 2013). That is, the design, implementation and analysis of research projects should be accomplished through a lens which prioritizes the need for this research as opposed to viewing the research as simply an "extension" of existing knowledge on non-Indigenous youth (see e.g., Shaffer, McCuish, Corrado, Behnken, & DeLisi, 2015). Specifically, a review of the literature indicates that often research in this area is conducted to demonstrate how an existing measure of concept can be modified in order to be adapted for an Indigenous sample rather than research which is aimed at identifying original measures and concepts related to this population (see e.g., Allard, Rayment-McHugh, Adams, Smallbone, & McKillop, 2016; Olver et al., 2009; Shepherd et al., 2014; Stathis et al., 2008)

Gender-Responsivity: If one were to describe the lack of culturally responsive research on Indigenous youth crime as a gap, then the lack of gender-responsive research on this issue would have to be described as a massive canyon. A review of the literature indicates that there has been only the most minimal attention paid to the challenges faced by Indigenous young females when it comes to crime and the criminal justice system. This situation is surprising given that there is a clear indication that Indigenous females are also overrepresented in the criminal justice system. In addition, recent research indicates that a number of the factors that have been identified as contributing to the challenges faced by young Indigenous males are now being experienced by females as well, such as gang affiliation and violence (Dhillon, 2015). It is essential that future research in this area not only strive to ensure that studies include females but should also be directed at identifying and responding to the unique challenges facing this group.

Technology: One final area that warrants mention relates to the need for research on how technology might be employed in assisting with the amelioration of the challenges faced by Indigenous youth in the criminal justice system. To date, the issue of technology and Indigenous youth crime has been limited to research involving the use of technology-based monitoring programs such as Global Positioning Systems and electronic monitoring (see e.g., Willoughby & Nellis, 2016). Although recent publications indicate a clear movement toward embracing technology as an educational and rehabilitative tool within the justice system (see e.g., King et al., 2017), there is very little relating to this movement with regard to Indigenous people. One exception is the *iTalk* program currently delivered by the Northern Territory Correctional Service in Australia, which seeks to assist Indigenous male offenders to give back to the community through the creation of computer-generated stories which reflect traditional beliefs and lore. Early assessment of this program indicates that participation has had a positive influence on the self-esteem, motivation, and cultural strength (Pfeifer, in review).

Conclusion

Although research relating to Indigenous youth crime appears to be limited at best, there is a strong consensus that the subject is one of importance to governments, youth justice agencies, and researchers internationally. As indicated throughout this chapter, there is a clear disconnect between the empirical attention paid to this issue and the magnitude of the challenge, especially when one considers the consistent and significant statistical rates of overrepresentation. Given this situation, aside from highlighting the need for additional scientific attention and insight into the area of Indigenous youth crime, this chapter seeks to provide researchers and others with a comprehensive overview of what has been done to date, where the gaps are, and a proposed framework for moving forward.

A review of the chapter indicates a number of guiding principles which might be useful for researchers, government agencies and frontline service providers working within the sphere of Indigenous youth crime. To begin with, any research initiative or intervention must be designed in a way that responds to the jurisdictional and contextual aspects of the population of interest. The information provided at the beginning of this chapter indicates that, although there are a number of identifiable consistencies across the various Indigenous peoples from the four countries examined (e.g., overrepresentation, impacts of colonization, and economic hardship), there are also very distinct historical, contextual, and jurisdictional differences which must be acknowledged as part of any research or intervention initiative. For example, the definitional ages of youth vary across jurisdictions, as do the constitutional issues and governmental approaches related to Indigenous populations. As such, it is important that researchers examine and understand the jurisdictional context related to specific Indigenous peoples when designing studies.

In addition to the above, future research should aim to clearly identify whether studies are aimed at affecting the systemic or individual contributing factors related to Indigenous youth crime. A review of the current literature on Indigenous youth crime indicates that the various identified contributing factors can be delineated as those which are systemic (e.g., colonization, cultural differences, discrimination) and those which are individual (e.g., education, alcohol/drug use, mental health/intellectual disability). Although it is clear that both systemic and individual factors affect Indigenous youth crime, future research should be designed in a way that allows for a direct link to the two overarching categories (i.e., systemic and individual) as well as one or more of the category factors (e.g., education, discrimination, drug/alcohol use).

Finally, future research should pay particular attention to the identified gaps in the literature. Specific attention should be paid to the fact that there is a strong need to design and implement research projects that address the specific needs of Indigenous youth who are involved in the criminal justice system. To date, a number of studies on youth crime appear to either exclude Indigenous samples or include Indigenous youth as a sub-sample of interest. Future research should ensure Indigenous youth are recognized as the sample of interest in order to ensure that the challenges faced by this population are more effectively met by both researchers and agencies. As noted by G. Stanley Hall in the opening quote to this chapter, an empirical understanding of youth and the challenges they face is incomplete if it does not highlight and include the Indigenous experience.

Acknowledgment The authors wish to thank Teagan Connop-Galer for her assistance with the preparation of this chapter.

References

Adler, F., Mueller, G. O. W., Laufer, W. S., & Gerkul, J. (2009). *Criminology* (Canadian ed.). Toronto: McGraw-Hill Ryerson.

Allard, T., Rayment-McHugh, S., Adams, D., Smallbone, S., & McKillop, N. (2016). Responding to youth sexual offending: A field-based practice model that "closes the gap" on sexual recidivism among Indigenous and non-Indigenous males. *Journal of Sexual Aggression, 22*, 82–94. https://doi.org/10.1080/13552600.2014.1003107

Amnesty International Australia. (2015). *A brighter tomorrow: Keeping Indigenous kids in the community and out of detention in Australia*. Broadway, New South Wales: Amnesty International Australia.

Andrae, D., McIntosh, T., & Coster, S. (2017). Marginalised: An insider's view of the state, state policies in New Zealand and gang formation. *Critical Criminology, 25*, 119–135. https://doi.org/10.1007/s10612-016-9325-8

Armstrong, T. L., Guilfoyle, M. H., & Melton, A. P. (1996a). Traditional approaches to tribal justice. In M. O. Neilsen & R. A. Silverman (Eds.), *Native Americans, crime and justice* (pp. 46–51). Boulder: Westview Press.

Armstrong, T. L., Guilfoyle, M. H., & Melton, A. P. (1996b). Native American delinquency. In M. O. Neilsen & R. A. Silverman (Eds.), *Native Americans, crime, and justice* (pp. 75–88). Boulder, CO: Westview Press.

Australian Institute of Health and Welfare. (2012). *Indigenous young people in the juvenile justice system: 2010-11. Bulletin 109 (Catalogue No. AUS164)*. Canberra, ACT: Australian Institute of Health and Welfare.

Australian Institute of Health and Welfare. (2014). *Youth detention population in Australia 2014. Juvenile justice series no. 16 (Catalogue No. JUV53)*. Canberra, ACT: Australian Institute of Health and Welfare.

Australian Institute of Health and Welfare. (2016). *Youth Justice in Australia: 2014–15. Bulletin no. 133 (Catalogue No. AUS198)*. Canberra, ACT: Australian Institute of Health and Welfare.

Australian Law Reform Commission (ALRC). (1997). Seen and heard: Priority for children in the legal process (ALRC Report 84). Retrieved from http://www.alrc.gov.au/publications/18-childrens-involvement-criminal-justice-processes/age-thresholds-criminal-justice-pro

Banks, C. (2000). Developing cultural specificity for a cultural criminology. In C. Banks (Ed.), *Developing cultural criminology: Theory and practice in Papua New Guinea* (pp. 15–50). Sydney, Australia: Sydney Institute of Criminology.

Barrett, M. S., & Baker, J. S. (2012). Developing learning identities in and through music: A case study of the outcomes of a music programme in an Australian juvenile detention centre. *International Journal of Music Education, 30*(3), 244–259. https://doi.org/10.1177/0255761411433721

Becroft, A. (2006). Children and young people in conflict with the law: Asking the hard questions. *Juvenile and Family Court Journal, 57*, 1–37. https://doi.org/10.1111/j.1755-6988.2006.tb00129.x

Becroft, A. (2012). Access to youth justice in New Zealand: "The very good, the good, the bad and the ugly". *Auckland University Law Review, 18*, 23–35.

Blagg, H. (1997). A just measure of shame? Aboriginal youth conferencing in Australia. *British Journal of Criminology, 37*, 481–501. https://doi.org/10.1093/oxfordjournals.bjc.a014193

Blagg, H. (2012). Re-imagining youth justice: Cultural contestation in the Kimberley region of Australia since the 1991 royal commission into Aboriginal deaths in custody. *Theoretical Criminology, 16*, 481–498. https://doi.org/10.1177/1362480611436360

Blagg, H., Morgan, N., Cunneen, C., & Ferrante, A. (2005, September). Systemic racism as a factor in the overrepresentation of Aboriginal people in the Victorian criminal justice system. Human Rights Commission. Retrieved from http://www.humanrightscommission.vic.gov.au/our-resources-and-publications/reports/item/1391-systemic-racism-as-a-factor-in-the-over-representation-of-aboriginal-people-in-the-victorian-criminal-justice-system-sep-2005

Blandford, J., & Sarre, R. (2009). Policing in South Australia's remote and rural communities: Preliminary observations from a novel police diversionary strategy for young Indigenous offenders. *Police Practice and Research, 10*, 187–197. https://doi.org/10.1080/15614260802381075

Borowski, A. (2011). In Courtroom 7 - the Children's Koori Court at work: Findings from an evaluation. *International Journal of Offender Therapy and Comparative Criminology, 55*, 1110–1134.

Bourke, C., & Cox, H. (1994). Two laws: One land. In C. Bourke, E. Bourke, & W. Edwards (Eds.), *Aboriginal Australia* (pp. 49–64). St. Lucia: University of Queensland Press.

Boyce, J. (2016). *Victimization of aboriginal people in Canada, 2014*. Ottawa, ON: Statistics Canada.

Brame, R., Mazerolle, P., & Piquero, A. (2010). Criminal career progression among serious youthful offenders in Australia. *Journal of Criminal Justice, 38*, 340–347. https://doi.org/10.1016/j.jcrimjus.2010.04.001

Browne, E. (1988). The Australian family 1788-1888-1988. *Australian and New Zealand Journal of Family Therapy, 9*, 1–8. https://doi.org/10.1002/j.1467-8438.1988.tb01283.x

Brzozowski, J. A., Taylor-Butts, A., & Johnson, S. (2006). Victimization and offending among the Aboriginal population in Canada. *Juristat,* 26(3). Catalogue no. 85-002-XIE.

Bull, S. (2004). 'The land of murder, cannibalism, and all kinds of atrocious crimes?' Māori and crime in New Zealand, 1853-1919. *British Journal of Criminology, 44*, 496–519. https://doi.org/10.1093/bjc/azh029

Bushway, S. (2010). Economy and crime. *The Criminologist, 35*, 1–5.

Caputo, T., & Kelly, K. (2015). Community level factors and concerns over youth gangs in first nation communities. *Journal of Gang research, 22*, 37–52.

Carney, T., & Myers, B. (2012). Effectiveness of early interventions for substance-using adolescents: Findings from a systematic review and meta-analysis. *Substance Abuse Treatment, Prevention, and Policy, 7*, 25–40. https://doi.org/10.1186/1747-597X-7-25

Carrington, K., & Pereira, M. (2009). *Offending youth: Sex, crime and justice*. Sydney, New South Wales: The Federation Press.

Cameron, H., & Telfer, J. (2004). Cognitive-behavioural group work: Its application to specific offender groups. *Howard Journal of Criminal Justice, 43*(1), 47–64. https://doi.org/10.1111/j.1468-2311.2004.00310.x

Chenhall, R., & Senior, K. (2009). Those young people are all crankybella: Indigenous youth mental health and globalization. *International Journal of Mental Health, 38*, 28–43. https://doi.org/10.2753/IMH0020-7411380302

Chettleburgh, M. C. (2008). *Young thugs: Inside the dangerous world of Canadian street gangs*. Toronto, ON: Harper Collins Pub.

Children's Court of NSW. (2016). Youth Koori court. Retrieved from http://www.childrenscourt.justice.nsw.gov.au/Documents/Youth%20Koori%20Court%20A4_Accessible.pdf

Clark, S. (2016). *Evaluation of the Aboriginal youth court, Toronto. Report prepared for the Ontario Court of Justice*. Toronto, ON: Ontario Court of Justice.

Cleland, A. (2016). Portrait of the accused as a young man: New Zealand's harsh treatment of young people who commit serious crimes. *The Round Table, 105*, 377–387. https://doi.org/10.1080/00358533.2016.1205360

Cleland, A., & Quince, K. (2014). *Youth justice in Aotearoa New Zealand: Law, policy and critique*. Wellington, New Zealand: Lexis Nexis New Zealand.

Clough, A. R., Kim San Lee, K., & Conigrave, K. M. (2008). Promising performance of a juvenile justice diversion programme in remote Aboriginal communities, Northern Territory, Australia. *Drug and Alcohol Review, 27*, 433–438. https://doi.org/10.1080/09595230802089693

Coalition for Juvenile Justice. (2008/2009). *Biennial report*. Washington, DC: Coalition for Juvenile Justice.

Cohen, M., Feyerherm, W., Spinny, E., Stephenson, R., & Yeide, M. (2013). *Disproportionate minority contact in the U.S juvenile justice system: A review of the DMC literature 2001–2010*. Washington DC: Office of Juvenile Justice and Delinquency Prevention.

Colenutt, A., & Toye, M. A. (2012). *Critical crossroads: Youth, criminal justice and literacy*. Calgary, AB: Bow Valley College.

Corrado, R. R., Kuehn, S., & Margaritescu, I. (2014). Policy issues regarding the over-representation of incarcerated Aboriginal young offender in a Canadian context. *Youth Justice, 14*, 40–62. https://doi.org/10.1177/1473225413520361

Cull, D. M., & Wehner, D. M. (1998). Australian Aborigines: Cultural factors pertaining to the assessment and treatment of Australian Aboriginal sexual offenders. In W. L. Marshall, Y. M. Fernandez, S. M. Hudson, & T. Ward (Eds.), *Sourcebook for treatment programs for sexual offenders* (pp. 431–444). New York: Plenum Press.

Cunneen, C. (2006). Racism, discrimination and the over-representation of Indigenous people in the criminal justice system: Some conceptual and explanatory issues. *Current Issues in Criminal Justice, 17*, 329–346. https://doi.org/10.2139/ssrn.2298241

Cunneen, C. (2007). The criminalization of Indigenous people. In T. D. Gupta, C. E. James, R. C. A. Maaka, G. E. Galabuzi, & C. Andersen (Eds.), *Race and racialization: Essential readings* (pp. 266–274). Toronto, ON: Canadian Scholars' Press.

Cunneen, C., & White, R. (2007). *Juvenile justice: Youth and crime in Australia*. Melbourne, VIC: Oxford University Press.

Dawes, G. (2002). Figure eights, spin outs and power slides: Aboriginal and Torres Straight Islander youth and the culture of joyriding. *Journal of Youth Studies, 5*(2), 196–208. https://doi.org/10.1080/13676260220134449

Dawes, G. D. (2011). The challenges of reintegrating Indigenous youth after their release from detention. *Journal of Youth Studies, 14*, 693–707. https://doi.org/10.1080/13676261.2011.580338

Development Services Group. (2016). *Tribal youth in the juvenile justice system: Literature review*. Washington, DC: Office of Juvenile Justice and Delinquency Prevention.

Dhillon, K. K. (2015). Indigenous girls and the violence of settler colonial policing. *Decolonization: Indigeneity, Education & Society, 4*(2), 1–31.

Doolan, I., Najman, J. M., Mills, R., Cherney, A., & Strathearn, L. (2013). Does child abuse and neglect explain the overrepresentation of Aboriginal and Torres Strait Islander young people in youth detention? Findings from a birth cohort study. *Child Abuse & Neglect, 37*, 303–309. https://doi.org/10.1016/j.chiabu.2012.12.005

Doolan, M. (2003). *Restorative practices and family empowerment: Both/and or either/or? Family Rights Newsletter*. London: Family Rights Group.

Dorgan, B. L., Shenandoah, J., Bigfoot, D. S., Broderick, E., Brown, E. F., Davidson, V., & Zimmerman, M. J. B. (2014). *Attorney General's advisory committee on American Indian and Alaska native children exposed to violence: Ending violence so children can thrive*. Washington, DC: U.S Department of Justice.

Dumont, J. (1996). Justice and native peoples. In M. O. Nielsen, O. Marianne, & R. Silverman (Eds.), *Native Americans, crime and justice* (pp. 20–33). Boulder, CO: Westview Press.

Durie, M. H. (1994). *Whaiora: Māori Health Development*. Auckland: Oxford University Press.

Education Counts. (2017). School leavers with NCEA level 3 or above. Retrieved from https://www.educationcounts.govt.nz/statistics/indicators/main/education-and-learning-outcomes/1891

Eitle, D., & McNulty-Eitle, T. (2016). General strain theory and delinquency: Extending a popular explanation to American Indian youth. *Youth & Society, 48*, 470–495. https://doi.org/10.1177/0044118X13499593

Faircloth, S. C., & Tippeconnic, J. W., III. (2010). *The rropout/graduation rate crisis among American Indian and Alaska native students: Failure to respond places the future of native peoples at risk*. Los Angeles, CA: The Civil Rights Project/Proyecto Derechos Civiles at UCLA. www.civilrightsproject.ucla.edu

Feldstein, S. W., Venner, K. L., & May, P. A. (2006). American Indian/Alaska Native alcohol-related incarceration and treatment. *American Indian and Alaska Native Mental Health Research, 13*, 1–22. http://dx.doi.org/10.5820/aian.1303.2006.1

Fergusson, D., Swain-Campbell, N. R., & Horwood, L. J. (2003). Arrests and convictions for cannabis related offences in a New Zealand birth cohort. *Drug and Alcohol Dependence, 70*, 53–63. https://doi.org/10.1016/S0376-8716(02)00336-8

Frize, M., Kenny, D., & Lennings, C. (2008). The relationship between intellectual disability, Indigenous status and risk of reoffending in juvenile offenders on community orders. *Journal of Intellectual Disability Research, 52*, 510–519. https://doi.org/10.1111/j.1365-2788.2008.01058.x

Galaway, B., & Hudson, J. (1996). *Restorative justice: International perspectives*. Amsterdam: Kugler Publications.

Goldsmith, A., & Halsey, M. (2013). Cousins in crime: Mobility, place and belonging in Indigenous youth co-offending. *British Journal of Criminology, 53*, 1157–1177. https://doi.org/10.1093/bjc/azt039

Goodwill, A., & Giannone, Z. (2017). From research to practice: Bridging the gaps for psychologists working in Indigenous communities affected by gangs. *Canadian Psychology, 58*, 345–353. https://doi.org/10.1037/cap0000091

Goran, S. (2001). Healing the victim, the young offender, and the community via restorative justice: An international perspective. *Issues in Mental Health Nursing, 22*, 137–149. https://doi.org/10.1080/01612840121244

Gover, A. R. (2005). Native American ethnicity and childhood maltreatment as variables in perceptions and adjustments to boot camp vs. "traditional" correctional settings. *Journal of Offender Rehabilitation, 40*, 177–198. https://doi.org/10.1300/J076v40n03_09

Grant, C. M., & Feimer, S. (2007). Street gangs in Indian country: A clash of cultures. *Journal of Gang Research, 14*, 27–66.

Grant, P. (2009). The children's Koori court in Victoria. Retrieved from https://www.childrenscourt.vic.gov.au/sites/default/files/Prato_presentation_final.pdf

Green, R. (2016). Understanding the Youth Criminal Justice Act. In J. Winterdyk & R. Smandych (Eds.), *Youth at risk and youth justice: A Canadian overview* (2nd ed.). Don Mills, ON: Oxford University Press.

Greenberg, H., Grekul, J., & Nelson, R. (2016). Aboriginal youth in Canada. In J. Winterdyk & R. Smandych (Eds.), *Youth at risk and youth justice: A Canadian overview* (2nd ed.). Don Mills, ON: Oxford University Press.

Grekul, J., & Sanderson, K. (2011). 'I thought peple would be mean and shout.' Introducing the Hobbema Community Cadet Corps: A response to youth gang involvement? *Journal of Youth Studies, 14*, 41–57. https://doi.org/10.1080/13676261.2010.489602

Grigorenko, E. (2012). *Handbook of juvenile forensic psychology and psychiatry*. New York, NY: Springer.

Hailer, J. A., & Hart, C. B. (1999). A new breed of warrior: The emergence of American Indian youth gangs. *Journal of Gang Research, 7*, 23–33.

Hall, G. S. (1904). *Adolescence: It's psychology and its relations to physiology, anthropology, sociology, sex, crime, religion and education (v.2)*. New York: Appleton & Company.

Harris, A. (2015). *Aboriginal corrections*. Ottawa, ON: Correctional Service Canada.

Hart-Mitchell, R., & Pfeifer, J. E. (2003). From jails to healing lodges: Evaluating the impact of correctional environments on offender adaptation. *Canadian Journal of Police and Security Services, 1*, 95–104.

Hartney, C. (2008). *Native American youth and the juvenile justice system*. Washington, DC: The National Council on Crime and Delinquency.

Higgins, D., & Davis, K. (2014). *Law and justice: Prevention and early intervention programs for Indigenous youth. Resource sheet no. 34. Produced by the closing the gap clearinghouse*. Canberra, ACT: Australian Institute of Health and Welfare.

Holland, C. (2015). *Close the gap: Progress and priorities report 2015*. Canberra, ACT: Close the Gap Campaign Steering Committee.

Homel, R., Lincoln, R., & Herd, B. (1999). Risk and resilience: Crime and violence prevention in Aboriginal communities. *Australian and New Zealand Journal of Criminology, 32*, 182–196. https://doi.org/10.1177/000486589903200207

Hudson, J., Morris, A., Maxwell, G., & Galaway, B. (1996). *Family group conferences: Perspectives on policy & practice*. Annandale, New South Wales: Federation Press.

Hughes, N., Clasby, B., Chitsabesan, P., & Williams, H. (2016). A systematic review of the prevalence of foetal alcohol syndrome disorders among young people in the criminal justice system. *Cogent Psychology, 3*, 1214213.

Ioane, J., Lambie, I., & Percival, T. (2016). A comparison of Pacific, Maori, and European violent youth offenders in New Zealand. *International Journal of Offender Therapy and Comparitive Criminology, 60*, 657–674. https://doi.org/10.1177/0306624X14560725

Jackson, M. (1988). *The Māori and the criminal justice system: A new perspective: He whaipaanga hou. Part 2 (Government Report)*. Wellington, New Zealand: Department of Justice.

Johnson, S. (2014). Developing first nations courts in Canada: Elders as foundational to Indigenous therapeutic jurisprudence. *Journal of Indigenous Social Development, 3*, 1–14.

Joseph, B. (2012). 8 key issues for Aboriginal people in Canada. Retrieved from http://www.ictinc.ca/blog/8-key-issues-for-aboriginal-people-in-canada

Joseph, J., & Taylor, D. (2003). Native-American youths and gangs. *Journal of Gang Research, 10*, 45–54.

Jones, R., & Day, A. (2011). Mental health, criminal justice and culture: Some ways forward? *Australasian Psychiatry, 19*(4), 325–330. https://doi.org/10.3109/10398562.2011.579613

Jweied, M. (2014). *Expert working group report: Native American traditional justice Practices*. Washington, DC: U.S. Department of Justice and U.S. Department of the Interior. Retrieved from https://www.justice.gov/sites/default/files/atj/legacy/2014/10/09/expert-working-group-report--native-american-traditional-justice-practices.pdf

Karmel, T., Misko, J., Blomberg, D., Bednarz, A., & Atkninson, G. (2014). *Improving labour market outcomes through education and training. Issues paper no. 9. Produced for the closing the gap clearinghouse*. Canberra: Australian Institute of Health and Welfare & Melbourne: Australian Institute of Family Studies.

Kenny, D. T., & Lennings, C. J. (2007). Cultural group differences in social disadvantage, offence characteristics, and experience of childhood trauma and psychopathology in incarcerated juvenile offenders in NSW, Australia: Implications for service delivery. *Psychiatry, Psychology and Law, 14*, 294–305. https://doi.org/10.1375/pplt.14.2.294

Kidwell, C. S., & Velie, A. (2005). *Native American studies*. Lincoln: University of Nebraska Press.

King, C. M., Heilbrun, K., Kim, N. Y., McWillimas, K., Phillips, S., Barbera, J., & Fretz, R. (2017). Tablet computers and forensic and psychological assessment: A randomized control study. *Law and Human Behavior, 41*, 468–477. https://doi.org/10.1037/lhb0000245

Kirmayer, L. J., Brass, G. M., Paul, K., Simpson, C., & Tait, C. (2007). *Suicide among Aboriginal people of Canada*. Ottawa, ON: Aboriginal Healing Foundation.

Koch, J., & Scherer, J. (2016). Redd alert! (Re)articulating Aboriginal gang violence in Western Canada. *Aboriginal Policy Studies, 6*, 34–62.

La Prairie, C. (2002). Aboriginal over-representation in the criminal justice system: A tale of nine cities. *Canadian Journal of Criminology, 44*, 181–208.

Latimer, J., & Foss, L. C. (2005). The sentencing of Aboriginal and non-Aboriginal youth under the young offenders act: A multivariate analysis. *Canadian Journal of Criminology and Criminal Justice, 45*, 481–500.

Latu, A., & Lucas, A. (2008). Discretion in the New Zealand criminal justice system: The position of Māori and Pacific Islanders. *Journal of South Pacific Law, 12*, 84–93.

Leiber, M. J., Johnson, J., & Fox, K. (2006). *An examination of the factors that influence justice decision making in Anchorage and Fairbanks, Alaska: An assessment study*. Alaska: Department of Health and Social Services, Division of Juvenile Justice.

LEVEL, Changing lives through law. (2017). Retrieved from https://leveljustice.org/en/youth-outreach

Livingston, M., Stewart, A., Allard, T., & Ogilvie, J. (2008). Understanding juvenile offending trajectories. *The Australian and New Zealand Journal of Criminology, 41*, 345–363. https://doi.org/10.1375/acri.41.3.345

Ludbrook, R. (2009). New Zealand's obligations under international law: What influence have they had on our youth justice system? In G. Maxwell (Ed.), *Addressing the causes of offending: What is the evidence?* Institute of Policy Studies: Wellington.

Lynch, M., Buckman, J., & Krenske, L. (2003). *Youth justice: Criminal trajectories*. Canberra, ACT: Australian Institute of Criminology.

Lynch, N. (2012a). *Youth justice in New Zealand*. Wellington, New Zealand: Brookers.

Lynch, N. (2012b). Playing catch-up? Recent reform of New Zealand's youth justice system. *Criminology and Criminal Justice, 12*, 507–526. https://doi.org/10.1177/1748895811432013

Mahuteau, S., Karmel, T., Mavromaras, K., & Zhu, R. (2015). Educational outcomes of young indigenous Australians. Report submitted to the National Centre for Student Equity in Higher Education (NCSEHE), Australia. National Institute of Labour Studies (NILS), Flinders University, Adelaide, Australia. Retrieved from https://www.ncsehe.edu.au/wp-content/uploads/2015/11/Educational-Outcomes-of-Young-Indigenous-Australians-Report.pdf

Malekieh, J. (2017). *Youth correctional statistics in Canada, 2015/1016. Juristat (Catalogue no. 85-002-x)*. Ottawa, ON: Statistics Canada.

Malvaso, C., Day, A., Casey, S., & Corrado, R. (2017). Young offenders, maltreatment, and trauma: A pilot study. *Psychiatry, Psychology and Law, 24*, 458–469. https://doi.org/10.1080/13218719.2016.1247682

Marchetti, E., & Daly, K. (2004). *Indigenous courts and justice practices in Australia (no. 277)*. Canberra, ACT: Australian Institute of Criminology.

Marenin, O. (1992). Explaining patterns of crime in the native villages of Alaska. *Canadian Journal of Criminology, 34*, 339–368.

Marie, D. (2010). Māori and criminal offending: A critical appraisal. *Australian and New Zealand Journal of Criminology, 43*, 282–300. https://doi.org/10.1375/acri.43.2.282

Martin, F. A. (2014). The coverage of American Indians and Alaskan natives in criminal justice and criminology introductory textbooks. *Critical Criminology, 22*, 237–256. https://doi.org/10.1007/s10612-013-9216-1

McKillop, D., & Pfeifer, J. E. (2004). Decision-making and young offenders: Examining the role of discretion in police judgments. *Canadian Journal of Police and Security Services, 2*, 209–214.

McLauren, K. (2000). *Tough is not enough getting smart about youth crime: A review of research on what works to reduce offending by young people*. Wellington, New Zealand: Ministry of Youth Affairs.

McRae, H., Nettheim, G., & Beacroft, L. (1997). *Indigenous legal issues: Commentary and materials*. North Ryde, New South Wales: LBC Information Services.

Melander, L. A., Sittner-Hartshorn, K. J., & Whitbeck, L. B. (2013). Correlates of bullying behaviors among a sample of North American Indigenous adolescents. *Journal of Adolescence, 36*, 675–684. https://doi.org/10.1016/j.adolescence.2013.05.003

Memmott, P., Nash, D., & Pasi, C. (2015). Cultural relativism and Indigenous family violence. In A. Day & E. Fernandez (Eds.), *Preventing violence in Australia: Policy, practice and solutions*. Annandale, New South Wales: Federation Press.

Ministry of Justice. (2010). *Child and youth offending statistics: An overview of child and youth offending statistics in New Zealand: 1992–2008*. Wellington, New Zealand: Ministry of Justice.

Ministry of Justice. (2013). *Youth crime action plan: Full report*. Wellington, New Zealand: Ministry of Justice.

Ministry of Justice. (2015). *Trends in child and youth prosecutions: Court statistics for 10–16 year olds in the year ended December 2015*. Wellington, New Zealand: Ministry of Justice.

Monchalin, L. (2016). *The colonial problem: An Indigenous perspective on crime and injustice in Canada*. Toronto, ON: University of Toronto Press.

Moore, E., Gaskin, C., & Indig, D. (2015). Attempted suicide, self-harm, and psychological disorder among young offenders in custody. *Journal of Correctional Health Care, 21*, 243–254. https://doi.org/10.1177/1078345815584849

Motivans, M., & Snyder, H. (2011). *Summary: Tribal youth in the federal justice system*. Washington, DC: U.S. Department of Justice (Office of Justice Programs - Bureau of Justice Statistics).

Moyle, P., & Tauri, J. M. (2016). Māori, family group conferencing and the mystifications of restorative justice. *Victims & Offenders, 11*, 87–106. https://doi.org/10.1080/15564886.2015.1135496

Munro-Harrison, E., Trounson, J. S., & Ironfield, N. (2016). A culturally safe education engagement model for Aboriginal and Torres Strait Islander men in prison. *Aboriginal & Islander Health Worker Journal, 40*, 34–35.

Nathan, L. (2009a). What works to reduce offending by Rangatahi Māori. In G. Maxwell (Ed.), *Addressing the causes of offending: What is the evidence?* Wellington: Institute of Policy Studies, Victoria University.

Nathan, L. (2009b). What works to reduce offending by Rangatahi Māori. In G. Maxwell (Ed.), *Impact on criminality: Māori youth perceptions*. Youth Justice.

Neilsen, M. O. (1996). Contextualization for Native American crime and criminal justice involvement. In M. O. Nielsen & R. Silverman (Eds.), *Native Americans, crime and justice* (pp. 10–19). Boulder, CO: Westview Press.

Nielsen, M. O., & Robyn, L. (2003). Colonialism and criminal justice for Indigenous peoples in Australia, Canada, New Zealand and the United States of America. *Indigenous Nations Studies Journal, 4*, 29–45.

Office of Juvenile Justice and Delinquency Prevention. (2016). Tribal Youth in the Juvenile Justice System. Retrieved from https://www.ojjdp.gov/mpg/litreviews/Tribal-youth-in-the-Juvenile-Justice-System.pdf

Ogloff, J. R. P., Pfeifer, J. E., Shepherd, S. M., & Ciorciari, J. (2017). Assessing the mental health, substance abuse, cognitive functioning, and social/emotional well-being needs of Aboriginal prisoners in Australia. *Journal of Correctional Health Care, 23*, 398–411.

Olver, M. E., Stockdale, K. C., & Wormith, J. S. (2009). Risk assessment with young offenders: A meta-analysis of three assessment measures. *Criminal Justice and Behavior, 36*, 329–353. https://doi.org/10.1177/0093854809331457

Ottawa Department of Justice. (2015). Aboriginal courtwork program evaluation. Retrieved from http://www.justice.gc.ca/eng/rp-pr/cp-pm/eval/rep-rap/13/acp-paa/p3.html

Parker, K., & Myrstol, B. A. (2013). *Juvenile justice referrals in Alaska 2003–2013*. Anchorage: Justice Center, University of Alaska.

Pavkov, T. W., Travis, L., Fox, K. A., Bear-King, C., & Cross, T. L. (2010). Tribal youth victimization abnd delinquency: Analysis of youth risk behaviour surveillance survey data. *Cultural Diversity and Ethnic Minority Psychology, 16*, 123–134. https://doi.org/10.1037/a0018664

Pennell, J., & Burford, G. (1996). Attending to context: Family group decision-making in Canada. In J. Hudson, A. Morris, G. Maxwell, & B. Galway (Eds.), *Family group conferences: Perspectives on policies and practices* (pp. 209–220). Annandale, New South Wales: Federated Press.

Perreault, S. (2014). *Admissions to youth correctional services in Canada, 2011/2012. Juristat (Cat. No. 85-002-x)*. Statistics Canada.

Perry, B. (2006). Nobody trust them! Under- and over-policing Native American communities. *Critical Criminology, 14*, 411–444. https://doi.org/10.1007/s10612-006-9007-z

Perry, B. (2009). *Policing race and place in Indian country*. Lanham: Lexington Books.

Perry, S. W. (2004). *American Indians and Crime*. Washington, DC: U.S. Department of Justice (Office of Justice Programs—Bureau of Justice Statistics).

Peters, A. M. F., & Corrado, R. R. (2016). The youth justice system in action. In J. Winterdyk & R. Smandych (Eds.), *Youth at risk and youth justice: A Canadian overview* (2nd ed.). Don Mills, ON: Oxford University Press.

Pew Research Center. (2012). One-in-four Native Americans and Alaska natives are living in poverty. Retrieved from http://www.pewresearch.org/fact-tank/2014/06/13/1-in-4-native-americans-and-alaska-natives-are-living-in-poverty/

Pfeifer, J. E. (2017). Police recruitment and Indigenous people: Examining the role of attitudes, perceptions and beliefs. *Journal of Australian Indigenous Issues, 20*, 31–47.

Pfeifer, J. E. (in review). Indigenous culture, corrections and technology: Assessing the effectiveness of the *iTalk* program in Northern Territory Corrections.

Poa, D., & Monod, S. W. (2016). A re-education initiative and its impact on reoffending among indigenous New Zealand youth. *Journal of Applied Youth Studies, 3*, 55–67.

Quince, K. (2007a). Māori and the criminal justice system in New Zealand. In J. Tolmie & W. Brookbanks (Eds.), *The New Zealand Justice System* (pp. 333–358). Auckland, New Zealand: Lexis Nexis.

Quince, K. (2007b). *Maori and the criminal justice system in New Zealand. Criminal Justice in New Zealand*. Auckland, New Zealand: Lexis Nexis.

Redding, R. E. (2010). *The impact of prosecuting youth in the adult criminal justice system: A review of the literature*. Los Angeles: University of California School of Law.

Restorative Justice Unit, & File Hills Qu'Appelle Tribal Council. (2010). *First nations community justice handbook*. Saskatchewan: Restorative Justice Unit, File Hills Qu'Appelle Tribal Council.

Rodriguez, N. (2008). *A multilevel analysis of juvenile court processes: The importance of community characteristics*. Washington, DC: National Institute of Justice.

Rojas, E. Y., & Gretton, H. M. (2007). Background, offence characteristics, and criminal outcomes of Aboriginal youth who sexually offend: A closer look at Aboriginal youth intervention needs. *Sexual Abuse: A Journal of Research and Treatment, 19*, 257–283.

Sahin, Q., & Maier, J. (2011). *Delinquency: Causes, reduction and prevention*. New York: Nova Science.

Sampson, R. J. (2009). Disparity and diversity in the contemporary city: Social (dis)order revisitied. *British Journal of Sociology, 60*, 1–31. https://doi.org/10.1111/j.1468-4446.2009.01211.x

Samra-Grewa, J., Pfeifer, J. E., & Ogloff, J. R. P. (2000). Recommendations for conditional release suitability: Cognitive biases and consistency in case management officers' decision-making. *Canadian Journal of Criminology, 42*, 421–447.

Senate Select Committee on Regional and Remote Indigenous Communities. (2010). *Indigenous Australians, incarceration and the criminal justice system (Discussion paper)*. Canberra, ACT: Commonwealth of Australia. Retrieved from http://www.aph.gov.au/Parliamentary_Business/Committees/Senate/Former_Committees/indig/index

Senior, K., Chenhall, R., & Daniels, D. (2006). "Stuck nose": Experiences and understanding of petrol sniffing in a remote Aboriginal community. *Contemporary Drug Problems, 33*, 451–472.

Shaffer, C., McCuish, E., Corrado, R. R., Behnken, M. P., & DeLisi, M. (2015). Psychopathy and violent misconduct in a sample of violent young offenders. *Journal of Criminal Justice, 43*, 321–326. https://doi.org/10.1016/j.jcrimjus.2015.05.008

Shepherd, S. M., Luebbers, S., Ferguson, M., Ogloff, J. R. P., & Dolan, M. (2014). The utility of the SAVRY across ethnicity in Australian young offenders. *Psychology, Public Policy, and Law, 20*, 31–45. https://doi.org/10.1037/a0033972

Shepherd, S. M., Ogloff, J. R. P., Pfeifer, J. E., & Paradies, Y. (2017). *Indigenous prisoners with cognitive impairment - is this the highest risk group*. Canberra: Australian Institute of Criminology.

Shepherd, S. M., Ogloff, J. R. P., Shea, D., Pfeifer, J. E., & Paradies, Y. (2017). Aboriginal prisoners and cognitive impairment: The impact of dual disadvantage on social and emotional wellbeing. *Journal of Intellectual Disability Research, 61*, 385–397. https://doi.org/10.1111/jir.12357

Sherwood, J. (2013). Colonisation – It's bad for your health: The context of Aboriginal health. *Contemporary Nurse, 46*, 28–40. https://doi.org/10.5172/conu.2013.46.1.28

Shoemaker, D. (1996). *International handbook on juvenile justice*. Westport, CT: Greenwood Press.

Shoham, S. G., Beck, O., & Kett, M. (2008). *Penology and criminal justice*. Boca Raton, FL: CRC Press.

Sickmund, M., & Puzzanchera, C. (2014). *Juvenile offenders and victims: 2014 national report*. Pittsburgh: National Center for Juvenile Justice. Retrieved from http://www.ojjdp.gov/ojstatbb/nr2014/downloads/NR2014.pdf

Silva, D., Colvin, L., Glauert, R., & Bower, C. (2014). Contact with juvenile justice system in children treated with stimulant medication for attention deficit hyperactivity disorder: A population study. *The Lancet: Psychiatry, 1*, 278–285. https://doi.org/10.1016/S2215-0366(14)70302-5

Silverstein, M. (2005). What's race got to do with justice? Responsibilization strategies at parole hearings. *British Journal of Criminology, 45*, 340–354. https://doi.org/10.1093/bjc/azh102

Singh, D., & White, C. (2000). *Searching for solutions: A review of research about effective interventions for reducing offending by indigenous and ethnic minority youth*. Wellington, New Zealand: Ministry of Youth Affairs.
Sittner-Hartshorn, K. J., Whitbeck, L. B., & Prentice, R. (2015). Substance use disorders, comorbidity, and arrest among Indigenous adolescents. *Crime & Delinquency, 61*, 1311–1332. https://doi.org/10.1177/0011128712466372
Skues, J., Pfeifer, J. E., Oliva, A., & Wise, L. (in press). Responding to the needs of prisoners with learning difficulties in Australia. *Journal of Bias, Identity, and Diversities in Education.*
Snow, P. C., Woodward, M., Mathis, M., & Powell, M. B. (2016). Language functioning, mental health and alexithymia in incarcerated young offenders. *International Journal of Speech-Language Pathology, 18*, 20–31. https://doi.org/10.3109/17549507.2015.1081291
Snowball, L. (2008). Juvenile diversion and Indigenous offenders. Criminology Research Council. Retrieved from http://criminologyresearchcouncil.gov.au/reports/200607-C02.pdf
Spiranovic, C., Clare, J., Clare, M., & Clare, B. (2013). Youth justice and child protection: The Children's Court in Western Australia. In R. Sheehan & A. Borowski (Eds.), *Australia's children's courts today and tomorrow* (pp. 143–162). Dordrecht: Springer.
Standing Committee on Aboriginal and Torres Strait Islander Affairs. (2011). *Doing time - time for doing: Indigenous youth in the criminal justice system*. Canberra, ACT: Parliament of Australia.
Stathis, S., Letters, P., Doolan, I., Fleming, R., Heath, K., Arnett, A., & Cory, S. (2008). Use of the Massachusetts youth screening instrument to assess mental health problems in young people within an Australian youth detention centre. *Journal of Paediatrics and Child Health, 44*, 438–443. https://doi.org/10.1111/j.1440-1754.2008.01324.x
Statistics Canada. (2015). Aboriginal statistics at a glance. Retrieved from http://www.statcan.gc.ca/pub/89-645-x/2010001/income-revenu-eng.htm
Statistics New Zealand. (2013). Population Census. Retrieved from http://www.stats.govt.nz/Census/2013-census.aspx
Statistics New Zealand. (2016). Apprehension statistics: Calendar year 2014. Retrieved from http://www.stats.govt.nz/tools_and_services/nzdotstat/tables-by-subject/new-zealand-recorded-crime-tables/apprehensions.aspx
Stewart, L. (1997). Approaches to preventing alcohol-related problems: The experience of New Zealand and Australia. *Drug and Alcohol Review, 16*, 391–399. https://doi.org/10.1080/09595239700186791
Stewart, A., Hayes, H., Livingston, M., & Palk, G. (2008). Youth justice conferencing and indigenous over-representation in the Queensland juvenile justice system: A micro-simulation case study. *Journal of Experimental Criminology, 4*(4), 357–380.
Suaalii-Sauni, T., Samu, K., Dunbar, L., Pulford, J., & Wheeler, A. (2012). A qualitative investigation into key cultural factors that support abstinence or responsible drinking amongst some Pacific youth living in New Zealand. *Harm Reduction Journal, 9*, 36–48. https://doi.org/10.1186/1477-7517-9-36
Taumaunu, H. (2014). Māori Law review. Retrieved from http://Māori lawreview.co.nz/2014/11/rangatahi-courts-of-aotearoa-new-zealand-an-update/
Tauri, J. (1999). Explaining recent innovations in New Zealand's criminal justice system: Empowering Māori of biculturalising the state? *The Australian and New Zealand Journal of Criminology, 32*, 153–167. https://doi.org/10.1177/000486589903200205
Tauri, J. (2005). Indigenous perspectives and experiences: Māori and the criminal justice system. In T. Bradley & R. Walters (Eds.), *Introduction to criminological thought* (pp. 129–145). Auckland: Pearson.
Tauri, J. (2012). Indigenous critique of authoritarian criminology. In K. Carrington, M. Ball, E. O'Brien, & J. Tauri (Eds.), *Crime justice and social democracy* (pp. 217–233). Basingstoke, UK: Palgrave Macmillan.
Tauri, J. M., & Webb, R. (2012). A critical appraisal of responses to Māori offending. *The International Indigenous Policy Journal, 3*(4), 1–16.
Te Puni Kōkiri. (2011a). *Addressing the drivers of crime for Māori*. Wellington: Te Puni Kōkiri.

Te Puni Kōkiri. (2011b). *He Pūrongo Arotake: Hard to reach youth (CART) evaluation report: Hard to Reach Youth (CART)*. Wellington, New Zealand: Te Puni Kōkiri.

Thompson, A. P., & McGrath, A. (2012). Subgroup differences and implications for contemporary risk-need assessment with juvenile offenders. *Law and Human Behavior, 36*, 345–355.

Thompson, A. P., & Pope, Z. (2005). Assessing juvenile offenders: Preliminary data for the Australian adaptation of the youth level of services/case management inventory (Hoge & Andrews, 1995). *Australian Psychologist, 40*, 207–214.

Thomson, S., De Bortoli, L., & Buckley, S. (2013). PISA in brief highlights from the full Australian report: PISA 2012 - how Australia measures up. Australian Council for Educational Research. Retrieved from http://research.acer.edu.au/cgi/viewcontent.cgi?article=1014&context=ozpisa

Toki, V. (2014). Indigenous children and youth: The case of marae courts in Aotearoa New Zealand. In W. Littlechild & E. Stamatopoulou (Eds.), *Indigenous people's access to justice, including truth and reconciliation processes* (pp. 243–254). New York, NY: Institute for the Study of Human Rights, Columbia University.

Totten, M. (2012). *Nasty, brutish, and short: The lives of gang members in Canada*. Toronto, ON: Lorimer Pub.

Totten, M. (2014). *Gang life: 10 of the toughest tell their stories*. Toronto, ON: Lorimer.

Totten, M. (2016). An overview of gang-involved youth in Canada. In J. Winterydk & R. Smandych (Eds.), *Youth at risk and youth justice: A Canadian overview*. Don Mills, ON: Oxford University Press.

Troth, G., & Grainger, J. (2000). The psychological impact of custody on the Aboriginal adolescent. *Psychiatry, Psychology and Law, 7*, 89–96. https://doi.org/10.1080/13218710009524974

Trotter, C., Baidawi, S., & Evans, P. (2015). Good practice in community-based supervision of Aboriginal youth offenders. *Australian Social Work, 68*(1), 5–18.

United States Census. (2010). Retrieved from https://www.census.gov/2010census/

Watt, E. (2003). *A history of youth justice in New Zealand 1-32*. Wellington, New Zealand. Retrieved from https://www.youthcourt.govt.nz/assets/Documents/Publications/Youth-Court-History-of-the-Youth-Court.pdf

Weatherburn, D., Fitzgerald, J., & Hua, J. (2003). Reducing Aboriginal overrepresentation in prison. *Australian Journal of Public Administration, 62*(3), 65–73.

Webb, R. (2009). Maori, Pacific peoples and the social construction of crime statistics. *Mai Review, 3*, 1–4.

Westcott, M. (2006). Murri courts – Research brief 2006/14. Queensland Parliament. Retrieved from http://www.parliament.qld.gov.au/documents/explore/ResearchPublications/ResearchBriefs/2006/RBR200614.pdf

Willoughby, A., & Nellis, M. (2016). "You cannot really hide": Experiences of probation officers and young offenders with GPS tracking in Winnipeg, Canada. *Journal of Technology in Human Service, 34*, 63–81. https://doi.org/10.1080/15228835.2016.1139919

Winterdyk, J. (Ed.). (2015). *Juvenile justice: International perspectives, models and trends*. Boca Raton, FL: CRC Press.

Workman, K. (2011). *Māori over-representation in the criminal justice system: Does discrimination have anything to do with it?* Wellington, New Zealand: Rethinking Crime and Punishment.

Workman, K. (2016). From a search for Rangatiratanga to a struggle for survival – Criminal justice, the state and Māori, 1985 to 2015. The 2015 JD Stout Lecture. *Journal of New Zealand Studies, 22*, 89–104.

Workman, K., & McIntosh, T. (2013). Crime, imprisonment and poverty. In M. Rashbrooke (Ed.), *Inequality: A New Zealand crisis* (pp. 120–131). Wellington, New Zealand: Bridget Williams Books.

Yessine, A. K., & Bonta, J. (2009). The offending trajectories of youthful Aboriginal offenders. *Canadian Journal of Criminology and Criminal Justice, 51*, 435–472. https://doi.org/10.3138/cjccj.51.4.435

Youth Justice Independent Advisory Group (IAG). (2009). *Practical ideas for addressing Māori youth offending* (Response to request by senior government ministers), 1-10.

An Empirical Analysis of Law-Psychology Journals: Who's Publishing and on What?

Krystia Reed, Kimberly S. Dellapaolera, Sarah Thimsen, and Brian H. Bornstein

As is implied by the name, law and psychology is an interdisciplinary field that incorporates research from both psychology and law. Contributions come from researchers in psychology, law, neuroscience, medicine, and other social sciences (e.g., political science, sociology). Furthermore, the research within psychology is diverse, with methods from cognitive, social, clinical, and developmental psychology being applied to legal issues. The primary means of disseminating psycholegal knowledge, as with any scientific discipline, is through publication in peer-reviewed journals. These journals both convey empirical research to the wider public and provide a measure of what leaders in the field (i.e., editors, editorial board members, reviewers) deem important. A knowledge of publication patterns can also help authors make informed decisions about where to submit their work. Thus, an examination of publication patterns in scholarly journals is one way of gauging what is going on in a particular field, in general, and where to publish in particular.

A History of Psychology and Law

In 1974, the American Psychology-Law Society (AP-LS; Division 41 of the American Psychological Association) met for the first time to focus on research at the intersection of law and psychology (Grisso, 1991). Within the first several years,

K. Reed (✉)
Cornell University, Ithaca, NY, USA
e-mail: Krystia.Reed@cornell.edu

K. S. Dellapaolera · B. H. Bornstein
University of Nebraska-Lincoln, Lincoln, NE, USA

S. Thimsen
South Dakota State University, University Center-Sioux Falls, Sioux Falls, SD, USA

M. K. Miller, B. H. Bornstein (eds.), *Advances in Psychology and Law*, Advances in Psychology and Law 3,
https://doi.org/10.1007/978-3-319-75859-6_9

members represented a multitude of disciplines and subdisciplines including social psychology, clinical psychology, community psychology, psychiatry, law, sociology, criminology, social ethics, political science, and anthropology (*see* Wylie et al., 2018). Although the field has become increasingly popular over the past 42 years (e.g., the AP-LS annual meeting has grown steadily, and new journals have been founded over the years), there has been a consistent call in the field of law-psychology to increase diversification in research. Indeed, it is a recurring litany of journal editors and other leaders of the discipline (*see*, e.g., Blumenthal, 2002; Brank, 2007; Cutler, 2007; Kovera, 2013; Lamb, 2013; Ogloff, 2000; Roesch, 1990; Saks, 1986; Skeem, 2014; Tremper, 1987; Wiener, 1997; Wylie et al., 2018).

One way to assess diversity in the field is to examine its publication patterns. Wylie et al. (2018) conducted a content analysis of *Law and Human Behavior* (*LHB*; the official AP-LS journal, currently published by the American Psychological Association) articles published since the journal's 1977 inception to assess the diversity of articles published in the journal. The analysis identified 19 primary research areas; however, 40% of studies involved one of two topics: jury/judicial decision making or eyewitness memory (Wylie et al., 2018).

Although the trends in *LHB* might be reflective of the law-psychology field, there are several other journals publishing work on law-psychology. Within a field, journals often vary in terms of what they publish, in terms of both subject area and type of article, and characteristics of the authors. For example, Bornstein (2016) found that *LHB* contained work conducted overwhelmingly by psychologists, whereas *Law and Society Review* was more broadly multidisciplinary but contained little work from a psychological perspective. And, although *LHB* publishes research from all over the world, as the official journal of the American Psychology-Law Society, it is likely less international in scope than journals based elsewhere. Thus, in order to understand fully what is being published within a particular field, it is important to look at a variety of journals. There are a number of additional influential law-psychology journals, and relevant research is of course also published in more general (especially applied) psychological journals. The present analysis focuses on three leading international and interdisciplinary journals: *Psychology, Crime and Law*; *Psychology, Public Policy, and Law;* and *Legal and Criminological Psychology*. Each of these journals has different publication goals and foci.

Psychology, Crime & Law: In 1994, the European Association of Psychology and Law established *Psychology, Crime & Law* (*PCL*). The founding editors of *PCL* indicated that the goal of the journal was both to provide another outlet to publish law-psychology research and to "encompass *all* aspects of psychology, crime, and law" rather than "to concentrate exclusively on one aspect of the field" (Hollin, van Koppen, & Lind, 1994, p. i; emphasis in original). The editors of *PCL* indicated that they were aiming for a breadth of coverage including "empirical studies, both full-length and brief reports; review papers, including meta-analyses; book reviews; and invited commentaries and papers" in addition to special editions focused on specific themes (Hollin et al., 1994, p. i). Similarly, the current goal of the journal is to publish "reviews and brief reports which make a significant contribution to the psychology of law, crime and legal behavior" and serve as a resource to professionals internationally (Taylor & Francis, 2016).

Psychology, Public Policy, and Law: In 1995, the American Psychological Association (APA) established *Psychology, Public Policy, and Law* (*PPPL*) under the editorship of Bruce Sales. The goal of *PPPL* was to "fill a significant void in psychology journals, law reviews, and interdisciplinary journals that publish articles relating to psychology and relevant information derived from related disciplines" (Sales, 1995, p. 3). Specifically, *PPPL* recognized that while the field is intended to be multidisciplinary, the current journals were not being disseminated to the "mainstream legal and policy communities" (Sales, 1995, p. 4). *PPPL* indicated the intent to engage scholars from multiple disciplines and encouraged submission of long, comprehensive pieces that did not necessarily include empirical studies (Sales, 1995). The current goal of *PPPL* is to "critically evaluate the contributions of psychology and related disciplines…to public policy and legal issues, and vice versa" (APA, 2017). *PPPL* emphasizes that the journal is read by a diverse group including legal scholars, legal professionals, public policy analysts, psychology researchers, and psychology practitioners (APA, 2017).

Legal and Criminological Psychology: In 1996, The British Psychological Society contributed an additional journal to the field, *Legal and Criminological Psychology* (*LCP*). The editorial in the first issue of *LCP* indicated the aim of the journal was "to advance scientific and professional knowledge in the wide-ranging field that its title defines" (McMurran & Lloyd-Bostock, 1996, p. 1). The editors acknowledged that because the journal was being published by The British Psychological Society, the primary discipline would be psychology (McMurran & Lloyd-Bostock, 1996). However, the editors simultaneously emphasized the multidisciplinary nature of the field: "both readers and contributors should be from a diversity of academic and professional backgrounds, including forensic psychiatrists, criminologists, lawyers, police, probation officers and prison personnel" (McMurran & Lloyd-Bostock, 1996, p. 1). The editors also indicated their desire that the journal be international, representing a wide geographical spread. The current editors also emphasize the goal of "publish[ing] original papers which advance professional and scientific knowledge in the field of legal and criminological psychology, defined broadly as the application of psychology to law or interdisciplinary enquiry in legal and psychological fields" (Wiley Online Library, 2017).

Present Study

The present study provides a useful point of comparison by examining these three leading law-psychology journals to determine the substantive topics and types of articles that they publish. In addition, because the field is interdisciplinary by definition and includes scholars active in a number of countries, we examined the disciplinary affiliation and institutional location of authors. We also investigated author gender because, as compared to many other sciences, women are well-represented in psychology graduate programs and on psychology faculties (see, e.g., Cynkar, 2007). The question remains, though, whether they are publishing at the same rate as their male colleagues. Some research indicates that female scientists publish less than male scientists (e.g., Rorstad & Aksnes, 2015); however, other research suggests that in younger generations, women are publishing more than men (van Arensbergen, van der Weijden, & van den Besselaar, 2012). It is possible that law-psychology journals will have more women publishing, particularly given that, unlike most other sciences, women are more represented in psychology than men.

Contemporary law-psychology scholarship is primarily an empirical endeavor. However, theoretical and conceptual articles are also an effective way of advancing science, and such articles tend to be more influential and more heavily cited (McLean, 2011). In the case of empirical research, law-psychology has not been immune to the vigorous debates over the extent to which results from student participants generalize to the population as a whole (e.g., Bornstein, 2017). Thus, we also examined the type of article and (for articles presenting original research) the type of sample.

Method

Sample

We coded all available articles published in seven full years (2010–2016) of three law-psychology journals: *PCL*, *PPPL*, and *LCP*. During this time period, *PCL* published ten issues per year, *PPPL* published four issues per year, and *LCP* published two issues per year. Initially, there were $N = 683$ articles, but after removing introductions to special issues, book reviews, comments, replies, announcements, errata, and obituaries, the final number of coded articles was $N = 633$, which included original data reports ($n = 528$), meta-analyses ($n = 16$), and nonempirical conceptual articles ($n = 89$).

Coding Scheme

All of the articles were coded by one of the authors, and a subset of articles was coded by an additional author ($n = 58$). An interrater reliability analysis was conducted for each variable to assess the degree to which coders were consistent. Percent agreement ranged from 74% to 100%. All of the variables had a Cohen's (1960) kappa indicating substantial or almost perfect agreement based on Landis and Koch's (1977) criteria. The lowest agreement variables were primary research area (74%) and sample type (75%). All of the remaining variables had agreement rates over 80% and 73% of the variables had agreement rates over 90%. When there was disagreement, the first author reviewed the data, giving deference to the primary coder.

Coded Variables

General publication information: Each of the articles was coded for general publication information including journal (*PCL*, *LCP*, or *PPPL*), publication year, and length (based on page numbers).

Author information: Each of the articles was also coded on a number of variables related to the authors. We coded the first five authors of each article for gender, institutional location, and primary disciplinary affiliation. Gender was determined by familiarity with gender naming. If there was doubt about the gender of any author, a Google search was conducted to determine if gender could be identified. In some cases, gender could not be confirmed and was coded as "unknown." Institutional location of the author was determined based on the location of the institution the author was affiliated with at the time of the publication. Finally, authors were coded for their primary disciplinary affiliation based on the first listed discipline with which the author was associated. If there were more than five authors, the article was coded as having more than five authors, but no additional author information was collected.

Article information: Each of the articles was coded on several factors: primary research area, article type, sample, and number of studies.

Each article was classified into a single research area based on the primary focus of the study. We coded for ten primary research areas, including: jury decision making, eyewitness, prisoners/offending, other mental health, public policy that does not fit into another category, policing, interrogation/confession, judicial decision making, other trial procedures, or other.

Articles were then coded for type of information presented. Each article was classified as one of three article types: original data report, meta-analysis, or concept/review/position paper. Articles that included original data were coded for the number of studies and the type of sample used. Sample type was divided into ten groups: college students, other students (e.g., high school, law), adult community members, offenders/prisoners, judges, attorneys, other professionals (e.g., experts), children/minors, other, or multiple sample types (e.g., the study was comparing different groups). If the article did not include original data, it was coded as such.

Results

General Publication Information

Out of the 633 articles, 265 (41.9%) were from *PCL*, 202 (31.9%) from *PPPL*, and 166 (26.2%) from *LCP*. In terms of publication by year, 79 (12.5%) were published in 2010, 85 (13.4%) were published in 2011, 103 (16.3%) were published in 2012, 117 (18.5%) were published in 2013, 70 (11.1%) were published in 2014, 69 (10.9%) were published in 2015, and 110 (17.4%) were published in 2016. On average, articles were 17.1 pages long (*range*: 5–81). Article length varied by journal, $F(2, 632) = 6.15$, $MSe = 48.84$, $p = 0.002$, $R^2 = 0.02$, with articles in *LCP* ($M = 15.54$, $SD = 5.69$) being significantly shorter than articles in *PPPL* ($M = 18.05$, $SD = 9.59$, $p = 0.001$) and *PCL* ($M = 17.32$, $SD = 6.26$, $p = 0.010$).

On average, it took 446.3 days ($SD = 260.4$, *range*: 50–1687) between the article being first received and first published. However, the journals differed in the type of information they provided and there were significant differences in review duration by journal. The total time from submission to initial publication was significantly longer for *LCP* ($M = 596.4$ days, $SD = 364.13$), followed by *PCL* ($M = 440.8$ days, $SD = 183.92$, $p < 0.001$), and significantly shorter for *PPPL* ($M = 329.3$, $SD = 172.54$, $p < 0.001$), $F(2, 617) = 56.53$, $MSe = 57483.53$, $p < 0.001$, $R^2 = 0.16$.

Author Information

On average, articles had three authors ($SD = 1.48$, *range*: 1–12); however, there were significant differences by journal, $F(2, 630) = 4.06$, $MSe = 2.16$, $p = 0.018$, $R^2 = 0.013$. *PPPL* tended to have significantly more authors per article ($M = 3.35$, $SD = 1.70$) than *PCL* ($M = 2.98$, $SD = 1.39$, $p = 0.008$), or *LCP* ($M = 3.01$, $SD = 1.35$, $p = 0.028$), but there was no significant difference between *PCL* and *LCP* ($p = 0.852$).

Author characteristics: Overall, first authors were primarily female (54.0%) (see Fig. 1) and were associated with psychology departments or mental health institutes (67.3%) (see Fig. 2) and were located in United States institutions (36.2%) (see Fig. 3). Because demographic information of additional authors was largely similar to that of the first authors (see Figs. 1, 2, and 3), we limit the following analyses to characteristics of first authors.

There were significant differences in author characteristics by journal. *PPPL* had significantly more male first authors (51.0%) than *PCL* (41.1%, $p = 0.002$), or *LCP* (37.3%, $p = 0.012$), $F(2, 630) = 5.55$, $MSe = 0.29$, $p = 0.004$, $R^2 = 0.02$. There was no significant difference between *LCP* and *PCL* ($p = 0.757$). *LCP* had significantly more first authors based in psychology departments (78.3%) than *PCL* (67.6%, $p = 0.021$) or *PPPL* (64.9%, $p = 0.005$), $F(2, 609) = 4.32$, $MSe = 0.21$, $p = 0.014$, $R^2 = 0.02$. There was no significant difference between *PCL* and *PPPL* ($p = 0.525$). In terms of author institutional location, *PPPL* was significantly less diverse, with 73.8% of authors employed by American institutions, than *LCP* (21.7%, $p < 0.001$), or *PCL* (16.6%, $p < 0.001$), $F(2, 630) = 127.76$, $MSe = 0.17$, $p < 0.001$, $R^2 = 0.29$. There was no significant difference between *LCP* and *PCL* in terms of author institutional location ($p = 0.207$).

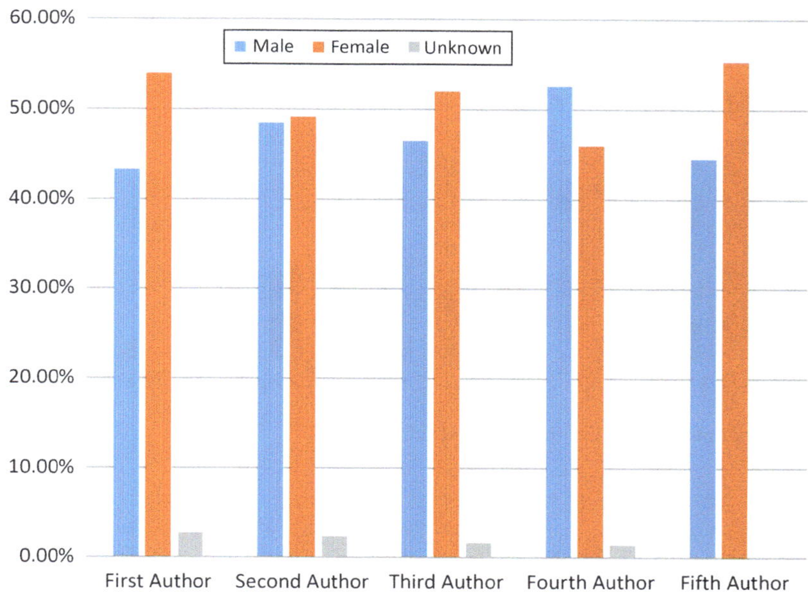

Fig. 1 Author gender based on author order

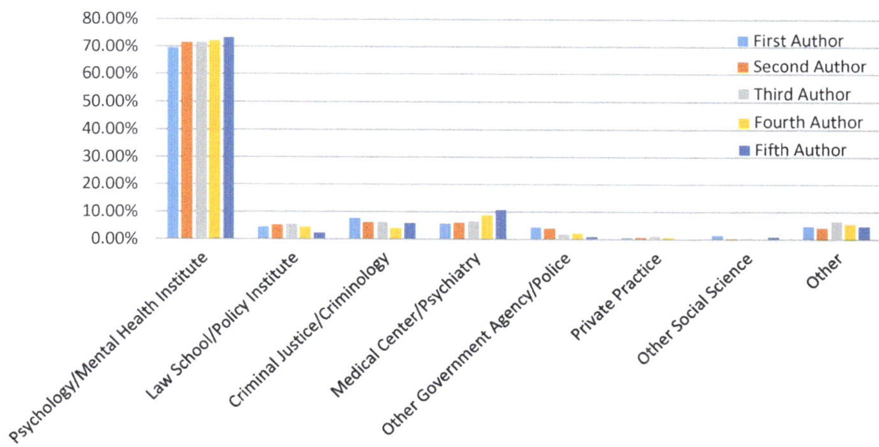

Fig. 2 Author discipline based on author order

Article Information

Overall, the most common research area was prisoners/offending (including risk assessment, predicting offending, reoffending, and recidivism), which constituted 34.1% of the articles (see Fig. 4). This was followed by "other" (12.6%), jury

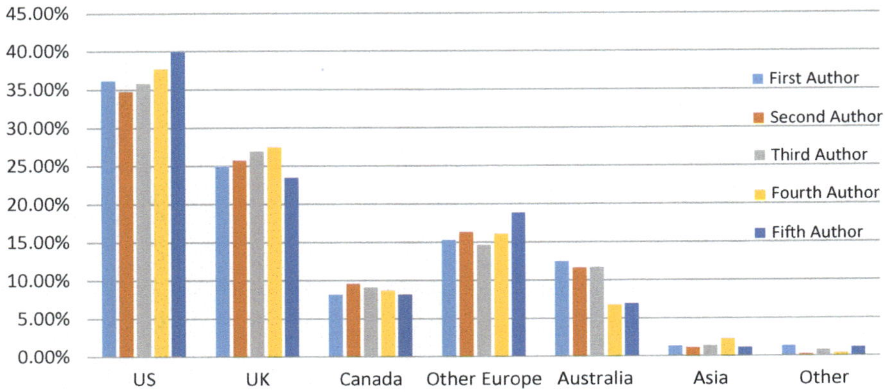

Fig. 3 Author institutional location based on author order

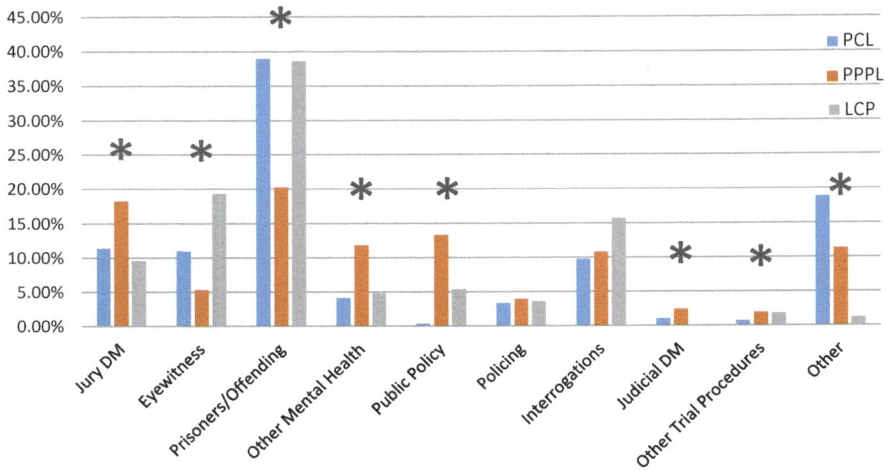

Fig. 4 Research area by journal

decision making (12.3%), interrogation (11.3%), and eyewitness (10.7%) in the top five most common types of research.

Out of the total sample, most articles were original data reports (83.4%) (see Fig. 5), with fewer concept/review papers (14.1%) and meta-analyses (2.5%). Original data reports used a wide variety of samples with adult community members (23.7%), offenders/prisoners (21.8%), and college students (19.5%) being the most common samples. The large majority of original data report articles included only one study (82.2%), and, at the other extreme, two articles included eight studies (0.4%). There were a number of significant differences on these measures by journal.

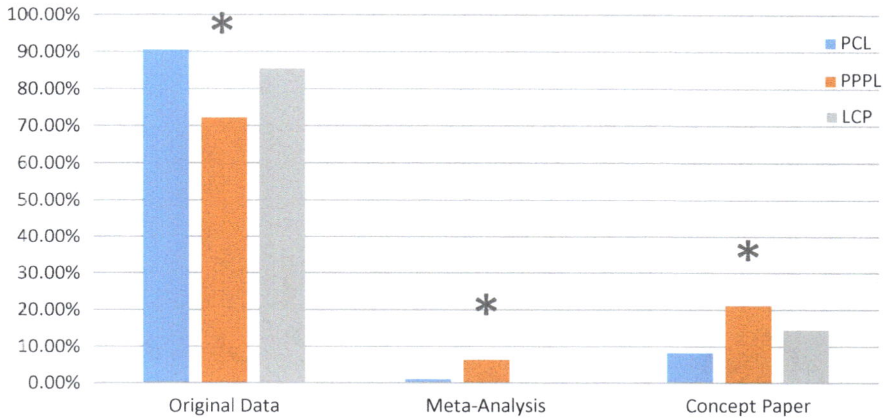

Fig. 5 Article type by journal

First, there were significant differences in primary research area by journal, $F(2, 629) = 6.46$, $MSe = 7.80$, $p = 0.002$, $R^2 = 0.02$. While prisoners/offending was a common research area in all three journals, *PPPL* tended to publish fewer articles on prisoners/offending (20.3%) than *PCL* (39.0%, $p < 0.001$) or *LCP* (38.6%, $p < 0.001$), $F(2, 629) = 11.03$, $MSe = 0.21$, $p < 0.001$, $R^2 = 0.03$ (see Fig. 4). *PPPL* was significantly more likely to publish on jury decision making (18.3%) than *PCL* (11.4%, $p = 0.027$) or *LCP* (9.6%, $p = 0.014$), $F(2, 629) = 3.65$, $MSe = 0.11$, $p = 0.026$, $R^2 = 0.01$. *PPPL* was also significantly more likely to publish on public policy that did not fit into another category (13.4%) than *LCP* (5.4%, $p = 0.001$) or *PCL* (0.4%, $p < 0.001$), $F(2, 629) = 18.49$, $MSe = 0.052$, $p < 0.001$, $R^2 = 0.06$. *LCP* published on public policy significantly more than *PCL* ($p = 0.026$). *PCL* included significantly more articles that did not fit into the identified topic list (i.e., categorized as "other"; 18.9%) than *PPPL* (5.4%, $p = 0.011$) or *LCP* (1.2%, $p < 0.001$), $F(2, 629) = 16.07$, $MSe = 0.10$, $p < 0.001$, $R^2 = 0.05$. *PPPL* published significantly more articles categorized as "other" than *LCP* ($p = 0.002$). Figure 4 shows additional differences across the other research areas.

There were also significant differences in type of article published by journal, $F(2, 630) = 11.79$, $MSe = 0.48$, $p < 0.001$, $R^2 = 0.04$ (see Fig. 5). Although all journals published more original data articles than meta-analyses or concept papers, articles in *PPPL* were significantly less likely to be original data articles (72.3%) than *PCL* (90.6%, $p < 0.001$) or *LCP* (85.5%, $p = 0.001$). There was no significant difference between articles in *LCP* and *PCL* ($p = 0.164$). *PPPL* had significantly more meta-analyses (6.4%) than *PCL* (1.1%, $p < 0.001$) or *LCP* (0%, $p < 0.001$). *PPPL* published significantly more concept papers (21.3%) than *PCL* (8.3%, $p < 0.001$) and marginally more than *LCP* (14.5%, $p = 0.059$), $F(2, 630) = 8.18$, $p < 0.001$, $R^2 = 0.03$. *LCP* tended to publish more concept papers than *PCL* ($p = 0.071$).

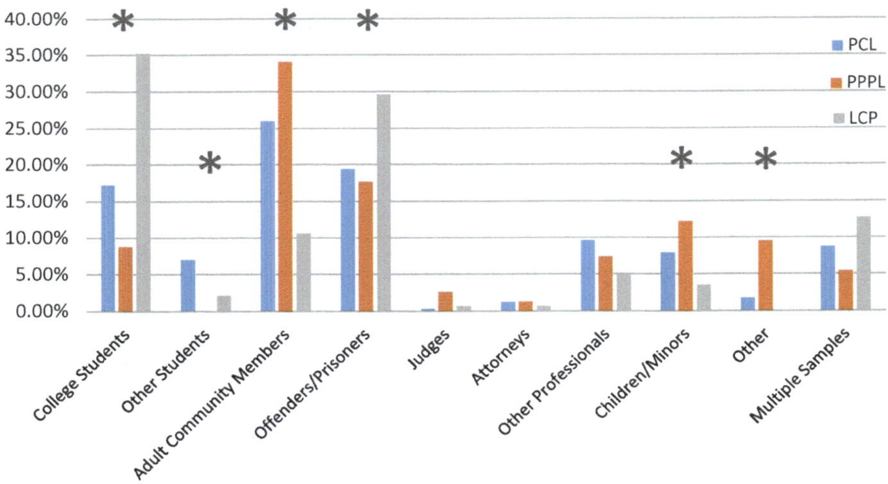

Fig. 6 Sample type by journal. Note: Asterisk indicates significant differences between journals, $p < 0.05$

For the original data reports, there was a significant difference in number of studies per article, $F(2, 525) = 4.98$, $MSe = 0.56$, $p = 0.007$, $R^2 = 0.02$. On average, *PPPL* articles included significantly more studies ($M = 1.40$, $SD = 0.93$) than *PCL* articles ($M = 1.27$, $SD = 0.89$, $p = 0.002$) and marginally more studies than *LCP* articles ($M = 1.12$, $SD = 0.59$, $p = 0.064$). *PCL* articles tended to have more studies than *LCP* articles ($p = 0.096$).

For original data reports, there were also significant differences in the type of sample used by journal, $F(2, 511) = 5.55$, $MSe = 44.53$, $p = 0.004$, $R^2 = 0.02$ (see Fig. 6). *LCP* was significantly more likely to have articles with data from college students (35.2%) than *PCL* (17.3%, $p < 0.001$) or *PPPL* (8.9%, $p < 0.001$), $F(2, 525) = 18.42$, $MSe = 0.15$, $p < 0.001$, $R^2 = 0.07$. *PCL* tended to have more articles with college students than *PPPL* ($p = 0.068$). On the other hand, *PCL* had significantly more articles (7.1%) with other types of students than *PPPL* (0%, $p < 0.001$) or *LCP* (2.1%, $p = 0.020$), which did not differ significantly ($p = 0.332$). *PPPL* had the most articles featuring community member samples (34.2%), significantly more than *PCL* (26.1%, $p = 0.027$) or *LCP* (10.6%, $p < 0.001$), which were also significantly different ($p = 0.002$), $F(2, 525) = 11.83$, $MSe = 0.17$, $p < 0.001$, $R^2 = 0.04$. *LCP* published significantly more articles using offenders (29.6%) than *PCL* (19.5%, $p = 0.009$) or *PPPL* (17.8%, $p = 0.014$), but there was no significant difference between *PCL* and *PPPL* ($p = 0.902$), $F(2, 525) = 4.11$, $MSe = 0.17$, $p = 0.017$, $R^2 = 0.2$. *PPPL* published significantly more articles with child samples (12%) than *LCP* (4%, $p = 0.005$) and slightly more than *PCL* (8%, $p = 0.085$), these were not significantly different from one another ($p = 0.159$), $F(2, 525) = 3.96$, $MSe = 0.07$, $p = 0.020$, $R^2 = 0.02$.

Discussion

Our findings regarding publication patterns in *PCL, PPPL,* and *LCP* in seven recent years, in conjunction with the *LHB* analysis conducted by Wylie et al. (2018), suggest that there are currently some common trends in publications in the field of law and psychology. However, differences also exist among the journals. Overall, authors publishing recently in all four journals were predominantly women and/or from psychology departments at American institutions. Although there are some differences by journal, in general the most common research area currently is prisoners and offending (e.g., risk assessment). Research on jury decision making and eyewitnesses was also common, but less frequent overall; *LHB* publication patterns also suggest that research on jury/judicial decision making and expert witnesses is becoming less common in recent years (Wylie et al., 2018). Moreover, articles overwhelmingly tended to include data from at least one original study, even though all of the journals accept nonempirical articles. This pattern is consistent with the publication patterns in *LHB*, which also primarily published empirical articles (Wylie et al., 2018). It is unclear whether this disparity reflects fewer nonempirical articles being submitted or a lower acceptance rate (unfortunately, we did not have access to data on submission or acceptance rates).

Although most articles published in *LHB* used a sample of college students (Wylie et al., 2018), overall there seemed to be more diversity in sample type in *PCL, PPPL,* and *LCP.* College students were the most frequent sample only in *LCP*, whereas *PCL* and *PPPL* were more likely to have articles using community members or offenders.

Thus, the commonalities in publications across the four journals can be seen as indicative of the current trends in law and psychology as a field. Conversely, the differences among the journals could be reflective of the differences in the goals of each individual journal. For example, because *PCL* was explicitly established with the goal of covering a breadth of topics, it makes sense that *PCL* includes significantly more articles that did not fit into the identified topic list (i.e., categorized as "other") than *PPPL* or *LCP*. Moreover, the fact that *PPPL* published more work from American institutions than *PCL* or *LCP* also makes sense because *PPPL* is the only publication by an American organization (APA), whereas *PCL* and *LCP* are published by European organizations (the European Association of Psychology and Law, and the British Psychological Society, respectively). However, with the exception of one of the three *PCL* coeditors (Jeffrey Neuschatz, who is in the United States), the current editors of all three journals are based in Europe.

Although each of these journals was established with the goal of increasing the multidisciplinary focus of the field, the common findings suggest that the calls for diversification in the field have not been heeded to any great extent. Roughly 70% of all first authors were affiliated with psychology or a mental health institute, and the second most frequent affiliation was a psychiatry department or medical center. Few authors came from law, policy, or other social sciences, and with the exception of *PPPL*, relatively little research focused on public policy (though other research topics undoubtedly had policy implications to varying degrees). Research published in *LHB* is also dominated by psychologists (Bornstein, 2016). Although *PCL* has the goal of publishing a variety of types of articles, in reality *PCL* published significantly more original data reports than *PPPL* or *LCP*. Similarly, both *PCL* and *PPPL* were established with the goal of representing more disciplines within the field of law and psychology (*LCP* acknowledged that psychology would be most common since the journal was based in psychology). Overall, our results indicate that the field is lacking the multidisciplinary perspective these journals call for, which can yield substantial scientific benefits (Bornstein, 2016).

Practical Implications

The present findings have a number of implications for scholars seeking to publish their work in law-psychology journals. Based on the analyses, it appears that authors using traditional (i.e., college student) samples would do especially well to consider publishing in *LCP*, as those samples constituted the majority of its publications. For researchers using community-based samples, *PCL* and *PPPL* might be more appropriate outlets. The direction of this relationship is unclear; however, it is not apparent if these journals are more likely to publish articles containing specific samples or if researchers using a specific sample are more likely to seek a particular publication outlet.

As for the content of the article, authors submitting research focusing on prisoners and offending and (to a lesser extent) decision making and eyewitnesses might find *LCP* and *PPPL* to be relatively more receptive to these topics. Research with a law-psychology focus that does not conform to the more traditional topics covered might most likely find a home in *PCL* which, as mentioned above, lists as one of its explicit goals to represent more disciplines within the field of law and psychology.

Published research does reveal trends in content, which can be an aid as well as an obstacle. Focusing on "hot topics" of the moment (e.g., policing) reflects an awareness of, and dedication to, studying the things affecting our societies at the moment. Following trends, however, might also impede the dissemination of important research not in line with the current fashion. For authors as well as editors, broadening the scope of participant samples and topics covered might open the doors for more of the kinds of interdisciplinary research that all of these journals call for. The fields of law and psychology do not have the sort of relationship that necessarily excludes other social science disciplines; rather, a more "open relationship" could let in other social sciences, to the benefit of all. This kind of broad interdisciplinarity is challenging for a number of reasons, such as conceptual and methodological differences (Bornstein, 2016). A deliberate effort on the part of law-psychology journals to expand the types of articles submitted and published (e.g., more concept papers and literature reviews) might help reach a wider audience across more disciplines.

Limitations

While the results of our analyses show some interesting trends in topics and sample type by journal, it is worthwhile to consider whether enough of the field's major publication outlets have been surveyed. We analyzed three leading journals in the field of psychology and law, which, in addition to the recent *LHB* analysis (Wylie et al., 2018) brings the grand total to four journals. These journals represent leading professional organizations in psychology and law (e.g., AP-LS, EAPL), but they are by no means exhaustive. Future research should include more psychology and law based journals, such as *Behavioral Sciences and the Law*; *Psychiatry, Psychology, and Law* (the official journal of the Australian and New Zealand Association of Psychiatry, Psychology and Law); *American Journal of Forensic Psychology*; and *Journal of Forensic Psychiatry & Psychology*, to name a few. In addition to a more inclusive list of journals, it would also be advantageous to track trends over a longer period of time. Extending the time period beyond 7 years would lead to a more meaningful longitudinal analysis of topics and trends in the field over time.

Future research should also examine other demographic characteristics of authors. Although we found that women authors were well-represented and there was a moderate degree of geographical diversity—which varied considerably across journals—it would be interesting to look at other author characteristics as well, such as race/ethnicity. Like other sciences (e.g., Tsui, 2007), psychology has a history of underrepresentation of racial and ethnic minorities—a pattern that continues today, despite recent gains (Lawson, Graham, & Baker, 2007). We did not code for authors' race/ethnicity, but we suspect that minorities would, indeed, be in the minority when it comes to publication in law-psychology journals.

Conclusions

The present study indicates that in general, law-psychology journals are very similar in terms of what they publish; however, there were several notable differences across law-psychology journals that might be related to the overall goals of the individual journals. *PPPL* tended to publish fewer articles on prisoners/offending and more articles on jury decision making and other public policy matters than *PCL* and *LCP.* On the other hand, *PCL* was more likely to publish original data articles than *PPPL* or *LCP*. And *LCP* was more likely to have articles using college student samples than *PPPL* or *PCL*. These differences in publications by journal can help direct authors as to where their articles might be more likely to be published.

Each of the journals was established with different goals, which encourages substantive diversification within the field generally. Although Wylie et al. (2018) found that *LHB* has diversified over time, our analyses of trends in recent publications suggest that further diversification is necessary. Our findings suggest that although some of these goals are being met, the field needs to continue encouraging a multi- and interdisciplinary focus.

References

American Psychological Association (2017). *Psychology, Public Policy, and Law description*. Retrieved from http://www.apa.org/pubs/journals/law/

Blumenthal, J. A. (2002). Law and social science in the twenty-first century. *Southern California Interdisciplinary Law Journal, 12*, 1–53. https://doi.org/10.2139/ssrn.355280

Bornstein, B. H. (2016). Law and social science: How interdisciplinary is interdisciplinary enough? In C. Willis-Esqueda & B. H. Bornstein (Eds.), *The witness stand and Lawrence S. Wrightsman, Jr*. New York: Springer.

Bornstein, B. H. (2017). Jury simulation research: Pros, cons, trends and alternatives. In M. B. Kovera (Ed.), *The psychology of juries: Current knowledge and a research agenda for the future* (pp. 207–226). Washington, DC: American Psychological Association.

Brank, E. M. (2007). Elder research: Filling an important gap in psychology and law. *Behavioral Sciences and the Law, 25*, 701–716. https://doi.org/10.1002/bsl.780

Cutler, B. L. (2007). Editor's note. *Law and Human Behavior, 31*, 1–2. https://doi.org/10.1007/s10979-006-9085-1

Cynkar, A. (2007). The changing gender composition of psychology. *Monitor on Psychology, 38*, 46.

Grisso, T. (1991). A developmental history of the American Psychology – Law Society. *Law and Human Behavior, 15*, 213–231. https://doi.org/10.1007/bf01061710

Hollin, C., van Koppen, P., & Lind, A. (1994). Editorial introduction to the first edition. *Psychology, Crime & Law, 1*, i–ii. https://doi.org/10.1080/10683169408411930

Kovera, M. B. (2013). *Law and human behavior update. American Psychology Law Society: Summer 2013 News*. Retrieved April 17, 2018, from http://www.apadivisions.org/division-41/publications/newsletters/news/2013/07/issue.pdf

Lamb, M. E. (2013). Inaugural editorial. *Psychology, Public Policy, and Law, 19*, 1–2. https://doi.org/10.1037/a0028996

Lawson, R. B., Graham, J. E., & Baker, K. M. (2007). *A history of psychology: Globaliazation, ideas, and applications*. Upper Saddle River, NJ: Pearson Prentice Hall.

McLean, G. N. (2011). Writing theory, conceptual, and position articles for publication. In T. S. Rocco & T. Hatcher (Eds.), *The handbook of scholarly writing and publishing* (pp. 209–221). San Francisco: Jossey-Bass.

McMurran, M., & Lloyd-Bostock, S. (1996). Editorial. *Legal and Criminological Psychology, 1*(1).

Ogloff, J. R. P. (2000). Two steps forward and one step backward: The law and psychology movement(s) in the 20th century. *Law and Human Behavior, 24*, 457–483. https://doi.org/10.1023/a:1005596414203

Roesch, R. (1990). From the editor. *Law and Human Behavior, 14*, 1–3. https://doi.org/10.1007/bf01055785

Rorstad, K., & Aksnes, D. W. (2015). Publication rate expressed by age, gender and academic position – A large-scale analysis of Norwegian academic staff. *Journal of Infometrics, 9*, 317–333. https://doi.org/10.1016/j.joi.2015.02.003; Sales, B. D. (1995). Editorial. *Psychology, Public Policy, and Law, 1*, 3–5.

Skeem, J. (2014). *Innovating psychology & law: Tackling bigger problems, more proactively*. Presidential address presented at 2014 American Psychology-Law Society Conference in New Orleans, Louisiana. Retrieved April 26, 2016 from https://www.youtube.com/watch?v=RKo8RO6-qFE.

Saks, M. J. (1986). The law does not live by eyewitness testimony alone. *Law and Human Behavior, 10*, 279–280. https://doi.org/10.1007/bf01047341
Sales, B. D. (1995). Editorial. *Psychology, Public Policy, and Law, 1*, 3–5.
Taylor & Francis (2016). *Psychology, crime & law aims & scope*. Retrieved from http://www.tandfonline.com/action/journalInformation?show=aimsScope&journalCode=gpcl20#.Vy_m2_krKUk
Tremper, C. R. (1987). Sanguinity and disillusionment where law meets social science. *Law and Human Behavior, 11*, 267–276. https://doi.org/10.1007/bf01044741
Tsui, L. (2007). Effective strategies to increase diversity in STEM fields: A review of the research literature. *The Journal of Negro Education, 76*, 555–581. http://www.jstor.org/stable/40037228
van Arensbergen, P., van der Weijden, I., & van den Besselaar, P. (2012). Gender differences in scientific productivity: A persisting phenomenon? *Scientometrics, 93*, 857–868. https://doi.org/10.1007/s11192-012-0712-y
Wiener, R. L. (1997). From the editor. *Law and Human Behavior, 21*, 1–3. https://doi.org/10.1023/a:1024809908861
Wiley Online Library (2017). *Legal and criminological psychology aims and scope*. Retrieved from http://onlinelibrary.wiley.com/journal/10.1111/(ISSN)2044-8333/homepage/ProductInformation.html
Wylie, L. E., Hazen, K. P., Hoetger, L. A., Haby, J. A., & Brank, E. M. (2018). Four decades of the journal law and human behavior: A content analysis. *Scientometrics, 115*, 655–693. https://doi.org/10.1007/s11192-018-2685-y

Index

M. K. Miller, B. H. Bornstein (eds.), *Advances in Psychology and Law*, Advances in Psychology and Law 3,
https://doi.org/10.1007/978-3-319-75859-6